The New Flesh

21st Century Horror Films A-Z, Volume 2

Stuart Willis

Special thanks to

Dave Drury for the amazing cover artwork (again), and for going beyond the call of duty in designing the wraparound cover.

Mark Savage for writing such a fantastic foreword.

Elliott Moran for all his help, technical and otherwise, behind the scenes.

Georgia, Esme and Nancy for their continued love and support.

Table of Contents

The Reviews

Foreword by Mark Savage

My first exposure, as a child, to a lesbian was to a lesbian vampire – a still from *Lust For A Vampire* (1971), if my memory serves me correctly. My awareness that nature *can* go berserk was shaped via movies like *Frogs* (1972), *Dogs* and *The Food Of The Gods* (both 1976). I developed my occasional distrust for the great outdoors thanks to classics like *The Hillis Have Eyes* (1977). I acquired my childhood fear of atomic power because of a giant lizard who was formed from its poisonous mist (*Godzilla, 1954*).

Like rain on the brim of a hat, we catch movies. Sometimes they stay with us, sometimes they evaporate. One person's favourite is another person's crashing bore. The movie I hate the most is the movie you own a dozen versions of on VHS, Beta, VCD, Laserdisc, DVD, BluRay and Digital. My favourite movie is the movie that made you question the very essence of my character. Nothing is more subjective than the way we filter movies through our own biases, prejudices, experiences, sexuality, fetishes, and fears. That's what makes them a source of endless debate.

When I was a kid, access to movies was determined by technology, availability, and being parented. I saw what I could, and dreamed of what I read about. I loved books that listed movies I hadn't seen. I loved the descriptions. I loved the stills. My appetite for all things fantasy and horror was fed more by the unseen than the seen. Books like Dennis Gifford's "A Pictorial History Of Horror Movies" (1974) and Alan Frank's 1977 tome "Horror Films" stimulated my imagination to the point of ecstasy. Once hooked on that heroin, the craving would never retreat.

My first exposure to horror films was via Australian TV and its super-limited channel menu – late night movies mostly, and a show hosted by a top-hatted freak named "Deadly Ernest". Deadly crawled out of a coffin on Fridays around 10:30pm and presented movies the local network had bought for cheap from dodgy American studios. Titles that played again and again were *The Beast With Five Fingers* (1946), *Them!* (1954) and Larry Buchanan's *It's Alive!* (1969). Oh, and *The Blob* (1958), which my mother called "far-fetched". In order to get my mother to let me stay up many hours past my bedtime and watch these confounded movies, I'd insist on drying the wishes, promise to hand-mow the lawn for six months, or make some outrageous guarantee that I'd go to bed early every night for the next thirty-five years. My manipulations were shameless and pathetic.

Eventually, I matured a little (marginally at best) and moved beyond parenting prohibition on late-night horror. But access remained the sticking point. Before VCRs, which hit Australia in the early 80's, you only had TV and the movies.

I vividly recall hearing about a kid in a nearby seaside town who had an uncut NTSC VHS of George Romero's *Dawn Of The Dead* (1978). The prospect excited my brother and I so much, we drove what seemed like hours to watch the movie, sat and watched it in this stranger's house, and left without saying more than a very sincere "Thank you"; I'd already seen the film in the US as I'd visited the country soon after turning eighteen, but my brother and some of our friends hadn't seen it, so making the trip was a necessary and important one. The horror fan's right of passage.

In the mid-80's, horror fandom was a semi-legal adventure in Australia (and England, too). It was the Video Nasty era. Famous and infamous horror movies coming into Australia usually followed that damn English convention of being cut – and cut to fuckin' shreds, too. A part of me died temporarily every time I learned a new, upcoming title was to be released in a censored version. It, literally, made my stomach ache.

So, while beginning to make movies myself that were the opposite of what Aussie censorship authorities would approve of, there also started an active underground in which resourceful fans began sourcing VHS tapes from more liberal destinations such as Venezuela and The Netherlands, making them available via mail order catalogue or a local flea market. The nastiest, most uncut version of Roger Watkins' *The Last House On Dead End Street* (1977) came from Venezuela.

The Netherlands provided the only version worth seeing of Ruggero Deodato's *House On The Edge Of The Park* (1980): the rapey one. And my mate Darren's 10th generation VHS dub of *Cannibal Holocaust* (1980) was routed from good old Venezuela, too. My first exposure to the infamous woman on a stick was through video tearing and rolling horizontals. But even THAT was amazing.

Back then, finding an uncut version of a notorious horror film was like finding buried treasure or hardcore Danish porn magazines strewn about in the nearby woods. Unlike today, where so-called "fans" are hoarding thousands of stolen files on hard drives, a real premium was placed back then on an uncut version of a hard-to-find film. What's changed now are several things, but mostly it's availability and how modern "films" are produced.

For indie horror flicks and anything featuring imagery that might get you tossed out of polite company, the mode of production these days is DIGITAL — which, of course, doesn't mean one thing, but suffices as a general term for what format images are recorded on.

It is true that digital cameras are somewhat more economical to shoot with because they don't churn expensive film stock (16mm, 35mm, or 65mm), but the much ballyhoo'ed evolution of recording mediums is, like politics, fraught with lies, misunderstandings, and a great deal of marketing bullshit. Once you add lenses, monitors, and technology that hangs like balls off the cameras, you arrive back at a budget figure that isn't too far north of what you'd pay to shoot on celluloid. On top of that, raw crew and cast costs, location fees, insurance, accommodation, and post-production premiums have declined barely at all.

But digital is here to stay, and the most extreme contemporary movies such as *A Serbian Film* (2010) are shot this way.

As many of the more extreme titles by-pass cinemas altogether due to the unbelievable dominance of Hollywood studios over movie theatres, we can thank digital for enabling the provision of pristine digital reproductions of movies we love on formats that faithfully reproduce a director's original intentions. On top of that, older titles shot on film are being digitally resurrected and preserved.

Books like the one you are about to read either reinforce the shared love of one man's trash and another man's treasure, or perform the act of enticing one with new cinematic delicacies that surely cannot be resisted.

Sinema, a drug for sure, comes replete with its own unique orgasm.

Mark Savage, cult filmmaker (*Marauders* [1986], *Defenceless: A Blood Symphony* [2004], *Stressed To Kill* [2016])
January 2017

Stills in order of appearance: *The Blob* (1958); *Defenceless: A Blood Symphony* (2004).

Introduction

Hello, welcome to *The New Flesh: 21st Century Horror Films Volume* 2.

My introduction to the first book opened with a quick summation of how contemporary horror cinema had evolved from 1960 through to the close of the 20th century. It was, I concede, an epigrammatic overview. I concluded my preface with a whistle-stop tour of the globe, remarking upon the genre-related creativity we were witnessing in this age, from Britain to America, Russia to Korea, Germany to Italy, and beyond.

All of which left me wondering how to introduce *Volume 2*. I could simply suggest it's more of the same.

But that takes up a line, no more.

So, after some thought, I decided to talk about my own relationship with horror films. Not in a narcissistic way. But just to give some insight into where these views and reviews are coming from, and to celebrate my own love of a genre that – despite cannibalising itself on frequent occasion – refuses to die.

To this end, I was born in October 1972. My dad left home when I was four, leaving me with my mother and two older sisters. We didn't have money but we were happy with our lot. We had a single small black-and-white television in our living room, and it's upon this that I watched my first horror film: Hammer's 1958 production of *Dracula*, starring two of my idols, Christopher Lee and Peter Cushing.

As I recall it, I was perhaps five years old. I'd complained to my mother about feeling poorly and she – doubtlessly lonely – had suggested that, if I was too ill to attend school the following morning, I could sit up late to watch a movie with her. I was thrilled. I was staying up later than my sisters, way past my bedtime, and getting to view a horror film – something I remember understanding even then as being taboo for kids.

Even without the benefit of its lurid colours, I adored *Dracula*. I was transfixed by its sense of danger right from the start. The moment Lee appeared on the screen as the titular character, I fell in love. I was like Joe Pesci's character in *Goodfellas* (1990) – rooting for the bad guy. Of course, I was scared. But, snuggling up to my mother, it was an exhilarating kind of fear, akin to riding a rollercoaster with your heart in your mouth but always knowing you'd be getting off safely a few moments later. Lee drew me in with his hypnotic presence, his charismatic portrayal of evil personified, his subliminal control over others. At least, this is how I recollect events: I realise I was only five at the time ...

Anyway, I was hooked. I fed my passion for horror films regularly after that, sitting up to watch double bills on television each weekend, which led to my discovery of classics like *I Walked With A Zombie* (1943) and *The Creeping Flesh* (1973). I received Dennis Gifford's 1974 book "A Pictorial History of Horror Films" for my 7th birthday – a life-changer – and Dick Smith's horror make-up set that Christmas. My mother, always a keen reader of the genre, had books and books of fiction on her shelf (James Herbert, Stephen

King etc) – all of which I gorged upon, if perhaps not always fully understanding their finer points at the time. I became a little obsessed by the escapism, the limitless possibilities of its dark fantasies, that horror offered.

In the meantime my mother remarried and the family relocated from North Wales to the North of England.

My love of late-night televisual frights continued up until 1982 when my parents bought a video recorder. Although we lived in a small village several miles from any major supermarket or sense of modern culture, a couple of video rental stores had already opened there. Back then, there was no policing of age: I was able to acquire a membership card for each store and rent whatever I wished.

So, seven days a week, I'd be renting videos. I started washing cars with my mate Gilly on a weekend to help pay for my habit. This was a revelatory time – it opened my eyes to a whole world of horror beyond the likes of Hammer, Amicus and the old Universal monster flicks. Suddenly I was watching stuff like *The Driller Killer* (1979), *Bloody Moon* (1981) and *Honeymoon Horror* (1982). The efforts of Cushing and Lee seemed positively twee in comparison!

Around this time I also started buying whatever magazines I could find which catered for my desires. Living in a Northern village, well before the advent of the Internet, this wasn't always easy. But mags like "Starburst" and Marvel Comics' short-lived 1982 publication "Monster Monthly" introduced me to the cinema of Lucio Fulci, Walerian Borowczyk and Dario Argento, among other things.

Randomly buying a copy of "Halls Of Horror", a quarterly publication that served as a resurrection of former magazine "The House Of Hammer" (also called "House Of Horror" at one stage), led to my discovery of a selection of video titles that were about to be banned. I believe it was here that a letter from Ramsey Campbell was printed, asking if the rumour of an impending ban was true and - if so - which titles were likely to be affected. In reply, the editor listed a handful of films deemed as obscene by the Department of Public Prosecutions.

Of course, I had to see them all. And see them all I did! I became an avid watcher and collector of the so-called video nasties, soon laying my hands on an official list of "banned" titles to use as my reference guide. As a consequence I was paying attention to titles that I'd have no doubt otherwise overlooked: *Blood Rites* (1968), *Mardi Gras Massacre* (1978), *Absurd* (1981), *Madhouse* (1981) …

I was a teenager. I was into loud, aggressive music (thrash metal and punk). I had long hair and wore Slayer T-shirts. I was collecting horror films deemed as being too disgusting for the general public's consumption. I was, in hindsight, a bit of a walking cliché. But my love for both the music and films was genuine and passionate: something which - I've come to realise via Internet forums, Facebook discussions, film festival gatherings and so on - is also true of so many other people of my era. At fourteen I probably revelled in the belief that I alone had these obsessions; as a man in his mid-forties, I love the realisation that I'm actually one of *many*.

However, I digress.

As the 1980s continued to unfold, horror came under more attacks for its graphic violence and attitude towards its female characters (the more vulnerable character is always going to elicit a greater sense of fear/empathy from the audience – something the tabloids would [knowingly?] misconstrue as misogyny). Censorship became more stringent. Anti-pornography groups lobbied outside screenings of movies in America. Filmmakers became more apologetic in their approach to the genre. Pick up any copy of American magazine "Fangoria" from around 1989, for example, and you'll be hard-pushed to find a director not trying to sell his film as a "psychological thriller", or "dark drama", or "pastiche" – anything other than admitting it's a dreaded, reviled "horror film".

All this adverse press and societal resistance resulted in distributors being reluctant to commission/release new genre flicks. So we got a tidal wave of light comedy-horrors, straight-to-video sequels and shameless micro-budget rip-offs instead. By the early 1990s, my feeling was that the genre had little left to offer. We still got the odd glimmer of promise, of course – *Begotten* (1990), *Der Todesking* (1990), *Braindead* (1992), *Man Bites Dog* (1992), *Nightwatch* (1994) – but these pearls were few and far between. Even old hands like Fulci and Argento were struggling to maintain their standards of yore, the arses having been torn from the budgets they were formerly used to toying with. As enjoyable as *A Cat In The Brain* (1990) and *The Stendhal Syndrome* (1996) are, they're undeniably inferior in quality when measured against the previous highs of these masters, such as *The Beyond* (1981) and *Tenebrae* (1982) respectively.

I was jaded. I'd collected just about everything I needed on videotape (along with some stuff I really, really didn't need – hello *Nightbeast* [1982] and *The Supernaturals* [1986]). Nothing new of any real interest was coming through, at least not anything that was easy to see in uncut form while living in the UK.

I cancelled my subscription to "Fangoria", disappointed with the films it was covering: if it wasn't some big budget gloss like *Interview With The Vampire* (1994), the pages were becoming increasingly filled with retrospectives which offered nothing I hadn't by that time already read (having discovered a small indie store in Middlesbrough which stocked the likes of "Video Watchdog" and "Deep Red" magazine in the mcantime).

My days of being an ardent fan and collector of horror movies were all but over, it seemed. Plus, I admit, I'd found other pastimes to partake in such as girls and booze (collectively described as "socialising" whenever listing hobbies in any job applications I submitted at the time).

One company, however, who maintained my interest in horror films of old during the mid-1990s were UK distributors Redemption Video. They were busy releasing (for their time) great VHS editions of old favourites such as *Deep Red* (1975) and *Martin* (1977), as well as introducing me to the until-then-untapped delights of *Flavia The Heretic* (1974) and *Black Candles* (1982). I rang their office in London one afternoon to enquire about forthcoming releases and got chatting to a very affable Marc Morris. This was some time in the late 1990s. He mentioned a new format called DVD which was gathering pace and set to storm the home video market. I took heed of Marc's advice and began investigating this promising new medium.

At around the same time I discovered the Internet. And, specifically, eBay. Which meant I could start selling my prized videotapes in anticipation of building a collection of these new-fangled "digital versatile disc" thingies.

Searching online, I soon became aware of the burgeoning import DVD market and made sure I bought myself a multi-region player (an entry-level ALBA model). I was ready to go. What I now needed were some reliable reviews of the discs I sought to buy. Were they uncut? English-friendly?

This is how I found Sex Gore Mutants, the site ran to this day by Alan Simpson. I believe my maiden visit to its pages was to check out their review for Sazuma's first DVD release of *Cannibal Ferox* (1981). I loved the informal approach to writing, the clear passion evident in the numerous reviews I went on to peruse, and the real sense of community felt in the site's forum pages. So I joined up. And bought myself a copy of *Ferox* in the meantime, of course.

A few months later I plucked up the courage to email Alan and ask if he accepted reviews from readers. He was extremely approachable, welcoming sample reviews for his consideration. I submitted write-ups of old favourites *Pink Flamingos* (1972) and *Axe* (1977).

I was thrilled (and surprised) when Alan published my two reviews and soon invited me to write more. Before long, I was receiving the odd screener disc through the post. At this point I was still very much stuck in the past, pining for a return to the raw, unapologetic horrors of the 1970s and 1980s. But it's through writing for Sex Gore Mutants - something I've incredibly been doing for sixteen years now - that

I've been exposed to post-millennial horror films in all its forms and guises. And I've learned a lot ... like how not to dismiss an entire generation of filmmakers based purely on a few lousy experiences at the beginning of the new Century.

And I most certainly *would* have passed over on a great deal of gems had it not been that I became committed to reviewing them for Al's site. Had I not been lucky enough for Al to send me discs from companies such as Sub Rosa Studios, Tartan Video, Hardgore, Tempe Video, Alternative Cinema etc - all of whom dealt in a whole plethora of early-2000s indie horror cinema - I doubt I'd have ever scratched the surface of the modern genre further than what the multiplexes and High Street magazines (which at that time were pretty much reduced to being a choice of either "Empire" or "Total Film") were telling me to see. I'd have stayed resolute in the belief that all modern horror, give or take the odd anomaly, was shit.

Thank God, then, for Alan and Sex Gore Mutants.

It's at this juncture that I try and think of some contemporary titles that reviewing has introduced me to, ones that I probably would've passed over but have contributed towards massively restoring my faith in the genre. And I'm struggling. For no other reason than there have been so many. Where do I begin?

The Undertow (2003)? *The Altruist* (2004)? *Antibodies* (2005)? *Poltergay* (2006)? *Amer* (2009)? *Bereavement* (2010)? *Saint* (2010)? *Cold Fish* (2010)? *Children Of A Darker Dawn* (2012)? *Nightmare Code* (2014)?

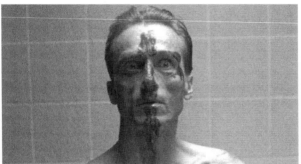

A random selection, certainly, but the list could go on and on and on. The fact is, reviewing for Alan's site taught me, and continues to remind me, that there is a lot of hope for the genre out there. Filmmakers are still striving to be creative, still determined to scare their audiences, and still more than capable of surprising us seasoned viewers. Of course, the volume of films being released has been amplified significantly thanks to the digital age, and the increase in avenues available for getting your completed film seen. And this means there's an awful lot of guff getting made. But scratching the surface and looking a little harder, casting your net a little wider than what those aforementioned High Street magazines tell us we should be watching, will - *does* - lead to some great finds. The genre is still well and truly alive.

Which leads to the incentive behind writing these books. They say you should write about what you know and, although I don't know many things, after sixteen years of reviewing post-millennial films online, I feel that I have a bit of knowledge stored in my brain somewhere! More than that, I still have my passion for the genre and that triggered me to write *Volume 1* a couple of years back: I was disappointed by the lack of books covering horror films post-2000 in any depth. The odd ones that did seemed to focus only on mainstream fare like *Saw* (2004) and *The Descent* (2005). Who was representing the abundance of independent filmmakers struggling to get noticed? Most of all, mixing with horror fans made me realise that the vast majority of them possessed the same sweeping prejudices against modern genre offerings that I once had. Something needed to be done about that ...

Whether or not my writing, either online or in these books, can turn sceptics onto the notion that not all contemporary horror flicks are piss-poor, I don't know. But I do hope I can at least intrigue the odd reader into checking something out that they perhaps otherwise would never have considered. And, you never know, they may even be pleasantly surprised. Likewise, it would be great for newcomers to venture a little deeper into the genre and find that there's more to modern horror than *Sinister* (2012), *The Conjuring* (2013) etc - and perhaps pick up on my hints peppered throughout in the meantime, redirecting them to classic terror films of yore ...

Stills in order of appearance: *Dracula* (1958); *I Walked With A Zombie* (1943); *Absurd* (1981); *Der Todesking* (1990); *Pink Flamingos* (1972); *Antibodies* (2005).

Portrait of the author as a zombie provided by Rees Finlay (Rees Finlay: Art & Design).

About the book ... a.k.a. Explanations and excuses ...

"What do the abbreviations mean?"

... asked no-one, I daresay.

Dir = Director. Scr = Screenplay. I apologise, I know that you knew this. But there it is, for anyone who possibly didn't.

"The reviews are a little short, aren't they?"

When reviewing DVD releases online I tend to keep my reviews somewhere between a thousand and fifteen-hundred words in length. Sometimes they'll be longer, but I am conscious that if a review is too long it becomes cumbersome and readers tend to scroll down to the final paragraph to get the gist. Be honest, you do. My online reviews include a synopsis, views on the film at hand and comments on the actual disc: the main feature's presentation, any bonus materials on offer etc. For these books, I'm focusing on the films alone, while attempting to keep synopses to a minimum (it may just be me, but I prefer not to have someone tell me everything that happens in a film before I see it).

While some films are easy to waffle on about, it's tempting to dismiss others in a single sentence. But I do believe that each movie within these pages deserves equal coverage. In hindsight I was overly conscientious when writing *Volume 1* in my pathological sweeping employment of this rule. As a result, I became focused on fashioning each review to three-hundred words. It may have worked. Certainly for me, from a writer's perspective, it was a canny exercise in cutting back on flannel and concentrating on that which was pertinent. But I concede that the reviews seemed at times a little short. The reviews in *Volume 2* follow a similar principle of equality but that neurotic need to cap everything at three-hundred words has been erased.

This has resulted in longer reviews - I think the longest here comes in somewhere around five-hundred words. My intention has been to give readers everything they need to know, while avoiding repetition and irrelevance (two traps that are easy for me to fall into once you get me chatting about films ...).

"Where's that foreign film I'm looking for?"

I've used the English titles for films where they exist. Original foreign-language titles are proffered within these pages, with redirection given in each case to the review under its English title. I hope that's okay.

"How do I see these films?"

I haven't provided details of how/where to best view each film because, well, that's a bit of headache.

How do *you* view films? Via the physical format? If so, you'll surely appreciate that so many titles get released, re-released, given the deluxe limited treatment etc - and attempting to inform a reader on the best way to view any given title becomes an awkward task which instantly ages the book. Each release gets superseded so quickly!

Plus, I'm not oblivious to the fact that while I'm of an era of folk who still enjoy collecting films physically, many of today's audience prefer to stream, torrent, whatever. They don't need my guidance ... they'll find their treasures online, by hook or by crook. That's not a criticism, I'm well aware of the times (even though I struggle to keep up with them).

14

And, dare I say it, does anyone actually venture out to support a major release at the *cinema* any more?

"Where's Saw? Hostel? Jeepers Creepers?"

If certain obvious films appear to have been overlooked, the chances are they were already covered in *Volume 1*. The above three certainly were. Failing that, if there's something you don't see here, it'll no doubt receive exposure in a future volume ...

"I've never heard of a lot of these films ..."

Good! One customer review on Amazon remarked that *Volume 1* covered too many obscure films. I understand their criticism - and I'm welcoming of any opinions, good or bad, that people want to throw my way after reading! - but I personally enjoy the idea of perhaps introducing even the more seasoned horror viewer to the odd film they may not have up-until-now encountered.

I did originally toy with the idea of writing a book solely on the 21st Century's indie/underground horror scene. But that seemed a bit limiting. Besides, where do you draw the line? At what budget does a film become "overground"? Is an indie film still an indie film once it's been picked up for widespread distribution by a major label?

For better or worse, I decided instead to try and encompass every aspect of the genre. The blockbusters, the remakes, the comedies, the no-budget backyard efforts, the anthologies, the pornos, the gornos ... Resultantly, you will find the likes of *Final Destination* (2000) sharing page space with something like *Flowers* (2015) in here.

The ambition with these books is to proffer a wide-ranging overview of post-millennial horror films which will both inform the curious and provide a feel for how the genre has evolved. Once again making use of that wondrous bastard we call hindsight, I can see that such an approach may have come across as somewhat random in *Volume 1*. I truly feel, however, that the vision is made clearer by the arrival of a second tome. We now have six-hundred films reviewed (over the course of both volumes), covering all sub-genres and hopefully working together to paint a picture of how much variation is out there, just waiting to be discovered.

"I wouldn't call that a horror film!"

As with *Volume 1*, there's the odd film to be found in these pages which isn't strictly "horror". Those non-horror pictures that, perhaps due to their unusually dark themes and/or unflinching moments of violence which prove just too much for mainstream audiences, are destined to find their way into the hearts and collections of horror fans everywhere.

Horror doesn't need to rely on Dracula, or zombies, or teenager-slashing psychopaths. Horror is in the mind. Horror lies within the body. The adjective "horrific" refers to something upsetting or shocking, and as such I present my flimsy case for including the occasional non-horror title which may, with any luck, be of interest to you. Indulge me ...

"The photos are a little dark and/or grainy at times ..."

True. Sorry about that. It's one of the perils of self-publishing. I've sourced the stills myself and gone for the highest resolution images I could find. But sometimes they don't turn out that well. This could be for a number of reasons. Sometimes the image is a little dark to begin with, so CreateSpace's printing methods struggle to bring out the clarity of that photo. In other cases, it's due to the fact that some of these films are deliberately lo-fi affairs, and as such any images from them are going to have a distressed, or grainy, look. Look at the still from *I Never Left The White Room* (2000) as an example. It looks like shit, but is perfectly indicative of how the film (intentionally) looks.

Anyway, all that's left for me to say is ... enjoy. I hope!

I sincerely hope there's something you can gain from reading this book. I hope it comes across that it's been written with a passion for the genre, not only for continually discovering new films myself but also for promoting these movies. I get a genuine kick from sharing whatever I can with others and if you come away from reading this with just one more film on your to-see list, I'll be ecstatic.

Cheers, Stu.

2LDK (2003)

Dir: Yukihiko Tsutsumi; Scr: Yukihiko Tsutsumi, Yuiko Miura; Cast: Maho Nonami, Eiko Koike, Daisuke Kizaki

One story is that while both were in Berlin attending the same film festival, Japanese filmmakers Tsutsumi and Ryuhei Kitamura (*Versus*, 2000) got talking over drinks. Striking upon a mutual appreciation of each other's work, a drunken bet came into place. Taking Tsutsumi's earlier *Chinese Dinner* (2001) as their template, the rules were simple: both had one week and an equal budget to make a film with minimal cast and a single location. The theme in each case was to be a duel to the death. The director whose film proved to be least successful was tasked with shaving their head in public.

Another, less adventurous take on this yarn is that producer Shin'ya Kawai had been sufficiently impressed with each filmmaker's efforts on his 2002 anthology *Jam Films*, that he commissioned both to make a flick restricted by the aforementioned stipulations.

Whatever the truth, the two movies emerged in 2003 and were commonly paired together as "The Duel Project". Kitamura's *Aragami* doesn't stray far from the style he'd already by that point established: kinetic, expertly choreographed and obsessed with violent swordplay. It looked good and held the attention quite well.

But Tsutsumi's *2LDK* - the title refers to Japanese lingo when advertising rental properties ("two bedrooms, living, dining and kitchen area") - is an entirely different beast. Shot in sequence over the course of eight days, it lacks the stylised aesthetics of its competitor but makes up for this in sheer, raw drama.

Koike is a quiet, ambitious wannabe actress from a humble background. She's attentive to tidiness and cleanliness, while appreciating the calm of running a simple life. Nonami, her flatmate and fellow aspiring thespian, is an outgoing, privileged girl-about-town. When both are shortlisted for a major role in an upcoming film, the tension in their apartment gradually escalates into violence.

Early scenes serve as a witty comment on Japanese mores, the girls maintaining a respectful politeness to each other's faces while their inner monologues clue us in on what they're really thinking. The black comedy is evident from the start, the girls' facade of friendliness slowly slipping throughout the course of one evening via annoyances over singing and accusations of using perfume without consent. Events go hurtling into overdrive midway through when a simple slap across the face unleashes maenadic Hell. Suddenly a slow start gives way to a tidal wave of violence utilising weapons as eclectic as a kettle, a bathtub, a sword and even a chain saw.

Graphic, violent, darkly humorous, perversely insightful: the two actresses are great too - funny and maniacal in equal measures. *2LDK* rises above its gritty sheen to also look great. It's clearly had some influence - the 2015 film *Roommate Wanted* (originally titled *2BR/1BA*) is a painfully obvious rip-off.

9 Lives Of Mara (2007)

Dir: Balaji K Kumar; Scr: Balaji K Kumar, Eric Massey; Cast: Pollyanna McIntosh, Chad Donella, Bret Loehr

Donella speaks from the mental institute in which he now resides, taking us back to his childhood where as a boy (as portrayed by Loehr) he came to suspect that new stepmother McIntosh was a witch. The child used Heinrich Kramer and James Sprenger's 1484 textbook "The Malleus Maleficarum" – an infamously paranoia-inducing (in its time) guide to recognising, capturing and executing witches - as a reference tool.

Was McIntosh, an alluring replacement for Loehr's mother, truly an evil sorceress? Or was the lad simply going insane?

The Oedipal references are obvious and Kumar wisely makes no effort to disguise them. From Loehr's reaction to his enticing new houseguest's scent to the curious hold he observes her having over his father, the balance between confusion, resentment and sexual awakening is astutely communicated.

Also intriguing is the manner in which Kumar has opted to convey his ostensibly simple story. He describes the style as "fairy tale noir", and it's easy to agree with this summation. Raymond Chandler is cited as an influence: the Los Angeles palm trees, the deliberate pacing and darkened, smoke-filled compositions are all testament to this. Shooting on 35mm lends the film that timeless quality it's striving for, as does an absence of contemporary trappings such as televisions, computers, mobile 'phones etc.

Kumar has also referenced the painters Henry Fuseli and Caravaggio in interviews, as well as the early cinema of Roman Polanski. The baroque style of the former two can be evidenced as events progress, as can the claustrophobic sense of obsession and distrust evoked in the latter's best works (*Repulsion* [1965] springs immediately to mind).

Shot over the course of eighteen days with many scenes being nailed in a single take for scheduling purposes, *9 Lives Of Mara* is an ambitious, beguiling indie feature which benefits from great performances and assured direction from the clearly talented Kumar.

It deserves to be more widely seen.

100 Feet (2008)

Dir/Scr: Eric Red; Cast: Famke Janssen, Bobby Cannavale, Ed Westwick

Imprisoned for murdering her abusive husband, Janssen is subsequently battered behind bars by fellow inmates. She's resultantly sent back home – the scene of the crime - and fitted with an electronic ankle bracelet preventing her from straying more than 100 feet from the premises. If she does, she'll be thrown back in the can … where further beatings surely await.

House arrest should be no biggie to her, she's seems resilient enough. But, lo, her home is haunted by a rancorous spirit. It's a bugger when that happens.

Points are scored for abjuring the cheap thrills of trendy gore. This concentrates instead on a slow-burning atmosphere which seeks to spook its viewer by way of bumps in the night and paranormal activity such as crockery smashing of its own accord.

Red's experience in the directorial field – he helmed a handful of films in the three decades leading up to this effort, the most popular of which is 1988's enjoyable crime thriller *Cohen And Tate* – undoubtedly helps the ghostly goings-on achieve impact. We may be thinking of *The Entity* (1982) at the time, but at least we're involved.

Janssen is a reliable lead. She's no stranger to the genre – *Lord Of Illusions* (1995) and *The Faculty* (1998) refer. But she'd also played with the big boys prior to this relatively low-key affair: check her out as the sexy Bond villain in 1995's *GoldenEye*, or as mutant superhero Phoenix in 2000's *X-Men* (a role she's reprised in several sequels).

She downplays her renowned glamour here, fulfilling her role as a dowdy, drab victim of circumstances. However, her character is too tough: there is little vulnerability in evidence, making her difficult to fear for.

A couple of plot points seem too convenient for comfort. Her abusive husband (portrayed in pivotal scenes by Uwe Boll regular Michael Pare) was a cop, and the officer assigned to enforcing her house arrest – Cannavale – is his grieving ex-partner; the inclusion of Westwick as the immediately-smitten buff delivery boy who has no knowledge of this local woman's murderous history, reeks of lazy screenwriting.

Oh, and can I really conclude this review before mentioning the unlikely scenario of the authorities arranging for a felon to remain captive in their crime-scene home while the walls are still spattered with the victim's blood? It transpires I can't.

A perfectly acceptable way of passing a rainy afternoon, *100 Feet* benefits from decent production values and a (vaguely) credible, restrained build-up prior to its sillier finale.

But Red's greatest contribution to the genre remains his screenplay to Robert Harmon's superlative sleeper hit *The Hitcher* (1986).

2001 Maniacs (2005)

Dir: Tim Sullivan; Scr: Chris Kobin, Tim Sullivan; Cast: Robert Englund, Wendy Kremer, Lin Shaye

Three oversexed teens split from school and head out towards Daytona Beach for their summer vacation (watch out for an enjoyable early cameo from Peter Stormare as a college lecturer). A makeshift detour in the road leads them to the remote Southern town of Pleasant Valley. The Valley's Mayor (Englund) advises of how the town is in the throes of a celebration and the travellers are to be their guests of honour. Encouraged by a bevy of horny local fillies led by the voluptuous Kremer, the boys agree to stay.

A short while later five more wayward tourists stumble upon the town. They too are enticed by the promise of cheap thrills, fine food and free ale. Of course, all is not as it seems in redneck-heavy Pleasant Valley …

Sullivan's remake of Herschell Gordon Lewis' early gore flick *Two Thousand Maniacs!* (1964) amplifies every aspect of that film's content. For a start, a $3 million budget assures a level of polish and professionalism here that was never previously evident. Whereas the original's play on sexuality as a weapon was understandably coy, this noughties model is free to exploit it to its fullest: buckle up for an array of pert breasts being exposed throughout, while the townsfolk don't merely flirt with their quarries anymore – they explicitly seduce them. The level of grisliness is upped considerably – fellatio ruined by metal-teethed violence, women pulled apart by horses - and benefits from the expertise of KNB EFX Group's wizardry along the way. Humour is more brazenly bawdy and racist this time around. Englund et al make for a far more proficient cast than the likes of Thomas Wood and Connie Mason in the progenitor.

But there's one thing you can't buy, and that's charm. Lewis' favourite film of his own may suffer from ugly photography, low production values and an erratic pace but it retains a curious charisma about its haphazard assembly. Perhaps it's due to its sense of innocence, or the amiably inept performances. Maybe it's because the protagonists of Sullivan's *teen-comedyesque* remake actually deserve to end up being the meat in Pleasant Valley's barbecue festivities.

One nice touch, however, is the effective use of Lewis' original song "The South's Gonna Rise Again".

A lesser sequel followed in 2010, carrying the puntastic sub-title *Field Of Screams*.

Ab-Normal Beauty (2004)

Dir: Oxide Pang Chun; Scr: Oxide Pang Chun, Thomas Pang; Cast: Race Wong, Roseanne Wong, Anson Leung

Race Wong stars as a promising art student who was molested as a child. This past begins to haunt her after she snaps photos of a dying man at the scene of a car accident. She subsequently becomes obsessed with capturing the act of death on her camera. Her friend, and object of unrequited love (Roseanne Wong), tries to help – but then a deranged stalker gets in on the action.

Pang Chun found international acclaim as one half of the Pang Brothers (alongside twin sibling Danny) with their collaborative effort *The Eye* (2002). That film, along with Oxide's solo effort *Bangkok Haunted* (2001), relied too heavily on slick, flashy visuals to successfully engage as raw drama. With *Ab-Normal Beauty*, the filmmaker tempers his MTV-esque editing style somewhat to produce a more satisfying narrative proposition.

The film's first hour explores some intriguing themes. Echoes of *Peeping Tom* (1960) abound as we're encouraged to identify with the lead protagonist's voyeuristic thrills. As she succumbs to her illness – a morbid fascination which hooks itself into her completely – she attracts the attentions of a snuff-loving psychopath, allowing the Pangs to challenge the audience's love of visceral kicks ... and suggest that their primary character is ultimately confronting her own dark desires in the form of her deadly pursuer.

A final third can't sustain the initial promise, however, and events do degenerate into overly stylised gory set-pieces which make little sense. The finale offers a glimpse of welcome black humour but, all said, it doesn't live up to the strong start.

Making for an interesting point of reference, not only in terms of the action onscreen but also as a parallel to the Pang brothers' possible motivations, the Wong girls are sisters. They enjoyed domestic success in the early 2000s as Chinese Cantopop duo 2R.

Danny Pang's *Leave Me Alone* (2004) can be viewed as a companion piece. It explores the opening crash, which was based on fact, in isolation.

The ABCs Of Death 2 (2014)

Dir/Scr: Various; Cast: Various

In 2012, US distributor Drafthouse Films and fledgling Australian company Timpson Films decided to venture into the tricky world of film production. They joined forces with the more established Magnet Releasing, and – based on an idea from Ant Timpson – emerged with *The ABCs Of Death*: a 26-chapter portmanteau of short films linked by the theme of death. Violent death, to be more precise. Attracting post-millennial talents as diverse as Noboru Iguchi, Ben Wheatley and Ti West, their gore-spattered compendium soon became a hit on international DVD.

A second instalment was inevitable.

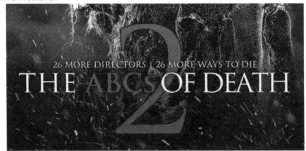

The formula remains the same: asked to choose a word beginning with a different letter of the alphabet, each director enlisted for this run was tasked with fashioning a brisk death-related yarn around it. Each segment averages a running time of around 5 minutes; brief animated title cards proffer a semblance of continuity at the close of the individual stories. The balance between irreverent humour and uber-gore is strikingly similar to that of its predecessor. Production values and visual presentation are on a par with the first instalment (that is, they're good).

If anything, the offerings here are generally more satisfying than what came before. Jen and Sylvia Soska have fun subverting a sub-genre in the pithy "T is for Torture Porn". Julian Gilbey's "C is for Capital Punishment" manages a brutal, affecting dramatic impact within its tight timeframe. "B is for Badger" is as entertainingly silly as you'd imagine from Julian Barratt, co-writer and co-star of surreal comedy show "The Mighty Boosh" (2003-2007). Alexandre Bustillo and Julien Maury keep fans of their *Inside* (2007) happy by employing Beatrice Dalle as a psychotic babysitter in the brutal "X is for Xylophone".

As is the curse of many an anthology, the quality is inconsistent throughout. Some entries are plain excruciating – hello to Todd Rohal's "P-P-P-P Scary!" and Lancelot Oduwa Imasuen's "L is for Legacy", to name but two. Overall though, the standard is improved over the 2012 batch, with just that little bit more attention being given to nurturing dramatic arcs within each ludicrously brief running time.

Abducted By The Daleks (2005)

Dir: Roman Nowicki; Scr: Billy Hartnell, Dave Stanley; Cast: Katarzyna Zelnik, Eliza Borecka, Lina Black

A quartet of comely fillies cruise along a lonely road one evening when their car hits something. Unbeknownst to them, it's a passing alien. Aware that a killer is loose in the area, they naturally opt to wander on foot into nearby woods. Why? There's no real explanation and, mere minutes into the fun, we know better than to ask.

The unfurling action sees each woman meander individually into the undergrowth, remove their (skimpy) clothing at some point and eventually be beamed up onto the titular rolling salt-cellars' spaceship. Scenes of softcore lesbianism and probing by alien plunger ensue.

Playing out in episodic fashion with very little plot, the amorphous storytelling does at least remember to eventually nod to the aforementioned killer and even provides an unlikely twist come its playful conclusion.

Unconvincing sets; stolen music on its soundtrack (specifically, two Pink Floyd tracks); dodgy performances which are further affected by English dialogue spoken in thick European accents: *Abducted By The Daleks* is as audacious in its use of copyrighted iconography as it is low-rent in its execution.

The opening titles sequence brazenly alludes to long-running television series "Dr Who" (1963 onwards – the Daleks are arguably its most famous villains), renaming crew members by amalgamating handles associated with the show ("Patrick Baker", "Billy Hartnell" etc). The intention is undoubtedly tongue-in-cheek; you get the impression the filmmakers found themselves with a Dalek at their disposal one weekend and decided to make this on the spot.

We get three of the trundling terrors on board their mothership. One, as mentioned above, appears to be the real deal – an official Dalek. The other two are clearly replicas, cheaper in design and differing in size (but at least they all have that famed staccato, ring-modulated bark). It's details like these, along with the fact that Black is inexplicably replaced by Maria Vaslova midway through the film (perhaps she objected to the copious nudity required of later scenes?), which inadvertently make this 55-minute calamity so amusing.

Smoky, well-lit woodlands scenes are more stylish than the material deserves; the women are uniformly beautiful. What else would you expect from Nowicki (directing under the pseudonym of Don Skaro here, but actually known to his friends as former Media Publications boss Trevor Barley), who previously gave us the *Fantom Kiler* films (1998–2008) and their hardcore *Fantom Seducer* sister flicks (2005)?

The BBC were quick to respond when distributors Teraz Films began selling a limited run of DVDs on eBay in 2005. They teamed up with the estate of Dalek creator Terry Nation to have the offending item removed. "Daleks do not do porn" argued estate director Tim Hancock. Barley & co responded by retitling their film *Abducted By The Daloids* …

Abducted By The Daloids
See *Abducted By The Daleks*

Adam Chaplin (2011)

Dir/Scr: Emanuele De Santi, Giulio De Santi; Cast: Emanuele De Santi, Chiara Marfella, Giulio De Santi

Chaplin (Emanuele De Santi) is forlorn when his wife is murdered by disfigured gangster Marfella's cartoonish henchmen. Actually, he's not so much pitiful as he is raging mad. Revenge springs to mind, and to this end he enlists the help of a diminutive demon (Giulio De Santi) – offering his soul in return for superhuman strength.

What follows is a remorseless cavalcade of vengeful bloodletting. Umpteen faces are punched into smithereens; heads are mashed into bloody pulps; jaws are thumped clean off; one victim is thrown against a wall with such force that their body literally explodes. All of which is presented in crisp digital HD.

The Italian filmmakers, working under their Necrostorm production house banner, have stated that their aim was to emulate the gory halcyon days of their home country's exploitation cinema in the 1980s. The end product is far closer in execution to the excesses of Japanese anime. As the muscular lead character literally wallops his foes into pools of goo, it's impossible not to recall the wildly entertaining *Story Of Ricky* (1991). And yet, *Adam Chaplin* lacks that film's knowing humour: it's a cynical slice of nonstop action striving solely to win the hearts of gorehounds everywhere.

If that's all you care about, the chances are you'll adore this film. The climactic battle alone is one of the grisliest spectacles you'll ever witness. But anyone else will by then most likely be a tad bored of the endless splatter; the frequency of the violence throughout soon acquires a nullifying effect.

Which leaves the film as a whole open to closer scrutiny. This is where narrative issues become more apparent: the poor acting, the one-dimensional characters, the plot's lack of substance. Once the gore ceases to distract (about ten minutes into proceedings, truth be told), even the blue-tinted colour-correction begins to vex.

Aftershock (2012)

Dir: Nicolas Lopez; Scr: Nicolas Lopez, Eli Roth, Guillermo Amoedo; Cast: Eli Roth, Lorenza Izzo, Nicolas Martinez

Six tourists revelling in a Chilean nightclub are traumatised when an earthquake brings the building crashing down around them. Digging their way out alive is one hurdle to overcome; the convicts newly escaped from the neighbouring maximum security prison are an even greater one.

Incorrectly sold as an out-and-out horror film, *Aftershock* owes more to the lavish disaster movies of the 1970s – an obvious reference point would be *Earthquake* (1974). This is true of the first half, certainly; after that, the film shifts genres and focuses on the threat of the escaped felons. Naturally, these aren't guys who're doing time for fiddling their taxes – we're talking murderers, rapists and the like. This is where the gore quotient is upped significantly, coincidentally at the same juncture where the screenplay loses all direction.

Working with a $2 million budget, *Aftershock* was shot on location in Chile, amid the rubble and ruin left behind by a quake that hit the country in 2010. This sense of authenticity and a heavy reliance on practical effects (courtesy of Sebastian Ballek and Mauro Contreras Villegas's team) both work in the film's favour. Points are also awarded for the manner in which Lopez takes pleasure in pulling the rug from beneath his audience's feet: no character is safe, the director reminding us that in a crisis scenario death can – and will - hit at random.

Narrative choices must come into question, however. The three male characters we're introduced to at the start are assumed as our protagonists but, while we strive to identify with them despite their arrogance, they're replaced midway and their female counterparts become the focal point. Suddenly, at a time where our connection with characters should be established, we're required to learn about these women if we're to feel any empathy towards them. But by then Lopez has given up on fleshing characters out, opting to let the well-orchestrated action take centre-stage.

Alleluia (2014)

Dir: Fabrice Du Welz; Scr: Fabrice Du Welz, Vincent Tavier, Romain Protat; Cast: Laurent Lucas, Lola Duenas, Helena Noguerra

Belgian filmmaker Du Welz made quite a splash with his 2004 feature debut, the subversive backwoods treat *The Ordeal*. His next movie, 2008's *Vinyan*, was an intriguing essay on love and loss co-starring Rufus Sewell and Emmanuelle Beart. Critics shrugged their shoulders; poor box office suggests the public did the same.

Such unjust snubbing led to Du Welz taking time over his next project. *Alleluia* came with no small amount of expectancy attached to it. Not least of all because it's loosely based on the true-crime exploits of Raymond Fernandez and Martha Beck, a.k.a. "The Lonely Hearts Killers", who preyed on lonesome women during the late 1940s. Du Welz doesn't make things easy for himself: the same tale also inspired the terrific movies *The Honeymoon Killers* (1969) and *Deep Crimson* (1996).

Alleluia updates the story to modern times, with serial rogue Lucas meeting impressionable Duenas online (though the Fernandez/Beck era is harkened to: Lucas is a fan of Humphrey Bogart and takes Duenas to see *The African Queen* [1951] at the cinema). She's so smitten that she willingly becomes his accomplice, helping to ensnare gullible singletons into courting him, then assisting in killing them once their assets are safely in their grasp.

There's a sense of urgency to Du Welz's camerawork here, all close-up and fidgety as his leads paradoxically saunter through scenes of alarming bloodshed and energetic sex. Conceptually this fits right in with the director's previous films, addressing the notion of unrestrained love, or obsession, with verve. The facts of the case are obviously discarded beyond the preliminaries: Du Welz ramps up the sex and violence while pandering aesthetically to the arthouse brigade in hope of adding weight to proceedings.

It doesn't wholly convince. Though *Alleluia* remains an entertainingly lurid ride, punctuated by committed performances and a propensity for moments of welcome dark humour (Duenas' demented jealousy; Lucas' discomfort with her increasing enjoyment of their crimes).

Amber Alert (2012)

Dir: Kerry Bellessa; Scr: Kerry Bellessa, Joshua Oram; Cast: Summer Bellessa, Chris Hill, Jasen Wade

For the unaware (or non-American), an "amber alert" is notification of a possible child abduction, or missing child, in the area.

Pals Bellessa and Hill harbour dreams of hosting their own reality TV series. They set off across the Arizonan highways scouting for locations to shoot from, soon realising that they're driving behind a car identified as having been posted on alert. Naturally they contact the police, and are warned away from making contact with the driver (Wade). Having passed on all relevant details, Hill suggests they let the cops do the rest; Bellessa, overcome with a sense of moral duty, insists they give chase.

I've neglected to mention that the whole thing is being filmed, in their car, by Bellessa's brother (Caleb Thompson). What we're watching, onscreen text tells us at the start, is edited footage recovered from the scene of an upcoming crime. Cue shaky cameras, high-volume bickering and a long haul to the close of this repetitive, largely ad-libbed clunker.

Filming mostly from the interior of a car can work - we've seen it being done successfully in Mario Bava's brilliant *Rabid Dogs* (1974) and, to a lesser extent, *Five Across The Eyes* (2006). The premise here is intriguing if somewhat tasteless. Yes, Bellessa spots a child in Wade's car.

What *Amber Alert* succeeds in doing with alarming swiftness is to remove any engagement, any sense of threat, from the viewing experience. Perhaps it's the terrible, camera-conscious performances that neuter the action. It could be that director Bellessa has no skill in editing with an eye to maintaining momentum, and lacks the hard edge required to rein his wife's annoying onscreen whining in. The aforementioned improvised dialogue undoubtedly hampers matters too: themes of moral obligation and the nature of heroism briskly give way to irritating squabbles over whether or not to continue pursuit of Wade's vehicle. A special mention must also go to the screenplay's reliance on characters doing the dumbest things imaginable (the protagonists contradict the police's advice with almost comical obliviousness; the cops don't seem remotely concerned about catching a potential kiddie fiddler).

An overwrought, laughably supernatural-tinged finale provides the unsavoury icing on an already most unappetising cake.

There's a pre-teen lad in this film called Mighty Swag (he also has small roles in *Fingerprints* [2006] and *Megan Is Missing* [2011]). I mention this because his mildly amusing acting name - he was born Evan Thomas Schwartz - is the most interesting thing about *Amber Alert*.

American Guinea Pig: Bouquet Of Guts And Gore (2014)

Dir/Scr: Stephen Biro; Cast: Caitlyn Dailey, Ashley Lynn Caputo, Eight The Chosen One

Dailey and Caputo are abducted, strapped to operating tables in a concentrated room and force-fed liquid LSD. Their incognito assailant (Eight - or Frank Pickarelli to his Facebook pals) then snips off their clothing and sets about dissecting the pair of them limb by limb. His actions are conducted under instruction from the similarly masked cameramen flanking him at either side.

The title is the giveaway: Unearthed Films head Biro's determinedly lo-fi shocker is a direct cousin of the infamous Japanese gore cycle *Guinea Pig* (1985-89) and in particular its second offering, 1985's *Flower Of Flesh And Blood*.

The latter, directed by Hideshi Hino, achieved infamy in 1991 when Charlie Sheen viewed it on VHS and, believing it to be an actual snuff film (!), reported it to the FBI for further investigation. Clearly, the tiger blood was having adverse effects even then ...

Three decades on, Biro's homage extends the short original to feature-length and revels in the ultra-realistic depiction of the goriest transgressions imaginable. Shot on a combination of Super 8mm and VHS, the self-consciously squalid gaze achieves a convincing snuff-like vibe. FX chief Marcus Koch supervises stripped skin, gouged eyes and various appendages being sawn off in unflinching detail. While it all flags midway through (yes, even boundary-pushing sadism can become nullifying), Biro is savvy enough to throw in a gut-wrenching finale as one final kick to the knackers.

Indie animator Jimmy ScreamerClauz provides the haunting score and sound design; as well as editing down the action (which was reportedly shot in real time), cult filmmaker Jim Van Bebber plays a key part in the film.

While the *Guinea Pig* films have inspired other imitations over the years - *Tumbling Doll Of Flesh* (1998) and the *Sadi Scream* series of films (2007, all five volumes) - the sheer proficiency of the clinical extremism here recalls the more polished *Aftermath* (1994). Little wonder that its director, Nacho Serda, is thanked in the closing credits – along with other noted gore purveyors such as Jorg Buttgereit, Olaf Ittenbach and Lucifer Valentine.

Amerikan Holokaust (2013)

Dir: Chris Woods; Scr: Chris Woods, John Miller; Cast: Jules Sceiro, Bob Glazier, Cyndi Crotts

Touted as a new level of extreme horror when first unleashed onto DVD by self-releasing label The Sleaze Box, *Amerikan Holokaust* isn't actually as graphic as its reputation suggests. Which may be a good thing, considering the themes covered – unless you *really* wanted to witness an infant being eaten (discussed but thankfully never shown)?

It follows the exploits of Sceiro and Glazier. They're veteran soldiers who served in Vietnam, whose unfavourable experiences since returning to their homeland have left them – inexplicably – with a penchant for raping and torturing young women. Naturally, this being the 21st Century, they're compelled to capture their activities on home video.

A $1,000.00 budget dictates that the film looks extremely grubby, a la Fred Vogel's *August Underground* (2001) – a clear influence on Woods, along with John McNaughton's superior *Henry: Portrait Of A Serial Killer* (1986). Having said that, *Holokaust* has the convincing FX work of Marcus Koch on its side, along with a script that at least attempts to weave a plot and characters into the succession of misogynistic set-pieces. Performances are generally strong too, with the middle-aged pairing of Sceiro and Glazier being particularly impressive.

Low resolution video photography may repel some, along with several moments of our aged antagonists cavorting naked in close-up. For those who stick it out, the curiously named Rue Goregrinder (she's probably called Gertrude on her birth certificate?) evens the balance somewhat by avenging the females who've been stabbed, disembowelled and raped (offscreen in the latter case) along the way.

Bookended by onscreen text attempting to convince viewers that what they're witnessing is actual footage retrieved from Sceiro's apartment by the police (increasingly a prerequisite of 'found footage' flicks), the occasional faux pas at the editing stage ruins the illusion of authenticity. Who's holding the camera during the final act of retribution, for example?

Choice moment? Has to be the scene where one character is castrated, and then beaten with his own disembodied cock before having it rammed down his throat. This should act as either a warning against or a recommendation in favour of *Holokaust*, dependent upon your sensibilities …

Among The Living (2010)

Dir/Scr: Alexandre Bustillo, Julien Maury; Cast: Theo Fernandez, Fabien Jegoudez, Zacharie Chasseriaud

An engrossing prologue reveals a family living in isolation from society, the father - Francis Renaud - a military veteran whose exposure to chemicals used as biological warfare has resulted in his four-year-old son Jegoudez being a fully-sized Michael Berryman lookalike. Heavily pregnant wife Beatrice Dalle doesn't want history to repeat itself, stabbing her own belly and slashing her throat after attempting to murder both husband and son. Renaud flees the scene, relocating his surviving family to a place they can live in anonymity.

The film picks up proper (and steadily goes downhill) two years down the narrative trail. Three friends bunk off the last day of school in favour of an afternoon frolicking in proximate fields. Their boredom leads them to a deserted film studio where they witness a masked figure dragging a screaming female victim into a basement-level hideout. Managing to escape after a foiled rescue attempt, the lads alert the police - but a subsequent search of the area reveals nothing untoward. Berated by the law and parents alike, the chastised kids retire to their respective homes ... where they're systematically hunted down by the genetically mutated antagonist. Yes, Jegoudez has grown into a murderous six-year-old, ready to carry out his paranoid dad's whims without question.

But ... how does a six-year-old kid, even one graced with the size and strength of an adult, become so resourceful that he can inexplicably trace strangers to their home addresses and cunningly sneak his way into their homes in a bid to kill them - and their families? And why does he feel compelled to do such things while completely naked? At what stage did this family, who have gone to such lengths to hide from society (to exist, secretly, "among the living"), suddenly progress to abducting and slaying innocent women? And, again, why?

A serious suspension of disbelief is required to engage in the tension Bustillo and Maury are attempting to provoke. Each set-piece is carefully shot and edited with an eye towards generating maximum suspense, even if they're polished to the extent that they more closely resemble mainstream horrors like *I Know What You Did Last Summer* (1997). But the sheer absence of logic throughout is enough to make any seasoned genre fan view every hackneyed scare tactic through cynical eyes.

It's a shame, because all the elements are otherwise there: a highly proficient cast (the child actors are great, especially Chasseriaud); Raphael Gesqua's sweeping score; Antoine Sarnier's delectable cinematography; Marc Thiebault's princely production design.

Bustillo and Maury wowed the horror community with their 2007 debut *Inside* (which also starred Dalle: her cameo here as an expectant psycho is a clear nod to such). Despite its far-fetched extravagances, that film was intense and brutal enough to singlehandedly cement their reputations as bright new genre hopes. But the lacklustre *Livid* followed in 2011, and *Among The Living* - skimping on the gore as well as credibility - does little to suggest they're likely to reach the high notes of their maiden outing again.

Apartment 1303 (2007)

Dir: Ataru Oikawa; Scr: Ataru Oikawa, Takamasa Sato, Kei Ohishi; Cast: Noriko Nakagoshi, Naoko Otani, Arata Furuta

Nakagoshi investigates when her sister moves into the titular apartment, only to throw herself from its balcony in front of her stunned housewarming guests. The dead girl's boyfriend insists it wasn't a suicide: he witnessed a tell-tale look in her eyes which suggested something more sinister was afoot. Enter a neighbouring child who discloses a shocking history behind the apartment: all of its female tenants have died in similar circumstances.

Naturally, Nakagoshi is compelled to spend a few nights in her sister's short-lived abode in a bid to uncover the truth. Cue flickering lights, strange noises in the night and shadowy figures flitting by in the background unseen by our witless heroine.

Oikawa had previously directed *Tomie* (1999) and *Tokyo Psycho* (2004) – two energetic, original films with style to spare. It's disconcerting, then, to see him go through such generic paces in a film that owes so much stylistically to *Ju-on: The Grudge* (2002). As in that movie, the malevolence here is housed by a building in which a violent history resides.

A succession of jump-scares, lank-haired female ghosts and flash-frame shocks play out like a "greatest hits" package of hackneyed J-Horror tropes. We're on to a loser here, even before we take into account the copious padding scenes of women tiptoeing furtively around darkened buildings.

The cause of our horror-minded pals in Asia rose significantly in profile during the 1990s, most notably with Hideo Nakata's refreshingly scary *Ring* (1998) and Takashi Miike's patient, perverse rug-puller *Audition* (1999). Alas, by 2007 the Japanese had fallen victim to what Western horror cinema has always done so well – and what our Eastern buddies initially seemed to be an antidote against: self-plagiarism in the pursuit of repeating a winning formula. Oikawa should know better, but he walks into every cliché with listless predictability.

As unlikely as it seems, *Apartment 1303* was deemed worthy of an American remake. Michael Taverna's 2012 adaptation is no better. It panders to the 3D crowd, along with throwing in the double threat of Mischa Barton and Rebecca De Mornay as headliners. It is, however, arguably worth seeing for the latter's overwrought maternal performance as a burned-out rock star: rein it in Beccy, the Academy aren't paying attention …

Apocalypse Of The Dead
See *Zone Of The Dead*

Applecart (2015)

Dir/Scr: Dustin Wayde Mills; Cast: Dave Parker Haley Madison, Allison Egan

Dustin Wayde Mills may well be the busiest filmmaker currently working in the indie horror scene. The Internet Movie Database credits him with having directed fourteen feature-length projects between 2010 and 2015, as well as several shorts. What's remarkable is that his output is always of an above-average standard, and details an interest in a diverse range of horror sub-genres (the irreverent comedic gore of *Zombie A-Hole* [2012]; the Cronenbergian body horror of *Skinless* [2013]; the arty torture porn of *Her Name Was Torment* [2014]).

In 2015, he announced via Facebook that his next film – the enigmatically titled *Applecart* – was going to be something different again. It is.

So, it's a portmanteau. Four stories, each of which stays true to the film's tagline "We all wear masks" by seeking to strip away conceptions of normalcy in everyday suburbia and examine what *really* goes on behind your neighbour's doors.

In one tale, a father spies on his daughter while she's engaging in a lesbian clinch with her pal. Another sees a female nurse tormenting an elderly male patient, pissing in his porridge and wanking in front of him for sadistic kicks. The third vignette surveys the cruel domination of a pregnant teenager by her devout Christian dad. Finally, we follow a besotted loser as he rescues the object of his affection from a twisted co-worker.

Clearly, in keeping with the title and the linking footage of apples (not to mention the continuation of this theme wherein characters feed on nothing but said produce throughout the film), the driving concept here is one of "forbidden fruit". Extending the parable of the Garden of Eden and Eve's unfortunate transgression, Mills delivers a twisted meditation on the contravention of recognised norms. As a statement of intent, it's worth noting that the title may well also allude to the expression "upsetting the applecart": an idiom used to describe the disturbance of routine.

Certainly, *Applecart* is anything but routine. Shot in stark monochrome and graced with a ragtime soundtrack, the film is boldly free from dialogue – save for the canned laughter and jeers of an off-screen audience. Each character wears an expressionless white mask and conveys their role via body language (very effective); there is little of the gore we've come to expect from Mills, though his penchant for full-frontal nudity remains unabated.

Can you handle frequent scenes of joyless masturbation (including the use of at least one prosthetic penis, courtesy of FX maestro Marcus Koch)? If so, *Applecart* will prove to be a rewarding, aesthetically rousing and genuinely subversive proposition for you.

Ascension (2002)

Dir/Scr: Karim Hussain; Cast: Marie-Josee Croze, Barbara Ulrich, Ilona Elkin

In a post-apocalyptic near-future, an unknown entity has killed God. Consequently, the world has been altered to such an extent that humans are now capable of performing their own miracles. Which sounds great, but for many this has resulted in life being a waking Hell. Three women – young Elkin, expectant Croze and the older Ulrich – climb the stairwells of an ominous building where they believe the guilty party lies waiting at the top. Their aim is to slay them, thus bringing this new world to an end.

Yes, really, that's the plot as I understood it. Portentous cod-psychology which accounts for over 90 minutes of footage detailing the female trio walking up the stairs, occasionally stepping over dead bodies, indulging in painfully slow philosophical discussions and sometimes sitting down for a breather.

Hussain first found infamy with 2000's *Subconscious Cruelty*, an arty examination of the brain's machinations which was as cerebral as it was disgusting. The film rightfully found notoriety. To his credit, Hussain's follow-up is anything but a hollow rehash of former successes. However, it's an endurance test which strives desperately to attain a higher meaning. The director wants this work to be likened to that of Russian filmmaker Andrei Tarkovsky (*Solaris* [1972], *Stalker* [1979] etc). Despite its decided anti-drama stance and appropriately plodding pace, the ghost of artifice looms large over the entire undertaking.

Hussain is a cinematographer first and foremost: visually, we know we're in good hands. But this is a short movie concept at best, which has been dragged out to a backside-bothering feature-length running time.

Just because people "don't get it" doesn't make it highbrow. Filling your film with self-indulgent repetition and pretentious dialogue shouldn't automatically earn it gravitas. Arguing that you're challenging conventions is sometimes not enough, especially when the ruminations contained within seem so artificial.

Atrocious
See *Atroz*

Atroz (2015)

Dir: Lex Ortega; Scr: Lex Ortega, Sergio Tello; Cast: Lex Ortega, Julio Rivera, Carlos Valencia

Ortega and Rivera are detained by police following a spot of drunk-driving which has resulted in a girl's death. Chief of police Valencia immediately recognises Ortega, which prompts him to search the latter's car. There, he finds a camcorder. Pressing 'play' takes us into the first of three home video-style shorts, each of which reveal more about Ortega's violent ways and the reasons behind these.

The first clip seen is actually a 2013 short from Ortega, a 17-minute assault on the senses also called *Atroz*. In it, he and Rivera stalk, abduct and ultimately kill a transvestite prostitute. Not content with merely committing murder, the hapless victim is punched, stabbed, smeared in their own shit and set alight first. The handheld video presentation, complete with interference and tape damage, is akin to that of *August Underground* (2001) – as is the unsparing, grimly realistic violence.

In the second segment, we follow our two antagonists as they further their obliteration of that which they fear most – female sexuality – by tearing an unwitting lap dancer apart. The third tape, found by the cops at Ortega's hideout following a brutal bout of police interrogation, takes us back in time where Carlos Padilla features as a younger version of the director and we learn of the horrible home life which helped create a monster.

From the high-speed opening montage of violence, homelessness and hookers openly flaunting their wares, Ortega paints an authentically threatening view of modern-day Mexico (he claims the film was inspired by stories that the country's authorities paid the producers of Bond feature *Spectre* [2015] to hide its "fucked up parts" while shooting their film). We realise from the start that the world he's about to drag us into is his country's seedier side. It's a poverty-stricken realm where crime is prevalent, sex sells and the police resort to tactics that fall just shy of butchery in a bid to control the unremitting sleaze.

Five minutes in to *Atroz* and your gut feeling will no doubt tell you not to expect a happy ending. But the journey to such a conclusion is an oddly compelling one: the lo-fi shorts serve more purpose in terms of narrative than we at first think; the framing present-day scenario is not only incredibly slick (shot in fluid digital HD with a tight command on editing) but also throws in a twist finale designed to hammer Ortega's political message home. Everyone is a victim in modern Mexico. The word "control" is used several times in the script, and that's what we see: the antagonists control their victims; their own sexual hang-ups are controlled by acts of hideous violence; control within a family environment; police control. Ironically, the underlying point is that virtually no-one has any control - these characters live in a world where everyone and anyone can become a victim, at any time.

Atroz comes recommended as a result – that is, if you can stomach the violence and insinuation that homophobia is ingrained in the Mexican mindset.

Attack Of The Cockface Killer (2002)

Dir: Jason Matherne; Scr: Jared Scallions; Cast: Mike Parks, Dana Kieferle, Bill Heintz

The titular phantom terrorises a small New Orleans community, armed with a blade and two dildos – one strapped to his chin (the correct term for this accessory is an accommodator, as any fetish freak will attest ...), another in hand. Oblivious victims consist of twentysomethings too busy getting either drunk or stoned to realise that once they engage in sexual activity, they're next on the madman's list.

Proclaiming to have been filmed entirely in "Tardo/Vision", Matherne's lowbrow, zero budget horror comedy comes on like Troma at their most fatuous. Fart gags and nudity galore, colourful characters often in wigs and bad make-up, a masturbating clown ... What more could you ask of a film whose killer wears a fake dick on his chin which sways from side to side as he chases his prey?

From the opening metal theme tune – attributed to The Pallbearers – through the ludicrous film-within-a-film "Stink Of Death", frequently seen on the revellers' televisions, to a climactic showdown between good guy Parks and Cockface which plays like something from a martial arts arcade game, this is stupefying in its childishness.

On the one hand, *Attack Of The Cockface Killer* is a real backyard effort, resembling what would happen if a group of friends gathered, cracked open a few beers and then proceeded to record an improvised play on camcorder. Naturally, it looks like shit. To say the cast exhibit signs of inexperience really is being too kind. But there's such a keen sense of the absurd that it's hard not to warm to.

Creative kills include nipple-slicing, castration, the disembowelment of one girl followed by strangulation by her own intestines, death by penis pump and more. The high body count provides an excuse for lots of rudimentary gore. A healthy quotient of sex adds to the lunacy. Matherne keeps the pace brisk and even demonstrates occasional flurries of cinematic style. As a result, *Attack Of The Cockface Killer* triumphs as being strangely watchable.

Matherne's production company Terror Optics self-released the film via a limited run of DVDs in 2005. I doubt they shifted many, but that didn't stop two sequels following: the marginally more structured *Goregasm* (2007) and *Grimewave: Cockface III* (2013).

The Autopsy Of Jane Doe (2016)

Dir: Andre Ovredal; Scr: Ian Goldberg, Richard Naing; Cast: Brian Cox, Emile Hirsch, Olwen Catherine Kelly

Coroner Cox is tasked with determining how unidentified corpse Kelly died. With a tight deadline imposed, he works overnight, reluctantly assisted by son Hirsch. As the evening draws on, they come across physical clues both disturbing (Kelly's tongue has been torn out, her genitalia mutilated) and anomalous (her clouded eyes suggest death occurred several days earlier; the blood that seeps from her torso when it's sliced open implies this is a fresh cadaver). More disconcertingly, they unearth evidence of possible witchery - which ties in with the strange power-cuts and random locking of doors they soon begin encountering.

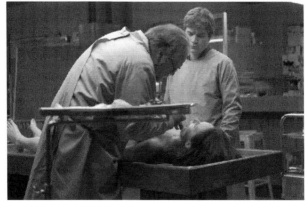

Having secured fans with his excellent *Troll Hunter* (2010), Norwegian filmmaker Ovredal made his English-speaking feature debut with this subtly chilling affair. Largely based in a single setting, it is - during its first half, certainly - an incrementally claustrophobic piece which worms its way into the viewer's mind with wily skill.

A lot of its power stems from the two lead performances. Hirsch impresses as the young trainee harbouring ideals of fleeing town for a life far removed from the one he's currently suffering. Cox excels in a role originally intended for Martin Sheen (he backed out due to conflicting shooting commitments). His is a cynical, set-in-his-ways character: the pragmatic old-timer initially disinclined to accept any notion of supernatural goings-on. To watch both characters evolve and have their beliefs not only challenged but turned upside-down becomes something rather beautiful to behold. Meanwhile, Ophelia Lovibond brings an extra depth to events as Hirsch's increasingly anxious love interest.

Themes of loyalty, faith, tradition and superstition rise to the surface as a result.

Matt Gant's production design is modest but persuasive. Roman Osin's cinematography fuels proceedings with a necessarily cool, austere aesthetic. Scott McIntyre's FX team provide splashy set-pieces, which Ovredal wisely measures out throughout the film to maximum effect.

Marred only by a weak final act, *The Autopsy Of Jane Doe* is nevertheless one of the more original and rewarding genre offerings in recent memory.

Awaken The Witch
See *Wake The Witch*

Bacterium (2006)

Dir/Scr: Brett Piper; Cast: Chuck McMahon, Alison Whitney, Benjamin Kanes

Having developed a form of biological warfare for the US army, scientist McMahon has since holed himself up in a remote forest-based cabin where he hopes to find a cure to his own creation. Four holidaying paintball enthusiasts stumble across his hideout, thus becoming unwilling test subjects. The covert military movement closing in on them has a more pragmatic approach: they plan to wipe out McMahon, his captives, and all trace of the wildly spreading virus.

As prolific with his no-budget special effects work as he is at filmmaking, Piper graduated via bargain basement schlock like *Mutant War* (1988) and *Draniac!* (2000) before enjoying a productive couple of years with EI Independent Cinema's Shock-O-Rama production house. *Bacterium* is the best film he made while with them.

What Piper brought to the table were a snappy, unapologetically corny script; an expertise in producing satisfyingly gooey old-school effects in the style of Chuck Russell's *The Blob* remake (1988); and the experience requisite for directing such action on a paltry $30,000.00 budget.

Okay, technical flourishes are restricted to Tarantino-esque 'retro' titles and adroit editing. These tend to be offset by some truly risible performances (McMahon takes top honours – or should that read 'bottom'?) and an undeniable cheapness to the overall look and feel.

But considering *Bacterium* was released onto US DVD with a family-friendly PG-13 rating, it scores remarkably high on the gore count. That's before we even consider the script's occasional expletives and a healthy dose of female nudity thrown in for no other reason than titillation.

The end results are breezily entertaining. Stylistic references to *The Crazies* (1973), along with a screenplay which alludes to the paranoia of *Invasion Of The Body Snatchers* (1956) and claustrophobia of *Night Of The Living Dead* (1968), simply add to the chaotic charm.

Bad Meat (2011)

Dir: Lulu Jarmen; Scr: Paul Gerstenberger; Cast: Mark Pellegrino, Elizabeth Harnois, Dave Franco

The most threadbare hospital room seen on screen since *Night Of The Demon* (1980) serves as the introduction to a badly incapacitated, heavily bandaged trauma survivor who details via flashbacks how they ended up in that state ...

Sequestered to a brutal summer camp at their despairing parents' behest, several teens were subjected to ridiculous disciplinary measures by administrator Pellegrino and his cohorts in the name of reconditioning: urine-coated alarm calls, hard labour, inedible slop for meals etc.

Then the kids discovered that their sponsored captors' luxurious dinners had been laced with contaminated meat. The nightmare intensified as the camp supervisors went suitably doolally.

Bad Meat suffered from a troubled production. Director Rob Schmidt (*Wrong Turn*, 2003) was attached to the project in 2007 until funding ran dry upon production team Capitol Films' collapse the following May. Crisis talks unsuccessfully fought to keep cast and crew members on board, who up until that point had completed two thirds of the movie for a promise of recompense that hadn't materialised.

Resultantly, the film - credited to the mysterious Jarmen who is, many suspect, Schmidt completing this ill-fated project under a pseudonym - applies unwieldy editing throughout and the aforementioned, unidentifiable narrator (their account is tapped onto a computer keyboard, handily) for the post-production linking sequences.

Such tactics are obvious and jarring, although there's still a fair amount to enjoy for the most part. Performances are strong (look out for Franco, brother of James), dark humour works well - though an S&M-themed interlude is perhaps *too* bizarre - and there's even a fair degree of tension elicited during the latter half. A queasy penchant for revelling in the excesses of bodily functions delivers the gross-out factor.

However, everything comes undone at the end. A bizarre jolting cut deprives the audience of any satisfying conclusion, shifting us abruptly from what would appear to be the beginnings of a climactic confrontation to the hospital where absolutely nothing is explained.

Baskin (2015)

Dir: Can Evrenol; Scr: Can Evrenol, Ogulcan Eren Akay, Cem Ozuduru, Ercin Sadikoglu; Cast: Ergun Kuyucu, Gorkem Kasal, Muharrem Bayrak

Based upon his intense 2013 short film of the same name, Evrenol's *Baskin* stands as the most high-profile Turkish horror film of the new millennium thus far.

In it, a group of cops - specifically troubled rookie Kasal and his seasoned partner Kuyucu - race to the scene of a supposed disturbance: a seemingly deserted building positioned in the centre of an Istanbul neighbourhood rumoured to be cursed. Searching the building, they stumble across a group of Satanists engaged in black mass practices ... and inadvertently open a portal to Hell. Much gory mayhem ensues.

Well, that's the gist. Much like its 11-minute progenitor, *Baskin* is a mess when it comes to storyline. Characters enjoy early cryptic conversations around the nature of dreams, strange occurrences from their past, pacts made with buddies who subsequently died, walking in on their parents having sex and so on. It's clear that there's a satirical bent to the lawmen's dodgy dealings. But quite what all of these early informational sequences have to do with the unfurling action remains vague, given Evrenol's penchant for hurling his protagonists through time loops which cast different slants on events that have already happened. Are the denizens of the Hell they unleash embodiments of Kasal's most traumatic memories? Possibly. Are they the sins of each corrupt cop coming back to haunt them? Could be.

Fear not. Even if the plot makes less and less sense as events progress, the film continues to delight on a purely visual level. I haven't seen such gleeful use of vivid primary colours since prime Dario Argento (*Suspiria*, 1977, for example).

Evrenol possesses a flair for filming everything, in fact, with oodles of colour and panache. Even the gore, of which there is plenty, is shot in a perversely considered, paradoxically beautiful manner. If you can say such a thing, that is, about nasty eye-gouging, disembowelments and the like.

The nightmare logic is just that - figuratively and literally. Forget about the plot (if you don't you'll only frustrate yourself) and enjoy the visuals. If you can do that, *Baskin* will thrill you - especially if you're a fan of Clive Barker's more unbridled fetishist excesses. Oh yes, the similarities are there ...

Beyond Re-Animator (2003)

Dir: Brian Yuzna; Scr: Jose Manuel Gomez; Cast: Jeffrey Combs, Elsa Pataky, Jason Barry

In 1985, theatre director Stuart Gordon and budding producer Brian Yuzna won the hearts of genre fans everywhere with *Re-Animator* – their witty, gore-soaked adaptation of HP Lovecraft's 1921-22 serialised tale "Herbert West: Re-Animator". A true breath of fresh air for its time, the film's winning combination of graphic gore, luminous performances and wild invention turned it into an instant classic. A sequel inevitably followed, 1989's *Bride Of Re-Animator*, which saw Yuzna take on directorial duties. Gorier and even more outrageous than its predecessor, the film did however rely too heavily on broad splatstick.

A period of quiet followed, during which time at least one mooted sequel toyed with the idea of placing its lead character in the White House, until finally *Beyond Re-Animator* surfaced.

The results are a mixed bag. The story finds titular protagonist Combs imprisoned. His scientific attempts at bringing the dead back to life, via a groundbreaking serum he's developed, have led to his incarceration following a murderous attack by one of his "zombies". Enter medical man Barry, whose girlfriend was the victim: now he wants to help Combs perfect his serum from behind bars. Much chaos ensues, via prison riots, gory undead assaults and more.

Yuzna's film is disposable fun which is best appreciated by unrepentant gorehounds. Shot entirely in Spain on a $3 million budget, *Beyond Re-Animator* doesn't do much to expand the initial premise (neither did the 1989 film, in fairness) and its nonsensical plot exists solely as a springboard from one splatterific punchline to the next. The Lovecraft references remain: Barry's character is called Howard Phillips, which were the author's first names; Pataky appears as a journalist called Olney – a surname first used in the 1926 short story "The Strange High House in the Mist".

Combs is reliable as ever as the enjoyably megalomaniacal Herbert West, though it's a shame Bruce Abbott – his reluctant assistant in the preceding two instalments – was too busy running a printing business in California to appear.

The film premiered on the Sci-Fi Channel in an edited version but was later released uncut onto DVD. The final scene leaves room for a sequel but, to date, there's been no sign of one coming.

Beyond The Black Rainbow (2010)

Dir/Scr: Panos Cosmatos; Cast: Eva Allan, Michael Rogers, Scott Hylands

In which the son of Italian-born filmmaker George P Cosmatos (*Massacre In Rome* [1973]; *Rambo: First Blood Part 2* [1985] etc) seeks to outclass his father's efforts with a single blow. This feature debut is certainly a beguiling experiment in its harkening of classic sci-fi cinema of yore.

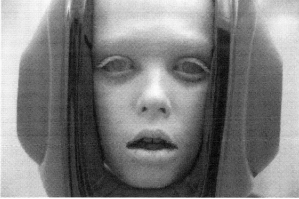

Telepathic Allan is held against her will in Hylands' clinically bare institute, where he conducts research in a bid to better understand her condition and ascertain as to whether he shares her gift. His assistant, Rogers, becomes obsessed with Allan - so much so that, when she escapes, he's compelled to take pursuit with a dagger in hand.

Events move at a glacial pace. This allows for the elegant set design and lush cinematography - all sparse interiors and empty, atmospherically icy compositions - to take centre stage. The painstaking visuals are congruent with the iconic aesthetics of Stanley Kubrick's masterful *2001: A Space Odyssey* (1968).

But this is one film that gets stranger and more ambitious as it progresses. Many have likened it to the cinema of David Lynch, such is its embracement of surrealism. It's more accurate to cite the colourful, openly metaphorical likes of Alexandro Jodorowsky (*The Holy Mountain*, 1973, springs to mind) and Luis Bunuel. Add a dash of Dario Argento at his most vivid and you should start to get the picture.

Complete with Jeremy Schmidt's droning synth score (which adds credence to the film being set in 1983) and extremely minimalistic plot, accusations of this Canadian production being a shining example of style over substance are unavoidable. One of the film's most portentous sequences is also one of its most memorable: a monochrome flashback which plays out as an acid trip of particularly nightmarish distinction.

Of course it's pretentious. Yes, it's dramatically lacking. But if you allow yourself to succumb to the duteous visuals and audio, you will be rewarded with a film of rich ambience and lasting visceral impact.

How cool is this film? The soundtrack also includes tracks by Venom and SSQ.

Beyond The Rave (2008)

Dir: Matthias Hoene; Scr: Tom Grass, Jon Wright; Cast: Jamie Dornan, Nora-Jane Noone, Sebastian Knapp

As comebacks go, this return to the fray by the justifiably famous Hammer Films brand – twenty-nine years after their previous incarnation's last production, *The Lady Vanishes* (1979) – is as inauspicious as they get.

British soldier Dornan is determined to enjoy his last night of civilian life before being shipped off to fight in Iraq. His revelry soon turns into a hunt for estranged girlfriend Noone - said to be living it up at an all-night-rave hosted by the enigmatic Knapp. With the help of his best pal (Matthew Forrest), Dornan sets about tracking her down. What he discovers upon locating the party proves to be a real pain in the neck.

Seeking a return to the romantic era of genre cinema where Peter Cushing and Christopher Lee hammed things up while fighting tooth and nail? Forget it. Don't even approach this expectant of the second-rate frights provided by *The Woman In Black* (2012). This is rubbish.

It began life as a series of twenty 4-minute webisodes screened via MySpace. These were brought together to make one 93-minute film, which was subsequently shat onto an unsuspecting world of DVD consumers in late 2010.

The episodic origins remain evident in the rapid-fire nature of the action: characters are hastily introduced and more often than not dispensed of just as swiftly, as the plot pile-drives unrelentingly onwards. There's little in the way of characterisation, emotional engagement or even continuity.

Ingrid Pitt makes a token cameo appearance – inadvertently forcing viewers to pine for the authentic Hammer pictures of her heyday (*The Vampire Lovers* [1970]; *Countess Dracula* [1971]). Other than her rather contrived inclusion, there's nothing here to suggest the heritage of Britain's greatest ever horror studio.

Instead we get supporting roles from Ray Winstone's daughter Lois, Primrose Hill has-been Sadie Frost and the usually reliable Leslie Simpson (*A Reckoning*, 2011). Perennial London hardnut Tamer Hassan is on hand to help events feel like a vampiric riff on Nick Love tropes – think *The Football Factory* (2004), *The Business* (2005) etc. It's all shell-suits, techno music and out-of-context expletives, and it soon becomes tiresome.

A blend of humour and gore works very occasionally. But, by and large, this is a travesty.

Hoene went on to co-write and direct the title-tells-all *Cockneys Vs Zombies* (2012) ...

Birdemic: Shock And Terror (2010)

Dir/Scr: James Nguyen; Cast: Alan Bagh, Whitney Moore, Danny Webber

Shot for less than $10,000.00 over the course of four years, *Birdemic* was something of a labour of love for Nguyen. If love means adopting a sloppy "that'll do" approach at every turn.

An eco-friendly crusade which takes its time to incorporate romance and an inordinate amount of feeble character-building into its meandering plot, the film holds the distinction of being widely received as one of the worst of its era (only Tommy Wiseau's 2003 indie hoot *The Room* comes close in terms of widespread scorn). But is *Birdemic* really that bad?

Yep. Set in a sleepy coastal town not too dissimilar to the Bodega Bay setting of Alfred Hitchcock's *The Birds* (1963), it's hard to imagine this train wreck of a movie being any more inept.

The actors are hardly Oscar contenders to begin with. Saddled with Nguyen's broken English script, they stammer and stall through nonsensical lines to such an extent that it's baffling to think the director (I use the term loosely) never called for additional takes. The clumsy deliveries and laughable dialogue – "the human species needs to stop playing cowboy with nature. We must act more like astronauts, spacemen taking care of spaceship Earth" – are equalled in their uselessness by zero continuity, out-of-focus camerawork, sloppy editing, an annoying repetitive score and a continually flagging pace.

And all of this is before the birds finally attack, about 50 minutes into the film.

When nature does eventually revolt (the signs have been there from the start: a TV anchor man warning of global warming's effects; a lovers' date which takes in a big screening of Al Gore's propaganda piece *An Inconvenient Truth* [2006]), prepare yourself for a new low in CGI-assisted action. The computer-generated bird assaults are epically shit.

Slow-moving vultures and eagles hover in superimposed fashion over actors too inexperienced to convincingly portray their fear of an imaginary threat. How anyone can wind up a fatality from such poorly staged scenes of "carnage" is beyond me. Luckily, our protagonists – two witless young couples – are armed with coat hangers. *Coat hangers.*

But, *Birdemic* is tremendous fun. Grabs some beers, grab some mates, and enjoy its absurdly incompetent charms in the company of likeminded souls. In this environment, it is perhaps the ultimate party flick.

Unfortunately, the success of Severin Films' blu-ray release (which looks like dung, given Nguyen's penchant for overexposed exterior shots) inspired the director to helm a 2013 sequel, *Birdemic 2: Resurrection*. Despite a bigger budget – reportedly $20,000.00 – and a leaning towards self-aware comedy which its predecessor lacked, the sequel proved that the joke wears thin quickly … especially when nice-but-dim Nguyen is in on it.

Black Mass Of The Nazi Sex Wizard (2015)

Dir/Scr: Lucifer Valentine; Cast: Hank Skinny, Sister S, Chalice

Did someone order a sequel/prequel to Lucifer Valentine's notorious "Vomit Gore Trilogy" (*Slaughtered Vomit Dolls* [2006], *ReGOREgitated Scarifice* [2008], *Slow Torture Puke Chamber* [2010])? No? Oh well, you've got one. Its alternate title is *Vomit Gore 4*.

It takes us back to the Christmas of 1996, where we witness – through the by-now expected façade of experimental (some may say *avant-garde*) non-linear, dreamlike sequences – how Valentine's bulimic muse Angela Aberdeen came to be possessed by demons. Cue disconnected set-piece scenes in which different actresses portray the character as her identity mutates during a downward spiral into Hell.

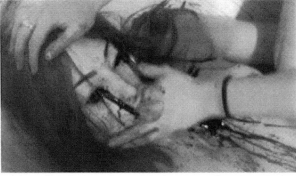

The score, by the filmmaker himself, is in keeping with the preceding instalments in the series and is ambient noise. It's highly effective in its jarring, nightmarish clatter. Valentine retains the artily jagged editing style of his earlier works, as well as the lo-fi aesthetic (furthered by his need to film on various formats here, necessitating an intermittent ratio change which may jolt some). The Satanic imagery of old is also inevitably recalled. Oh, and do you remember the haunting snippets of archive home videos in *Dolls*, evoking a sense of "innocence lost"? A similar tactic is employed here, utilising vintage cartoon clips at choice moments. There remains an air of distasteful tragedy as a result.

Cheap excessive gore maintains a presence too. A woman's face is peeled away from her skull; breasts and eyes are hacked away and devoured. None of it is terribly convincing, nor can any of it claim to be as remotely extreme as the copious vomiting and acts of genuine self-mutilation being served up throughout.

In fact, there are very few new ideas emergent during *Black Mass*'s long sixty-six minute haul.

Harmony Korine, David Lynch and Larry Clarke are cited among Valentine's influences. Squint extremely hard and you still may have a hard time joining the dots between his skid row fetish philosophising and any of these authentically gifted filmmakers' successes.

The director – whose true identity remains a secret to most, though at the time of writing he traverses Facebook using the moniker Thompson Edward - made a rare personal appearance at 2015's Slaughter in Syracuse festival, where *Black Mass* was premiered and a notice was given that this may be the only time it would be screened publicly. Of course, this threat was never carried out and Austrian label Black Lava Entertainment offered the film on DVD via online sales shortly afterwards.

The Black Waters Of Echo's Pond (2009)

Dir: Gabriel Bologna; Scr: Gabriel Bologna, Michael Berenson, Sean Clark; Cast: Danielle Harris, Sean Lawlor, James Duval

A group of pals gather to let their hair down in a cabin located on drunken co-star Robert Patrick's privately owned island. You'd be right to expect the customary cattiness, sexual frissons and boozing. But there's a background to these characters too: underlying animosities are apparent during early scenes. These are brought to the fore when the grouping discover a board game capable of invoking antagonistic visions of former transgressions each has previously suffered at the hands of a fellow player. Naturally, this leads to vengeful murder ... and demonic possession.

The casting is impressive. Harris has obviously carved a genre-specific niche for herself over the last couple of decades, making an impact in everything from *Halloween 4: The Return Of Michael Myers* (1988) and *Halloween 5* (1989) to *Stake Land* (2010) and *Chromeskull: Laid To Rest 2* (2011). Patrick will always be best-known for his villainous role in *Terminator 2: Judgement Day* (1991). Duval has pedigree too: *The Doom Generation* (1995), *Donnie Darko* (2001) etc.

Such experienced hands are given short shrift by sloppy, unimaginative direction and a clichéd screenplay. It's not so much that the cabin-in-the-woods scenario has been done to death (though it has). The problems here include an inconsistent tone (is this dark horror or a comedy – or is the latter unintentional and purely due to the ill-advised speaking roles given to Robert Rodriguez's identical-twin nieces, Electra and Elise Avellan?), characters unworthy of caring about and a ludicrous plot twist which exercises a complete absence of inspiration on the filmmakers' part.

The film isn't bad-looking on a photogenic level. There's some decent practical gore too (chain saws and rakes are employed to good effect). And those seeking cheap thrills can rest assured that Mircea Monroe's breasts are more than willing to titillate the needy. Beyond that, and despite an appearance by malevolent god Pan, this fails to convince either as drama or horror.

But what do I know? The film won the Audience Choice Award at HorrorHound magazine's Ohio-based festival in 2009.

Blood Oath (2007)

Dir: David Buchert; Scr: David Meier Smith; Cast: Natalie Hart, Roger Horn, Jamie Reynolds

Two couples extend their camping festivities to incorporating the search for a cabin where, urban legend promises, a beautiful murderess tends to her psychotic parents and disfigured twin. Guess what happens?

Picked up for US distribution by his company, Lloyd Kaufman declared this to be "better than anything Troma ever made". That's debatable but, as with *Blood Junkie* (2010), it does qualify as a title superior to many of their in-house productions.

One of the many post-millennial throwbacks to the slasher style of the early 80s (though the inclusion of mobile telephones and mention of eBay place it firmly within a contemporary setting), *Blood Oath*'s plot is - of course - derivative hokum. Tellingly, even its working title was *Stalk 'N' Slash*. But the sub-genre it owes its design to was hardly renowned for its capricious nature; docking points here for unoriginality seems inequitable.

Buchert compensates for a lack of surprises by way of unravelling his simplistic yarn with gusto. Well-lit compositions, considered camerawork and copious gore - delivered with verve by Gray Creasy - add to the frequent set-pieces. Cameos from latter-day scream queens Tiffany Shepis and Tina Krause don't harm the film's credibility any.

Considering all concerned donated their services for free, no small amount of effort appears to have been involved here. Each gory action sequence was meticulously prepared via storyboards; suitable locations were scouted out months ahead of the shoot; actor Patrick Holt endured 3-hour make-up sessions in order to transform into the deformed killer. Even the acting's above par.

Perversely, it may be *Blood Oath*'s proficiency that renders it ultimately forgettable. Diverting, yes - but only fleetingly so. Had it been abominable it would have been remembered as being so (perhaps even in an enjoyable sense). As it stands, it simply treads overly familiar ground in an accomplished bur rarely exciting manner.

Blood Of The Werewolf (2001)

Dir: Joe Bagnardi, Bruce G Hallenbeck, Kevin J Lindenmuth; Scr: Stephen C Seward; Cast: Tony Luna, Mia Borrelli, Bruce G Hallenbeck

A trio of tales, each of which celebrates the concept of lyncanthropic terror.

The first, Hallenbeck's "Blood Reunion", sees horror novelist Luna return to his hometown in the hope of winning the heart of his childhood crush (Mary Kay Hilko). As their love blossoms, her over-protective grandmother warns of a family curse and the locals fret over the succession of mutilated corpses that start turning up. Substandard effects, ugly video aesthetics and amateurish acting set a tone that will continue throughout.

Lindenmuth's "Old Blood" is arguably the best of the shorts on offer, thanks to slightly more proficient performances, more fleshed-out characters and tighter editing - though that's not saying a great deal. It introduces us to Roberta (Borrelli). She's a shape-shifter desperately trying to suppress her condition with drugs, in order that she can maintain a relationship with human lover Charlene (Sasha Graham).

Rounding things off, Bagnardi's rather pedestrian "Manbeast" takes far too long to reach its predictable "twist" conclusion. It stars Hallenbeck as a man infected from a werewolf's bite, on the run and pursued through greenery by two hunters.

Of the three filmmakers involved in *Blood Of The Werewolf*, Lindenmuth undoubtedly has the largest profile. His rudimentary gorefests *Vampires And Other Stereotypes* (1994) and *Addicted To Murder* (1995) were notable titles during the last hoorah of mainstream VHS retail. He's also no stranger to shaggy dog horror movies - having also directed the likes of *Rage Of The Werewolf* (1999) and one section of *Bites: The Werewolf Chronicles* (2002). Bagnardi and Hallenbeck have made a handful of nondescript no-budget genre flicks between them. The latter is best known for cult documentary *Fangs! A History Of Vampires In The Movies* (1989).

Rosa Hallenbeck (Bruce's wife) is responsible for the special effects in the first and third segments. I use that term extremely loosely. Actors race around in rubber wolf masks, while plastic limbs which have clearly been bought from toy stores are employed wherever dismemberment has been written into the screenplay. Mike Strain Jr of Fantasy Creations provides the marginally better FX work for Lindenmuth's effort.

Minor points of interest: the film opens to a monochrome prologue shot by Gabriel Campisi, in which infamous director Ted V Mikels (*The Corpse Grinders* [1971], *Blood Orgy Of The She-Devils* [1973] etc) introduces the action; *Fangoria* scribe Michael Gingold and latter-day scream queen Debbie Rochon have extremely brief cameos in "Old Blood".

Bloodrape (2011)

Dir/Scr: Tucker Bennett, Taeer Maymon, Zach Shipko; Cast: Tucker Bennett, Brooke Candy, Chris Corrente

All-girl hardcore punk band Bloodrape return from an extended period of hibernation, intent on wreaking havoc wherever they play on their comeback tour. The girls also just happen to be vampires, which means that as well as piercing eardrums they're out to puncture necks where possible. Along with mutilating genitals, vomiting, drug-taking and much more. A pair of hapless youths are spared their lives in order that they can document the band's reckless antics on camcorder (it would appear bloodsuckers haven't yet fathomed how to work these things).

Following on from their curious 2009 DIY debut *Why Are You Weird?*, student filmmakers Bennett and Shipko returned – newcomer Maymon in tow – with this mockumentary shot on various formats: HD camcorder, Hi-8, Mini DV and even a few moments of 16mm. The low grade look complies with Bennett's appreciation for transgressive artists such as Nick Zedd and Richard Kern in interviews.

Lending a further feel of no-budget, no-wave cinema to proceedings, iconic underground filmmaker George Kuchar (*Hold Me While I'm Naked* [1966], *I, An Actress* [1977] etc) appears in what was to be his final cameo role: he died in September 2011.

Written and shot over the course of sixteen months and made with no official budget (unofficially, the filmmakers reckon they forked out somewhere between $300 and $500 during this time, mainly on beer and pizza for their cast), *Bloodrape* makes no attempt to hide its shoddiness – from the failure to disguise the fact that the concert venue we first see the band playing in is far more likely to be someone's living room, to the amateurish splatter effects later on.

An uncanny level of high energy, along with a boisterous soundtrack – co-written in part by Bennett and Shipko, alongside contributions from the band Felt Drawings – helps *Bloodrape* hold the interest. It's also worth a look for the inclusion of charismatic former heroin addict-turned-wannabe rap star Candy as the band's leader.

The filmmakers released a strictly limited DVD/magazine/CD soundtrack combo of the film back in 2012, via their Next Wave Video Productions site. Good luck tracking down one of those!

One piece of advice: it's perhaps not a good idea to run searches for this title online while at work …

Bug (2006)

Dir: William Friedkin; Scr: Tracy Letts; Cast: Michael Shannon, Ashley Judd, Harry Connick Jr

Lonely waitress Judd escapes an abusive marriage and walks straight into a relationship with outsider Shannon. Oh, Ashley, the frying pan probably doesn't seem so bad, now that you're sitting in the fire?

Inveigled into his life and then his motel room home, Judd not only learns of Shannon's neuroses – he's a war veteran who may or may not have been experimented on by the Army, and now exists in a state of intense paranoia – but grows to share it. First he sees insects everywhere, crawling over his flesh (they're invisible to us, the audience), and then she begins to see them too. Their four-wall surroundings become a prison of aluminium foil and airtight sealants as they struggle to keep the bugs, both literal and metaphorical, out of their habitat.

Adapted for the screen by Letts from his own 1996 play of the same name, *Bug*'s first masterstroke was to carry over Shannon, who'd made the lead role his own on the stage. His performance is a powerhouse of fevered psychosis, a man whose delusions intensify to such an extent that he *needs* someone else to see them. Judd is convincingly downtrodden and unglamorous as the former victim willing to be that "someone". Never merely an account of *delusional parasitosis*, the film examines the modern world's issues with security: we are not safe anymore, we feel, even in our own homes.

Admittedly, *Bug* does suffer a little from its (predominantly) single-setting scenario. The sparse set design may be curiously effective in its claustrophobic feel but the film's stage origins are obvious at times. Friedkin's direction often lacks the imagination required to keep things visually interesting. Despite reports that the director whizzed through the shoot, keen to complete it in as few takes as possible, this is all very much held together by the conviction of its lead actors.

The film made the British tabloid press when, in June 2007, London-based millionaire businessman Alberto Izaga murdered his two-year-old daughter a week after seeing the movie in an American cinema. At the subsequent court hearing, the Old Bailey was told Izaga had become "obsessed" with the film and convinced that his family were possessed by the Devil (ironic, perhaps, as Friedkin also directed the world's most renowned film about demonic possession, *The Exorcist* [1973]).

Friedkin and Letts would work together again on adapting one of the latter's plays for the cinema, with 2011's well-received *Killer Joe*.

Buried (2010)

Dir: Rodrigo Cortes; Scr: Chris Sparling; Cast: Ryan Reynolds, Samantha Mathis, Jose Luis Garcia Perez

American trucker Reynolds has been working as part of a convoy delivering supplies in the Iraqi desert. Having an affair with a colleague and being subsequently sacked by his employer are the least of his worries: in the meantime he's been kidnapped by loyalists and buried alive in the arid plains, inside a coffin. Equipped with only a cigarette lighter and Blackberry 'phone, he sets about trying to initiate his own rescue mission.

Buried is notable for its especially minimalist approach: filmed in sequential order, in a single setting and with only Reynolds ever appearing on screen (all other players are heard in voice only), the simplistic premise is a daring one which puts a great deal of pressure on its leading man to carry the drama. Remarkably, the chiselled star of insipid romantic comedies like *Just Friends* (2005) and *Definitely, Maybe* (2008) pulls it off.

He makes for a convincing everyman: flawed, arrogant, vulnerable, charming, scared. We believe in him, and we want him to survive as the action unfurls. Sparling's taut script helps the cause, ladling on the tension from the get-go. It drip-feeds sub-plots which reveal more of our protagonist's background and builds steadily towards a nail-biting twist climax.

It's Cortes who threatens to let the side down. Even if silly lapses in logic, such as Reynolds constantly using his lighter (burning up precious oxygen *and* wasting its fuel) or him being unable to remember an emergency number (and not thinking to have stored it in his 'phone) but capable of recalling every other useless number, stem from Sparling's mind it's up to the director to iron out such calamities. He doesn't; the action is almost entirely undermined as a result.

Fortunately, the suspense of the grim scenario and Reynolds' surprisingly committed turn salvage affairs.

Busanhaeng
See *Train To Busan*

The Butchers
See *Death Factory*

Buzz Saw (2005)

Dir/Scr: Robin Garrels, David Burnett; Cast: Stephen J Heffernan, Jason Allen Wolfe, Lisa Ann Harness

Don't you just hate it when the boss goes away, and you're left in charge of maintaining a block of apartments - only for the tenants to start getting bloodily bumped off? This is the situation Heffernan finds himself in. His sole ally is friend and colleague Wolfe.

Each murder employs use of power tools from Heffernan's personal collection. Could he really be responsible, as per the local sheriff's suspicions? Or perhaps there is some credence to Wolfe's claims of having seen an alien spacecraft in the neighbouring woods? That would at least explain the strange green-faced children (Jodi Wurm and Jeffery McCoy) who witness each atrocity while taking notes.

Unfortunately Heffernan is a drunk, while Wolfe's drug addiction has him renowned for being a paranoid wreck ... so who's going to believe a word these two say?

One of those films where almost everyone appears to have doubled up on chores - actors chipping in behind the scenes, crew members proffering onscreen cameos - *Buzz Saw* overcomes its penurious digital look by virtue of this sense of it being a labour of love. It's unabashedly strange, though brimming with confidence and creativity.

Much less the rip-off of *The Toolbox Murders* (1978) than it may sound, it does however begin much akin to a traditional body count movie. Before long, it's mutated into a hybrid of black comedy and offbeat horror which is not a million miles away from the weirdness of David Lynch.

Tonal shifts from one scene to the next play havoc with any sense of continuity. It's difficult not to imagine that this isn't Garrels and Burnett's intention, given that they appear to enjoy subverting audience expectations (the humour works best during the unlikeliest, darkest moments; our two protagonists are dysfunctional to the point of chronic self-destruction; how many slasher films segue successfully into sci-fi territory?). This staccato approach to delivery results in events rarely having any relevance to their preceding scenes. It shouldn't work but, curiously, it all adds to the demented glee with which the co-writers toy with us.

Buzz Saw is also gory - though perhaps not as much as you initially think. The aftermath of a bathtub electrocution; multiple stabbings; a power-saw disembowelment: clever editing skirts around the pratfalls of no-budget special effects, deceiving our brains into seeing more than our eyes do.

One drawback is that Garrels and Burnett's oddity, as enjoyable as it is, can't fully sustain its 97-minute running time.

Cabin Fever (2002)

Dir/Scr: Eli Roth; Cast: Cerina Vincent, Jordan Ladd, Rider Strong

Roth's calling card to the genre harks back to the cinema of the 1970s and 1980s. It does so awkwardly, flitting between the go-for-broke gruesomeness of the former and the apologetic humour of the latter's later years.

A quintet of young adults travel out to a remote cabin for their summer holiday. It's quickly established that this takes these city slickers into territory popularised by *Deliverance* (1972). Upon arrival they're accosted by a local hick who's been bitten by his dog, thus contracting a curious flesh-eating disease. The youths despatch of their aggressive visitor in predictably excessive fashion, ultimately dumping his charred corpse in the nearby reservoir. Alas, their cabin's water supply stems directly from the same lake.

With five individuals holed up in the sticks while succumbing one-by-one to malevolent forces, the plot pilfers unabashedly from *The Evil Dead* (1981) - at least during its first act. To his credit, Roth fleshes out his characters more roundly than Sam Raimi ever bothered to. As the action unfolds, paranoia akin to that experienced in *The Thing* (1982) adds a fresh twist.

Cabin Fever can also boast of Scott Kevan's crisp photography, Ryan Folsey's nimble editing and satisfyingly gooey effects from KNB EFX Group. The cast are sexy and unexpectedly likeable in the main, despite Roth's penchant to fill their mouths with crass pubescent one-liners.

But the balance of humour and horror never quite gels, the former often coming across as smug and the latter feeling somewhat restrained. For all the gloopy practical FX work, there's a sense that Roth is holding back in a bid to secure an R rating. An anticlimactic conclusion also works against the film.

The movie spawned a couple of sequels, most notably 2009's *Cabin Fever 2: Spring Fever* – directed by Ti West. 2016 also saw the release of Travis Zariwny's unexpected, unwarranted and inferior remake.

The Cabin In The Woods (2012)

Dir: Drew Goddard; Scr: Drew Goddard, Josh Whedon; Cast: Chris Hemsworth, Kristen Connolly, Fran Kranz

Five pals embark into the great outdoors, venturing towards a boondocks-based holiday cabin – despite warnings against doing so, courtesy of a typically feral local gas attendant.

Upon their arrival, the cellar door mysteriously bursts open of its own accord. Inspecting the cellar, the group discover an array of cryptic curios. Among these is a dusty old book which, when read from, is capable of raising a family of cannibals buried in the surrounding woods.

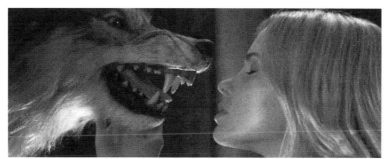

You *think* you know the story. Or at least, the two or three components which combine to provide the plot thus far (most glaringly, 1981's *The Evil Dead*). However, *The Cabin In The Woods* has a couple of tricks up its sleeve.

From its cloyingly uninspired title to a cast of empty-headed, finely chiselled young actors portraying clichéd characters (the buff hero, the slut, the puritanical final girl, the stoner comic relief dude), Whedon and Goddard desperately hope to sucker their audience into expecting "just another dumb horror film".

The first of two major twists comes early into proceedings, as we learn the true nature of this game long before these unwitting protagonists do. This allows for a healthy amount of *meta* musings, the conventions of the genre being laid bare and scrutinised in a consciously self-referential manner. "What makes a horror film scary?" the co-writers appear to be asking, while fashioning a movie devoid of whatever the answers may be.

For *The Cabin In The Woods* is never fearsome. Intermittently amusing, yes. Even surprising in where it cribs its ideas from on occasion (could the scene utilising a goat's hoof *really* be a nod to *The Last House On Dead End Street* [1977]?!). It wears its attractive production values on its sleeve – including some righteous FX work during the final act - and boasts a good-looking cast of competent, if unremarkable, actors.

But, no, it's never frightening. It's "horror 101" for people with a passing – and quite probably rather condescending – regard for the genre. The second twist is as outlandish as it is smugly delivered, dividing viewers into those who will laugh and applaud its "originality" (i.e. those who've never sat through *Thir13een Ghosts* [2001 – a remake of William Castle's 1960 film *13 Ghosts*] or *Scooby-Doo 2: Monsters Unleashed* [2004]) and those declaring this emperor as being stark bollock naked.

Camp Massacre (2014)

Dir: Jim O'Rear, Daniel Emery Taylor; Scr: Daniel Emery Taylor; Cast: Jim O'Rear, Daniel Emery Taylor, Bree Olson

Failed TV talk show host O'Rear engineers a reality programme in which ten obese male contestants are required to sweat it out at a woodlands-based boot camp, the eventual winner being promised a hefty $1,000,000.00 cash prize. Inevitably, a psychopath is in their midst – and the body count rises steadily.

It's essentially TV's "The Biggest Loser" meets *Friday The 13th* (1980).

On paper, *Camp Massacre* probably sounded like a grand idea. Especially back when the script went by its original title, the superior *Fat Chance*. Fusing comedy of the one-liner and occasional slapstick variety with old-school slasher movie keynotes (a flash of boob – both female and male – here; a splash of practical gore there) must've seemed like a formula that couldn't possibly fail.

Well, pluses include attractive HD photography and proficient technical aspects. The supersized cast members are game for ribbing themselves via Taylor's sometimes caustic script. Terror set-pieces are filmed with an agreeable degree of flair, striving to recall the style set out in templates such as *The Burning* and *My Bloody Valentine* (both 1981). The opening titles sequence has fun summarising the film's action in cartoon form, a la *Grease* (1978). Oh, and then there's G Larry Butler. He gets the best lines and the most opportunities to leave an aggressive impression as the club's merciless coach.

Olson is a bit of a coup, I suppose, for such a clearly small production. Making her bid to leap from a prolific background in hardcore porn – *Barely Legal: Straight To Anal* (2008) refers, along with many other titles – to more mainstream fare (beginning by lampooning her adult persona in *Don Jon* and *Not Another Celebrity Movie*, both 2013), she featured prominently in *Camp Massacre*'s advertising campaign. In truth she only appears in a 5-minute prologue which is disembodied from the remainder of the plot. Naturally, she provides the film's obligatory full-frontal shower scene.

Practically everything is undone, however, by the film's bum-numbing 129-minute running time. The plot is too thin, characters too under-developed and the jokes far too repetitive to sustain or justify such a length. Throw in a killer who isn't scary (aping the goofy guise of former Guns 'n' Roses guitarist Buckethead – you know, the guy who wears a KFC bucket over his face – was a bizarre stylistic choice), and you're left with a film that peters out well before reaching the finishing line.

Ironically considering its synopsis, *Camp Massacre* is in dire need of shedding a good deal of its own excess baggage.

Capture Kill Release (2016)

Dir: Nick McAnulty, Brian Allan Stewart; Scr: Nick McAnulty; Cast: Jennifer Fraser, Farhang Ghajar, Jon Gates

Fraser and Ghajar are the married couple who derive their kicks from plotting to abduct and kill a random person, all of which they plan to capture on camera. Their video diary documents the preparation and lovemaking which punctuate the build-up to the main event, along with the consequential fallout as the gravity of their deeds hits home.

Just when you thought the found-footage sub-genre truly had ran its course, along comes something like *Capture Kill Release* to breathe fresh life into its flea-bitten carcass.

The strength here lies not only in McAnulty's tight script, which addresses the moral implications of playing God with equal measures of humour and dark drama, but also the rather extraordinary performances of the two leads. Their chemistry is palpable from the off: early conversations debating the merits of various power tools as murder weapons and whether it's ethical to kill gays or the handicapped are delivered with expert semi-comic timing and gleeful, sincere energy.

As our antagonists settle on a potential victim – affable hobo Gates – the tone shifts seamlessly into one of despair, hostility and paranoia. The comedic interactions subside and an aura of claustrophobia permeates throughout the film's final third as we enter torture-porn territory reminiscent of *August Underground* (2001).

Proceedings do indeed become extremely gory and an unhappy ending seems inevitable from an early juncture. But the calibre of the thought-provoking screenplay and naturalistic acting help this rise above its comparatively vacuous brethren. And for this reason, we can ignore the numerous instances of lapses in logic (why insist on filming such banal everyday occurrences? Why edit the most grisly moments, or film them from blind spots [other than to give the FX team a break, of course]?) and continuity.

The Card Player (2004)

Dir: Dario Argento; Scr: Dario Argento, Franco Ferrini; Cast: Liam Cunningham, Stefania Rocca, Silvio Muccino

British cop Cunningham is called in to help Rocca track down a killer taunting police in Rome by luring them into games of online poker. The stakes are high – he murders a fresh hostage each time the cops lose a game.

The script's first draft was originally intended as a sequel to *The Stendhal Syndrome* (1996), and was to be called "The Dark". Instead, Argento ditched those plans and went on to make arguably his worst film, *The Phantom Of The Opera* (1998). Reeling from a string of commercial and critical failures throughout the 1990s, the director then bounced back with 2001's *Sleepless* – a low-budget 'greatest hits' package of motifs and riffs from classic films of his such as *Deep Red* (1975) and *Tenebrae* (1982). A minor hit resulted, allowing Argento to revisit his abandoned script of several years earlier …

Argento surrounds himself with talent for *The Card Player*. Claudio Simonetti, of rock band Goblin, provides a typically ambient score. Benoit Debie went straight from his sterling work on Gaspar Noe's *Irreversible* (2002) to handling cinematography duties here. Renowned Italian FX artist Sergio Stivaletti supervises his team through delivering the intermittent gore.

The results aren't as strong as the above ensemble may suggest. It's tough to put a finger on why that is, though it's undeniable that the meticulous care taken into creating each frame of a vintage Argento flick like *Suspiria* (1977) – both visually and aurally – has gone. Much of the film is shot in a flat style. The old flair only rears its head on occasion nowadays, usually during the violent set-piece scenes. Even those moments lack the heightened operatic intensity of old. However, this is most likely due to the significant drop in budgets that the maestro has to work with these days.

Performances are decent enough. Cunningham carries himself well against a mostly European cast which also includes Argento's eldest daughter Fiore. Mathieu Kassovitz, director of the excellent *La Haine* (1995), was originally offered the lead role but turned it down in favour of helming his English-language debut: 2003's tepid *Gothika*.

What emerges, then, is a passable horror-thriller with only a few instances of taut direction and style befitting of someone revered as one of the genre's great directors. It's not that the film is bad *per se* – it actually qualifies as a respectable evening's entertainment – it just pales in comparison to Argento's early body of work.

Il Cartaio
See *The Card Player*

Cat Sick Blues (2015)

Dir: Dave Jackson; Scr: Dave Jackson, Andrew Gallacher; Cast: Matthew C Vaughan, Shian Denovan, Noah Moon

Vaughan falls to pieces when his beloved cat dies. Under a cloud of depression, he determines that he can bring the moggy back ... by claiming the souls of nine luckless human victims. So begins the Catman's reign of terror: Vaughan dresses himself up in feline mask, clawed gloves and a huge dildo in preparation of embarking on his killing spree. In the meantime, introverted Denovan loses her own cat during an altercation with a rapist. She just needs someone to share her grief with. Can you guess who she gravitates towards?

This odd little fucker is the result of a successful Kickstarter campaign, which allowed Jackson and Gallacher's 2013 effort - a 10-minute short of the same name - to be developed upon. Backers can rejoice: every penny of the 15,000 Australian dollars raised - just over £9,000.00 - can be seen on the screen.

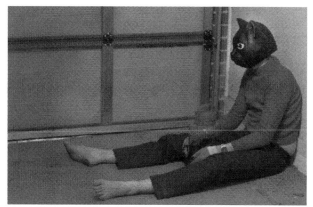

From the fine performances to the subtly-lit ambience, to the colourful art design and noteworthy (largely practical) special effects work, *Cat Sick Blues* takes its warped theme and manages to fashion something truly stylish and affecting from it. Not only that, it's also as weird as Hell.

As it flits unpredictably between scenes of brutal violence and pitch-black humour, it should be easy to accuse Jackson's film of being difficult to warm to. Thankfully we have assured direction, a wonderfully eclectic score and fabulous turns from the lead actors. Consequently, a seamless handling of moods recalls another highpoint of transgressive Aussie cinema, 1993's *Bad Boy Bubby* (and, no, *not* because both protagonists had a cat ...!).

The emotional connection between cat lovers and their four-legged companions is clearly examined, as is the phenomena of people uploading videos of pets onto social media (Denovan's dead pussy was a celebrity in this regard). But, let's be honest, as much as we can chalk this one up as an essay on grief, loneliness, etc - which it is - it's going to be best-remembered for those jaw-dropping moments where you *really* didn't think they were going to go there ...

Cue bloody throat-slashings; decapitations; a show-stealing hostel massacre; savage dildo violence; a gory face-mashing. All wrapped up in a vaguely surreal, arthouse dressing which, while flirting with mordant humour, impels its unhappy characters through a riveting version of Hell on Earth.

Chained (2012)

Dir/Scr: Jennifer Lynch; Cast: Vincent D'Onofrio, Eamon Farren, Evan Bird

Based on a screenplay by Damian O'Donnell, Lynch - daughter of David - reworked the material to her own ends and delivered this surprisingly effective serial killer study.

It opens with a mother (Julia Ormond; underused) taking her son, Bird, to the cinema one afternoon. The father (Jake Weber) has given her some extra cash to get a taxi, thus avoiding having to walk home past the usual riff-raff. Alas, they hop into the worst cab imaginable and wind up as the latest unwilling houseguests of murderous D'Onofrio.

Ormond is killed off pretty quickly; Bird is kept as D'Onofrio's slave-cum-protégé. The years pass by, so much so that Farren takes over the mantle from Bird as the lad grows into his teens. Conditioned over time, he's resigned to flinching as his captor brings back fresh victims to rape and kill, and dutifully cleans up the mess afterwards. D'Onofrio finally recognises the boy's primal needs and begins to educate him in biological matters, even going so far as to hunt for a suitable victim worthy of Farren losing his virginity to. This changes everything.

Parallels between *Chained* and *Bereavement* (2010) are unavoidable. Both charter the grooming of a child living in the shadow of a serial killer. Whereas the latter predicts a life in slaughter for its young protagonist, *Chained* remains ambiguous in the main as to how his imprisonment will affect Farren's outcome in life. It's a most curious journey.

Thankfully Lynch handles such delicate material adeptly, eschewing onscreen atrocities in favour of focusing on the tormented reactions of her young lead. Farren is excellent in this role. He's keenly supported by low-key production design and an ever-present sense of ominous foreboding. D'Onofrio, who was fantastic in 1987's *Full Metal Jacket*, spoils the milieu somewhat with his hackneyed portrayal of evil: dirty vest, beer constantly in his mouth, unexplained Austrian accent.

A frankly ridiculous coda deducts further points, despite making some sort of sense in its own daft, circular way.

Chakushin Ari
See *One Missed Call*

The Children (2008)

Dir/Scr: Tom Shankland; Cast: Stephen Campbell Moore, Eva Birthistle, Hannah Tointon

Campbell Moore, wife Birthistle and her three kids – surly teenager Tointon and two younger siblings - drive through heavy snow to spend New Year with Birthistle's sister (Rachel Shelley) and her clan at their secluded country estate. Upon arrival, minor tensions are evident: an unspoken rivalry between the two husbands, Tointon's obvious physical attraction towards her uncle (Jeremy Sheffield) and so on.

Alas, Shelley's youngest child has fallen ill and is in no mood to play with the visiting cousins. Before long, the youngsters have contracted the bug too: symptoms include nausea, cold sweats and screaming tirades. With both sets of parents dismissing their children's increasingly violent behaviour as mere side-effects of their illness, Tointon is the first to realise something more sinister is afoot.

Expanded from an original idea by Paul Andrew Williams (director of the same year's *The Cottage*) *The Children* opts for a flab-free approach, restricting its action to a single isolated location (Worcestershire's 13th Century nunnery-turned-Grade 2 listed building Cookhill Priory is used to impressive effect) and keeping tidy explanations at bay. In visceral terms, this works.

Shankland showed promise with killer thriller *WAZ* (2007) and expands on it here, evoking a low-key build-up briefly reminiscent of classic 1970s horror cinema. In particular, the suggestion of terror before it actually transpires is deftly handled, calling to mind similar techniques employed by the likes of *The Exorcist* (1973) and *The Omen* (1976).

Once the kids are exposed as being possessed by *something*, the action shifts several gears and never lets up from thereon in. Their violence, aided by Paul Hyett's practical effects work, is occasionally grisly (the first instance of the minors attacking the adults is shocking) but never excessive, and usually comes underpinned by dark humour. Once the grown-ups realise they must fight back to survive, their merciless retaliations stir troubled emotions in the viewer which are similar to those provoked by the superior *Who Can Kill A Child?* (1976 – remade in 2012 as *Come Out And Play*).

The child actors are excellent, as is Tointon – best-known to UK audiences at the time for her role in long-running soap opera "Hollyoaks". The twist-ending disappoints, as does the lack of insight into the adults' relationships once the shit has hit the fan. Considering Shankland claims to have gone through fifty-five script drafts before filming, there's very little coverage of expected themes (innocence lost; unconditional parental love; the fear of one's own brood turning against them).

But in terms of well-executed suspense, the film plays out proficiently.

A Christmas Horror Story (2015)

Dir: Grant Harvey, Steven Hoban, Brett Sullivan; Scr: Jason Filiatrault, James Kee, Sarah Larsen, Doug Taylor, Pascal Trottier; Cast: William Shatner, George Buza, Zoe De Grand Maison

A compendium of interwoven stories, all bound by being set on Christmas Eve in the sleepy town of Bailey Downs (also the setting of werewolf flick *Ginger Snaps* [2000] and TV series "Orphan Black" [2013 onwards], both of which share Canadian production connections with this film).

Tipsy DJ Shatner provides the anchor between the four tales: Santa's (Buza) preparations are hindered by a zombie virus infestation in his elfs' workshop; a trio of teens break into the local school determined to solve a murder mystery from a year earlier; a bickering family are attacked by legendary Yuletide monster the Krampus (Rob Archer); a couple's plight to illicitly obtain a Christmas tree turns sour when their son shows signs of having become possessed during the trip.

Slickly produced and handsomely mounted from the off (Santa's workshop in particular is a triumph of production design), even Alex Khaskin's score sweeps and stirs in the tradition of a big budget studio picture. And yet the pin-sharp digital visuals and unapologetic use of tongue-in-cheek gore suggests a campier, more genre-savvy proposition. The film aims itself at horror fans, and wants to give them fun.

Considering there were three directors here, the end results are surprisingly fluid. The tone teeters between irreverent comedy and dark horror, certainly, but the balance is handled deftly throughout. The gore is delivered via a mix of CGI and practical effects – most of which is pretty effective.

Characters bob and weave between each tale, a la another recent holiday anthology *Trick 'r Treat* (2007). What works for that film, however, often dissipates any sense of tension in this case. All too often, an intriguing storyline (the school-based one is the best) is cut short at a crucial suspenseful moment, only for us to cutaway to a far less involving scenario (the tale of demonic possession fails to engage due to poorly written characters). The result is a movie which provides an excellent source of entertainment at times, but is all-but undone by too many stops and starts.

The film's title caused offence to US store Wal-Mart, who insisted on retitling display DVDs as *A Holiday Horror Story*. The retail giants are clearly becoming increasingly sensitive of late (see also *Deathgasm*, 2015).

Citizen Toxie: The Toxic Avenger IV (2000)

Dir: Lloyd Kaufman; Scr: Lloyd Kaufman, Trent Haaga, Gabriel Friedman, Patrick Cassidy; Cast: David Mattey, Joe Fleishaker, Heidi Sjursen

The fourth instalment in the popular superhero franchise which was kick-started when put-upon janitor Melvin fell into a vat of chemical waste in *The Toxic Avenger* (1984), only to resurface as a hideously deformed, pumped-up vigilante with superhuman strength.

The first film was a breakout hit for Kaufman's Troma Entertainment brand, so it's entirely predictable that a succession of sequels would follow. *The Toxic Avenger Part 2* and *The Toxic Avenger Part 3: The Last Temptation Of Toxie* (both 1989) bloated the original concept, their overreaching sense of ambition threatening to kill off the series - which had by this point also extended to include a family-friendly animated TV show. *Citizen Toxie* redresses the balance somewhat.

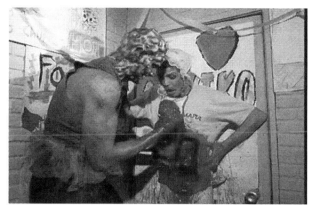

A synopsis seems hardly necessary: the plot serves merely as an excuse for puerile gags involving vaudeville performances, cheap excessive bloodletting and, inevitably, boobies. For what it's worth, our titular hero (Mattey, but voiced to comic effect by Clyde Lewis) teams up with obese sidekick Fleishaker to take on the local mafia, who've kidnapped a classroom of Tromaville's special needs kids and are holding their safe return to ransom. The ensuing conflict results in an explosion which opens up a parallel universe housed by evil doppelgangers of the film's main characters - Toxie's nefarious double (also portrayed by Mattey) is known as the Noxious Offender ... or Noxie, for short.

Castration, toilet humour, politically incorrect diatribes, gratuitous nudity, crude gore ... it's a Troma film and you know what you're getting. But a lot of the sight gags and one-liners work surprisingly well, while there's a real sense of true independent cinema at play here. Everyone involved emits a degree of spunk we don't often see on the screen nowadays. The energy put into this production is palpable.

Kaufman, naturally, enjoys a spirited cameo. You should also keep a keen eye out for appearances from Corey Feldman, Ron Jeremy, Lemmy, Debbie Rochon, Tiffany Shepis, Eli Roth, Synapse Films' head honcho Don May Jr and Hugh Hefner in an uncredited role as the American president.

Claustrofobia (2011)

Dir: Bobby Boermans; Scr: Robert Arthur Jansen; Cast: Carolein Spoor, Dragan Bakema, Thijs Romer

Spoor is a veterinary student and aspiring actress. Having just moved into her own apartment, she has plenty of pressing matters to keep her occupied: odd neighbours; a stalking ex-boyfriend; her diabetes. All of which pale into insignificance when, following a night on the razzle, she retires to her bed ... only to wake up shackled to it, albeit in the centre of a completely different room.

Who is her captor and what is their motive? Say, could it have anything to do with the atmospheric prologue in which a young girl cons a horny boy into sleeping in the local morgue – you know, as a practical joke?

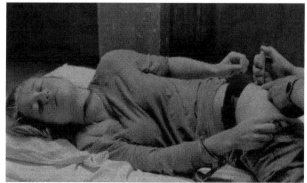

Claustrofobia is a modest yet solid Dutch thriller which benefits from a better standard of acting than films with budgets this low usually attract. Performances are very naturalistic, complementing Boermans'

unobtrusive direction and allowing plenty of room for the viewer to emotionally invest. The scenario may scream "torture porn" but, although there is some gore, happily the film shies away from such formula. Spoor's captor begins his ordeal by blaring loud music to her distaste; when he later starts siphoning blood from her arm, you *will* want to stick around and discover why.

The measured build-up of the first half works best; the film's latter half descends into bouts of cat-and-mouse cliché. Even then, Boermans and Jansen have a couple of workable twists up the sleeve – while lead players Spoor and Bakema are never anything less than watchable.

Boermans is an interesting character. He's a graduate of both the Dutch Film Academy and the American Film Institute, was winning music video awards in his teens and went on to direct *Claustrofobia* – his feature debut – at the age of 29. The movie has the prestige of being the first Dutch film designed to be viewed as a free online download. Positive word of mouth did, however, later win the film DVD releases in several territories – including the UK and the US.

The Cloth (2013)

Dir/Scr: Justin Price; Cast: Kyler Willett, Justin Price, Eric Roberts

Lothario Willett has no interest in ecumenical matters. He'd rather indulge in fast cars and loose women. That is, until he's inducted into The Cloth – a secret society ran by Roberts behind the Vatican's closed doors. It turns out that Willett, as unlikely as it seems, is the Catholic Church's "chosen one": his mission is to rid the world of demons. In particular, Satan's general (Price) is walking the Earth. He has seven days on this mortal soil in which time he aims to claim as many souls as possible. It's up to Willett to stop him.

Priests throwing kicks around and shooting guns loaded with holy water. That's the standard of fare here. The plot brings together elements of *The Ninth Gate*, *The Matrix* (both 1999) and *Constantine* (2005), while managing to resemble none of these.

Where to start with a film like *The Cloth*? It's bad. Really bad. Not just "Nicolas Cage on a bad day" bad, but really fucking terrible. I love the word "lamentable" but don't like to use it too often. *The Cloth* is lamentable.

Price can't direct. His actors are given free rein to deliver truly risible performances (support players Lassiter Holmes and Cameron White appear to be in competition with one another to see who can muster the most wooden acting). Willetts is the cheesiest, least charismatic lead imaginable – wholly unconvincing either as a playboy stud or holy avenger. Roberts looks bored, drugged or both. Danny Trejo may be plastered all over the DVD cover but he has a small cameo; to say his is the best performance in the film really should be speaking volumes to you.

There's no consistency to the pace. The action sequences are poorly choreographed and further blighted by some of the worst CGI this side of an Uwe Boll movie. The dialogue is so rum that I wasn't sure whether or not this was intended as comedy. I'm guessing not – there's nothing to suggest it's *intentionally* funny – but things get so bad that it's nigh-on impossible to gauge the tone Price was aiming for.

Looking for slick visuals? Look elsewhere, the camerawork here is as shoddy and amateurish as the lousily recorded audio. Honest to God, this isn't even so-bad-it's-good.

Avoid.

Cloverfield (2008)

Dir: Matt Reeves; Scr: Drew Goddard; Cast: Michael Stahl-David, Odette Yustman, T J Miller

A New York penthouse party is interrupted by news that a monster is attacking the city. Resourceful reveller Miller records the ensuing pandemonium on his video camera.

"Something has found us", ran the tagline. Or could that be "Something has found (the) US"? Perhaps *the* archetypal post-911 alarm film, *Cloverfield* – or *01-18-08*, as clever marketing called it while teasing eager audiences online months ahead of its official release date – indulges in rather obvious allegory: we're witnessing horror cinema from an America attuned to the threat of terror attacks on home soil.

The panic is palpable; paroxysmal camerawork disorientates the viewer while events – dialogue, sound design, pulses – quickly accelerate, rarely slowing or quietening along the way. The message is clear: America is unprepared.

Fundamentally inspired by *Godzilla* movies (various versions, released between 1954 and 2014), the monster is wisely kept hidden for a large part of the film. Interestingly, the production was shrouded in secrecy, to the point that cast members were hired without knowing the nature of the script. This had more to do with ensuring audiences were kept in the dark, than with keeping actors on their toes.

Cloverfield was shot on a range of HD cameras on an estimated budget of $25,000,000.00. A mixture of CGI and animatronics were employed to achieve the effect of the devastation the monster causes to the city. Certainly, this is as polished a "found footage" picture as you're ever likely to see.

A bare minimum of exposition keeps the pace taut, perhaps to accommodate the rather gimmicky desire for the film to clock-in at 80 minutes in length (the length of a MiniDV tape). The film is action-packed as a result, but a lack of character depth robs it of much suspense.

Director Reeves met *Cloverfield* producer J J Abrams back in the 1980s when they were both teenagers. Forming an allegiance founded on their mutual love of film, they cut their teeth making shorts which aired on public-access cable television during the early 1990s, before co-creating popular US sitcom "Felicity" (1998-2002). This latter show – followed by a couple of minor TV movies - also gave Reeves ample opportunity to develop his growing directorial skills, while Abrams made a name for himself as co-creator of the hit series "Lost" (2004-2010).

Following *Cloverfield*'s success, Reeves remained in the genre for his next gig, helming Hammer's *Let Me In* (2010), an alternate adaptation of the John Ajvide Lindqvist novel which was more popularly translated to the screen in 2008 as *Let The Right One In*.

Screenwriter Goddard, who came from a background in TV (including Abrams-produced shows "Alias" [2001-2006] and "Lost") hit paydirt writing and directing 2012's well-received *The Cabin In The Woods*.

And Abrams? Meh. His workload became more obscure, taking in little-heard-of oddities such as *Star Trek* (2009) and *Star Wars: The Force Awakens* (2015). He was, however, the only returning name to the credits for 2016's sequel-in-name-only, *10 Cloverfield Lane* (which he co-produced alongside Lindsey Weber).

Clown (2014)

Dir: Jon Watts; Scr: Jon Watts, Christopher D Ward; Cast: Andy Powers, Laura Allen, Christian Distefano

When the clown (Eli Roth in a cameo) scheduled to appear at son Distefano's birthday party doesn't show up, Powers is keen to conciliate the situation. Fortunately, he's found an old clown's outfit in a house he's currently selling. However, following a successful shindig, Powers finds himself unable to remove the costume – and increasingly succumbing to outlandish urges. Like wanting to eat children, for example.

Tracking down the outfit's former owner (a show-stealing turn from Peter Stormare), Powers learns that it's been made from the skin and hair of a demon. Whoever wears it becomes possessed, and can only be freed by feeding the monster the infants it so craves.

Watts originally filmed a fake 1-minute trailer in 2010, for an imaginary film claiming to have come "from the Master of Horror, Eli Roth". Roth saw this effort on YouTube. He was taken both by the budding filmmaker's audacity and the creepy style at play. He stepped in, co-producing the script's development to feature-length.

What emerges is a "body horror" drama along the lines of vintage Cronenberg (in particular, parallels can be identified between this and the latter's 1986 remake of *The Fly* – the good protagonist overwhelmed by unnatural urges, creating a sympathetic monster), as written by Stephen King.

Merging the fear of the anatomy rebelling against one's own mental desires with good old-fashioned coulrophobia sounds like a sure-fire recipe for horror success. Throw in the dark, troubling matter of Powers's conflict of interest as he finds it harder and harder to resist devouring children (a possible allusion to repressed paedophilic impulses?), and this could've been one of the scariest films imaginable.

In other hands.

Alas it's all a tad sedate, playing safe in terms of bona fide scares and onscreen violence. Watts directs in workmanlike manner, ensuring the film never looks like much more than an unusually polished TV pilot. The cast are good and the clown make-up is suitably sinister, but ultimately the tepid screenplay never fulfils the promise of the wonderfully macabre concept. At best, there's enough here to sustain a short film - but not a full-length feature.

Cold Grip (2005)

Dir/Scr: Javier Barbera; Cast: Anna Lluch, John Davidson, Alejandro Cardenas

Davidson is a travelling businessman who meets the alluring Lluch at Los Angeles airport. Following a few drinks and light conversation, she ends up back at his hotel room for a night of energetic sex. When he next wakes, she's gone. All that's left behind is a macabre missive scrawled on the bathroom mirror in lipstick: "HIV". Ouch.

Yes, Davidson has been duped by a floozy intent on spreading her disease among as many one-night-stands as possible (her motive is unclear). Cue lots of anguish on the wronged male's part, before he determines to do some investigating and locate Lluch – a serial seductress with a penchant for picking up her victims at the airport - with retribution in mind. This he does, in the meantime acquiring and modifying a lock-up that will serve as a prison in which he intends to punish her. Inevitable complications ensue.

A simple premise is afforded a no-frills approach, Barbera safeguarding his film's lean running time against any unnecessary sub-plotting. The cast are reliable and the sheen of the film, despite an obvious modest budget and digital aesthetic, is attractive.

But ... the intriguing set-up has potential which is never satisfactorily explored. This is, in essence, a rape-revenge flick in reverse. Davidson has been complicit, certainly, but he's been conned into sex by a conniving succubus who mates with the express intention of inflicting incurable illness upon her prey. The fact that his payback degenerates into unimaginative (and fairly mild) torture porn is a major disappointment given where a more astute director could've taken such material. There are no politics at play here, simply a desire to shock.

Capped off by a silly woodlands chase scene, *Cold Grip* blows its chance at exploring uncomfortable moral territory and instead wallows in unpleasantness. It's not extreme enough to attract the gore ghouls, nor is it cerebral or polished enough to appeal elsewhere.

Colin (2008)

Dir/Scr: Marc Price; Cast: Alastair Kirton, Daisy Aitkens, Leanne Pammen

An undead apocalypse rages through the streets of South London. This bedlam is surveyed by the newly-turned titular zombie (Kirton) as he fails to grasp what is happening to him.

Virtually plotless, the first fifty minutes amount to little more than a succession of vignettes. We watch as Kirton dies from a bite wound and gradually returns to life (a patiently affecting sequence); stumbles around the devastated streets seeking to recognise his surroundings; falls foul of looters and a vigilante group who see the undead as targets for their violent fantasies; happens upon a huddle of survivors which includes sister Aitkens – who tries desperately to jog his memory and tap into his inner human. A narrative develops hereon in.

Taking on a role requiring him to be mute save for the occasional snarl, Kirton breathes sympathetic life into his ambling, grunting creature – not dissimilar to how Boris Karloff's performance helped us identify with the monster in James Whale's *Frankenstein* (1931). Seeing his new world through confused, childlike eyes, Kirton's intelligent reading of his role is key to *Colin*'s realisation. Aside from him, there's virtually no characterisation during the course of the film. Each set-piece races by briskly, most participants appearing fleetingly on screen and many of them not deemed worthy of character names in the credits.

Is Kirton a man or a monster – or something in-between? The "they are us" concept isn't the only thing linking *Colin* to Romero's zombie films. The actor openly admits to taking inspiration for his character from Bub, the semi-domesticated ghoul in *Day Of The Dead* (1985). Sharp-eyed viewers will also notice a newspaper headline proclaiming "The dead walk" – a further nod to a similar moment from the aforementioned *Day*.

Themes of loss, instinct, memory, desire and especially identity run throughout. Price keeps the tone bleak and the sporadic outbursts of violence suitably grim. Michelle Webb supervised the impressive grisly FX work, much of which – as with the extras – was fulfilled by volunteers donating their time on the shoot for free.

The above supported the film's claims to have been made on a budget of just £45.00 – most of which, according to Price, went on tea and biscuits for his cast. If this is true, the end results are quite remarkable. While shot on DV, *Colin* is an unexpectedly handsome prospect: the practical effects work well; a violent street riot comes across as convincingly chaotic; performances are dedicated across the board.

If you're looking for shortcomings … This would've made a better short: padding it out to a feature running-time results in a lot of dull passages where nothing much happens. Too much shaky camerawork can make a viewer nauseous. Oh, and the pop song that plays over the end titles is preposterously ill-chosen.

Celebrated as heralding in a novel approach to undead drama with its zombie perspective storytelling, *Colin* was actually pipped to the post by Andrew Parkinson's *I, Zombie* back in 1998. Prior to that, Bob Clark's *Dead Of Night* (1974) had encouraged sympathy for its undead lead character.

Concrete (2004)

Dir: Hiromu Nakamura; Scr: Hiroshi Kannu; Cast: Miki Komori, Sosuke Takaoka, Katsuya Kobayashi

Hey kids, do you want to be depressed? Great. Gather round and I'll tell you the horrific story of Junko Furuta.

Furuta was a sixteen-year-old Tokyo schoolgirl who was abducted by four juvenile acquaintances in November 1988 and held captive in one of their parents' homes for over forty days. The lads made her call her own parents and tell them she was staying with a pal, before inviting their mobster contacts round regularly to help torture and rape her countless times. She was beaten repeatedly, had hot wax burned onto her eyelids, suffered foreign objects rammed into her vagina and anus, was hung from the ceiling and used as a punch bag: the last days of her life were surely a living Hell. Her ordeal only ended when she was battered with an iron barbell by the lads and then set alight; her body went into shock and she died several hours later. The killers hid her corpse in an oil drum filled with concrete.

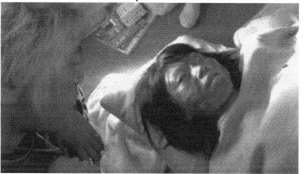

Now that I've most likely ruined your day (the full facts of the case are mortifying - only Google it if you want to feel really shitty about humanity), I'll boot you where it hurts by telling you the lads were given relatively light sentences because they were too young to be tried as adults and face possible death sentences.

As tragic as a case like this clearly is, it's also inevitably going to attract unscrupulous artists hoping to capitalise upon the public outrage concerning its most shocking elements. At least three books and a Manga series have been based upon the case. Katsuya Matsumura - director of the misanthropic *All Night Long* quadrilogy (1992 - 2009) - exploited the crime's more sadistic facets in his hard-hitting 1995 film *Concrete-Encased High School Girl Murder Case*. This was followed by Gunji Kawasaki's equally messed up *Juvenile Crime* (1997).

Nakamura's film takes one of those aforementioned books, Atsumi Joji's "Age 17, Chronicle of Evil", as its inspiration. In a bid to explore the antagonists' backgrounds, he focuses on the build-up to the crime during the film's first half, via their lives of petty crime and wannabe gangster tropes.

Concrete isn't as obviously horrible as its predecessors as a consequence. But it is inescapably grim. It doesn't shy away from the grisly, misanthropic details of the case (the names of those concerned are changed, at the very least). Moments of dark humour fit uneasily amongst such dark subject matter; having said that, Nakamura succeeds in unsettling his audience and pile-driving towards a powerful finale which continues to resonate long after the film has reached its depressing conclusion.

The Conjuring (2013)

Dir: James Wan; Scr: Chad Hayes, Carey Hayes; Cast: Patrick Wilson, Lili Taylor, Ron Livingston

Livingston and Taylor contact psychic investigators Wilson and Vera Farmiga when their newly acquired Rhode Island home shows signs of being haunted.

In 1971 the Perron family made the headlines, claiming they were being spooked in their Harrisville farmhouse. The otherworldly culprit was said to be the home's former occupant, a 19th Century witch. Paranormal researchers Ed and Lorraine Warren were called in to assist with the matter (they would later also become involved in a 1976 case of ghostly goings-on at a certain home in Amityville). The unfolding palaver was documented by Andrea Perron in her book "House of Darkness, House of Light". It's this source material, along with on-set consultancy from Lorraine Warren, which forms the basis of Wan's film.

Taking his cues from the likes of *The Haunting* (1963) and – of course – *The Amityville Horror* (1979), Wan eschews graphic excesses in favour of subtler scares of the "things that go bump in the night" variety. Aided by great performances across the board (the five child actors portraying Livingston's daughters show considerable promise) the director takes a potentially tired formula and revives it with assured direction; his control over pacing and tone is expertly measured.

Focusing on the investigators' relationship as well as the central family's is a shrewd move. Wilson and Farmiga enjoy good onscreen chemistry, enabling the viewer to really root for them too. Occasional comic relief in-between the moments of unease is never obtrusive; when the scares come, they're delivered with imposing precision.

The handsome production design evokes the early 70s setting convincingly, lending the film a welcome look of *The Exorcist* (1973). Sound design, meanwhile, skilfully maximises tension. Camerawork – including virtuoso spinning shots and ghoulish point-of-view sequences – is oft-times superlative while being careful not to allow such stylistic flourishes to eclipse dramatic impact.

Events being shot in chronological order perhaps helped *The Conjuring* to successfully gather momentum where a lot of modern horror outings tend to peter out. The escalation of creepy paranoia is persuasive; Wan wisely holds back on hackneyed jump-scare tactics for the most part.

Fair enough, no fresh ground is being covered. And the finale ties up loose ends a little too swiftly, given the extended running time and disciplined build-up. Such gripes seem trifling considering the film's overall success: the American ratings board, the MPAA, gave *The Conjuring* an R-rating based solely on its ability to scare (there's no profanity, sex or gore in the film).

A massive hit at the international box office, more of the same was inevitable: an offshoot, *Annabelle* (2014), followed along with 2016's mandatory sequel, the cunningly titled *The Conjuring 2*.

The Cottage (2008)

Dir/Scr: Paul Andrew Williams; Cast: Andy Serkis, Reece Shearsmith, Jennifer Ellison

Serkis and Shearsmith are brothers who spend most of their time bickering like some old married couple. They're also hopeless small-time hoods. Between them they hatch a plan to kidnap a local gangster's daughter – busty Ellison – and hold her for ransom on an isolated farmhouse cottage. This not only sets two hitmen on their trail, but brings the brothers into contact with the cottage's psychotic owner.

Very much a film of two halves, *The Cottage* begins as a typically quirky British comedy – caricature characters, situational farces, acerbic banter – before catapulting full-pelt into gory horror during its final forty minutes. The shift of milieu is handled deftly, the expert male leads finding a tonal balance between absurd humour – its darkness is in keeping with Shearsmith's presence, harking to the TV series "The League Of Gentlemen" (1999-2002) which made him a household name – and palpable escalating tension.

Former British soap queen and lads' mag favourite Ellison has great fun chewing scenery as their feisty, foul-mouthed hostage. Hers is an intentionally grating performance, creating a character so intolerable that, much like the kidnappers in *Ruthless People* (1986), you suspect Serkis and Shearsmith have bitten off far more than they can chew (the only surprise is that, in this case, her safe return is actually wanted).

Serkis is excellent as the often incredulous straight man to Shearsmith's bungling patsy. Crooks with hearts, unconvincing bad guys, petulant idiots: there's a lot of physical humour from this pair, including some wonderfully expressive facial gymnastics.

Frequently funny, at times unexpectedly grisly and making great visual use of Crispian Sallis's unfussy production design, *The Cottage* was unfairly received by disappointed punters who'd expected more intense drama from Williams following his gritty feature debut *London To Brighton* (2006). It's a different kettle of fish, clearly, but is no worse for it.

The Crazies (2010)

Dir: Breck Eisner; Scr: Scott Kosar, Ray Wright; Cast: Timothy Olyphant, Danielle Panabaker, Radha Mitchell

A plane crashes, leaking a mysterious toxin contaminant into a small Iowan town's water supply. Drinking the infected liquid renders most of its populace deranged. Sherriff Olyphant strives to save his family from meeting a similar fate.

A remake of George A Romero's 1973 potboiler, Eisner's film retains its forefather's political edge – the incoming virus can still be read as a product of harmful scientific "progress", or as a metaphor for both pollution and the threat of invasion by a foreign body.

But who are the crazy ones? Those infected by the tainted water, given to sexual psychosis before an early death greets them? The frantic surviving locals whose inability to pool together in the face of crisis begs comparisons to Romero's general cinematic oeuvre (*Dawn Of The Dead* [1978] being a prime example)? Or the US military, who are called in to oversee a heavy-handed containment operation – which they implement with ruthless efficiency?

Eisner may provide more questions than answers, but the fun is very definitely in the spectacle. There is tension, but no fear: this is horror of the action movie variety. And it's slick at that - a $20 million budget ensures as such. Expect solid performances, tautly edited set-pieces and a script that knows better than to ruin its Multiplex audience's enjoyment by developing its characters.

A fine blend of social commentary, creeping paranoia and exhilarating violence – appreciably upping the ante in this latter regard when compared to its source material – Eisner's *The Crazies* is that rare thing: a superior remake.

Look out for one of the original's stars, Lynn Lowry, in a fleeting cameo as a passing cyclist.

Creepshow 3 (2006)

Dir: Ana Clavell, James Glenn Dudelson; Scr: Ana Clavell, James Glenn Dudelson, Scott Frazelle, Pablo C Pappano, Alex Ugelow; Cast: Stephanie Pettee, A J Bowen, Camille Lacey

The original *Creepshow* (1982) was an affectionate, colourful homage to the EC horror comics of the 1950s that its co-creators - director George A Romero and writer Stephen King - had grown up on. Flawed but fun, it made for a boundlessly entertaining anthology held together in the guise of five short stories which came to life from within the pages of the titular comic book. Its sequel, Michael Gornick's *Creepshow 2* (1987), was less credible but had its moments. At the very least, it retained Romero and King in writing capacities.

Creepshow 3, a shameless attempt at utilising a renowned franchise name in the hope of finding an audience for its cable television-bound shenanigans, lacks either of its predecessors' charms.

This time around, cheap TV movie-type visuals abound as a spooky hotdog vendor acts as the tenuous link between a quintet of terrible tales: a surreal take on Lewis Carroll's "Alice In Wonderland"; a murderous prostitute's ill-fated tryst with a vampire; a radio that compels its owner to kill; a professor's wife who may or may not be a robot; a cruel doctor's comeuppance at the hands of a haunted hotdog (seriously).

Greg McDougal's special effects work is committed to maintaining a level of sterile safety which even Gornick's largely toothless second instalment rose above.

Far more prolific over the last four decades as a distributor, Dudelson's company Taurus Entertainment have been no stranger to delving into the murky waters of film production during recent years. Their name can also be found on the credits of other 21st Century genre debacles like *Horror 102: Endgame* (2004) and *Day Of The Dead 2: Contagium* (2005). It guarantees Dudelson work as a director, sadly.

True to form, Taurus worked "in association with" one-hit-wonders Creepy Films Productions to excrete the sorry mess that is *Creepshow 3* onto an unsuspecting horror community. Even Tom Savini, who provided the FX work on the original and portrayed the iconic Creeper in its sequel, dismissed this turd as "unofficial" while pointing people in the direction of *Tales From The Darkside: The Movie* (1990) as a preferred alternative.

Cybernatural
See *Unfriended*

Daddy's Little Girl (2013)

Dir/Scr: Chris Sun; Cast: Michael Thompson, Christian Radford, Billi Baker

We're off to Australia now, for a cheery tale of child abduction, rape and retribution.

Thompson is distraught when his six-year-old daughter (Baker) is kidnapped. She's eventually found murdered. The police are ineffectual in their investigations, uncovering no forensic evidence whatsoever. It's only when he uses brother Radford's computer that Thompson's suspicions are aroused ... and swiftly confirmed, as he discovers his sibling's diary detailing the abuse he'd put the girl through.

With the cops still chasing their tails, Thompson holds Radford hostage, tying him to a pool table and making good of his promise to him: "For every year (my daughter) was alive, I'm going to torture you for a day".

This fantasist reactionary scenario - the persecution of a paedophile/suspected paedophile at the hands of a vengeful father - has been deployed several times in recent years: take *7 Days* (2010), *Big Bad Wolves* and *Prisoners* (both 2013) as examples. The difference between those latter two titles and Sun's film is that Thompson *knows* who molested and killed his daughter. Even worse, the culprit is someone painfully close to home - making a mockery of any "stranger danger" notions.

The horror of discovering a trusted family member could hurt one of your own; the guilt of not recognising this threat sooner; the moral quagmire surrounding those who take the law into their own hands, as opposed to waiting for the judicial system to potentially fail them ... *Daddy's Little Girl* sets itself up to examine plenty of thorny, discussion-baiting issues. And then fails to do so.

Instead we get a highly implausible premise (Thompson seeks informal advice from local medics on how to keep torture victims alert; the cops are not only dumb, they're indifferent; why don't they act sooner when the sketch of an eyewitness' account blatantly points them in Radford's direction?), terribly wooden acting and a pace that stalls more times than my first car used to.

All of which is before the final hour of wall-to-wall, unengaging sadism. If pulverised kneecaps and sawn-off limbs are your thing, then look no further. Such transgressions, courtesy of Steven Boyle's Slaughter FX team (of which Sun is a member), qualify as this production's most professional moments.

The film's look is perplexing. Lighting and editing are proficient, and there's some inventive camerawork occurring - crane shots and the like. But then, the framing of characters is frequently iffy, with tops of heads being lopped off in many instances (most likely, the film was shot in a broader ratio before being cropped to 2.35:1 for its home video debut). The audio hasn't been recorded well either, with dialogue often suffering from uneven and muffled characteristics.

Dard Divorce (2007)

Dir/Scr: Olaf Ittenbach; Cast: Martina Ittenbach, Daryl Jackson, Barrett Jones

Ittenbach juggles her time between drinking, caring for her kids and practicing as a lawyer. She's also in the throes of a messy divorce with Jones. On the eve of a decision which is sure to award her full custody of their two children, Jones turns up bloodied at Ittenbach's home explaining that the kids are being held hostage by gangsters. As he dies, we learn that he's been accused of stealing money and cocaine from the aforementioned crooks. Little surprise then when they soon appear at Ittenbach's door wanting their ill-gotten gains back. They're ready to torture her in the belief that she knows of their whereabouts. As for the kids? They may or may not have been butchered, depending which lowlife criminal's flashback story you believe.

Dard Divorce begins slowly, the opening expositional twenty minutes being seriously impaired by atrocious dialogue and even worse acting. The director casts his wife in the lead role with catastrophic results: as with all the other players here, she's appalling. A German production spoken in the English language, the European cast members speak in monotone staccato style while their American counterparts behave like they're delivering lines at a school play.

The script is juvenile – one tormentor warns Mrs Ittenbach: "I'm going to amputate all your extremities ... and drop you off at a centre for the disabled". Ironically, it's a blessing that the film's audio has been so ineptly mixed: the lacklustre electronic score is so prominent on the soundtrack in later scenes that it drowns out key lines of stupid dialogue. Elsewhere, overloud post-production sound effects such as footsteps and clinking glasses provide unintentional comedy.

A crime-horror hybrid, it's the action that will draw the more unforgiving gorehound to this otherwise almost meritless feature. No character leaves *Dard Divorce* unharmed. Whether it be repeated punches to the face, a needle in the eye, the nefarious use of a drill, a jawbone destroyed by a hammer, a shotgun to the head ... mega gore is guaranteed. This being an Olaf Ittenbach film, you've probably guessed that already.

A prominent figure in the modern German horror scene, Ittenbach is most prolific as a special effects artist (gun-for-hire jobs include *Seed* [2006], *Barricade* [2007]) and *Prison Of Hell: K3* [2009]) but has racked up a few interesting directorial achievements too. 1997's *Premutos* is arguably the best of these.

We can count on the affable filmmaker for some fine FX work. True to form, he delivers the gory goods here. It's all practical, and it's frequently insane in its level of grisliness - from brutal beatings to infanticide.

Well-shot and lit but painfully stilted by its shitty cast and script, the film – shot largely in Ittenbach's own home, with a handful of exterior shots lensed on location in America for effect – exists solely for its adept, torture-porn inflected violence.

Still, at least I learned that "dard" is Persian for "inflict pain". So all is not lost.

Dark Divorce

See *Dard* Divorce

The Day Of The Dead (2007)

Dir/Scr: Ricardo Islas; Cast: Rosa Isela Frausto, Cyn Dulay, Jim Kirwan

Hard times in Mexico. Careworn local girl Frausto aspires for a better life, and so relocates to Chicago with a gritty determination to make this happen. Reality is often crueller than dreams and such is the case here: she's housed in a rathole apartment and begrudgingly taken on by an agency who do next-to-nothing to help find her minimum wage employment.

An even greater concern is the gang who are terrorising the area raping homeless women. One such early victim has her breasts hacked off post-attack. Inevitably, as she embarks on a tour of lower class homes in search of cleaning jobs, Frausto falls foul of said wrongdoers. Their philosophy is that no-one will miss an immigrant.

But that's only half the story ... as these kill-for-sport punks soon learn.

The title will no doubt lead many to expect another uninspired zombie flick. In actuality, *The Day Of The Dead* - the title is a reference to Mexico's annual remembrance holiday - is an alarmingly grim take on the treatment of immigrants in America; class systems and their flaws across universal territories; ineffectual policing; poverty; and today's violent, disaffected youth.

Islas has been a prolific filmmaker since the mid 1980s. Other output of his includes *Headcrusher* (1999) and *Zombie Farm* (2009). His experience certainly shines through in this bleak outing, which purports to take inspiration from a true story. He knows how to fashion a good-looking feature on a $100,000.00 budget; his assured direction carries the film through from its gloomy thriller beginnings and into a final act of gore-soaked Japanese-style mayhem with nary a hint of contrivance.

The dual-language dialogue (Spanish and English at equal turns) could either be perceived as an annoyance or a commendable attempt at authenticating the action. When considered against the self-consciously lo-fi aesthetic and Frausto's dowdy mien, it's easier to agree with the latter. Though Xavier Quijas Yxayotl's melodramatic score may work against a great deal of Islas' otherwise assiduous scene-setting.

Hidden upon its 2014 US DVD release in a multi-film set from MVD Visual entitled "The Killer 4 Pack", here is a film that has been unjustly overlooked by many. It may not be a classic, but its ambition and confident execution ensure that it's certainly worth a gander.

Not to be confused with the 2013 zombie stripper short *Dia De Los Muertos*. Or, for that matter, either of the *Day Of The Dead* films (George A Romero's 1985 classic; Steve Miner's not-so-classic remake from 2008) ...

Dead Birds (2004)

Dir: Alex Turner; Scr: Simon Barrett; Cast: Henry Thomas, Nicki Lynn Aycox, Patrick Fugit

A sextet of outlaws hole up in an Alabama plantation after robbing the local bank. Their plan is to flee to Mexico the following day – all they need is overnight shelter from the thunderstorm outside. Unfortunately the plantation is haunted by the spirits of its grim past; one by one, the outlaws are driven to madness and compelled to turn against each other.

You don't get a great deal of American genre films based in the 19th Century (*Premature Burial* [1962], *The Tomb Of Ligeia* [1964], *An American Haunting* [2005], *Bone Tomahawk* [2015] … they do exist). *Dead Birds* – filmed on sets left over from the shoot of Tim Burton's *Big Fish* (2003) - is a carefully measured, slyly eerie little number which ably justifies the need for more. It's all about the atmosphere here, which broods nicely throughout. Turner achieves valuable mileage from reliably scary scenarios such as wanders through overgrown cornfields, a clan of spooky white-clad children, and an ill-fated stay in an old abandoned farmhouse.

A fine cast also includes the likes of Michael Shannon and Isaiah Washington, both of whom proffer solid turns. Thomas, best-known as the annoyingly cute Elliott in *E.T. The Extra-Terrestrial* (1982), holds his own well alongside such an impressive ensemble, oozing casual charisma while convincingly portraying the robber with a heart. His wide-eyed expressions as events escalate are persuasive at conveying terror: he proves his adult chops once and for all.

An opening bloody shootout aside, the film's power derives chiefly from its austere, Gothic-tinged chills. With superior production values, taut editing and Peter Lopez's astute, haunting score, it's fair to say that *Dead Birds* is something of an oft-overlooked gem.

Dead Clowns (2004)

Dir/Scr: Steve Sessions; Cast: Brinke Stevens, Debbie Rochon, Eric Spudic

Five decades earlier, a hurricane tore through the sleepy Florida town of Port Emmett and forced a tugboat to collide with a train carrying members of a travelling circus. A carriage containing several

clowns fell into the nearby sea, at which point the town's residents deemed it too costly an exercise to try and recover their bodies. Back in the present, a fresh hurricane arrives and, as the locals prepare to weather the storm, brings with it the vengeful zombified corpses of said clowns.

The watery ghosts of wronged travellers, returning to claim revenge upon a sleepy coastal town? True, this premise may cause you to think back to John Carpenter's *The Fog* (1980). That's hardly surprising, as Sessions cites it as one of his all-time favourite horror films - alongside Andrea Bianchi's *Burial Ground* (1981), which should give a fair indication of what this movie's ghouls look like.

In fact, the cheap goofy make-up consisting of rubber masks and patently fake blood comes across like an extremely low-rent variation on the work Giannetto De Rossi put into creating the sterling monsters of both Bianchi's flick and Lucio Fulci's superior *Zombie Flesh Eaters* (1979).

Stock footage of hurricanes opens the film in an inauspicious manner. From there, the story is painfully slow to start and further harmed by a complete lack of characterisation. Sessions introduces us to several of the townsfolk as they go about their business (snorting cocaine, securing their homes etc) but we learn nothing about them, nor do we care.

When the zombie clowns eventually attack - which is a fantastic concept, on paper at least - their cannibalistic assaults are gory but incompetently staged. A couple of stand-out sequences include a bloody hammer death and an eye-gouging which gives anything the aforementioned Fulci lensed a run for its money.

Shot on video, *Dead Clowns* is often lit too dimly. This problem gains more significance due to the fact that most of the action occurs at night. Audio isn't the most reliable either, helping make Sessions' micro budget effort a chore to sit through.

As basic as it is, his feature debut - 2001's guiltily enjoyable genre anthology *Cremains* - is more fun.

Dead Daughters (2007)

Dir/Scr: Pavel Ruminov; Cast: Darya Charusha, Ekaterina Shcheglova, Mikhail Dementyev

Charusha is accosted by a stranger one afternoon, who tells her he is being hounded by the ghosts of three children. She manages to flee him, only to discover he died a short while later. Sharing this story with a group of friends, she learns that the spectral girls behind the man's death now have their sights set on her. Her pals unwittingly gain the curse too. Legend has it these ghouls monitor their targets for three days before passing judgement on whether or not they deserve to die. Only the good shall survive.

Can our protagonists prove their virtue during the next seventy-two hours?

Ruminov's film is, on the one hand, a morality tale. The cursed individuals each begin proceedings as materially minded, self-centred and vacuous. They personify the director's satirical swipes at contemporary Russia. As events progress, each one determines to better their ways. This entails quitting smoking, being honest to colleagues at all times and so on. The type of things that allow awkward, ill-fitting humour to rear its ugly head.

On the other hand, *Dead Daughters* really wants to be embraced by Western audiences. What could've resulted as engrossing ethical observation instead too often panders to tropes of both Japanese (the moral aspect of the premise; the lank-haired girls recalling the ethereal monster from *Ring* [1998]) and American horror cinema (the attractive young cast; a succession of stereotypical, *me*-generation characters; that ill-fitting humour). Inspired, I'd guess, by the breakout success of fellow countryman Timur Bekmambetov's more bombastic *Night Watch* (2004), Ruminov clearly hopes for a crossover.

But, once the set-up is established, the film becomes a long haul towards its half-satisfying conclusion. It all gets very talky as we explore each protagonist – the problem with this being that none of them are particularly interesting.

Colours are de-saturated to create a pastel-like aesthetic, visually conveying a bleak view of present-day Moscow. Consequently, *Dead Daughters* is at the very least frequently atmospheric. The shaky handheld camerawork should annoy but is more in the vein of Lars Von Trier's verite works than formulaic "found footage" swill.

Wisely, Ruminov and producer Ruben Dishdishyan ditched plans to lace their film with CGI spookiness in post-production. The earthy qualities of what they'd achieved during principal photography were sufficient to persuade them towards a grittier, more low-key approach.

Dead In Three Days (2006)

Dir: Andreas Prochaska; Scr: Thomas Baum, Andreas Prochaska; Cast: Sabrina Reiter, Nadja Vogel, Julia Rosa Stokl

A group of attractive young adults each receive a sinister message on their respective mobile 'phones, warning that they'll be dead within the next three days. Initially dismissed as a joke – the obligatory nerdish outsider, desperately keen to penetrate their inner circle, being the prime suspect – the survivors begin to panic when one of their number is subsequently killed.

Austria is hardly prolific when it comes to its contributions to the horror genre. So it's unsurprising that, come the 2006 release of Prochaska's big screen debut (following on from a decade of directorial gigs on domestic TV), *Dead In Three Days* was hailed by some as the country's first full-blooded terror flick. On the contrary, the odd times Austria has dipped its toes in the genre, it's done so with considerable purpose: Robert Weine's influential *The Hands Of Orlac* (1924), Peter Patzak's controversial 1975 thriller *Parapsycho – Spectrum Of Fear* (Marisa Mell and genuine autopsy footage in the same film: why hasn't this acquired a greater cult following?) and Gerard Kargl's peerless *Angst* (1983) are but three examples of how significant their efforts can be.

What Prochaska's film *can* arguably claim to be is his country's maiden venture into slasher territory. Making respectable use of its budget (reportedly 2 million Euros), cinematographer David Slama turns his 35mm lens on to the natural beauty of the Ebensse setting and captures the magnificent Lake Traunsee in all its icily foreboding glory. Such rich visuals go some way to distracting viewers from the rather middling performances.

The major issue, of course, is a lack of originality. Much like Norway's *Cold Prey* (also 2006), *Dead In Three Days* offsets its distinctive locations against tired conventions. A surplus of suspects, obvious red herrings … all the usual tropes of the genre are wheeled out in time-honoured fashion. There are few surprises. Even the fact that the ensuing murders are tied to an accident witnessed by the group several years earlier is a plot device which many have likened to 1997's *I Know What You Did Last Summer*.

To its credit, this film is far more able than its American predecessor when it comes to eliciting tension. Though it similarly skimps on the gore – barring one stand-out decapitation set-piece.

The film's Austrian title, *In 3 Tagen Bist Du Tot*, more accurately translates as "In three days, you'll be dead" – the menacing missive received by each of the protagonists.

A hit on its home turf, Prochaska directed a more violent sequel in 2008. The sequel's script was originally to have been written by Jorg Buttgereit but his draft was shelved in favour of the director's own efforts. That's a shame: I imagine the creator of *Nekromantik* (1987) would've come up with something far more challenging …

Dead Man's Shoes (2004)

Dir: Shane Meadows; Scr: Paddy Considine, Shane Meadows, Paul Fraser; Cast: Paddy Considine, Toby Kebbell, Gary Stretch

Considine, a soldier returning to his home town under mysterious circumstances after serving in action abroad, has a score to settle. Though they don't initially know it, he's targeted the local drug dealers – a bunch of aimless miscreants led by lowlife Stretch.

Staffordshire-born filmmaker Meadows had already developed a niche for himself at this point: purveyor of witty, human dramas which flirted with crime in a very everyman manner to help get across their ultimately accessible themes. *Small Time* (1996), *24 7: Twenty Four Seven* (1997) and *Once Upon A Time In The Midlands* (2002) refer. With *Dead Man's Shoes*, he ventured into extremely dark drama with a hidden supernatural element. Even so, a wealth of well-drawn characters and wry humour rescue it from drowning in its otherwise relentless revenge theme.

Performances are exceptional. Former boxer Stretch is far better than you'd expect as the slightly effeminate, casually callous gang leader. Considine is outstanding. The fire that burns in his eyes, and the

fury with which he spits out obscenities in his enemies' direction, are both menacing and heart-breaking in their regretful conviction.

Meadows tends to revisit one experience from his youth – a bad egg adversely influencing a close-knit group of pals within the context of a small Midlands town – time and again in his filmography (*A Room For Romeo Brass* [1999] and *This Is England* [2006]) but garners far more insight and dramatic impetus here from Considine's input. Together – with Fraser credited as providing "additional material" – they've fashioned a script that tackles loss, guilt and dislocation to an extent of almost immeasurable resonance.

Some light relief is necessary in a film this intense. As stated above, there is humour: perhaps the most amusing scene comes during a raid on Stretch's drug-addled pals. Anyone who's ever tripped before will know how astutely this set-piece has been realised.

Filmed around the Derbyshire countryside, the film can also boast gorgeous cinematography from Danny Cohen. The soundtrack – containing tracks by Aphex Twin, Calexico and Danger Mouse among others - sits perfectly.

But it's Considine's searing conveyance of sadness manifest as rage beyond reason, and Meadows's sagacious observations of everyday working class folk, that will linger - even as the body count rises.

A beautiful, haunting masterwork.

Deadly Revisions (2013)

Dir/Scr: Gregory Blair; Cast: Bill Oberst Jr, Mikhail Blokh, Cindy Merrill

One of the busiest genre actors around, The Internet Movie Database claims Oberst Jr loaned his talents to 10 feature films during 2013 – along with making appearances in two shorts and a couple of TV shows. What's remarkable is that, despite such a work rate, the actor remains consistent in delivering strong, memorable performances across the board.

Prolific actor Blair's directorial feature debut is no exception. Oberst Jr's mentally fragile character is a popular screenwriter of horror movies who, following an incident in the home, awakes from a six-week coma with chronic amnesia.

Did he murder his estranged wife (Lise Hart)? Or did the fictional villains of his horror scripts really come to life and do the dirty deed, as per his haunting visions? Pal Blokh aims to help him find the answers, by (a) donating use of his secluded country cabin for solitary convalescence and (b) enlisting the assistance of sexy psychotherapist Merrill to hypnotise Oberst Jr in a bid to unearth the truth.

What could possibly go wrong?

A psychological thriller with horror undertones, *Deadly Revisions* impresses by virtue of solid performances – the wooden Merrill aside – and a refreshing focus on restrained chills over overt

grisliness. Fusing the paranoid fractured flashback storytelling of *Memento* (2000) with old-school bumps in the night a la *The Changeling* (1980), Blair's interest is in keeping his audience guessing as to the true state of Oberst Jr's mind. Fortunately the actor is on typically fine form, delivering a commanding, persuasive and finely balanced performance of ambiguity and vulnerability.

Perhaps the conclusion rushes too much to tie everything up tidily. But the fun is in the insidiously distrustful memories that lead Oberst Jr – and us – there; as an examination of writer's block and the threat of one's creative writing taking over their concept of reality, *Deadly Revisions* successfully recalls the finer stabs of Stephen King's literary allusions to the same.

Death Factory (2014)

Dir: Steven Judd; Scr: Stephen Durham, David McClellan; Cast: Semi Anthony, Damien Puckler, Cameron Bowen

A busload of stereotypes – truculent Goth lovers, vacuous busty bimbos, the fitness fanatic, the religious zealot, a middle-aged black woman (perhaps the most racist character written into a horror script for an age) – breaks down in the desert. They're stranded in an area with – surprise! - no mobile 'phone coverage. Their nearest port of refuge is the remote, titular attraction: a shambolic museum focusing exclusively on the world's most notorious serial killers. Presuming it to be deserted, they disband and explore the place.

The museum has actually just been acquired, through ill means, by shady Anthony – who seeks to resurrect murderous subjects such as Jeffrey Dahmer and Albert Fish in order to usurp their evil powers. Of course, bringing such attractions to life (something the Goths inadvertently do while reading a book of spells which they hope will get them in the mood for sex) brings nothing but trouble.

Death Factory dispenses with exposition in a bid to establish its wafer-thin premise without delay. The action comes thick and fast during the relatively short (under 80 minutes) running time. Taking its cue not so much from the classic *House Of Wax* (1953) but more likely its overblown 2005 remake and the superior *Waxwork* (1988), the notion of a bunch of figurines based on nefarious villains springing into life is a concept rife with possibilities.

But you can abandon hopes that this potential is sufficiently explored.

An aura of the jejune permeates through Durham and McClellan's screenplay from the start. The broad nature in which each protagonist is written ensures none of them are cultivated beyond being mere caricatures. The character of Auntie May (Mara Hall) is the most apparent offender. A constantly cussing and belligerent loudmouth, a condescending object of God-fearing ethnic labelling, she's the living embodiment of the fat black momma who would chase her cat with a broomstick in antiquated "Tom and Jerry" cartoons.

The killers are outlandish exaggerations too, all hulking muscle-bound presence and unfeasible strength. Save for Jack the Ripper, who's revealed as being a hot temptress in a G-string (Mary LeGault) with a penchant for seducing other women and speaking in a risible English accent (gauchely voiced by Katy Silvester). Why? God only knows.

If you want blood you've got it: cheap but marginally effective practical effects. How cheap? One actor tucks a blade under his arm and stands side-profile to pretend it's ran him through. Some poor CGI helps (hinders?) during more occult-weighted moments; eleventh-hour set-pieces rely on bizarre hand-to-hand combat scenes which help further confuse an already muddled screenplay. It's one of those films that you can actually see falling to pieces as its plot advances.

Worryingly, *Death Factory* leaves itself open for a sequel.

Judd's film bears no relation to the 2002 Brad Sykes movie of the same name. Distributors perhaps anticipated potential mystification, as the film has been retitled at least twice: in the UK it became *The Factory*; US DVD consumers will know it better as *The Butchers*.

Deathgasm (2015)

Dir/Scr: Jason Lei Howden; Cast: Milo Cawthorne, Kimberley Crossman, James Blake

... or *Heavy Metal Apocalypse*, as it came to be known in Wal-Mart stores across America. They took exception to the original title's sexual connotations along with a poster campaign containing a pentagram (their solution was to create new artwork in which a gun featured prominently. Because, you know, America has a lot less problems with shootings than it does with Satanism ...).

Cawthorne is the teenaged metalhead misfit who's begrudgingly relocated to staid suburbia when his mother is institutionalised. Bullied in his new school, he seeks to escape the daily drudge by forming a rock band - Deathgasm - with the resident nerds and cool delinquent Blake. Cawthorne's hope is that this may help win the attention of school stunner Crossman. Rather, he unwittingly unleashes demonic forces when attempting to play the "lost tune" of his metal idol, which also doubles up as a Satanic spell ...

Deathgasm has the hip heavy soundtrack (New Zealand band Bulletbelt provide the rousing theme tune, aided by director Howden on backing vocals) and energetic surplus of visual ideas required to propel its simple plot in brisk fashion. Employing various storytelling techniques (narration, onscreen text used to introduce characters, the occasional breaking of the fourth wall), *Deathgasm* is aesthetically engaging and frequently amusing.

Crossman is the obligatory resilient female, cute and coy in early scenes but a dab hand with an axe as soon as the locals start turning into zombies. Cawthorne, all bug-eyes and wiry awkwardness, makes for a convivial underdog protagonist. Blake takes on the role of the surly antihero with an unspoken hint of inferiority complex, and does so with agreeable conviction.

Metal and horror are longstanding bedfellows. Their shared outsider appeal has spoken in volumes to legions of self-perceived outcasts over the decades. This connection has been exploited in films before: *Hard Rock Zombies* (1985), *Trick Or Treat* (1986), *Black Roses* (1988) etc. But Howden's movie is the first to truly feel sincere in its adoration of both pursuits. Anyone who's been the long-haired fashion loner at school will recognise the alienation being felt; bands referenced include less mainstream choices like Anal Cunt, King Diamond and Cannibal Corpse; the absurdly bloody violence recalls another great Kiwi horror, Peter Jackson's clearly influential *Braindead* (1992).

The numerous gory sight gags mostly employ impressive practical techniques. Highlights include a possessed lecturer vomiting unfeasible amounts of plasma over his horrified students, and a jaw-dropping set-piece where demons are fought off with their own sex toys.

Is it all trying a little *too hard* to win our affections? Yes, probably. There is a whiff of desperate calculation about it all. But it's still great fun. It gets more likeable upon subsequent revisits (trust me), which is to its credit.

Several of the cast members, including Cawthorne and Crossman, are veterans of various offshoots of the "Power Rangers" TV show.

Deliver Us From Evil (2014)

Dir: Scott Derrickson; Scr: Scott Derrickson, Paul Harris Boardman; Cast: Eric Bana, Olivia Munn, Edgar Ramirez

Troubled cop and lapsed Catholic Bana, whose complicated past is having adverse effects on his own family, has his faith tested while investigating apparently supernatural crimes on New York's mean streets. Unconventional Jesuit priest Ramirez lends a hand.

Based very loosely on cop-turned-demonologist Ralph Sarchie's 2001 book "Beware The Night", co-written by Lisa Collier Cool, *Deliver Us From Evil* is even harder to swallow than that so-called factual account of demonic possession and law-enforcing exorcists.

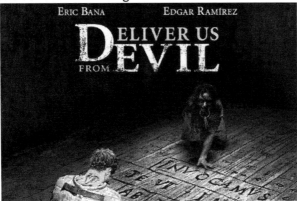

Derrickson pitched the film as "*Serpico* meets The Exorcist (both 1973)". His previous directorial credits include *The Exorcism Of Emily Rose* (2005) and *Sinister* (2012). Bolstered by flashy Jerry Bruckheimer production values, *Evil* retains their rather pedestrian approach to the genre, while significantly upping the "silly" factor in terms of set-piece spectacle.

The handsome priest who likes to shag, smoke and booze; the cop's wisecracking buddy partner (Joel McHale) who inevitably ends up taking a bullet; Bana's wife (Munn) and child, mandatorily neglected by him as he throws himself further into his job ... It's as if the director sat down with Boardman and said "right, how can we make this more clichéd?".

As if consciously trying to buttress this sense of formula, the production design diligently apes that of *Se7en* (1995): the New York backdrop is one of perpetual gloom, where it's permanently dark and always rains heavily. In a bid for eeriness, the sound design resorts to ethereal screams lacerating through the soundtrack akin to those in *Suspiria* (1977), and slowed-down voices droning in reverse a la *The Evil Dead*

(1981). The climactic scenes of exorcism may as well have been lifted from outtakes for *The Exorcist*, they're so devoid of their own ideas.

Even the running thread of references to rock band The Doors, including use of four of their songs (three original recordings; one cover by punk band X), echoes the superior use of a Rolling Stones song in *Fallen* (1998). Don't even ask what purpose they serve here, as I don't honestly know.

Worst of all though - worse than the by-numbers direction, insultingly stupid script and trite jump-scare tactics – is Bana. The Australian stand-up comic whose transition to serious acting - in 2000's Mark Brandon Read biopic *Chopper* – suggested more brilliance to come, is bizarrely bad here. Looking to be concentrating solely on mastering his Brooklyn accent, he fails to connect with anyone. It's rare to see an established actor so incapable of mustering chemistry with *any* of their co-stars. But Bana achieves this ignoble accolade, perhaps due to disinterest: his casting was an eleventh-hour announcement, following intended star Mark Wahlberg's decision to leave the project.

Bafflingly, dishearteningly, *Deliver Us From Evil* still proved to be a box office success – raking in over $9 million on its opening weekend in the US alone.

The Devil Of Kreuzberg (2015)

Dir: Alex Bakshaev; Cast: Sandra Bourdonnec, Ludwig Reuter, Suleyman Yuceer

Reuter and Bourdonnec are young and in love. However, recurring nightmares in which she mutates into a murderous demon during lovemaking lead him to believe she may actually be a succubus. Rather unreasonably, perhaps, he asks best friend Yuceer – a hitman with an emerging conscience – to kill her.

Despite its 50-minute running time, *Kreuzberg* finds ample opportunity to showcase both Bakshaev's skills behind the camera and his love for European cinema. As evidenced in his 2008 debut *Naked Trip*, the Russian-born filmmaker has a deep passion for the language of film. Be it toying with European tropes such as eschewing linear storytelling conventions, or expertly capturing locations that tell their own tales; his works take in influences as disparate and exciting as Jean-Luc Goddard and Jean Rollin.

Kreuzberg once again marries a definite arthouse aesthetic to grindhouse sensibilities, albeit with a more Gothic-flavoured leaning. Thrillingly, there's a definite Jesus Franco vibe to the chiefly visual, dreamlike storytelling. The candidness afforded to voyeuristic moments of relationship dissection brings John Cassavettes directorial triumphs such as *A Woman Under The Influence* (1974) to mind.

Filmed predominantly, as the title suggests, in the Berlin borough – a hive of counterculture activity where immigrants are plentiful - Bakshaev shot largely in the early hours over the course of 16 days. An eerie sense of dislocation is achieved. Frequent collaborator Pippo Schund's story is simplistic in requirements: three characters (a fourth, played silently by Bakshaev, serves solely to help demonstrate Yuceer's vocational confliction), limited locations, big themes writ small. Minimal dialogue is muttered in German.

The plot advances much more directly once it's been established who the central characters are in relation to one another. Even then, it acts as a mere backdrop to the rich visuals and borderline-surreal atmospherics which bring that Franco style to the fore.

Performances are intriguingly unusual throughout, the principal players looking to have been cast for their striking onscreen presences as much as anything else. Come the sublime, haunting cemetery-based denouement – which brings us back to Rollin territory, circa *The Iron Rose* (1973) - it's Bourdonnec who leaves the greatest impression. Along the way, Reuter and Yuceer amuse with their vaguely homoerotic bond. They even get to shake a few moves during the most bizarre spot of impromptu all-male disco-dancing seen on screen since *The Bad Samaritan Must Die!* (2012).

El Dia De Los Muertos
See *The Day Of The Dead*

Diary Of The Dead (2007)

Dir/Scr: George A Romero; Cast: Michelle Morgan, Shawn Roberts, Joshua Close

Night Of The Living Dead (1968): a game-changer. Horror cinema was dragged kicking and gorily screaming into a bold new age, establishing an ecological conscience which has been expanded upon within the genre as an accusatory argument for man's tribulations with the undead ever since. *Dawn Of The Dead* (1978): the definitive statement on zombies as a mirror of society, nudging themes of xenophobic paranoia while allowing Tom Savini's FX work to rewrite the rulebook in terms of splatter. *Day Of The Dead* (1985): a post-apocalyptic setting, a fatalistic tone and more gore than censors of the 1980s could handle. Who is the greater monster, *Day* asked, man or zombie?

Equally cerebral and visceral, to an extent largely unparalleled within the genre at their time, Romero's original living dead trilogy will endure for many as the zenith of zombie cinema. Bolstered by the success of the *Dawn Of The Dead* remake and Edgar Wright's sincere comedy *Shaun Of The Dead* (both 2004), the resolutely Pittsburgh-based filmmaker returned to the subject with 2005's *Land Of The Dead*. It afforded Romero the opportunity to finally realise his ambition of pitching conditioned ghouls against their increasingly advanced but undomesticated brethren – a concept envisaged for *Day* but shelved due to budgetary difficulties. However, its corny action movie tropes and clumsily written characters (along with zombies that were inexplicably capable of underwater tourism) - were generally met with derision from long-term fans.

Pointedly, *Diary* ignores its predecessor's false steps and reintroduces the notion of a zombie outbreak to a fresh group of youngsters. Here, they're a bunch of wannabe horror filmmakers toiling in local woodlands at night to shoot a pitiful gore flick. The undead attack. While fleeing for the safety of a close-by hospital, our protagonists determine to capture as much of this as they can on their trusty digicam.

Occasionally ferocious in terms of violence, where *Diary* lacks bite is in its commentary. Romero no longer seems to care about his characters, so trite observations such as "If it didn't happen on camera, it's like it didn't happen" – a clear comment on today's mobile 'phone-obsessed, YouTube-uploading generation – don't stir a great deal. The social satire in this instance is so blunt and devoid of human emotion that it feels sorely forced.

Shot on handheld Panasonic HD camcorders, Romero conveniently eschews the need for the polish of earlier works while also begging entry into the New Wave of "found footage" flicks. He's even adopted a whole load of post-modernism in his script, attempting to tear apart tired genre conventions while observing the making of the aborted film-within-a-film. But it's all been done before.

Who are the zombies, *Diary Of The Dead* asks in-between its predictable shaky-cam exploits and shouted dialogue. The flesh-eating ghouls recently risen from the dead? The surviving hipster-generation waifs given to documenting everything in life on their portable devices rather than experiencing it first-hand? Or Romero, struggling for relevance while onlookers shudder at the lack of commitment felt in later works such as this?

Donkey Punch (2008)

Dir: Oliver Blackburn; Scr: Oliver Blackburn, David Bloom; Cast: Jaime Winstone, Sian Breckin, Nichola Burley

While holidaying in Majorca, three girls – the charmless triptych of Winstone, Breckin and Burley – accept an invitation onto a yacht where four well-groomed boys promise an evening of non-stop revelling. When one member of the party is accidentally killed (a consequence of the titular action, in which the male thumps his partner heavily on the back of the neck during anal sex in a bid to make their sphincter muscle involuntarily contract), the survivors squabble over how they should best deal with the situation.

Exterior scenes shot in Cape Town and Malaga, additional interior footage lensed at London's famous Pinewood Studios: if nothing else, *Donkey Punch* makes every attempt to ensure its £900,000.00 budget can be appreciated on screen. Shooting on 35mm film inveigles maximum vibrancy from each sun-kissed composition.

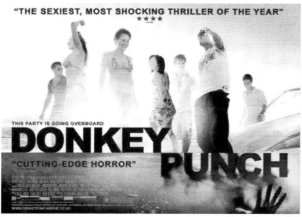

And yet, all this proves is that there needs to be more to a decent film than a bit of spit 'n' polish. While *Donkey Punch* may look the bee's knees – as colourful and superficial as an MTV beach party special, complete with a cast of anatomically impeccable simpletons – it soon comes undone in virtually every other respect.

Each character is obnoxious to the point of being detestable. Performances are offputtingly smug, especially from Winstone (daughter of Ray) – who I assume the filmmakers hoped we would empathise with. The annoying hip soundtrack, which includes the likes of Nightmares on Wax, Bloc Party and Peter,

Bjorn & John, conspires with the "controversial" subject matter and absurdly profanity-laden script to convince us that Blackburn et al are striving way too hard for coolness.

The screenplay makes no attempt to flesh out its wafer thin foundation; instead of taking the opportunity to explore likely themes of sexual politics and moral obligation, Blackburn and Bloom throw us headlong into a succession of flatly conceived chase and/or fight scenes. Given the potentially claustrophobic setting a la *Dead Calm* (1989), you'd hope for some tension perhaps. However, there is none.

Resultantly, *Donkey Punch* materialises as being far less "sexy" or "shocking" than its advertising campaign pledged.

Don't You Recognise Me? (2015)

Dir/Scr: Jason Figgis; Cast: Darren Travers, Matthew Toman, Jason Sherlock

Toman makes online documentaries. For his latest venture, he's aiming a little higher: he wants to find an interesting subject and film their life in the aim of editing and selling the results to television. Through an open appeal for interviewees he meets Sherlock, a loose cannon living in a rundown flat on one of Dublin's rougher estates. Toman and his two-strong crew set out to document Sherlock and his young wannabe-gangster mates - but events take a sinister turn when the filmmakers are led to a lock-up and introduced to Sherlock's brother, Travers.

Figgis began his career working on animation (early credits include the Steven Spielberg-produced *An American Tail: Fievel Goes West* [1991]) before switching to producing and directing live-action documentaries for Sky TV in the early 21st Century. Following his maiden foray into feature filmmaking - 2009's relentlessly violent *3Crosses* (later retitled *Once Upon A Time In Dublin*), Figgis began to focus more on honing his skills for strong narratives and eliciting extraordinary performances from his actors. Subsequent films *Children Of A Darker Dawn* and *The Ecstasy Of Isabel Mann* (both 2012) ably demonstrate his evolution in these regards.

Don't You Recognise Me? flexes those muscles further, while upping the tension considerably and also maintaining a keen eye on more technical issues such as attractive photography, tight editing, intelligent sound design etc.

The economic plot - it begins as pseudo-documentary but soon evolves into something more riveting - works in that a minimum of exposition allows for Toman's predicament to become nail-biting very quickly; a twist midway through alters our perception of events and challenges our concepts of both class and morality. Who are the more honourable - the privileged or the downtrodden? Who are the real bad guys? All of which may sound a tad vague, but it's best going into Figgis's film not knowing what's about to hit you.

That said, there's a whole heap of cathartic violence and emotional outpouring in the film's second half, helping to lift the intense drama out of the torture-porn trap it flirts terribly closely to. Some may find the constant grief overwhelming; others are likely to find themselves straining in a bid to understand the increasingly broad Irish accents.

But it's all worth it. Performances are astonishing in their naturalistic power. Travers in particular is on fire here: he deservedly won Best Performance at Starburst magazine's 2016 Fantasy Awards. Michael Richard Plowman's understated electronic score pulsates with menace as the action grows evermore claustrophobic. Figgis even turns up in later scenes to deliver the film's most frightening, violent punchlines.

Dumplings (2004)

Dir: Fruit Chan; Scr: Pik Wah Lee; Cast: Bai Ling, Tony Ka Fai Leung, Miriam Chin Wah Yeung

Extended from a much shorter version which originally accounted for one third of the director-showcasing portmanteau *Three ... Extremes* (2004). Chan returns to helm this feature version.

Ling is a cook famous for her special dumplings, which are said to restore the youthful looks of those who eat them. She has a very exclusive clientele. Yeung is a former TV actress who's reeling from the revelation that husband Leung is cheating on her with a younger woman. Inevitably the two ladies enter into a contract together.

Yeung is delighted with the results and wants more. But the secret ingredient in Ling's dumplings isn't easy to come by.

Beautifully and considerately shot by acclaimed Australian-born cinematographer Christopher Doyle (other credits in this field include *Chungking Express* [1994] and *In The Mood For Love* [2000]), *Dumplings* takes a potentially sickening concept and dresses it in an enticing aesthetic gumbo of warm colours and scrupulous production design.

Chan makes the nature of the dumplings' secret ingredient clear from an early juncture. The disturbing premise echoes stories of Ecsedi Bathory Erzsebet, a Hungarian countess who murdered countless young women between 1585 and 1610, and who is rumoured to have bathed in the blood of virgins in a bid to retain her youth.

Of course, what it all boils down to thematically is vanity. We first meet Yeung as she's at the arse-end of a career in an industry demanding of glamour, spitting its victims out once they're considered as being past their prime. Leung is a health fanatic and serial womaniser, as narcissistic as his wife but for more self-serving reasons. Chan handles such material with unexpected delicacy: we're never invited to mock these characters. Indeed, in Yeung's case, her desperation to regain her husband's interest and feel worthy once more is little short of heart-breaking.

Though not as explicit as its reputation may suggest, *Dumplings* gradually increases in terms of graphic content. It's a slow-burner, but all the more rewarding for it.

Ed Gein (2000)

Dir: Chuck Parello; Scr: Stephen Johnston; Cast: Steve Railsback, Carrie Snodgrass, Carol Mansell

When it comes to their influence on horror cinema, Ed Gein is undoubtedly the most significant killer of them all. A lonely Texan farmer-handyman whose crimes began with grave-robbing in the 1950s (excavating his mother's corpse so he could keep it at home for company) before escalating to murder. It was the gruesome details attached to the case that no doubt captured imaginations: Gein had made ornamental furniture out of human bones and skin, and even wore attire he'd fashioned from the flesh of corpses.

Filmmakers were quick to spy the dramatic potential in Gein's story: *Psycho* (1960), *Deranged* (1974), *The Texas Chain Saw Massacre* (1974) and *The Silence Of The Lambs* (1991) are arguably the four most renowned examples of many, many films to have taken cues from this loner's crimes over the decades. Countless documentaries have been produced, and several dramatised biographies exist – ranging from Kane Hodder's curious take on the character in *Ed Gein: The Butcher Of Plainfield* (2007) to the frankly bizarre *Ed Gein: The Musical* (2010).

Parrello's effort feels a tad too workmanlike to wholly convince, coming across as a TV drama with added violence and cursing. But it remains the most accurate account of the facts to date. More of a psychological study than an exploitation vehicle – Johnston's script aims to explore Gein's background, rather than the sensational details of his crimes – allowing the alarming tragedy behind the case to shine through.

Railsback, most familiar to genre fans for his portrayal of another notorious figure in American crime history, Charles Manson, in the made-for-television film *Helter Skelter* (1976), is excellent at imbuing his character with a quiet, plausible streak of sympathy. Domineered by his religious zealot of a mother (Snodgrass), persuaded by her that all other females are evil, and then lost when she passes away: he offers a convincingly and well-rounded balance of naivety and insidious threat.

Parello attempts a creepy atmosphere and is intermittently successful, compensating for the lack of overt graphic re-enactments. It makes for a biopic of some worth – but the definitive cinematic account of Gein's wrongdoings (and their motivations) still eludes us.

The Editor (2014)

Dir: Adam Brooks, Matthew Kennedy; Scr: Adam Brooks, Matthew Kennedy, Conor Sweeney; Cast: Adam Brooks, Paz de la Huerta, Samantha Hill

A horrific mishap leaves world-renowned film editor Brooks with four wooden fingers. Recovering from both disfigurement and the mental breakdown he'd suffered as a consequence, he eventually makes a comeback-of-sorts, splicing together scenes for tacky low-budget exploitation flicks. When the lead actor of the film he's currently working on is murdered, Brooks becomes the prime suspect. As the slayings mount, a bungling macho detective (co-director Kennedy) snoops, and resentful crackpot wife de la

Huerta snarls, can Brooks hold it together long enough to prove his innocence, unmask the killer and complete his latest editing job?

Formed in 2007 by Brooks and Kennedy, Canadian production team Astron-6 is a five-strong ensemble of DIY filmmakers, which also includes Sweeney, Jeremy Gillespie and Steven Kostanski. Their objective from day one has been to instigate a renaissance in the love of golden-era VHS schlock.

A series of proficient shorts accounted for their earliest works, titles like *Insanophenia* (2007) and *Inferno Of The Dead* (2009) demonstrating from the off their penchant for strikingly accurate 70s and 80s homages tempered by healthy doses of both style and sardonic wit. Their transition to features came in the form of 2011's enjoyably dumb *Manborg*. This was swiftly followed by the same year's gore-drenched revenge comedy *Father's Day*. When word got out that these indie stalwarts were taking on the giallo genre with *The Editor*, expectations were understandably high.

There's a lot to enjoy here. Unlike other recent *neo-giallo* offerings like *Amer* (2009), this is far more plot-driven, more accessible. It also helps that this isn't all strictly gialli-worship: the film enjoys tackling *poliziotteschi* and Italian horror tropes too.

Well-considered colour-correction and other post-production manipulation techniques enable the HD digital photography to attain a - for the most part - convincing filmic quality akin to the vintage flicks it's striving to evoke. Every scene is swathed in agreeable Bava-esque primary-coloured lighting. Claudio Simonetti contributes towards a pitch-perfect, atmospherically retro-style score. The casting is great: as well as the Astron-6 guys lapping up the chance to indulge in their own knowingly daft dialogue, we get modern genre luminaries Tristan Risk and Laurence R Harvey alongside legend Udo Kier in a small role as a psychiatrist. de la Huerta stands out as the protagonist's increasingly demented spouse.

The straight-faced comedy largely succeeds, save for a couple of recurring gags which do grow tiresome (this includes the intentionally clumsy dubbing). The film feels perhaps fifteen minutes too long. Still, with ample nudity and gore punctuating its weaving plot, and canny references to classics such as *The Strange Vice Of Mrs Wardh* (1971), *Don't Look Now* (1973) and *The Beyond* (1981) peppered throughout, *The Editor* provides too much fun for us to hold the occasional shortcoming against it.

En Las Afueras De La Cuidad
See *Hidden In The Woods*

Enemy Of The State
See *NF713*

Evil Aliens (2005)

Dir/Scr: Jake West; Cast: Emily Booth, Jennifer Evans, Jamie Honeybourne

Booth hosts a TV show intent on exposing phony UFO and alien sightings. Her and a small crew venture to an isolated Welsh island when they hear of a local girl there (Evans) who claims to have been abducted and impregnated by extra-terrestrials. Upon arrival Booth and co are startled to discover evidence of a genuine alien presence; the prospect of fame and fortune prompts them to stay and continue filming, regardless of the consequences ...

Evil Aliens is a consciously tasteless, cheesy mash-up of sci-fi, horror and comedy tropes from the director of *Razor Blade Smile* (1998) and *Doghouse* (2009). Though quintessentially British in its exaggerated delivery, it's easy to see the influence it draws from the likes of Peter Jackson's silly, phenomenal *Braindead* (1992). As in that film, the performances here are knowingly broad and consequently nigh-on impossible to assess.

West enjoys littering his action with references to favourite films along the way. Keep your eyes peeled for nods towards *Jaws* (1975), *Re-Animator* (1985), *Aliens* (1986) and *Predator* (1987) among others – as well as an obvious homage to the *Watchmen* graphic novels, themselves translated into film form courtesy of Zack Snyder's 2009 movie of the same name.

If you're looking for excess, you've come to the right place. Albeit most of this is presented in a tongue-in-cheek manner. Even so, you can look forward to intrusive anal probing, cross-species sex, dismemberment, eye-gouging, mutilation of humans and animals, and more. Tim Berry and Llyr Williams' twenty-strong effects team serve up a plethora of inventive, squishy nastiness. There's no emphasis on realism: from clumsy CGI to outlandish practical gore, the cartoonish visual gags are in keeping with the script's fast-paced, farcical tone. A show-stopping set-piece set to The Wurzels' classic song "I've Got a Brand New Combine Harvester" sums the film up perfectly: gory, trashy, silly, no fucks given.

Is any of this any good? It's fun, and it's proficiently shot. But West's strengths remain in the sterling work he's done producing and directing featurettes on key exploitation movies for Nucleus Films (a company he co-runs with film historian Marc Morris). His 1980s retrospective *Video Nasties: Moral Panic, Censorship And Videotape* (2010) is one of the best documentaries out there.

Evil Dead (2013)

Dir: Fede Alvarez; Scr: Fede Alvarez, Rodo Sayagues; Cast: Jane Levy, Shiloh Fernandez, Lou Taylor Pucci

Four friends venture to a remote country cabin with Levy, where it's hoped they can help her recover from heroin addiction. Upon the discovery of an ancient Book of the Dead in the cabin's cellar, they unwisely recite an incantation from within its pages. This stirs malevolent demonic forces lurking in the woods outside: one by one, the friends – and their dog – will succumb to their terrors.

Sam Raimi's original *The Evil Dead* (1981) was so much more than the poster boy of the video nasty era. It was an energetic, wildly imaginative feature debut which owed as much to the physical comedy of the Three Stooges as it did to Grand Guignol horror excesses. It also introduced Raimi as a directorial force to be reckoned with – a promise that saw him go on to direct, among other things, a box office-dominating *Spider-Man* trilogy (2002-2007).

Uruguayan filmmaker Alvarez was apparently handpicked for this project by co-producer Raimi. His previous credits include a small handful of shorts, of which 2009's *Panic Attack!* is arguably the most accomplished.

Here, the up-and-coming director gets to play with a reported $17 million budget. He does a credible job of setting the scenario in flab-free fashion, arousing tension, and bringing on the expected rivers of gore (though Alvarez has stated that 70 gallons of blood were used on the shoot, whereas the original purports to have gone through more than 200).

Shot on 35mm and processed in HD, this reboot (don't call it a remake, we're told) certainly looks a lot snazzier than Raimi's $375,000.00 budgeted, 16mm DIY effort. The FX work, most of which is of the practical variety, is gruesomely stunning. The script (refined in terms of language by Diablo Cody, whose screenwriting credits also include *Juno* [2007] and *Jennifer's Body* [2009]) stays true enough to its source material, while throwing in the clever device of Levy's addiction: when she's the first to become possessed, her friends assume her disposition is due to withdrawal symptoms. The cast are reliable, if not always thoroughly likeable. Pacing, lighting, editing: all technical aspects are highly proficient.

Alvarez is even savvy enough to throw diehard fans a few bones: the original's star, Bruce Campbell, makes a very brief eleventh-hour cameo; the iconic "boomstick" from the earlier sequels (a double-barrelled shotgun) comes back into use.

But for all its intensity, for all of its gore, it's difficult to make favourable comparisons between Alvarez's taut studio picture and the unbridled lunacy of Raimi's go-for-broke progenitor. *Evil Dead* is a solid horror film, but is unlikely to attain cult classic status.

An extended cut of the film was erroneously broadcast on UK television in January 2015, though – at the time of writing – this is yet to rear its head on home video.

Evil Eyes (2005)

Dir: Shripal Morakhai; Scr: Sagar Pandya, Anjum Rajapali; Cast: Urmila Matondkar, Anuj Sawhney, Malavikka

Twenty years of blindness are brought to an end when Matondkar receives a revolutionary cornea transplant. Alas, her celebrations are short-lived: it transpires that her new eyes possess supernatural capabilities – such as seeing dead people. With these powers comes great danger, forcing Matondkar into a quest to discover the true nature of her mystery donor.

The screenplay is based on a story credited to director Morakhai, though *Evil Eyes* is quite clearly an unacknowledged remake of Danny Pang Phat and Oxide Pang Chun's *The Eye* (2002) - which, of course, was also reimagined by Hollywood in 2008. As is not uncommon with Bollywood productions, this copies several scenes from its source of inspiration scene-for-scene (the spooky guy lurking in the elevator; the little girl who appears to Matondkar in her hallway ...).

Plus points include an efficient supporting cast, an agreeable lead in the beautiful Matondkar and a polished style which at times evokes the sheen of *The Sixth Sense* (1999). What little efforts are made to incorporate Indian values – themes of duty, rebirth and comfort in religion – are welcome variations on a theme, if somewhat undersold. It will perhaps serve as a blessing to some that the patented musical routines which pepper so many Bollywood efforts are absent here.

Waging war against the good are a complete lack of central character development (Morakhai brushes over the two decades Matondkar spends sightless, thus robbing the audience of early empathy; a romantic sub-plot feels rushed and therefore redundant), a handful of questionable special effects – the make up on the ghost of a cancer-stricken girl is laughable, blatant skullcap and all – and a climax which would've impacted quite well, were it not for it being tagged on as an afterthought.

The film premiered at Cannes Film Festival in 2005 as part of their *Marche du Film* section.

The Evil Within (2017)

Dir/Scr: Andrew Getty; Cast: Frederick Koehler, Sean Patrick Flanery, Dina Meyer

Mentally challenged Koehler is cared for by older sibling Flanery, who harbours a guilty secret relating to his brother's condition. When Flanery temporarily stores an antique full-length mirror in Koehler's room, it triggers a sequence of events in which the latter's murderous alter-ego appears as his reflection, compelling the lad to kill those closest to him.

The Evil Within's shoot began in 2002 and lasted for six long years. A labour of love for oil heir Getty, the production was plagued with funding issues, cast disputes and a revolving door of crew members (just check out the huge list of grips, best boys, production assistants etc during the end titles).

By the time the shoot had ended, Getty was dependent on methamphetamines. This no doubt played a part in the gruelling seven years of editing which followed, the director's increasingly obsessive attempts at sculpting a masterpiece ultimately resulting in the film remaining incomplete when his addiction led to a fatal ulcer in 2015. Enter producer Michael Luceri, who completed editing on the film ahead of its 2017 release.

The result is a fascinatingly cluttered puzzle. Elements of Lewis Carroll's 1871 novel "Through The Looking-Glass, And What Alice Found There" grapple with hints of doppelganger and evil twin themes, while a strong surreal bent is introduced by way of Koehler's frequent, barmy nightmares. These lend events a hyper-stylised whiff of everything from *Phantasm* (1979) and *Café Flesh* (1982) to *A Nightmare On Elm Street* (1984) and *The Cell* (2000).

There are glimpses of unexpectedly focused character development. But for the most part Getty piles on the horror tropes, from feverish schizophrenia to ungodly puppet creatures borne of dismembered body parts which can't help but call to mind KNB EFX Group and John Carl Buechler's outlandish FX designs for *Bride Of Re-Animator* (1989). This is horror written as a fever dream, ill of logic but chock-full of internal monologues, inventive camerawork (sometimes obtrusively so) and insane, outwardly random set-pieces.

Koehler is unintentionally amusing in his dual role. One of his personas is a stammering, insecure wreck; the other is a domineering creep with sunken eyes and sneering grin. Flanery and love interest Meyer suffer the expositional exterior moments which are shot with all the panache of a daytime TV soap. Cameos from the likes of Michael Berryman, Brianna Brown and Tim Bagley are noted but varying in degrees of impact.

The whole thing comes on like a severe headache committed to 35mm. Somehow, it works. If nothing else, you've never seen anything quite like it.

The Eyes Of My Mother (2016)

Dir/Scr: Nicolas Pesce; Cast: Kika Magalhaes, Diana Agostini, Will Brill

Having cut his teeth shooting music videos, Pesce makes the leap to feature filmmaking with this auspicious debut.

Split into chapters - "Mother", "Father" and "Family" – it follows the travails of demure farm girl Magalhaes. Bearing witness to an act of horrific violence as a child, she's since lived a reclusive life on her family's ranch. Her own son (Joey Curtis-Green) observes, as she did in her youth, the strange goings-on which come from living in an environment free from steadfast role models.

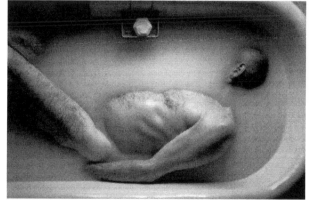

By the time Magalhaes makes contact with the outside world, it's apparent that no good will come of this. To say any more runs the risk of doing *The Eyes Of My Mother* a disservice. This is partly due to the film's non-linear approach, opening with a flash-forward and then settling back to take us on the minimalistic journey to that point. But it's also because here is a quietly sobering little film (76 minutes in length) which genuinely does reward first-time viewers who aren't opposed to going into it knowing as little as possible.

Shot in Cooperstown, New York on digital HD (utilising the Red Epic Dragon camera), Zach Kuperstein's black-and-white cinematography deserves special mention. Every nuance in Magalhaes's intense, almost-smiling face is captured candidly through expert use of light and shade; a rich Gothic atmosphere oozes through almost every scene; the film feels arty even during its more gruesome moments - but never pretentious. Ariel Loh's understated score shouldn't pass by without praise either: it's a perfect complement to the lyrical visuals.

Extended passages of quiet and a generally parsimonious attitude towards dialogue work in the film's favour, affording its audience ample opportunity to burrow into our leading lady's psyche. Portugese Maghalaes is excellent: simultaneously placid and seething with craving rage; a mess of repressed monstrous urges; the product of a sad history.

Beyond its great performances, sublime photography and bouts of shocking gore (mostly suggested rather than overtly shown), *The Eyes Of My Mother* is an impactful essay on the fundamental human need for companionship, and a meditation on how one's character is moulded by their childhood experiences and surroundings. Haunting.

The Factory
See *Death Factory*

The Fall Of The Louse Of Usher (2002)

Dir/Scr: Ken Russell; Cast: James Johnston, Tulip Junkie, Ken Russell

When his wife is murdered, Johnston becomes the prime suspect. He's incarcerated in the local asylum, where mad doctor Russell subjects him to various "treatments" in a bid to reveal the truth.

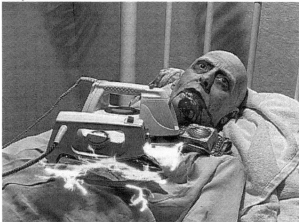

Russell began his filmmaking career as a documentarian in the late 1950s and graduated to helming features in 1964 with *French Dressing*. He made a name for himself in 1969 with his D H Lawrence adaptation *Women In Love*; despite the controversy raised by its scenes of nudity and celebration of that era's bohemian politics, the film was lauded by critics. It was ultimately nominated for four Academy Awards (Glenda Jackson won one, for Best Actress).

The successes – and controversy – continued in the 1970s: *The Music Lovers* (1970), *The Devils* (1971), *Tommy* (1975) … all essential additions to any film library. Over the next two decades, titles like *Crimes Of Passion* (1984) and *Prisoner Of Honour* (1991) maintained the director's artistic flair but raised far fewer eyebrows. Come the 21st Century, Russell had been reduced to using his minor celebrity status to self-finance experimental homemade films.

Which brings us to *The Fall Of The Louse Of Usher*. Shot on a handheld digital video camera in his own garage-studio, the filmmaker feeds his eroticised take on Edgar Allan Poe's classic story to a bunch of friends and neighbours.

Freed from the constraints of nervous producers breathing down his back, Russell lets his wild side run riot here. He's clearly having a ball as the demented asylum keeper, complete with dodgy German accent and manic leer. Everyone concerned is enjoying themselves, and why wouldn't they be – it's not every day you get to frolic among blow-up dolls or run around in a gorilla costume terrorising your co-stars.

The expected Russell ingredients of old are all here: music (Johnston also provided the Goth-tinged songs via his rock band Gallon Drunk), flamboyant use of colour, surrealism and – of course – a great deal of sex. A warped sense of humour is also unsurprisingly present, delivered with theatrical energy by the winking cast. Look out for references to other Poe tales throughout, including "The Facts in the Case of M Valdemar", "The Murders in the Rue Morgue" and "The Tell-Tale Heart".

Attractive to look at, snappily edited and unexpectedly emergent as a credible thriller, *Usher* does however make you realise that the days of lavish productions like the glorious *Mahler* (1974) were far behind Russell.

Indeed, prior to his death in 2011, the filmmaking legend was probably best-known to this generation for briefly appearing as a contestant alongside Jade Goody and Donny Tourette on TV's "Celebrity Big Brother" (2007).

Family Portraits: A Trilogy Of America (2003)

Dir/Scr: Douglas Buck; Cast: Nica Ray, Gary Betsworth, Sally Conway

A troika of short films shot between 1997 and 2003, re-edited and grouped together as a searing two-hour anthology. Collectively they takes savage swipes at the very notion of American life at its most intimate.

Presented in chronological order, the movie version – which enjoyed a limited theatrical run Stateside – opens with *Cutting Moments* (originally 1997). It's a powerhouse introduction, a former festival favourite which juxtaposes quiet moments of intense unrest with scenes of gory excess that compelled famed FX artist Tom Savini (*Dawn Of The Dead* [1978]; *Maniac* [1980]) to call it "an extremely disturbing cinematic experience".

In it, Ray is the mousy housewife who silently despairs over how her husband – Betsworth – no longer acknowledges her, instead choosing to sneak into their young son's bedroom at night and sexually abuse him. She takes drastic measures to deflect the attention back onto her. Hide the garden shears, this ends badly.

Home (first completed in 1998) has previously been described by Buck as a loose remake of the above. It tells much the same story, albeit this time from the perspective of the father – again portrayed by Betsworth. Flashbacks reveal how his tormented upbringing have prevented him from settling into the comfort of family life, despite his best efforts. A more subdued affair than the preceding episode, its best moments are those of understated tension: the wife shaking with fear over the prospect of potentially spilling her husband's cup of coffee, and so on.

2003's *Prologue* is a longer and slower proposition. Conway is the teenage girl left paralysed and without hands following a tragedy she can barely remember, but slowly starts to piece together upon returning to her bucolic home. As the truth gradually comes to the fore, she struggles within herself to find forgiveness toward her aggressor. Get past the fact that Conway bears an uncanny resemblance to Sarah Polley in *The Sweet Hereafter* (1997) – even down to the wheelchair confinement – and this is an absorbing, oddly optimistic essay on the human condition ... via a great deal of misfortune and angst, of course.

Bleak, disquieting drama of the darkest order, *Family Portraits* is also beautifully shot and painstakingly measured in its matter-of-fact asceticism. What it says about everyday life – that we all suffer in silence – is dispiriting. But the punch is worth taking, if you like your cinema so grim and skilled in equal measures.

Buck's work has been wildly erratic ever since. His 2006 remake of Brian De Palma's *Sisters* (1973) suffered from somnambulistic performances from the usually reliable Chloe Sevigny and Stephen Rea; his contribution to 2011 anthology *The Theatre Bizarre* was quite exquisite. Hopes remain high for more essential cinema to come from this intriguing filmmaker.

Fat Chance
See *Camp Massacre*

Fear Clinic (2015)

Dir: Robert Hall; Scr: Aaron Drane, Robert Hall; Cast: Robert Englund, Fiona Dourif, Angelina Armani

Five victims of the same violent crime seek the help of shady doctor Englund. He'd previously developed a revolutionary "fear chamber" capable of summoning and controlling the inner phobias of its subjects. Having shut up shop a year earlier following a tragedy directly related to his invention, Englund is persuaded by former patient Dourif to bring his contraption back into action. Which, of course, spells bad news for all concerned.

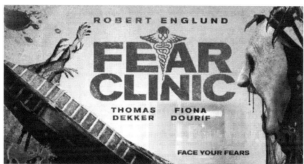

In 2009 Hall and Crane shot five episodes for a star-studded web series of the same name. Alongside Englund, horror luminaries such as Kane Hodder and Danielle Harris were drafted in. Only the former returns for this feature-length expansion of its themes.

Working with a partially crowd-funded $1 million budget, Hall is careful to convey the healthy production values across the screen. If nothing else, *Fear Clinic* often looks great: keenly designed sets, stylish colour-filtered lighting and so on. It's only when the set-piece terror scenes spring into action that events take on the ropy form of B-movie cheapness.

Englund, looking haggard, is dependably sinister. Kevin Gage exudes his usual screen presence in a supporting role. Dourif, daughter of cult actor Brad, makes for a good-natured if slightly pedestrian lead. You want to warm to her, but she's just a little too dull to make that happen. Armani – Hall's girlfriend at the time of shooting – delivers on the obligatory topless scene.

More noteworthy, perhaps, is the inclusion of rock singer Corey Taylor in the cast. Appearing in his first film role, the Slipknot/Stone Sour vocalist actually acquits himself well. Predictably, his band Stone Sour contributes towards the soundtrack.

Veteran FX artist Steve Johnson oversaw the mainly decent special effects, reining back on the levels of gore Hall had established in *Laid To Rest* (2009). With otherworldly hallucinations and fear manifesting itself as various creatures, Johnson at least makes good on Hall's pre-production promise of the film following a more "surreal" slant.

But it never quite gels. Performances are erratic, the muddied plot can't sustain its balance between reality and dream, and Hall is yet to master the art of successfully sustaining suspense.

Ambitious but lacking the fine tuning to fully realise its aspirations, then, *Fear Clinic* never amounts to the sum of its intriguing premise, canny production design and attractive casting choices.

Feed (2005)

Dir: Brett Leonard; Scr: Kieran Galvin; Cast: Alex O'Loughlin, Gabby Millgate, Patrick Thompson

Thompson, a cop with personal issues, sets his sights on tracking down force-feeding fetishist O'Loughlin. Having witnessed his antics online, via a site catering for fans of this odd practice, he's convinced his quarry is up to even more sinister deeds ...

Galvin's script was developed from an original idea by co-stars Thompson and O'Loughlin. Their concept stemmed from the very real and sometime favourite subject of TV shockumentaries: those with a bent for feeding their consenting partners to excess, encouraging a level of obesity where the eater becomes totally dependent upon their feeder.

An attention-grabbing prologue in which two men prepare to feast upon a severed, grilled penis also manages to explicitly allude to the curious case of Armin Meiwes, a German guy who in 2003 made headline news for killing and partially eating Bernd Brandes – a voluntary victim he'd met online. This latter scenario also inspired Marian Dora's troublesome *Cannibal* (2006), a film rumoured to have used genuine human blood for its gore.

Leonard doesn't go that far, but nor does he shy away from grossing his audience out. An obvious talking point is the moment O'Loughlin masturbates over his latest lust object (Millgate) whilst watching her trough. Full-frontal male nudity is used as a means of confrontation, it feels, while the sight of a healthy man getting it on with a forty-two stone woman is surely designed to make viewers gag. And if you do vomit, you're not the only one – Millgate goes there too. But however far *Feed* pushes in its bid to have you wince, there's always an air of polished "safeness" evident. The production is slick, and Leonard is too much of a professional – previous hits of his include *The Lawnmower Man* (1992) and *Virtuosity* (1995) – to wallow for too long in depravity.

The filmmaker is perhaps most fondly remembered by genre fans for his likeable 1989 romp *The Dead Pit*.

Feher Isten
See *White God*

Fetus (2008)

Dir/Scr: Brian Paulin; Cast: Brian Paulin, Nette Detroy, Joe Olson

Paulin is distraught when he loses both wife Detroy and new son following a mishap during childbirth. As you would, he turns to necromancy in a bid to reanimate them, while harbouring thoughts of seeking revenge against the doctors he feels failed them.

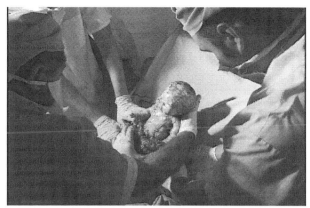

Such a straightforward premise is rendered absurdly complicated, thanks to a mixture of ill-placed flashbacks and Paulin's shortcomings as a storyteller. A trippy sense of dislocation which comes and goes without clear purpose, a lack of plot consistency, lapses into extended sequences of gore which serve to effectively kill narrative progression: it's as if *Fetus* is trying extremely hard to test its audience's patience.

For those willing to endure such inadequacies, the film does make good on its promise of delivering the nastiness. Abortion, castration, innards splattered across the screen ... *Fetus* ensures gorehounds don't go without. And with such a provocative title, you're probably thinking this film is willing to indulge in fantasies of an even sicker nature? You'd be right. Look forward to outlandish delights such a bathtub scene involving the gory self-mutilation of a woman's crotch and subsequent cannibalisation of a baby's head, along with the (I think) unique sight of a man giving birth through his penis. No need to reread that; you got it right first time.

Auteur Paulin not only wrote and directed *Fetus*, he also handled the editing and cinematography, as well as co-writing the gialloesque score with Matt Meserve. Shooting on mini-DV with a reported budget of $10,000.00, the film looks about as good as you could expect it to. Unforgiving cineastes are sure to balk at the poverty-stricken visuals; in their own curious way, they do add to the unpleasantness.

The filmmaker's strongest asset is his special make-up effects work. Having studied under the late great Dick Smith (*The Exorcist* [1973], *Taxi Driver* [1976] etc), Paulin's work is pretty good. Limited on occasions by lack of funds, of course, but generally effectively in their own grubby way.

Where Paulin really falters, more so than as a screenwriter, is as an actor. We're not expecting Oscar-worthy workouts, of course. However, the performances are horrible across the board. You'd think Paulin in particular would've accepted his limitations in this regard following the terrible turn he contributed to his 2004 zombie flick *Bone Sickness*. But no, he's clearly oblivious to the fact that he will never convince as a thespian...

The director cites Japanese splatter/punk movies as the initial influence behind *Fetus*, but concedes that the finished film more closely resembles the extremities of the original *Guinea Pig* series (1985-89).

Films From A Broken Mind (2016)

Dir: Bazz Hancher; Scr: Bazz Hancher, Pauline Winks, David Stokes; Cast: Richard Robotham, Kevin Varty, Richard Taylor

Kidderminster-based filmmaker Hancher began making short horror movies in 2004 with the gory DIY effort *The Deadwoods*. Several eclectic ventures followed in proceeding years - 2006's home invasion ode *Number 50 Peel Street*; 2008's protest against domestic violence *Liquid Sadness* etc - before his 24-minute shocker *Leon's Broken Mind* (2011) garnered real underground attention.

This anthology opens with the latter, grouping it with three other Hancher shorts of old - in order of appearance: *Bonjour Monsieur Trepas* (2010), *Darkest Secrets* (2013) and *The Rogue Filmmaker* (2012 - directed under the pseudonym Hank B Marvelous). For the initiated, Matt Lee features in stylishly shot new framing scenes as Satan, introducing us to each vignette with equal measures of wit and menace.

Broken Mind follows man-child Robotham as he struggles to cope with the loss of his mother. His late father abused him as a child and returns in visions taunting him, suggesting that acts of random murder will set him free from the voices inside his head. This leads to a barrage of excess: wanking off over violent horror DVDs; eating an eye out of one victim's skull; stabbing a heavily pregnant lady in the gut; slashing a dog's throat (watch out for Hancher in a cameo as the mutt's hapless owner). Downward spirals tend to end in similar fashion and this one is no different ... along the way we get the anal rape of a physically disabled male. Which you don't see every day.

The kick is that *Broken Mind* is a genuinely well-made proposition. It's well-lit, tightly edited, performed with spirit and courage (look out for fellow filmmaker Tom Lee Rutter as a tramp), and boasts an incredible 80s-esque score courtesy of Matthew Wright. While intended as a commentary on "the moral state of the society in which we live", there's also a fair amount of dark British humour in place to help keep things from ever becoming too oppressive.

Trepas follows a similar theme, albeit in a slightly less confrontational manner. The messages here are never to judge a book by its cover, and that you never know who your seemingly innocuous neighbour/workmate/pal truly is. In this instance, mild-mannered Varty is well-spoken in public, but a right cunt behind closed doors. "Does this rag smell of chloroform to you?" - indeed. Another highly accomplished effort (shot on a budget of £20? Really?!), there's a neat twist in store for those giving this a punt.

Secrets pares back much of the mordant humour punctuating the first two tales. This gangster thriller is more ambitious in terms of storytelling. More characters, more plot strands, more locations. It gets a little muddled at times but the advancement in editing, photography and general writing is soon evident. Violence is used more sparingly, achieving surprising impact as a result (in one shocking scene a young girl is shot in the head [the hitman is played by returning Robotham]).

Rogue is a summation of everything that's been witnessed thus far, a convincing mockumentary in which a host of Hancher's participants speak to the screen, berating their filmmaker as an unprofessional bully and a "psycho". Even his own mother delivers a wonderfully straight-faced character assassination. Replete with gory clips from earlier films, an amusingly accurate mock-American narration and a last-minute appearance from Hancher himself, it's a wonderfully silly conclusion to events.

Final Destination (2000)

Dir: James Wong; Scr: James Wong, Jeffrey Reddick, Glen Morgan; Cast: Devon Sawa, Ali Larter, Kerr Smith

On board a flight destined for France, student Sawa receives a premonition warning that the plane will crash. Convincing a handful of his classmates that they're all in danger, he and a small group of pals manage to get themselves evicted minutes before take-off. They watch in horror as, moments later, the plane erupts into a ball of flames.

But, can you cheat Death? Apparently not: when your time is up, your time is up. No matter what you do to try and prevent it, Death will find a way of claiming you once your number's been called. Sawa and friends learn this the hard way as, one-by-one, they start dying in evermore convoluted ways.

Originally conceived as a concept for an episode of TV series "The X-Files" (1993 onwards), budding writer Reddick's draft screenplay was picked up by two of the show's regular scribes, Wong and Morgan, who saw the potential in developing it as a feature-length endeavour.

With financing secured courtesy of New Line Cinema, the film finally went into production six years after Reddick had originally submitted his draft for consideration. The fascinating cast also boasts Sean William Scott, Daniel Roebuck and Tony Todd.

Final Destination is a slasher film where the killer isn't a visible entity. Death moves in increasingly inventive ways (a mishap involving kitchen utensils; decapitation by flying car wreckage shrapnel ...), but this remains in essence a teen-kill body count movie – replete with an attractive young cast and the designer gore that's come to be expected of the genre.

Sufficiently glossy and "Hollywood" in finish to appeal to fans of the *Scream* series (1996-2011), Wong's film inspired a franchise of its own (four sequels to date, the last instalment being 2011): each subsequent chapter has been sillier and gorier than the last.

Flowers (2015)

Dir/Scr: Phil Stevens; Cast: Anastasia Blue, Bryant W Lohr Senior, Colette Kenny McKenna

Six murder victims "awaken" individually in the crawlspace of their killer's abode. Each woman scuttles on her belly during their own vignette, wading past the grime and gore found in the narrow tunnels they must negotiate. Their journeys are punctuated by fragments of their final memories, and glimpses of their murderer (Lohr Senior) at play with his latest quarry.

Stevens' film is a bold surreal nightmare, told in non-linear fashion. There is no dialogue. As debut features go, these are audacious stylistic choices.

Each girl's plight is delivered in abstract style. Their semi-naked bodies are bloodied and bruised, merging into the convincingly squalid set design as they crawl through slew consisting of unimaginable horrors.

It's easy to read a suggestion of rebirth into their painful odysseys; a metaphorical purgatory seems more likely though, as they each make their way towards either redemption or damnation.

The hulking, largely inexperienced Lohr Senior has tremendous presence. This ensures his antagonist – acting, it's hinted at, upon the wishes of sharp-suited benefactors who observe his actions via monitors – can menace without ever slipping into overcooked psycho territory. Watching the childlike giant gut one victim, smear her fresh blood onto his dick for lubrication and then fuck her corpse is not only disturbing, it's intense and persuasive.

It goes without saying that each actress gives a brave, soul-baring performance. Without uttering a word between them, they brilliantly convey the heartache of realising death becomes them, and the panic with which they rush to flee their own murder scenes. Wading on their hands and knees through yards of blood and spunk can't have been pleasant, either.

Shot on an apparent budget of just $20,000.00, *Flowers* is clearly a labour of love. Scene after scene after scene, each composition has been painstakingly thought through and realised. Stevens not only writes and directs the action, but is credited as co-producer, art designer, cinematographer and helping to decorate the sets. Many of the cast doubled up on behind-the-camera chores too. Associate producer Ronnie Sortor – himself a name that will be known to fans of no-budget horror, having helmed the 1997 DIY splatter fest *Ravage* – is responsible for the outstanding, ambient sound design.

A crowd-funded prequel followed in 2016, entitled *Lung II*.

Fluid Boy (2016)

Dir/Scr: Jason Impey, Wade Radford; Cast: Samantha Keller, Jason Impey, Wade Radford

Aspiring actress Keller attends an audition for a role in zombie flick "The Orgasmic Dead". Director Impey and his leading man Radford (performing as Dylan Jake-Price) greet her. In a barren room, she's required to place herself on a seat in its centre while Impey sits opposite and films her on a handheld camera. Arrogant Radford bounces around the room in surly, agitated fashion, creating a Herzog/Kinski-like tension between the two men. It's all a little too much for Keller, especially when she's aggressively required to fellate a banana. Upon attempting to exit she's knocked out cold by Radford. When she comes to, she's tied to the aforementioned chair and her captors are discussing how to go about making their snuff film ... of which she's now the star.

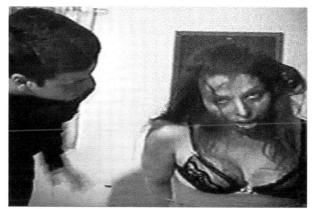

Filmed in Impey's home town of Milton Keynes on an apparent budget of just £50.00, *Fluid Boy* makes for an absorbing addition to the usually dull faux-snuff genre popularised by the likes of *August Underground* (2001). It's territory prolific no-budget filmmaker Impey has explored previously, in *Suicide Snuff* (2008) and *Snuff Film* (2011 – Impey directed this under the pseudonym Joe Newton, his character's name in *Fluid Boy*).

Six cameras are employed for this largely one-location film. This helps immeasurably when it comes to both style and pacing: continuity is consistent; the action is tightly edited throughout. The evolution of Impey's technical proficiency over earlier efforts such as *Sick Bastard* (2007) is evident from the start.

The barrage of humiliation and misogynistic dialogue may prove too much for some stomachs, as will scenes of Radford shitting into his victim's face and battering her senseless. We know it's all faked, of course, but that doesn't make it any less discomfiting – especially when it's all executed so persuasively.

What lifts this one above depressing torture-porn shallowness, aside from its superior editing, is the power-play between its male characters. As in a previous successful collaboration of theirs, *Twink* (2014), Impey is largely off-screen while acting as the calm to Radford's onscreen storm. Placed as an impartial observer who steadfastly refuses to help either victim or aggressor, Impey can often be heard berating his star's vitriolic outbursts: it has been suggested, and is entirely feasible, that the two characters are halves of the same psyche.

Radford is as reliable as ever – a ball of nervous energy and spunky bellicosity. But it's Keller who takes top honours as the beleaguered victim: brave and resilient in her role, vulnerable and convincingly terrified in her performance.

The Forbidden Four (2012)

Dir/Scr: Tom Lee Rutter; Cast: Shane Moroney, Tom Lee Rutter, Luke Coates

Rutter is an author, struggling to find the impetus to finish his latest book. Threatened by his publishers, he retreats to an isolated cottage where he hopes to find a cure for his writer's block. This comes in the form of a giant mutated lobster, which latches itself onto Rutter's skull and promises to awaken the four chambers of his exposed brain by secreting fresh stories into each one. All of which allows for a quartet of short yarns to unfold in rapid succession …

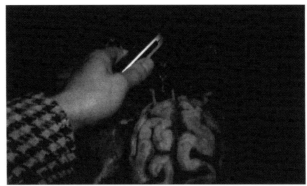

The first, "Antigone and Polyneices", takes on the Sophocles tragedy, via keen location scenery, masked actors and a healthy dose of inexpensive expressionism. "A Child's Toy" is a monochrome exercise in surrealism involving striking stop-motion animation which brings dolls to life at night. "The Catalyst" flirts with conformist storytelling techniques as an artist discovers murder can help bring the most out of a picture. "Solstice at the Midlife Circus" finds Coates as a man who's reached a crossroads in life, battling inner demons in an effort to find internal peace.

With shooting sites spanning Greece, Portugal and England, *The Forbidden Four* demonstrates ambition on its amiable director's behalf (his latest movie, 2016's *Stranger*, is equally audacious in choosing English and Welsh beaches for its acid-Western setting). This sense of grand motivation extends to the narrative here: unconventional and setting out to be creepily bizarre at every turn, these shorts are nothing if not bold in their experimental drive.

Kenneth Anger, Ken Russell and Lloyd Kaufman are cited among primary influences – imagine an unholy hybrid of the three, a marriage of the psychedelic and the irreverent, and you'll almost be there.

The miniscule budget has its restrictions, the biggest victim of which is the audio. There are passages of dialogue that are compromised to the point of virtual incomprehensibility. Luckily you don't really need to pick up every line (and a couple of the stories are largely speech-free): the film's strength lies within its creative, nightmarish visuals.

Coloured lighting filters and skewed camera angles create an aura of otherworldly unease; tight framing at choice moments amplifies the claustrophobia stifling our lead character. The circus story feels like a bad hallucinatory trip committed to digital. Odd characters, paradoxically frivolous music, leering faces ... the whole thing authenticates the suffocating nature of night terrors by virtue of ill-logic and go-for-broke eccentricity.

The Forbidden Four was released onto DVD independently by Rutter's Carnie Film Productions fold.

Forced Entry (2002)

Dir/Scr: Lizzy Borden; Cast: Rob Zicari, Michael Stefano, Valentino

This Extreme Associates production caused ripples upon its release for marrying gore with hardcore sexual violence – a controversy also courted by the movie it takes its inspiration from, Shaun Costello's notorious 1973 roughie of the same name.

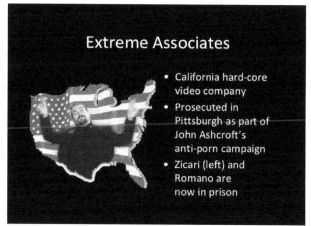

The original saw tortured Vietnam War veteran and gas station attendant Harry Reems stalk female customers, break into their apartments and violate them before taking their lives. Borden (born Janet Romano; Zicari's wife at the time of filming) ups the ante by having Stefano's rapist-murderer flanked by two accomplices and a copycat killer (Valentino). There's also slightly more plot on offer here. *Slightly*. Zicari is the roving reporter hot on the trail of devil-worshipping Stefano; the villain taunts victims and media alike with his love for infamous serial killer Richard Ramirez (cue our lead wearing a homemade AC/DC cap).

Forced Entry is in essence just over two hours of raw, brutal extended vignettes in which women are spat at, expletives are screamed in their face, and every orifice is desecrated in persuasively ruthless fashion. The first victim gets a face full of cum and piss moments prior to being suffocated. The second unfortunate is a pregnant lady who takes a disconcertingly authentic-looking beating before her gang rape and murder (thankfully actress Taylor St Claire wasn't *really* up the duff). A violent coda half-heartedly attempts to redress such ill deeds by doling out harsh justice on Stefano – none of which is filmed with the same level of gusto as the go-for-broke savage sex.

Low production values and unconvincing gore effects don't alter the fact that the performances are cogent in their intensity; the fear in each victim's eyes and screams rings true, as does the venom with which their aggressors dole out the unsparing punishments.

Zicari, who at one time side-lined as a pro-wrestler, is better known in the adult industry as Robert Black (his character here is called Roberto Negro). It's under this name that he produced a string of violent pornos while garnering attention from wandering documentarian Louis Theroux and American television distributors PBS. Theroux walked off the set of a simulated rape being shot by Zicari and Romano while filming his account of the American porn industry for the BBC in 1997. Similarly, PBS balked while visiting the shoot of *Forced Entry* a few years later – their consternation heightened by Romano's on-camera claims that actress Veronica Cainc had no idea she was about to be hurt and abused for real.

The exposure ultimately led to Zicari's offices being raided by the FBI in 2003. A lengthy court case ensued, resulting in he and Romano being imprisoned in 2010: the sentence for each was one year, the charge was distribution of obscene material. The pair went on to work on more innocuous parody fuckfests such as *Reservoir Doggs* (2011).

Found (2012)

Dir/Scr: Scott Schirmer; Cast: Gavin Brown, Ethan Philbeck, Phyllis Munro

Based on Todd Rigney's 2004 novella of the same name, Schirmer has fashioned an admirably discomfiting coming-of-age drama on a budget of just $8,000.00.

In it, 12-year-old Brown's world crumbles when he discovers his older brother Philbeck is a serial killer. Bullied at school and ignored by his parents, the horror-obsessed youngster inevitably develops a morbid fascination with his sibling's nocturnal activities.

The harrowing prospect of inherited racism is implied, their father's xenophobic rants indicated as an influence on Philbeck's penchant for beheading African-American women on a weekly basis. Even more absorbing are the themes of innocence lost, the painful confusion of puberty and – most potent of all – the imprint that you never know what's happening in someone else's home behind closed doors. In fact, equally disturbingly, we're alerted to the fact that many parents don't even realise what their kids are up to under their own roof.

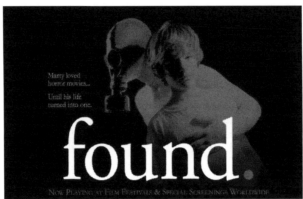

The perennial debate over the impact of youths watching violent videos is addressed, Brown pilfering a VHS atrocity from his brother's bedroom and drooling over its excesses while slowly detaching from reality. It's an interesting sub-plot but it's hardly in the league of Michael Haneke's *Benny's Video* (1992): first-timer Schirmer's directorial inexperience is exposed in this regard, as he fails to deliver a satisfying statement for or against said argument.

Brown is fantastic. He's required to carry the film, both on screen and via narration. He does both with heart-breaking honesty. Philbeck acquits himself well too, straddling a fine line between antisocial adolescent and reluctant role model to his browbeaten sibling. Regrettably, the fine performances stop there: much of the outlying cast are shockingly bad (that's mainly aimed at you, Louie Lawless – the dad).

Shot using the Canon 7D digital camera, the film looks highly professional for the most part. There are occasions where the good work is let down by a cheap aesthetic but, considering its budget, the feel of *Found* is often cinematic.

One question: what era is this supposed to based in? An emphasis on watching videotapes on a small CRT set suggests a 1980s backdrop, as do the many VHS titles in Philbeck's collection. But if that's the case, placements of posters for the likes of *Wild Zero* (1999) are clearly specious ...

That aside, *Found* (relax, it's not a 'found footage' effort) is a dark study of suburban terror and deserves to be seen for its tense familial drama. If anything, its gory excesses – the video footage, which includes breast-hacking and decapitated skull-fucking, along with the framing story's grim finale – aren't necessary in getting the film's point across. Such scenes were largely missing from the censored UK and Australian releases of the movie.

The film-within-a-film as viewed on VHS by Brown proved so popular that it was developed, via a successful Kickstarter campaign, into its own 2015 full-length movie – the outrageously gruesome *Headless*.

Francesca (2015)

Dir: Luciano Onetti; Scr: Luciano Onetti, Nicolas Onetti; Cast: Luis Emilio Rodriguez, Raul Gederlini, Silvina Grippaldi

Detectives in Rome are not only baffled by a series of murders which make reference to Dante Alighieri's epic poem "The Divine Comedy"; they're also being taunted by the paradoxically puritanical killer. Eventually linking each victim to the disappearance of a young girl fifteen years earlier, they realise their only hope of solving the case is to discover what became of Francesca.

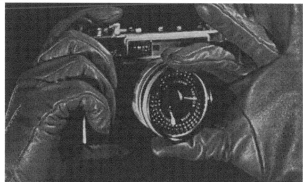

The first thing you'll notice when watching *Francesca* is how perfectly it mimics Italian cinema of the 1970s. Argentinean director Onetti's cinematography captures the angular editing and skewered camerawork of trusted gialli with meticulous attention to detail. The film simultaneously concentrates on ensuring all the expected motifs are present: the leather-gloved killer; sadistic animal-harming kids; creepy dolls; wheelchair-bound victim-cum-suspects; operatic kill sequences. And, of course, the obligatory bottle of J&B. All of which is greeted by a fitting prog rock score heavily reminiscent of Goblin's heyday (again, the work of the director).

More of a full-on love letter than mere homage, worshipping the tropes of a genre popularised by the likes of Sergio Martino (*All The Colours Of The Dark*, 1972) and Dario Argento (*Deep Red*, 1975), *Francesca* triumphs in being more accessible than recent films which have built their love of all things gialli around arthouse frameworks - the neo-giallo brigade, which incorporates films such as 2009's *Amer* and *Berberian Sound Studio* (2012). The narrative is far more clearly presented here.

This is also a significant step forward in technical terms when measured against the Onetti brothers' previous film, the similarly themed but more experimental *Deep Sleep* (2013). A tighter script and greater understanding of how to use visuals to enhance mood (the digital photography has undergone colour correction and other tinkering to afford proceedings the most authentically vintage look imaginable) make this a feast for the eyes and ears of giallo followers everywhere.

Are there shortcomings? Why, yes. Despite a greater emphasis on storytelling, the end result still smacks of all style and very little substance. The opening act is little more than a montage of abstract flashbacks and suggestion: beautifully constructed but emotionally cold. Although things settle somewhat in this regard, what follows still values emulation of classic styles over the spinning of an involving yarn. It's akin to those sitcoms which employ umpteen writers all obsessed with making every single line funny; the Onettis are unhealthily preoccupied with creating punchline after punchline, which in this case means ensuring every scene nails the design of their creative forefathers.

For all, then, that *Francesca* is an impressive achievement, replete with its deceptively simple mystery and moments of stunningly captured sexualised violence (keep watching after the end credits for the most alarmingly eroticised moment), the whiff of superficiality is never far away.

Freeze Me
See *Freezer*

Freezer (2000)

Dir/Scr: Takashi Ishii; Cast: Harumi Inoue, Shingo Tsurumi, Kazuki Kitamura

As a young woman Inoue was raped by three men. Rather than face the humiliation of reporting the crime, she decided to flee her small town and relocate to Tokyo. There, she embarked upon a new life. Now happily engaged to a workmate, all seems well - until a face from her past, Kitamura, forces his way into her apartment and the nightmare returns. He's brandishing a videotape containing footage he and his pals shot while having their way with Inoue. The plan is, now that he's tracked her down, she will oblige in a "reunion" - or the tape gets shown publicly. Kitamura's partners in crime are also on their way, she's told.

A subsequent showdown with Kitamura at her workplace costs Inoue her job and her fiancé (Tsurumi). Retreating to her apartment, Inoue's fragile mental state further deteriorates as she awaits each one of her aggressors' arrivals. Once the bodies start piling up, she begins ordering large freezers in which the corpses are stored. This causes her fresh problems ...

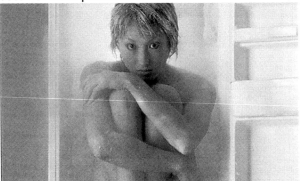

On paper *Freezer* could easily be dismissed as just another rape-revenge flick. *I Spit On Your Grave* (1978) is a clear template. Shot with typical Japanese formality, however, it is immediately - on a visual level alone - far slicker and more considered than your average grindhouse fare. Inoue's apartment becomes a prison of clinical, madness-inducing claustrophobia which helps the film superficially recall Roman Polanski's masterful *Repulsion* (1965).

Ishii, who's explored the concept of wronged women avenging their male antagonists before and since (see also *Black Angel Volume 1* [1998], *Flower And Snake* [2004] and *Sweet Whip* [2013]), keeps the actual rape scenes - largely seen through clips of Kitamura's videoed footage - brief and non-explicit. The tone of Inoue's violence is stark and brutal, eschewing the cathartic action movie-type tropes of similar Western fantasies.

Speaking of Inoue, the model-actress-sometime-pop-star is remarkable in the lead role. Capable of conveying vulnerability, shame, anger, confusion and sadness with equal degrees of persuasion, she realises her character to an extent which surpasses that which is expected of this traditionally ignoble sub-genre. Traces of subtle humour don't harm her cause.

It's a shame then that Ishii - creator of the infamous "Angel Guts" graphic novel - doesn't appear interested in saying anything of substance beyond the slick visuals, frequent nudity and bone-shattering violence. If this is commentary on the contradictory nature of Japanese society's manners, he disguises it well.

His most well-known film to date is arguably the Takeshi Kitano-starring gangster flick *Gonin* (1995).

Friend Request (2016)

Dir: Simon Verhoeven; Scr: Simon Verhoeven, Phillip Koch, Matthew Ballen; Cast: Alycia Debnam-Carey, Liesl Ahlers, William Moseley

Popular student Debnam-Carey accepts an online friend request from oddball Ahlers. Bad move. The latter is not only a cyber-stalker but, as Debnam's pals start dying around her, potentially something far more sinister.

The evils of social media. *Unfriended* (2015) was the big hitter a year earlier, so it was perhaps inevitable that similar films would swiftly follow. In the case of *Friend Request* (renamed from the ridiculously nondescript *Unknown Error*), we have a German production which – for commercial purposes - was shot in South Africa with English-speaking actors.

Debnam-Carey, who made her name during 2015-16 in the TV series "Fear the Walking Dead", rescues this film from being utterly redundant. Just. Her demure persona possesses a plausible vulnerability which gets the audience quickly onside. Whether being diplomatic with unwanted suitors or growing increasingly anxious when the police won't accept her stories of online terrors, she turns a potentially flat character into someone worthy of empathising with.

Her performance aside, watching *Friend Request* is a fairly demoralising chore. The concept of the remote tormentor transpiring as a witch is novel but insufficiently explored; Debnam-Carey's friends are uniformly one-dimensional non-entities – the type that have saturated far too many slasher flicks over the decades; Verheoven clearly mistakes frequent, telegraphed jump-scares for legitimate frights.

It's ironic that a film which embraces modern technology to such an extent (the usual social media interfaces, dodgy uploaded videos and so on) should feel so tired and conventional. At least *Unfriended* had the gimmick of its action unfurling in real time, exclusively via its protagonist's laptop screen.

And that "ambiguous" ending? *Please.*

Verhoeven is the grandson of filmmaker Paul. No, not *that* one: German actor and director Paul Verhoeven, whose behind-the-camera credits included *The Big Shadow* (1942) and *Heart Of Stone* (1950).

Frontier(s) (2007)

Dir/Scr: Xavier Gens; Cast: Karina Testa, Aurelien Wiik, Estelle Lefebure

As with the other big French horror film of 2007, *Inside*, the action here is set against the backdrop of that country's political unrest. On this occasion, the specifics are riots stemming from the controversial result of an election. Both films are also fronted by a pregnant lead character.

In this instance, Testa is the expectant mother-to-be. She, along with lover Wiik, her brother and a few friends, have opted to flee for the border following a botched robbery and head for a more stable life in Amsterdam. Alas, they foolishly take refuge from the pursuant police by detouring to a remote inn-cum-abattoir en route. Lured in by the promise of free shelter and sex, the group soon realises its mistake: this establishment is ran by a family of neo-Nazi cannibals.

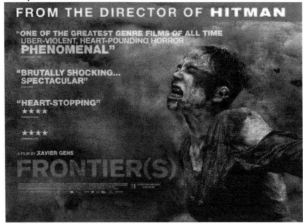

The appointment of a right-wing politician into a position of domestic power; a multi-cultural group of protagonists; a violent, inbred family of racists sired by a former SS officer and war criminal (Jean-Pierre Jorris) ... there's little doubt that Gens' muscular film is setting out its stall as a commentary on France's racial meltdown (see also the likes of Mathieu Kassovitz's *La Haine* [1995], a caustic reaction to the death of the director's ethnic friend while held in police custody).

For a while, the film convinces as such. We're even persuaded in earlier scenes that Testa's unborn child represents the hope of a more tolerant, educated future generation living in a Utopia borne of cosmopolitan harmony. But ...

Gens, whose biggest hit to date remains the pugnacious game adaptation *Hitman* (also 2007), soon ditches all aspirations of political allegory and instead ladles on the gory platitudes.

The flesh-eating family comes straight out of *The Texas Chain Saw Massacre* (1974), even going so far as to stage an excruciating victim/tormentors dinner scene akin to the infamous set-piece centre of Tobe Hooper's classic. The slick production design echoes more recent fare such as *Saw* (2004) and *Hostel* (2005).

Typically though, for a Gallic New Wave entry, *Frontier(s)* dramatically increases the level of onscreen brutality. Multiple stabbings, shootings and removals of body parts are shown in lovingly graphic detail.

Any statement being made may consequently get lost in the final hour's mayhem, and it may leave you with a feeling of having seen it all before, but *Frontier(s)* still delivers in terms of its succession of well-orchestrated torture-porn tribulations.

An ambiguous finale may suggest a return to social commentary come the end of the drama, but the whole thing reeks of style over substance. Again, much like *Inside*. Not so much of a criticism in terms of entertainment; merely an observation.

Frustre (2013)

Dir/Scr: Jacques Vendome; Cast: Christophe Cerdan, Marianna Voronkova, Camille Bardery

Dishevelled loner Cerdan feels increasingly isolated from society: belittled by workmates and seemingly unable to speak of a single true friend. He's taunted by billboards and other forms of advertising which sedulously sell a notion of sex unattainable to someone as socially inept as him. The closest he gets to nookie is fucking a mannequin in his fleapit apartment.

Eventually Cerdan's inner psychoses spill outwardly, as he takes to the streets with rape and murder in mind.

Dark conceptually and literally, this lo-fi serial killer study echoes Abel Ferrara's *The Driller Killer* (1979) in its premise of an individual's detachment from his environment escalating into violent madness, and William Lustig's *Maniac* (1980) with regards to the squalid production design and leering central character. The preoccupation with necrophilia - coupled with the French dialogue of course - also draws patent comparisons to Belgian nasty *Lucker The Necrophagus* (1986).

All three of the above films offer gritty, unsparing character studies of sadistic killers whose unforgiving city surroundings can be accountable both for their mental rejection of empathy towards others, and a perfect hiding place in which to go about their nefarious deeds unnoticed. *Frustre* ("frustrated" in English) plays very closely to these principles.

While successful in being intermittently haunting, Vendome's effort struggles to rivet its viewer due to a lack of insight into its protagonist's twisted inner workings. He has a monotonous factory job, fair enough. His fetid abode reflects his antisocial deportment, we get it. But what compels a man – even someone who feels as alone and humiliated as Cerdan's character – to violate and destroy innocent women? *Frustre* bypasses attempts at answering such questions.

It is, however, quite well-acted and shot in a convincingly filthy manner which at least manages to drag us into the killer's hellishly claustrophobic existence (if not his mind). It's also boldly amoral in a way which recalls superior assessments of past such as *Angst* (1983) and *Henry: Portrait Of A Serial Killer* (1986).

Furizu Mi
See *Freezer*

Game Over (2009)

Dir/Scr: Timo Rose; Cast: Debbie Rochon, Raine Brown, Nicola Fiore

Shot in Rose's home country of Germany but featuring English dialogue, *Game Over* begins in deceptively sedate manner as Brown and Fiore arrive in said country to visit their American pal Rochon on her birthday. The trio enjoy catching up for a short while – about twenty minutes to be more precise – before the tone shifts dramatically and the girls are abducted by a demented sadist. His basement is, handily, primed for the ensuing torture.

The bulk of the action takes place in this singular space. What we therefore get, after a promising opening, is an hour of repetitive torture porn for the German gore crowd. In one respect, it's commendable that *Game Over* makes no attempt at disguising itself as anything but.

On this level, the film delivers what its audience demands. The splatter quotient is high, boasting solid special effects work from Rose and co-star Manoush. Violence is doled out upon our three hapless leads almost constantly once we're in the basement. Along with slicings and beatings galore, Rose remembers to throw in a couple of brutal rapes for good measure (though these are not as explicit as I'd expected – a flash of breasts is the most female nudity on offer). A final act of vengeance will leave gorehounds with a satisfyingly nasty taste in their mouths.

Rochon and Brown are highly competent, prolific professionals. The material doesn't really allow for them to show off their skills here, other than to accentuate how effectively they can emulate being in pain. The aforementioned Manoush, an insanely busy actress herself (she's worked with Rose before, in the likes of *Barricade* [2007] and *Fearmakers* [2008]), stands out in a meaty scenery-chewing role. Also keep your eyes peeled for cameos from fellow German filmmakers Andreas Schnaas and Marc Rohnstock.

The Gateway Meat (2008)

Dir/Scr: Ron DeCaro; Cast: Ron DeCaro, D Whitney, Turibia Fradoca

DeCaro's "Brightside Trilogy" began in 2005 with the self-explanatory 28-minute *Eating Razors*. A year later, a keener sense of narrative and greater command of cinematic style informed the 11-minute shocker *The White Lie*. This employed chilling sound design and inventive use of suggestion to overcome budgetary limitations and get under its viewers' skin. It demonstrated real potential on DeCaro's part: expectations were high for its follow-up.

That arrived in the form of *The Gateway Meat*. With a $20,000.00 budget and a 69-minute running time, it's an epic undertaking for the director's small 'For The Better Of Mankind' production team.

In it, DeCaro portrays a family man living a seemingly normal life in a sleepy seaside town (shooting took place in Tucson, Arizona). He loves his wife and daughter, both of whom are played by his offscreen kin. But all is not as it seems. Behind closed doors, he's just inherited the mantle from his late Satanist father – necessitating that he rape, torture and kill as many people as possible in order to attain unholy powers and unlock a portal to Hell. Mother and daughter are complicit in the crimes, allowing for some harrowing (albeit cleverly edited) scenes in which the youngster appears to be taking part in alarmingly cruel deeds.

That's it in terms of plot. There's a little political allegory here (an alternate reality imagining the US president had been assassinated by religious extremists, which the Satanists see as a sign for their bloodletting to begin) and a smattering of surrealism there (an intentional vagueness to narrative, as much as it may irk some). But there's minimal character development and no comfort blanket of scene-setting elucidation. Indeed, the devil-worshipping aspects of the ensuing degradation are explained solely by introductory text and a pentagram painted on one of the family's walls.

On a technical front, it's DeCaro's most accomplished feature. The editing is slick, while the cinematography – by Jared Silva with a little help from Jessica Pratt and co-producer Drew Snelson – is frequently striking. A couple of stylised dream sequences lend further gravitas. Instances of poorly recorded audio and substandard acting weaken the dramatic impact somewhat.

But then there's the gore. The over-the-top, realistic gore. Eyeball violence, hammer attacks, bloody gunshots, multiple stab wounds to the face … the excellent effects were created by DeCaro alongside twins Aaron and Ben LaBonte. DeCaro captures their impressive results in raw, handheld style. Be warned, though, this is nasty stuff: prepare to witness sex with a pregnant corpse, for example.

Fellow gore purveyors Fred Vogel (*August Underground*, 2001) – whose films this resembles in terms of unrelenting, plotless sadism only - and Brian Paulin (*Bone Sickness*, 2004) have vocal cameos, heard over radio frequencies during the film.

German Angst (2015)

Dir: Jorg Buttgereit, Michal Kosakowski, Andreas Marschall; Scr: Jorg Buttgereit, Goran Mimica, Michal Kosakowski, Andreas Marschall; Cast: Lola Gave, Andreas Pape, Kristina Kostiv

Three tales of love, sex and death in modern-day Berlin, as mused over by German filmmakers Buttgereit, Kosakowski and Marschall.

The big draw here is most likely Buttgereit. He found infamy with 1987's splatter-art epic *Nekromantik*. His first foray into the horror genre since 1993's masterful serial killer flick *Schramm*, the opening segment here - "Final Girl" - is a short meditation on the relationship between pet (a guinea pig in this instance) and owner, and the similarities between their two personalities. Of course, there's more to proceedings than that ... though not much. Tightly edited and impressively photographed, there is however an aura of slightness to Buttgereit's offering, even if it does culminate in some pretty nasty scenes of torture.

Kosakowski, who helmed the absorbing documentary *Zero Killing* (2012), achieves more substance with the longer "Make A Wish". The highpoint of this portmanteau, this focuses on a deaf and dumb Polish couple who turn to a charmed necklace for help when they're accosted by racist thugs. Germany's deep-rooted history of racial prejudice comes to the fore in this astutely observed, painfully honest and hauntingly sad piece. Needless to say, its more graphic moments are resolute in their bone-crunching impact.

Marschall goes for explicit nudity and deep primary hues in closing segment "Alraune". It tells of a man who visits a club (called Mabuse!) in search of the ultimate thrill. He finds it, to his expense, by accepting to be blindfolded and drugged ...

Though heavy on the T&A and stylised camerawork, "Alraune" meanders badly. It's most interesting facet is that fellow directors Buttgereit and Kosakowski appear in tiny cameo roles.

Adhering to the unwritten rule that all horror anthologies must be wildly inconsistent in quality, the visually slick *German Angst* boasts several points of interest while managing to remain a decidedly mixed bag.

Get Out (2017)

Dir/Scr: Jordan Peele; Cast: Daniel Kaluuya, Allison Williams, Catherine Keener

Williams takes new boyfriend Kaluuya back to her family home in order for her parents to meet him. On the eve of the journey, she confesses she's neglected to tell her folks that her beau is black. This puts Kaluuya a little at unease: it's a sense of discomfort which grows when he reaches the parents' exclusively white, upper-class neighbourhood and realises that the only black people in sight are there to serve as maids, gardeners and the like. Following an unsettling hypnosis session with Williams' therapist mother Keener (claiming she can help him quit smoking), Kaluuya becomes convinced that every minute he stays with his girlfriend's weird, overly-friendly family is a threat to his very existence.

A prolific television actor, it's hardly surprising that Peele's greatest strength in his directorial debut are the performances he elicits from his cast. Briton Kaluuya is a strong, sympathetic lead; Williams is likeable as, ostensibly, the film's most grounded character. Keener and Bradley Whitford have fun hamming things up as her permanently smiling guardians, as do an array of interesting, sinisterly near-comical neighbours.

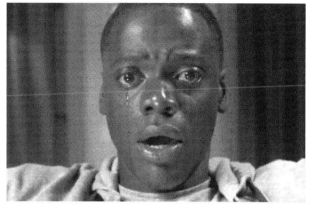

The screenplay has things to say about race relations and thinly disguised prejudices in modern society. Almost everyone Kaluuya meets over-compensates by singing the praises of black personalities (Jesse Owens, Tiger Woods etc) in his company - and initially intrigues with its simple but potent premise.

As the movie unfolds, it becomes less interested in having anything of note to say and more focused on ticking exploitation boxes. Hence the potentially appealing plot soon derails into clichéd elements such as slave-like creatures akin to something from *The Stepford Wives* (1975), Williams' frankly ridiculous redneck brother (Caleb Landry Jones) and Kaluuya's annoying - not to mention thoroughly unnecessary - comedy sidekick (LilRel Howery). There's also a whiff of Cronenberg - specifically *Videodrome* (1983) - thrown in during the final act as we finally realise what's going on behind the scenes.

Get Out resultantly winds up being a film very much of two halves: a first half where we ponder over the true meaning of the movie's title (is it a plea for Kaluuya to escape while he still can, or a clear racist message from the white neighbourhood directed at our hapless hero?), followed by a second half where we're invited to forget such subtleties and tolerate an uneven mix of dark comedy and predictable scares.

By the time the film suddenly ends, any early promise of substance has long since been retracted.

A Girl Walks Home Alone At Night (2014)

Dir/Scr: Ana Lily Amirpour; Cast: Sheila Vand, Arash Marandi, Mozhan Marno

Shot over the course of 24 days in Taft, California, Amirpour's feature debut is an assured, darkly humorous proposition merging Western motifs and indie quirkiness with stylish horror traditions. In an Iranian setting.

Marandi works assiduously to maintain his beloved sports car. It's the one thing of beauty he can admire in his otherwise bleak, desolate hometown of Bad City. That is, until he meets lonesome figure Vand. Equipped with a skateboard as mode of transport and Chador as headdress, she soon has our hapless protagonist beguiled.

But in Bad City, the fact that Vand is a vampire is the least of these star-crossed lovers' worries. Everyone has a violent agenda – not least of all prostitute Marno's thuggish pimp, who also happens to have stolen Marandi's car ...

A twee indie soundtrack (Kiosk, Radio Tehran, White Lies), crisp monochrome cinematography and characters introduced in the credits as "The Pimp", "The Junkie" etc: *A Girl Walks Home Alone At Night* tries extremely hard to be hip. It manages this, in a contrived manner which brings to mind the superficial cinema of Jim Jarmusch (*Mystery Train*, 1989; *Dead Man*, 1995). Style over substance.

It seems unfair to accuse the Farsi dialogue as an extension of the film's pretentiousness, given (a) where the action is set and (b) the fact that Amirpour is Iranian-American herself. But there's a definite whiff of smug "cool" about proceedings; resultantly, for all that it looks great in Digital HD and undeniably possesses its share of interesting visual ideas, *A Girl* emerges as being very difficult to warm to. It's an achievement to be admired, rather than a drama to become engrossed by.

A series of graphic novels began in 2014, serving as both prequel (the first release) and sequels which elaborate on the stories of Vand's titular creature and Bad City as a larger canvas. All-rounder Amirpour – she's also a painter, sculptor, keen skateboarder and sometime rock singer – worked with artist Michael DeWeese on these stylish creations.

The film premiered at 2014's Sundance Film Festival to glowing reviews. It went on to win several awards at prestigious events such as Sitges Film Festival.

Goksung
See *The Wailing*

Goodnight Mommy (2014)

Dir/Scr: Severin Fiala, Veronika Franz; Cast: Lukas Schwarz, Elias Schwarz, Susanne Wuest

The original title, *Ich Seh, Ich Seh*, translates literally as "I See, I See".

Nine-year-old twin brothers Lukas and Elias (the Schwarz siblings) await the return of their mother, Wuest, from hospital. Upon her arrival at their remote home, the boys sense something's off: Wuest's face is covered by bandages, having undergone extensive cosmetic surgery. Her actions seem unfamiliar to the lads. Could it be that the woman beneath the dressings is an imposter?

This Austrian film, shot on 35mm, is often beautiful to behold. Its muted colour schemes, long static shots and skew-whiff camera angles come together to produce a film as aesthetically clinical as it is attractive.

The icy veneer, scarce employment of music on the soundtrack and matter-of-fact sense of anti-drama also conspire to make this play like "Michael Haneke gone horror". Wuest's bandaged visage offers clear visual allusions to *Eyes Without A Face* (1960). The marriage of such styles musters undeniably atmospheric results.

Themes of trust and identity are deftly dissected, helping the co-directors to skilfully elicit an aura of persuasive escalating uncertainty rather than opting for the easier route of overt scares and gore.

An interesting side-note concerning the film's production is that the cast were shielded from the script and each scene was filmed in chronological order. Even with this in mind, however, there is a twist to proceedings that many will see coming within the action's first third. Alas, it's a "shock" revelation which has been used several times in genre films (no spoilers!) – and one which, once sussed, threatens to undermine any tension that may remain.

It's a real shame, because all the other elements are in place (well, barring a finale that feels slightly rushed and out of synch with the more austere build-up).

Fiala and Franz previously shot the acclaimed 2012 documentary *Kern*, which focused on controversial Austrian actor-director Peter Kern.

Grave
See *Raw*

Graveyard Of The Living Dead (2008)

Dir/Scr: Marc Rohnstock; Cast: Lars Rohnstock, Alexander Reckert, Marc Rohnstock

Reckert and director Rohnstock are a pair of bungling scientists employing brainwaves to resurrect a recent corpse in the hope of determining the brain's activity after death. Unsurprisingly, their endeavours go tits-up and they have a ravenous zombie on their hands. Infected by their undead creation, they make for the local graveyard where a gang of Goth teens have decided to throw a party. A massacre follows, resulting in contaminated blood seeping into the soil and rejuvenating the long-since dead.

It's *Re-Animator* meets *The Return Of The Living Dead* (both 1985), by way of gory Italian excesses such as *Zombie Creeping Flesh* (1980). And, this being a German splatter flick, you can bet that the Rohnstock brothers don't short-change us with the red stuff.

On the contrary, this fast-moving digital effort is crammed with enthusiastic gore. Axe dismemberments; umpteen gunshots to zombie heads; disembowelment galore; gut-munching ... the director provides the elemental homemade effects in abundance, red, raw and dripping. The zombie make-up brings to mind Giannetto De Rossi's convincingly crusty work on Lucio Fulci's *Zombie Flesh Eaters* (1979).

Co-star Ramon Kaltenbach also provides an appropriately atmospheric score with Martin Rudel, while a significant amount of the action is bolstered by a clutch of Goth-punk tunes from the likes of Godforsaken, The Other and Blitzkid.

Graveyard Of The Living Dead is overlong and unapologetically embraces the shortcomings of no-budget filmmaking: risible performances, home video aesthetics and a distinct lack of originality. But it's never dull - and, in technical terms, mark a definite progression when measured against Rohnstock's earlier *Dungeon Of Evil* (2005).

It's perhaps also worth noting that, other than a funny scene where the Goths rip open their dead pal and various zombies in a search for their missing car keys, the film possesses much less humour than your average German gore flick.

The Greasy Strangler (2016)

Dir: Jim Hosking; Scr: Jim Hosking, Toby Harvard; Cast: Michael St Michaels, Sky Elobar, Elizabeth De Razzo

Elderly Michaels and his equally odd son run a walking tour of disco landmarks around the streets of Los Angeles. When De Razzo visits their attraction, both men are smitten and a bout of father-son rivalry ensues. This coincides with an oily stranger stalking the neighbourhood at night preying upon innocents. Could the two events be related?

Elobar certainly believes so, as he grows increasingly convinced that his dad may be the greased-up, huge-cocked killer ...

The Greasy Strangler enters into a curious alternate take on working-class America, filtered through an air of surrealism which brings to mind both David Lynch weirdness (particularly *Eraserhead* [1977] and *Blue Velvet* [1986]) as well as the quirky trailer-trash comedy of the more recent *Napoleon Dynamite* (2004). British-born Hosking cites television programmes from his own upbringing as influential too: that he claims to worship the irreverence and offbeat anarchic style of "The Young Ones" (1982-1984) comes as no surprise.

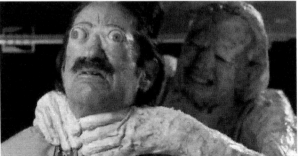

Far from being a simple mish-mash of the above, however, director Hosking's feature debut (following several well-received shorts) adds elements of early John Waters tastelessness and video nasty-style violence to produce something uniquely peculiar. Add a ton of full-frontal male nudity - thankfully all phalluses are prosthetic - and a truly singular score by Andrew Hung which sounds like it belongs on a Japanese video game, and you have a film as unclassifiable as it is rewarding.

Who knows - or cares - what it all means? Just revel in the sight of the then-72-year-old Michaels (genre fans may recognise him from 1987's cheap 'n' gory *The Video Dead*) partaking in all manner of onscreen deviance. It's a film where even the repetition of everyday words such as "potato" can tap into instances of hilarity.

Elijah Wood, Ant Timpson and Ben Wheatley are among this crazed film's co-producers.

The Green Inferno (2015)

Dir: Eli Roth; Scr: Eli Roth, Guillermo Amoedo; Cast: Lorenza Izzo, Ariel Levy, Daryl Sabara

First announced at the 2012 Cannes Film Festival, Roth's $6 million-budgeted folly was billed as a love letter to the Italian gut-muncher movies of the 1970s and early 1980s. It was originally scheduled for a US theatrical release in September 2014 but was delayed by a year when production company Worldview Entertainment began experiencing "financial difficulties". Blumhouse Productions came to the rescue via their multi-platform release offshoot BH Tilt.

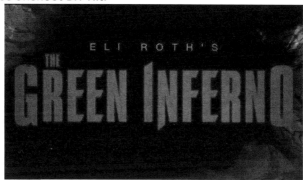

Izzo is an idealistic American student who's enticed into travelling to the Amazon jungle with social activist pals and filming footage of loggers at work. Their hope is to raise global awareness of the danger indigenous tribes in the area are being placed under. Irony is their enemy as one such clan duly captures them ... and is revealed to be of the primal, flesh-eating variety.

Roth had previously awarded fellow filmmaker Ruggero Deodato a cameo role in his *Hostel Part 2* (2007). The latter's celebrated *Cannibal Holocaust* (1980) is clearly a major influence, as is Umberto Lenzi's trashier *Cannibal Ferox* (1981). Whereas those films portray exploitative Westerners as the catalysts for the natives' violence – "who are the real cannibals?" we're asked of society in *Holocaust* – Roth flips the dynamic here by having a bunch of tree-hugging do-gooders become the prey. At the very least, any disturbance they cause to the locals during their visit is unintentional.

And that's arguably the most interesting thing *The Green Inferno* has to offer. Yes, the Peruvian locations are beautifully captured (though the director hasn't quite managed to evoke the imagery of Werner Herzog [*Aguirre, The Wrath Of God*, 1972, etc], as was his stated intent). Certainly the gore runs red during the film's latter half: eviscerations, dismemberment, anthropophagy – all present. Another plus note is that the film abjures the most notorious aspect of films like *Cannibal Holocaust*, meaning there is no ugly animal violence here.

But Roth still can't write congenial characters. He hasn't yet mastered the art of crafting a screenplay which moves at a consistent tempo. And the veneer is too polished to convincingly deliver the threat of its infamous forefathers. Plus, is it me or is *The Green Inferno* incredibly coy when it comes to nudity (another major ingredient of its predecessors)?

What we're left with is a film whose most noteworthy facets occurred behind the scenes: tales of Roth locating a genuine Peruvian tribe and enlisting their services; showing them a HD screening of *Cannibal Holocaust* to demonstrate what a "movie" is; the natives offering one of their own infants to the production company as a thank you; and so on.

The Green Inferno isn't the travesty that video nasty purists insist. Nor is it anything more than a well-shot but plodding (impatient viewers will be itching for the flesh-eating to begin) and only mildly engaging update of racist Third World exploitation flicks. A couple of moments of ill-considered schoolboy humour - one character masturbating in full view of fellow captives, for example, in an attempt to alleviate the stress he's under - reveal that Roth, at heart, is seeking the approval of the frat boy element.

Green Room (2015)

Dir/Scr: Jeremy Saulnier; Cast: Patrick Stewart, Anton Yelchin, Macon Blair

Small-time punk band The Ain't Rights accept a gig at a club in the backwoods of Portland. It's not enough that they choose to antagonise the right-wing skinhead audience by opening their set with a cover of Dead Kennedys' "Nazi Punks Fuck Off"; they're unfortunate enough to witness a murder in the green room too. Enter club owner Stewart, a cool calculated psychopath who insists all witnesses must perish. Can the group, locked in the titular backstage area, survive the night and escape unscathed?

Back in 2007 I reviewed the DVD release of that year's *Murder Party*, Saulnier's feature debut (he'd made a couple of shorts previously). I recall that it successfully balanced irreverent humour with gory horror and showed potential from the then-29-year-old director. Indeed, I concluded my review by saying it was "well worth checking out". Saulnier has made good on that initial promise, scoring an indie hit with 2013's convention-subverting revenge thriller *Blue Ruin* and then this, a taut action-horror which went down extremely well with festival-goers and critics alike.

In terms of pacing, its claustrophobic setting and the tone - dark but infused with necessary humour in all the right places - *Green Room* brings to mind early John Carpenter works, in particular *Assault On Precinct 13* (1976). With blasts of hardcore punk and death metal littered throughout for good measure. Saulnier professes to be a former punk rocker himself, and the bands referenced along the way - Fugazi, TKO, Misfits, The Cro-Mags etc - demonstrate his familiarity with the music. Better still, the authentic piss 'n' sweat vibe of Stewart's club (and the protagonists' gig, in which the actors all played their own instruments) rings true of the world inhabited by underground music scenes.

Tension is elicited quickly and, for the large part, sustained. If the film sags at any point, this is due to a tendency for characters to mumble their dialogue in disengaged fashion. From what I gather, everyone had fun making the film, but it was Saulnier's choice to have his actors behave against type. True, his screenplay and direction bring extra dimension to Stewart's character, along with his henchman Blair (returning from his superlative lead turn in the aforementioned *Blue Ruin*), by stripping them of overt menace and giving them human concerns. But there's a low-key approach to much of the action, in keeping with Brooke and Will Blair's subtly groaning score, which prevents pulses from ever seriously racing.

The film is gory in fits and starts, stylishly shot (cinematographer Sean Porter makes good atmospheric use of Portland's unexpected shit weather) and benefits from being fronted by a likeable bunch of idealistic, wet-behind-the-ears good guys.

Russian-born Yelchin was forging a great career for himself, having won praise for roles in *Star Trek* and *Terminator Salvation* (both 2009) and *Odd Thomas* (2013). Alas he died in June 2016, run over by his own jeep after leaving it in neutral on a hill.

Grotesk (2015)

Dir/Scr: Peter J Bonneman; Cast: Heine Sorensen, Jorgen Gjerstrup, Mai Sydendahl

An American spacecraft crash-lands off the coast of Denmark, having recently completed a clandestine mission to the moon. On board is a mysterious slime which the astronaut (Jack Jensen) scraped from the moon's surface. As it leaks out of the wreckage and into the Oresund strait, it mutates into a malevolent man-creature ... spelling bad news for a whole host of witless locals. Cue a heavily armed SWAT team in hazmat suits. Can they save the day?

Allusions to *The Green Slime* (1968) and *The Incredible Melting Man* (1977) are clear. But, working on an evidently shoestring budget, Bonneman is aware of his limitations: he himself bills the film as Denmark's answer to Ed Wood Jr's famously inept *Plan 9 From Outer Space* (1959). *Grotesk* is deliberate in its expressionless acting, stonewashed colour grading and atrocious dubbing. It also wears its gaudy and enthusiastic gore proudly upon its sleeve.

Speaking of which, fans of the red stuff definitely don't go without. Though the director has cited the cinema of Herschell Gordon Lewis as an influence (*Blood Feast* [1963], *The Wizard Of Gore* [1970] etc), the rampant gore is more akin to the entertainingly crude, OTT work witnessed in Peter Jackson's *Bad Taste* (1987). Brains are spattered here, there and everywhere; the creature wields an axe with ferocious efficiency; blood squibs literally explode whenever anyone is shot at. The gore is excessive to the point of absurdity, and - within the context of Bonnneman's zany script - is all the better for it.

Clocking in at just 64 minutes in length, *Grotesk* manages to be both righteously violent and amiable: it's very much a "beer and pals" kind of flick. Beneath all the filthy fun and self-conscious trashiness, however, it's also worth noting that Bonneman has an unexpected flair for stylish visuals and tight editing.

Grub Girl (2006)

Dir: Craven Moorehead; Scr: Edward Lee; Cast: Brittney Skye, Charmane Star, Teanna Kai

In 1994 rock singer Glenn Danzig founded the publishing company Verotik, their speciality being the production of comic books aiming to provide adult readers with imagery of both a sexual and/or violent nature. One of Verotik's most popular creations remains Edward Lee's "Grub Girl" series, the first issue of which was originally published in June 1997.

Danzig teamed up with director Moorehead to produce this no-holds-barred adaptation in 2006.

In it, Skye takes on the lead role – a hooker in a near-future apocalyptic world, whose exposure to radiation has left her zombified. Realising her condition renders her immune to both disease and pain, she sets about fucking all she can while exacting revenge on the pimp who did her wrong.

Alt-porn has been on the rise in recent years, possibly serving as a kick against the increasingly tired formula of the "gonzo" filth proffered online. Merging adult action with horror tropes has become a virtual cottage industry, with titles such as *Re-Penetrator* (2004), *The XXXorcist* and *Porn Of The Dead* (both 2006) providing typical examples of what to expect.

Grub Girl can claim to have better production values than most. It's a good-looking, filmic offering with a clear aesthetic eye on the cinematic stylings of the 1970s. Skye is a credible lead: feisty and sexy, strong enough in presence to fulfil the fantasies of pubescent viewers making that leap from superhero comics to wank material.

Born as Doug Brewer, Moorehead has been a hugely prolific filmmaker in Porn Valley during the 21st Century – he's made over 100 videos with cumshot legend Peter North alone. The director described *Grub Girl* in interviews as a "sick, twisted mix of horror, rock music and great sex scenes". He certainly films the action at an agreeable pace, ensuring the fuck set-pieces – there are four in total – aren't too drawn-out. Cunnilingus, fellatio and penetration are the order of the day. Gore is thin on the ground by comparison, save for a show-stopping moment of sticky cock-munching.

The Grudge
See *Ju-on: The Grudge*

Gun Woman (2014)

Dir/Scr: Kurando Mitsutake; Cast: Asami, Noriaki Kamata, Kairi Narita

Mobster's son Kamata is a bug-eyed sexual lunatic. He inherits a fortune when his father dies. But there's one condition: he must leave Japan for good. Hence he heads to Los Angeles, where he tracks down Narita - the wealthy doctor who failed to cure his dad's mystery illness. As an act of vengeance, Kamata cripples Narita before raping and murdering his wife in front of him.

Naturally Narita wants revenge too. Having heard of Kamata's regular visits to a heavily protected exclusive club for necrophiles, he "buys" junkie Asami off the street and sets about training her into becoming a highly skilled killing machine. His plan is to conceal a gun and a round of bullets into two wounds cut into her torso, and then administer a drug to her which replicates signs of being dead. Once smuggled into the club by an insider, Asami is to awaken and rip her wounds open, giving her twenty-two minutes to locate and slaughter Kamata before she herself bleeds to death.

The concept is brilliant. Bonkers but brilliant. There's no room for logic in this world where the lead avengers have seemingly limitless resources and the biggest chips conceivable on their shoulders. To scrutinise events on such grounds really would be missing the point. Simply sit back and enjoy the spectacle.

Enjoy the unrelenting action as Asami is put through her paces in training montages not unlike those in *Rocky IV* (1985). Enjoy Dean Harada's emotive electronic score, echoing Giorgio Moroder's efforts from *Scarface* (1983) - a similarly excessive film about friends torn apart by greed, whereas *Gun Woman* focuses on people brought together by their hunger for revenge. Enjoy the ludicrous amount of female nudity on offer (alongside beautiful former porn actress Asami, there's a totally gratuitous shower-based opening kill and a show-stopping sequence in which a naked woman stands bleeding to death during an arguably unnecessary demonstration of the twenty-two minute rule).

Well-shot and lit, gory as Hell and utterly crazy (Kamata is one of the most enjoyably repugnant villains in recent memory), the Manga-style *Gun Woman* also manages to stir unexpected emotions, thanks to Asami's uncanny ability to evoke warmth and empathy in a largely silent role.

A smidgeon of ham-fisted CGI and a clumsy American wraparound story aside, *Gun Woman* comes highly recommended.

The BBFC objected to five seconds of Kamata showing signs of arousal during one scene of violence. Considering the extreme nature of the film as a whole, this cut (for the UK DVD release) seems redundant.

Gut (2011)

Dir/Scr: Elias; Cast: Jason Vail, Nicholas Wilder, Sarah Schoofs

The enigmatically named Elias (a.k.a. Biff Juggernaut) first shook the underground horror scene with his bombastic short *The Voice Inside* (2001) – an angry slice of monochrome body horror which ladled on the gore while suggesting allusions of an arthouse persuasion.

Fast-forward a decade, and the auteur's feature debut traverses similar terrain.

It focuses on Vail, a jaded husband and father whose transition into responsible adulthood is met with an apathy which suggests he'd rather go back to watching horror films with old pal Wilder. The latter is the concerned pal who fears that he's forever lost his friend to the rigmaroles of parenthood and regular work.

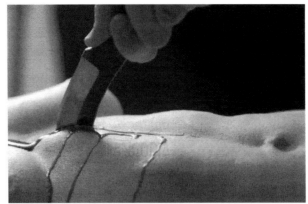

In an attempt to relive their glory days, Wilder gets the beers in and orders a dodgy horror film over the Internet. While watching it together, the lads are simultaneously intrigued and repulsed by what they witness: seemingly genuine footage of a naked female's stomach being sliced open, the innards contained within the cavity subsequently fondled.

The experience has psychological repercussions for Vail in particular; as the dodgy DVDs keep coming, his disturbed state of mind spells trouble for well-intended wife Schoofs and their daughter.

A fascination with snuff broadcasts which awakens something up until then lying dormant in the protagonist: *Gut* can at times be loosely compared with *Videodrome* (1983). The Cronenberg connection runs deeper, however, via the examination of bodily obsessions manifesting themselves in horrifying manner. Or, at the very least, it can be said that the focus on morbid self-attention which came with many of the Canadian director's seminal early works is also present here.

A slow-moving plot reinforces the fact that *Gut* is driven by its detached characters, rather than its gore (which is infrequent and quite repetitive). The action is surprisingly downbeat throughout.

Though unsuccessful as a meditation on the psychology of being a horror fan and the implications of enjoying vicariously violent thrills, Elias' film packs a fair wallop once it finally gathers pace and the disturbing denouement delivers.

Gvozdi
See *Nails*

Gwoemul
See *The Host*

Hack Job (2011)

Dir/Scr: James Balsamo; Cast: James Balsamo, Michael Shershenovich, Dave Brockie

A prologue finds a pretentious arthouse director extolling the virtues of his latest masterpiece (the entirely fictitious "The Life And Death Of An Avocado") for a live TV interview, only for the transmission to be interrupted midway through - the gatecrashers being Balsamo and Shershenovich, two deranged horror fans who blame highbrow art cinema for holding their beloved genre back.

Their diatribe is sufficiently demented to convince the Devil (Michael Perillo) that he's found a pair idiotic enough to turn his dreadful horror anthology script into a movie. Sure enough, Balsamo and Shershenovich are excited at the prospect of directing an indie film which promises "tits, cheesy monsters and more tits".

And so, the three short films-within-the-film commence with the Nazi-versus-mummies madness of "Tomb of the SS". Set in Mumbai but actually shot in New York and Los Angeles, this sets the tone perfectly: zealous overacting, intentionally crappy FX work and some truly risible one-liners. Oh, and lots of lots of crunching metal on the soundtrack.

"Earth is on the Menu" sees the late Brockie - better-known to rock fans as GWAR lead singer Oderus Urungus - as a seedy diner owner who becomes the first fatality of an alien newly arrived on the planet. For unknown reasons, other than to perhaps highlight a few of the many bands featured on the soundtrack, the carnivorous space creature opts to single out a local Battle of the Bands contest for its prey.

Finally, "The Mark" pits a demonically possessed loser against a televangelist. This one provides some nice pastiche of religious bullshit, and some truly nasty pipe music.

Balsamo takes the lead in each of these vignettes. As with the wraparound yarn, his performance - and those of everyone else involved, for that matter - is crassly theatrical. His script is busy; endlessly spewing forth gags of both a lyrical and visual nature. Some are funny (cameo star Lloyd Kaufman's bout of drug-induced flatulence), most others are painful in their broadness. The appeal is that this is endlessly energetic and deceptively inventive fare.

Hack Job also benefits from an impressive supporting cast. Alongside Kaufman - his appearance is entirely understandable, given the film's Troma-esque tone and the inclusion of both the Toxic Avenger and Sgt Kabukiman in one punchline - genre faves such as Lynn Lowry and Debbie Rochon also turn up to join in the low-budget fun.

This isn't going to appeal en masse. It's very lo-fi in its finish, and enormously stupid for the most part. Gleefully so. It also delivers on its early promise of nudity, gore and cheesiness. Albeit, everything is so crude and ugly that you're advised to wash this down with beer for maximum appreciation.

That aforementioned soundtrack is certainly rousing, containing the likes of Death by Stereo, The Creepshow and - providing a boisterously up-tempo title tune - Bloodsucking Zombies from Outer Space.

The Hagstone Demon (2009)

Dir: Jon Springer; Scr: Jon Springer, Harrison Matthews; Cast: Mark Borchardt, Nadine Gross, Cyndi Kurtz

Borchardt retreats into alcoholism following his wife's suicide. In-between drinking, he barely manages to function as caretaker for an apartment block on the brink of being condemned. He finds a glimmer of hope in attractive new tenant Kurtz, but a spate of murders in the building bring suspicions - and demons from the past - Borchardt's way.

Springer has over twenty years' experience as a cinematographer (*Made In Berlin* [1998], *America's Next Felon* [2009] etc) and he puts those skills to valuable use here. The monochrome photography captures the ambient setting well, accentuating shadows in almost every composition while revelling in tested expressionism elsewhere. Bursts of colour are effective in their representation of Borchardt's dreams. A $2,000,000.00 budget helps, of course: visuals are crisp and clear, adding just the right degree of polish to the affair.

Casting Borchardt in the lead role is an inspired move. The witless star of the excellent *American Movie* (1999), which documented his attempts to break into the movie industry by finally completing the no-budget horror flick he'd started and then abandoned some years earlier, Borchardt retains his quirky nerdish demeanour to become a rather unconventional, inharmoniously identifiable protagonist.

Lung Leg, the punk icon who made a name for herself in Richard Kern shorts such as *You Killed Me First* (1985) and *Death Valley '69* (1986), also appears in a supporting role. Following a lengthy spell out of the limelight she resumed her acting career in 2005's *Sewer Baby*, which happens to have been directed by Springer's pal Mike Etoll. Etoll supervises the FX work on *The Hagstone Demon*.

Ties between Borchardt's crumbling mental state and the condition of the building he manages are tenuous at best: ignore them and focus instead on the fine selection of idiosyncratic characters being proffered. Traces of black comedy are handled with deftness, Springer's borderline-surreal style at times recalling early David Lynch (specifically *Eraserhead*, 1977) while serving up a confident blend of film noir and insinuated terror. When the movie shifts gear during its final act to reveal a more overtly supernatural leaning, it's impossible not to liken proceedings to *Rosemary's Baby* (1968).

The film garnered mixed responses from audiences, but was generally well-received by critics. It even won the Best Feature prize at the 2009 Atlanta Horror Festival.

Don't let the generic title (Hagstone is the name of the apartment block) or Pacific Entertainment's horrible photoshopped US DVD cover put you off: Springer's film offers good-looking paranormal drama and one of the most interesting casts in recent memory.

Hanger (2009)

Dir: Ryan Nicholson; Scr: Ryan Nicholson, Patrick Coble; Cast: Nathan Dashwood, Ronald Patrick Thompson, Debbie Rochon

Coat-hangers ... they bring out the child in you.

Pimp Thompson is furious when one of his girls, hooker-with-a-heart Rochon, falls pregnant. So much so that he performs a coat-hanger abortion on her. But ... the child survives. Eighteen years down the line, the kid has grown to become Dashwood. With the help of his father (Dan Ellis), he gets himself a job at the local scrapyard and rents an apartment, where he sets about plotting his revenge against Thompson.

Canadian filmmaker Nicholson has a style he's made his own. He farts in the face of political correctness and rarely if ever believes that there's such a thing as "going too far". There are two things which distinguish him from most other purveyors of extreme cinema. One is that he's an established special effects make-up artist, having worked on over two hundred projects since 1995 including *Final Destination* (2000) and *Scary Movie 3* (2003). Even when he's not handling the FX on his own films, you know you can rely on a certain standard. The second is his irreverent sense of humour which, as tasteless as it is, lends a wicked sense of fun to what would otherwise be unrelentingly grim material.

His best film to date is probably 80s throwback *Gutterballs* (2008). It's a kinetic neon-drenched rape-revenge-cum-slasher flick with more "f" words than *Scarface* (1983) and a penchant for outrageous sexual violence. *Hanger* can't compete with that rollercoaster of madness, but gives it its best shot.

Smashed heads, torn-off titties, cannibalism, tampon fetishes, female masturbation, rape, buggery, jokes made at the expense of people with physical deformities (almost every male character wears, for unexplained reasons, facial make-up to appear disfigured) ... no stone is left unturned in Nicholson's bid to challenge boundaries. The broad comedy and cartoonish characters conspire to make it resemble a Troma film; Lloyd Kaufman even cameos as a predictably flamboyant transvestite.

A superficial likeness to *Street Trash* (1987) arises from the scrapyard setting and the gallery of freaks who inhabit this shady world. But the low-res video aesthetics and try-too-hard approach to the endless succession of "shocks" cause *Hanger* to fall short of such greatness.

I do like a film with reassuring credits though: "No genitalia were harmed in the making of this birth".

Hangman (2015)

Dir: Adam Mason; Scr: Simon Boyes, Adam Mason; Cast: Jeremy Sisto, Kate Ashfield, Eric Michael Cole

Inspired by a news article which told of a homeless man who'd be living secretly in the crawlspace of a family's home for months, *Hangman* marks the latest of several collaborations between Britons Mason and Boyes (*Broken* [2006], *Blood River* [2009] etc).

In it, a family of four return from holiday to discover their home has been broken into. The police dismiss the crime as being the work of pranksters. The parents, Sisto and Ashfield, do their utmost to shrug the event off and get their lives back on track. However, unbeknownst to them, their intruder (Cole) has never left: he's set up home in their attic and now watches their every move via an array of strategically placed hidden cameras.

The set-up is strikingly similar to that of 2011's *388 Arletta Avenue*, while Cole's masked assailant brings to mind the sinister Tooth Fairy from *Manhunter* (1986). The invader's subtle tormenting of the family – moving household items in their absence and the like - and voyeuristic viewing of their resultant anxieties elicits memories of Michael Haneke's *Hidden* (2005). And, naturally, there's more than a whiff of *Paranormal Activity* (2007) about the found-footage aesthetics.

Everyday objects getting misplaced, unexplained noises from upstairs: Mason mounts the sense of unease gradually and subtly. Sisto and Ashfield are likeable leads, making the sombre spectre of inevitability all the more insidious. *Hangman* evokes a feeling that too few modern horror movies do: fear.

Some will no doubt find the pace too sluggish, or bemoan the fact that not much happens – even scenes such as Cole pleasuring himself while watching the parents make love are downplayed. But for those who can attune to the matter-of-fact scariness of the situation and the cool, calculated manner in which Mason confidently builds to a harrowing denouement, *Hangman* will be recognised as a superior addition to the conceptually troubling "home invasion" sub-genre.

Hard Splasher
See *Fetus*

Hate Crime (2012)

Dir: James Cullen Bressack; Scr: James Cullen Bressack, Jarret Cohen; Cast: Jody Barton, Tim Moran, Ian Roberts

A Jewish family celebrate their youngest son's birthday, the father filming the event on his camcorder. Within minutes their home is stormed by a trio of masked, Crystal Meth-abusing neo-Nazi thugs. A night of terror follows, the most salacious parts of which are captured by the hoodlums on the handheld camera.

Hate Crime wastes no time in getting down to its nasty business. The plot, for what it's worth, boils down to the family being new to the neighbourhood, and their aggressors not taking kindly to their arrival. What's problematic about such a lack of exposition is that no time is invested in the victims. We know too little about them to feel genuine concern. Also, horror impacts greater when it has a build-up; there is none here, Bressack's approach being one of constant assault.

A home invasion film presented in "found footage" fashion: *Hate Crime* proffers two modern sub-genres for the price of one. From this angle, the entire thing could be perceived as an elongated version of Otis and Henry's notorious attack on a family in *Henry: Portrait Of A Serial Killer* (1986). The end results aren't half as effective here: a combination of clumsy editing and unconvincingly staged violence - rape, infanticide, an eye gouging etc - geld much of the film's potential power.

What we get, then, is a lot of (partially improvised) hullaballoo. A great deal of the dialogue either suffers from characters shouting over one another, or antagonists spitting out racist bile largely muffled by the masks they're wearing. Anti-Semitic profanities are used with such abandon that, after a short while, their shock value has diminished and they end up sounding like the desperate rants of unimaginative ad-libbing.

Performances are credible by and large. Only Roberts is truly memorable, though, as a hulking baddie with unexpectedly interesting foibles.

The son of three-time Emmy Award winning writer Gordon Bressack and voice actress Ellen Gerstell, the director was just 20 when he helmed *Hate Crime*. Of Jewish lineage himself, he shows potential in terms of generating moments of claustrophobic fear and threat. But he has a lot to learn when it comes to spinning yarns populated by three-dimensional characters. The text coda explaining the fates of those still breathing come the end of the slim 71-minute running time is something of a copout, providing further evidence of lazy writing that all-but diminishes any impression left by the preceding action.

Submitted for a UK DVD release by The Horror Show Ltd, Bressack's film was rejected outright by the BBFC in March 2015. Their concern was due to the "unremitting manner in which *Hate Crime* focuses on physical and sexual abuse, aggravated by racist invective". It's not the first time the classification board has objected to a film on such grounds: the enjoyably trashy "video nasty" *Fight For Your Life* (1977) remains banned in the UK at the time of writing.

Head Case (2007)

Dir/Scr: Anthony Spadaccini; Cast: Paul McCloskey, Barbara Lessin, Brinke Stevens

A documentary-style account of married couple McCloskey and Lessin, whose home videos have apparently been edited together here to reveal a household of bickering, marital routine and the occasional murder.

Spadaccini employs his home state of Delaware as the setting for these tawdry goings-on, the geeky-looking McCloskey addressing the camera with blasé pride as he explains how, having taken a break from killing for several years in order to raise his kids, he's now back in the saddle ... with his cold-hearted wife joining in the fun. After all, it's so much easier abducting, raping and dismembering transients when there's two of you at it.

In the meantime the couple walk inconspicuously among their unsuspecting community: to the outside world they are churchgoers, loving parents and unassuming neighbours.

Shot on a mix of Super 8mm and video, on a reported budget of $5,000.00, *Head Case* is almost entirely drained of colour. It's an odd, dreary look to begin with, but one which makes sense when married to the extremely naturalistic performances and moments of jarring matter-of-fact violence.

Camerawork is intelligent in its openness and unfussy manner, allowing for the sparing use of effective make-up effects to achieve maximum grisly impact during wider shots. The killings are often underpinned by traces of dark, subtle humour. Lessin hectors her husband over the mess he's making as he commits his foul deeds, causing this viewer to ponder: is this how Fred and Rose West carried on?

Ultimately disturbing in its examination of what lies beneath the facade of normalcy, behind your neighbours' curtains, and man's capacity for casual brutality, *Head Case* offers more than the usual faux-snuff platitudes.

The film was well-received at festivals local to it and the US DVD rights were soon sold as a consequence. Little wonder then that Spadaccini has revisited this plot several times, returning to these characters in follow-ups *The Ritual* (2009), *Post-Mortem* (2010) and *Head Cases: Serial Killers In The Delaware Valley* (2013).

Headless (2015)

Dir: Arthur Cullipher; Scr: Nathan Erdel; Cast: Shane Beasley, Kaden Miller, Kelsey Carlisle

Beasley lives as a recluse on a rundown farm. His only contact with the outside world are the women he abducts and decapitates, for the purpose of fornicating with their severed heads. Flashbacks reveal an abusive childhood as being the root of his problems.

Remember that "lost" horror film from 1978 called "Headless", as seen in Scott Schirmer's *Found* (2012)? The film-within-a-film footage proved so popular that a fundraising campaign was soon set up to help develop it into a feature-length entity of its own. This proved to be highly successful, and ... *voila*.

Schirmer returns, helping to edit this film as well as co-producing alongside screenwriter Nathan Erdel and his wife Kara. Cullipher, who worked as FX artist on Schirmer's movie and oversees a crew of twelve effects wizards on this occasion, also graduates to directorial duties.

The late 70s setting - complete with 70s fashions, big hair and a refreshing lack of political correctness - superficially recalls *Gutterballs* (2008). An occasional distressed look has been applied in post-production, though this isn't entirely successful due to the fact that the film was shot on a Canon 7D digital HD camera. A certain degree of artifice resultantly prevails.

In terms of plot, there's not much to it. The background story is lazy, and there is no character development whatsoever. Carlisle, as the luckless heroine destined to meet with Beasley, works at a roller rink and has a stoner boyfriend: that's essentially all we learn of her. Her promiscuous pal Ellie Church is far more interesting though underused. Miller, as the young version of Beasley's character (referred to as Skullboy for reasons that will become obvious) is a striking addition. Beasley's own role is low on dialogue – he's a killing machine, simply.

Which brings us to the violence. It's gory, reliant solely on practical effects and oft-times reasonably convincing. If a tad repetitive.

Heavy Metal Apocalypse
See *Deathgasm*

Her Name Was Torment (2014)

Dir/Scr: Dustin Wayde Mills; Cast: Allison Egan, Dustin Wayde Mills, Jackie McKown

Mills is a doctor of some description, addressing masked Patient 394 (Egan, appearing as Allison Fitzgerald in the film's credits) in a sparsely furnished room. We soon learn that she's a serial killer and, through flashbacks, we witness the fate of her last victim (Mills regular Brandon Salkil, who's as dependable as ever in his very physical role). Mills' questioning provokes Egan to claim her murders have been committed at the behest of an alien being known only as The Overlord.

This prolific director is eclectic in style, having tried his hand at everything from wacky puppet mayhem (*The Puppet Monster Massacre*, 2010) through sci-fi schlock (*Skinless*, 2013) to arthouse shockers (*Applecart*, 2015). Here he enters the ignoble arena of torture porn.

Her Name Was Torment was conceived as the maiden voyage of Mills' Crumpleshack label, set up specifically to cater for a more uncompromising, brutal form of horror film. He delivers on this promise with graphic scenes of fingers being hacked off by pliers, eyes getting yanked out and corpses being fucked.

Shot in a grainy, shaky found-footage manner on an estimated budget of $500.00, the film is presented predominantly in black-and-white. Colour is employed sparingly to unexpectedly impactful effect. The results are often arty, at times surreal and rarely far away from being convincingly grubby. This being a Mills movie, you can also rest assured that there is plenty of female nudity in attendance throughout.

The whole thing is only 50 minutes long. This was a shrewd move, as by that point the events of the film are bordering on becoming aimless. The sub-plot concerning The Overlord is ill-fitting; the intrigue surrounding Egan's character begins to dissipate.

But in terms of clammy atmosphere and disconcerting violence, Mills nails it.

The Hexecutioners (2015)

Dir: Jesse Thomas Cook; Scr: Tony Burgess; Cast: Liv Collins, Sarah Power, Timothy Burd

You know that feeling when a new law is passed making euthanasia legal and you take on a job at a suicide-assisting agency, only for things to go well and truly tits up? No? Well, place yourself mentally into that scenario – if you can – and you'll have better chance of swallowing what follows.

Collins is the rookie death aide. Her first job goes badly, and so she's paired with surly veteran Power for her next excursion: a jaunt out to a rural mansion where writer Burgess cameos as a disfigured eccentric in search of an aerial burial. Why does he wish to be fed to the birds after death? Because he doesn't want to incur the wrath of the Death Cult, whose suicides he inspired en masse on his premises some time earlier. What could possibly go wrong?

Abominable title aside, *The Hexecutioners* actually isn't too shabby. It benefits from keen cinematography throughout which uses the mansion setting to ample ambient effect. Performances rely on astute observations, resulting in a healthy amount of chemistry achieved between the two female leads. Their relationship goes from strained, to reliant, to close when the shit starts hitting the fan. There's even a brief moment where the girls get intimate. Each degree of their association is plausible, such is the calibre of acting on offer.

Instances of minor gore and a fleeting topless scene (thank you Ms Power) will keep the exploitation contingent happy. Those seeking a serious meditation on the for-and-against arguments around the thorny issue of euthanasia will be sorely disappointed: Cook and Burgess use the concept as a backdrop to their spooky story, nothing more.

A muddled screenplay pulls things down; it's inescapable that nothing later in the film equals the salvo of the opening ten minutes.

Hidden In The Woods (2012)

Dir: Patricio Valladares; Scr: Patricio Valladares, Andrea Caveletto; Cast: Siboney Lo, Carolina Escobar, Francois Soto

Lo and Escobar think they've escaped from a life of isolation and abuse when their violent, drug-dealing dad (Daniel Antivilo) is imprisoned after slaughtering a couple of cops with his chain saw. But their trial is just beginning: uncle Soto, a hardened criminal, is on the warpath. He's on the hunt for the safe return of his "merchandise" – a stash of narcotics which daddy supposedly hid somewhere in the local woods. The girls hide out in a nearby cabin with their deformed brother (Jose Hernandez, a product of incestuous rape); a bloody showdown with Soto and his cronies is however inevitable.

This Chilean production was shot over the course of thirteen days, on digital HD format, with a modest budget of $57,000.00. According to Valladares, the bulk of the funding came direct from the Chilean government, on the understanding that he would make a drama capable of selling on to overseas markets. Retreating into the woods with a small crew, the director returned with something much grimmer than his financiers had ordered. However, it *did* sell well overseas (and holds the distinction of being the first Chilean film to screen at FrightFest in the UK – where it received applause over the end titles).

Loosely based on a true story, Valladares elicits strong performances from his female leads, while Soto makes for a formidable foe. The relationships shared between these three are highly convincing, even as the action becomes increasingly brutal.

And brutal it is. Nasty rape scenes? Check. Chain saw violence? Yes, present. Cannibalism. You bet. All captured in raw handheld style and with enough blood to drown a horse in.

The screenplay often makes little sense and the editing is a little choppy at times. But by-and-large *Hidden In The Woods* is a stylish, stylised slice of modern exploitation which takes few prisoners.

Valladares returned in 2014 for a US remake with the same title, co-starring Michael Biehn and William Forsythe. It's nowhere near as intense as the original.

The Hills Have Eyes (2006)

Dir: Alexandre Aja; Scr: Alexandre Aja, Gregory Levasseur; Cast: Aaron Stanford, Kathleen Quinlan, Billy Drago

The remake machine continued to churn out new models of classic cult films well into 2006 with Aja's "reimagining" of Wes Craven's great 1976 original. The late director served as co-producer on this outing.

An all-American family travel across the desert while on vacation. They embark on a detour which takes them into an isolated stretch of land once used by the US government as a nuclear testing zone. Naturally, the family's vehicle breaks down there and then … which would be bad enough, were it not the fact that they're not as alone as they think they are. Up in the surrounding hills, an alternate family lives: Drago's clan of mutated cannibals.

Shooting in the Moroccan desert (doubling up for the American southwest), the slick veneer and sun-kissed hues suggest a hollow horror to appease the MTV crowd. In actual fact, *The Hills Have Eyes* takes itself satisfyingly seriously.

The original film was a gritty 16mm experience, and was also one of the key American horror films of the 1970s. It tapped into the counter-culture anxieties of the time while exploring Craven's favourite territory: the threat comes to your own home (in this case, a mobile home). The cannibal family were famously based on the 16th Century Scottish figure Alexander "Sawney" Bean, who is said to have lived in a cave with his incestuous family and preyed on travellers – robbing, murdering and eating them.

From the opening montage of babies born with physical defects (genuine footage which actually relates to children of men exposed to Agent Orange chemicals during the Vietnam war), it's clear that the 21st Century model has a different source of inspiration – a true "nuclear family".

The notion of civilised man tapping into his root violent nature in order to combat his primitive aggressor is retained, and upped significantly in terms of viscera. Aja was riding high off the success of *Switchblade Romance* (2003) – a taut, bloody homage to slasher flicks of yore. The levels of gore in his *Eyes* remake are in keeping with his breakthrough hit. If anything, they're even more brutal.

One of the new Century's better remakes.

A Holiday Horror Story
See *A Christmas Horror Story*

Holocaust Cannibal (2014)

Dir/Scr: Bill Zebub; Cast: Erin Brown, Lydia Lael, Vanna Blondelle

Onscreen text opens the film, advising us of a plane filled with Nazi officers which escaped Germany at the end of the Second World War. As lightning struck, the plane was forced to crash-land "on an island, just off the coast of South America".

It's a canny way of avoiding unnecessary exposition - and, of course, of saving on recreating a plane crash on a shoestring budget.

Once on the island, it takes the Nazis all of two minutes to establish that it's inhabited by cannibals. This allows the broad comedy to take centre-stage - there are a surprising number of successful one-liners to be enjoyed - while an increasingly insignificant "plot" propels the viewer from one outrageous pastiche of jungle capers and Nazisploitation excesses to the next.

It's always good to see natural beauty Brown at work, even if her output is less prolific nowadays than several years ago when she went under the moniker of Misty Mundae and was a poster girl for Seduction Cinema (*Spiderbabe* [2003], *The Girl Who Shagged Me* [2005] etc). She's underused here, alas.

Still, we get plenty of female nudity to keep the exploitation fans happy, Zebub being shrewd enough to know that naked flesh was always an integral ingredient of both ignoble sub-genres. Along with gore, of course. Yes, the red stuff is present - though it's only fair to warn you that Tom Savini didn't handle the special effects work. On the contrary, body parts here look like pieces of a shop mannequin which have been covered in raw mince and ketchup. Oddly, along with the curiously ill-fitting slow-motion combat sequences, it all adds to the demented fun.

Zebub, self-proclaimed "King of the B-movies", produces films as frequently as other people take a dump. His shtick is controversial exploitation with a comedic slant - as titles such as *Jesus Christ: Serial Rapist* (2004) and *Dickshark* (2016) no doubt suggest. *Holocaust Cannibal* is a fitting addition to the auteur's canon. For this reason it's probably going to be best appreciated by those already initiated.

As fun as this film is, the 96-minute running time does stretch the joke too thinly.

Las Horas Del Dia
See *The Hours Of The Day*

The Host (2006)

Dir: Joon Ho Bong; Scr: Joon Ho Bong, Won-jun Ha, Chul-hyun Baek; Cast: Kang-ho Song, Ah-sung Ko, Hie-bong Byeon

Onlookers are aghast when a giant creature emerges from the Han River, causing chaos among the picnickers before settling on young Ko as its captive. Her frantic family, headed by surly grandpa Byeon and Ko's bungling father Song, join ranks to pursue the monster to its hiding spot and recover their frightened relative.

On the surface, *The Host* is a dark comedy with a strong sentimental thread running through its core. Dig a little deeper, however, and what initially comes across as two hours of entertaining action actually has a great deal more to offer.

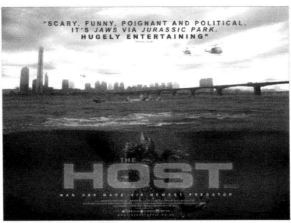

Bong's concern is clearly political from the off. The creature is a mutated product of dangerous toxins dumped into the Han River – by reckless Americans, no less. This plot point echoes an instance from February 2000, in which a US military civilian employee was accused of dumping huge amounts of formaldehyde into the Korean stretch of water. No monsters have been reported in the river though ... yet.

As well as addressing a favourite theme of Korean cinema, family, Bong has fun satirising his own government's ineffectual response to calamity (the sloppy handling of crisis centres; the panicked search for a non-existent virus) and the country's more pressing concern of over-population. On a wider scale, many have seen the film as a reaction to the unwanted continual presence of US troops on Korean soil: Seoul being the "host" of the title.

Sinking your teeth into the sundry allegories and satirical swipes makes for a delicious, rewarding experience. However, Bong's direction is assured enough to ensure *The Host* works on more primal levels for those who simply want to be thrilled. Some early reviews likened the film to *Jaws* (1975), and it's easy to see why: not only for boasting a formidable monster – brought to life here by employing a combination of digital effects, animatronics and puppetry, the bulk of such work being handled by Orphanage Inc, Weta Workshop and John Cox's Creature Workshop – but for realising the importance of populating the 35mm action with warm, believable characters and skilfully manipulating ever emotion from the viewer. You'll laugh, you'll cry, your heart will skip a beat.

Plus, referencing Steven Spielberg takes us back to that "strong sentimental thread". It's here, only Bong's penchant for irreverent humour tempers it somewhat better than his Western forefather.

As beautifully constructed as *The Host* is, its one flaw is perhaps that nothing later in the film can match the monster's early attack on the river banks.

The Hours Of The Day (2003)

Dir: Jaime Rosales; Scr: Jaime Rosales, Enric Rufas; Cast: Alex Brendemuhl, Agata Roca, Vicente Romero

Brendemuhl is an unassuming kind of guy. He lives with his widowed mother in a Barcelona apartment, running her family boutique and plodding along quite nicely with girlfriend Roca. In his spare time he's open to helping pal Romero expand his fledgling business. And every now and then, Brendemuhl is given to killing random strangers with his bare hands.

Rosales's film is devoid of music and pathologically avoids any hint of sensation. Many scenes are self-consciously drawn out, forcing us to watch drab characters make small talk across the dinner table and the like. For Brendemuhl, this banality of existence is punctuated occasionally by the act of killing - though, chillingly, these moments are filmed in the same cold, detached manner as everything else.

Performances are disarmingly naturalistic. Rosale shoots on 35mm in a matter-of-fact manner, framing everything attractively but tightly in a claustrophobic 1.37:1 ratio. His deliberate pace captures the phenomena of a human being's capacity for violence, while hiding it in plain sight amid the routine of everyday life.

Many may find this examination of an outwardly normal person too boring to warm to. The murders are powerful in their casual brutality despite being gore-free. They come without warning. *The Hours Of The Day* is carefully resistant to analysis on the subject of the killer's psyche: why he does what he does seems a moot point, given his character is afforded no development whatsoever. It's not as if Brendemuhl shows signs of release, of being more alive, when taking another's life.

The impassive, numbed reality of it all echoes Krzysztof Kieslowski's masterful *A Short Film About Killing* (1988), minus that movie's condemnation of the judicial system and capital punishment. In fact, Rosales offers no moral stance at all - his film is simply a snapshot of someone's mundane life. Someone who happens to be a murderer. It's akin to what would result if Michael Haneke was commissioned with remaking *Henry: Portrait Of A Serial Killer* (1986).

House At The End Of The Street (2012)

Dir: Mark Tonderai; Scr: David Loucka; Cast: Jennifer Lawrence, Elisabeth Shue, Mac Thieriot

Recently divorced Shue relocates to a new town with her teenaged daughter Lawrence. Their new property is huge and would usually be well out of their price range, were it not for the macabre history of the house next to theirs - located at the end of the street, of course. The story goes that a crazed girl stabbed her parents to death there several years earlier. When Lawrence befriends surviving family member Thieriot, the missing girl's sibling, she begins to realise there's more to this tale than initially met the eye.

Having won over the art brigade with her magnificent turn in the autumnal *Winter's Bone* (2010) and courted mainstream adulation in *The Hunger Games* (2012), Lawrence was fast becoming the face of her age. Her pretty, slightly chubby-cheeked girl-next-door looks and proven acting chops were alluring for many smaller Hollywood productions looking for a bright new star to head their show. *House At The End Of The Street* was one of the first movies to successfully capitalise on the Kentuckian actress's popularity.

She acquits herself well, lending gravitas to Loucka's somewhat by-the-numbers screenplay - based on a story by *Terminator 3: Rise Of The Machines* (2003) director Jonathan Mostow - where a lesser actor would've undoubtedly been buried beneath the succession of clichés and predictable, derivative twists.

Decent production values (a $7 million budget has been disclosed) and solid support from Shue help things tick over nicely, while Tonderai - the British filmmaker who gave us the excellent suspense vehicle *Hush* in 2008 - knows how to elicit tension here and there.

But with a large debt to *Psycho* (1960) casting an undeniable shadow, a ridiculous baddie and a Multiplex-conscious sense of reservation when it comes to the genre's more exploitative elements, *House At The End Of The Street* feels more teledrama than edge-of-seat cinema fare.

House Of The Dead (2003)

Dir: Uwe Boll; Scr: Mark A Altman, Dave Parker; Cast: Jonathan Cherry, Ona Grauer, Tyron Leitso

Based on the Sega series, Boll's movie – lensed in his favoured place of filming, Canada – acts thematically as a prequel to 1997's popular "The House Of The Dead" videogame. With the benefit of a reported $7 million budget and shooting on 35mm, it's not inconceivable that fans would have approached this upon release with cautious optimism. Oh, what a disappointment they must've had in store!

The story is pure trash. A party of five take a ride in a smuggler's boat to an island hosting a rave. Upon arrival they discover the shindig to be deserted. While one couple separate from the group to make out (yes, this ends badly for them) the others investigate their surroundings until they happen upon an isolated house. Here, they learn that their fellow revellers have been slain by zombies. It seems the whole debacle is down to the exploits of a 15th century Spanish priest (David Palffy) and his experiments in the pursuit of immortality.

Terrible dialogue, atrocious performances and some of cinema's most pitiful CGI hamper virtually every scene. Is it so bad it's good? No, not really. The pace is far too erratic and Boll's pop video aesthetics make this feel like an arrogant disaster as opposed to an amiably misguided romp.

It's easy to slate Boll and I don't like to. His reputation as the world's worst director is down to puerile internet nastiness. He's emerged in an era where filmmakers are forced to mature publicly, but later films of his such as *Tunnel Rats* (2008) and *Rampage* (2009) exhibit a talent for telling dark dramas.

However, *House Of The Dead*, his eighth feature film, is undeniably catastrophic in all regards. Or is it? It went on to gross almost twice its budget and spawned Michael Hurst's better-received 2005 sequel, the ingeniously titled *House Of The Dead 2*.

Boll apparently conceded to his critics in 2008 with the release of a "director's cut" which went to lengths to highlight the film's silliness, adding fresh lines of knowingly corny dialogue, graphic inserts from the original videogames and even the odd moment of pop-up commentary.

House On The Hill (2012)

Dir: Jeff Frentzen; Scr: Jeff Frentzen, Nicole Marie Polec; Cast: Stephen A F Day, Naidra Dawn Thomson, Sam Leung

On June 6th 1985, gun-obsessed former US Marine Leonard Lake was arrested on a firearms offence. While in custody, he ripped out the cyanide pills that he'd sewn into his clothing and ended his life right there.

Upon the subsequent search of his remote Californian cabin home, police found a collection of videotapes in which Lake boasted of the kidnapping, torture and murder of several women. The recordings also implicated his associate Charles Ng, who was arrested a short while later.

Frentzen's disturbing micro budget effort intrigues from the off by fusing recreations of their crimes with genuine footage from Lake's videotaped confessional monologues. It makes for a morbidly fascinating mix of fact and fiction.

Day and Leung are credible in the roles of Lake and Ng respectively. The calm with which they re-enact the abduction of random women, followed by their casual requests that the prisoners hand over their bank details and provide the men with a constant supply of "washing, cooking, cleaning and fucking", is quietly chilling. In a custom-made dungeon Lake had prepared on the side of his cabin, the women were kept as slaves to their captors' every whim ... until death released them, and fresh victims took their places.

The action plays out in the form of sketches which detail Lake and Ng's atrocities in morose, matter-of-fact fashion. There's a distinct lack of sensation applied to the violence being doled out - check out the scene where the aggressors relax with beers while nonchalantly watching as a stab victim slowly chokes to death. Jonah Kraut and Robert J Walsh's gloomy synthesiser score adds to the miserable tone. The sadism is rarely graphic - when it is, Day's clumsy application of a retractable blade spoils the effect.

The oppressive mood is compromised occasionally by ill-advised monochrome segments in which a badly-acted detective (Kevin McCloskey) fictionally interviews a survivor in the present day. These scenes, along with some inappropriately melodramatic library music here and there, are at loggerheads with the film's overall grim drive; the clips of the real Lake addressing the screen are used just enough to keep things compelling.

The BBFC insisted on a whopping 7 minutes and 12 seconds of cuts in order for Lighthouse Digital Media Ltd's 2015 UK DVD release to obtain an 18 rating. The cuts were made to rather tame "scenes of sexual and sexualised violence". MVD Visual's US DVD is uncensored.

Housebound (2014)

Dir/Scr: Gerard Johnstone; Cast: Morgana O'Reilly, Rima Te Wiata, Cameron Rhodes

O'Reilly is placed under house arrest following the botched robbery of a cash machine which resulted in her boyfriend's death. Clearly in need of assistance in kicking her drug habit, she's charged with returning to her eccentric mother Te Wiata's farmhouse – the place she grew up in, and which she hastily fled from the moment she'd grown her wings. Social worker Rhodes pops in occasionally to ensure she's progressing on her road to recovery and rehabilitation.

Before long strange things start happening – crockery inexplicably repositions itself, disconcerting noises are heard coming from within the house's walls – and it becomes clearer why O'Reilly was so keen to leave there in the first place. Te Wiata insists her home is spooked.

What begins as seemingly a riff on 2008's *100 Feet* threatens to let its "haunted house" premise peter out by the midway point. However, a neat twist occurs at precisely the right moment, shifting the film's final half into high-octane splatstick with more than a faint whiff of *The People Under The Stairs* (1991) about it.

Mahuia Bridgman-Cooper's score is skilled at eliciting tension. The central performers are brilliant in measuring the dual tones of Johnstone's screenplay, aiding the frequent transitions between black comedy and played-straight suspense with their knowingly deadpan deliveries. Te Wiata is genuinely funny. O'Reilly specifically impresses as the gutsy heroine, in a warming lead role which should by rights see her follow Guy Pearce as a successful big-screen proposition first-seen in Australian soap opera "Neighbours" (1985 onwards).

This being a modern genre production from New Zealand, it's unsurprising to learn that Ant Timpson acted as executive producer. One half of the brains (the other being Tim League) behind *The ABCs Of Death* anthologies - 2013 and 2014 respectively - he's also played a significant role in bringing contemporary genre favourites such as *Turbo* and *Deathgasm* (both 2015) to realisation. Those latter two movies, along with *Housebound*, adhere to a quirky New Zealand sensibility when it comes to delivering their low-budget thrills. Gore, humour and idiosyncratic characters are all high on the agenda in each case – this new generation of Kiwi filmmakers following a template laid down by the early works of their last home-grown success story, Peter Jackson (*Braindead* [1992] has evidently been of particular influence). Like Jackson in his pre-Hollywood days, Johnstone and co know how to entertain an exploitation audience.

Analysing it, the plot is rather threadbare and doesn't hold up to close scrutiny in terms of logic. But if you're willing to ride with its combination of spiky dialogue, lovingly prepared production design and climactic gore fest – as hilarious in its casual absurdity as it is splashy in its Grand Guignol excess – then there's no reason why *Housebound* shouldn't contribute towards a perfect evening in front of the TV.

New Line Cinema announced plans to produce an American remake, in early 2015.

The Human Centipede 3: Final Sequence (2015)

Dir/Scr: Tom Six; Cast: Dieter Laser, Laurence R Harvey, Bree Olson

Deep in the heart of the sweltering Texan desert, Laser presides over America's most disreputable jail. While his brutal eccentricities keep individual prisoners in line, he's concerned that governor Eric Roberts will rob him of his title unless he can devise a way to control all 500 of his inmates. Fortunately his accountant Harvey is a fan of Six's first two *Human Centipede* films (2009 and 2011 respectively), and has an idea ...

Six is wise to the controversy caused by his preceding features and uses this third instalment to torment the Daily Mail readers etc who'd spent the past few years demonising him. Testes are manually carved out of ball-sacks; a colostomy bag is torn out and a gun thrust into the bloody stoma; our antihero feasts on dried clitorises in a superstitious bid to gain superhuman strength ... Indeed, Six goes all-out to ensure *Centipede 3* lives up to its tagline, "100% politically incorrect".

Former porn actress Olson (choice titles include *Swallow My Squirt 5* and *Fuck My White Ass 3*, both 2007) acts cute and dumb as Laser's habitually abused secretary. It's a far more substantial role for her than the cameo in *Camp Massacre* (2014), even though she's here purely as a patsy to her chief's increasingly outlandish outbursts. Harvey perspires heavily as he beholds his boss' cigar-chomping, violent eruptions and obscene invectives ("even the corpse of a spastic would turn you down" he seethes at one point, in an exaggeratedly pronounced drawl).

The director cameos as himself, drafted in to help Laser and Harvey achieve their dream of stitching 500 inmates together mouth-to-anus. He ribs his own persona gently, feeding the *meta* qualities of a screenplay which cleverly acts as both sequel and bizarre commentary on the whole *Centipede* phenomenon.

For all its excesses, the film is a satire – a series of irreverent skits which fall somewhere between the cultural mockery of John Landis' *The Kentucky Fried Movie* (1977) and the gleefully old-fashioned mischief of TV's *The Benny Hill Show* (1969-1988). The broad pantomime-like performances only add to the madness.

Six swipes at his franchise's reputation, its critics, and what he perceives as being most brutal of all – modern American society. From its crazed judicial system through its public's need for violence and its objectification of women (Olson's character is named Daisy, and is presented to us in a guise recalling the iconic character of the same name from *The Dukes Of Hazzard* [1979-1985]), the points being made are obvious – even before "The Star-Spangled Banner" plays over the closing moments.

I Am A Ghost (2012)

Dir/Scr: H P Mendoza; Cast: Anna Ishida, Jeannie Barroga, Rick Burkhardt

Ishida toils around her family's spacious home, fulfilling daily chores in a mundane daily cycle. This routine is repetitive and seemingly never-ending. That is, until a disembodied voice - Barroga's - begins communicating with her, offering to help unlock mental secrets and thus find a way to break the spell holding Ishida as prisoner.

Just in case you missed the clue in the title ... Ishida is a ghost. A demure young lady with a dark past which remains buried, suppressed somewhere in the recesses of her brain. Barroga is the clairvoyant who establishes a patient-therapist relationship with Ishida, seeking to rid the house of her inadvertent hauntings by unlocking said past and helping our amiable ghoul come to terms with a history of violence.

Mendoza's film, shot on a reported budget of $10,000.00, is a supremely controlled piece. It starts off slow and deliberate, the cyclic rigmarole of Ishida's daily "life" - stretching as she rises from her bed, solemnly preparing herself eggs for breakfast and so on - coming across as tedium-inducing for those not willing or able to look a little deeper and understand from the start the subtle differences between each take. Once Barroga is introduced we get a semblance of plot and, even better, some interesting metaphysical sparring between her and Ishida. "Shouldn't the living be able to haunt houses as well?" muses our lead, suggesting a further thematic link to the opening text words of poet Emily Dickinson: "One need not be a chamber to be haunted. One need not be a house. The brain has corridors surpassing material space". How true, and how astutely explored by Mendoza in this carefully crafted, perfectly acted austerity piece.

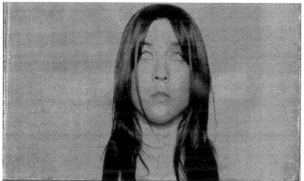

The house is successfully spooky. Ishida exudes a warm innocence about her which immediately gets us on side. The pace is set out in expert fashion. An ambiguous ending can be easily explained with a little thought. There are only the ill-fitting shock tactics and lousy make-up effects of the final act that let the side down somewhat.

All in all, though, *I Am A Ghost* - terrible title aside - is deserving of a wider audience.

I Am Legend (2007)

Dir: Francis Lawrence; Scr: Mark Protosevich, Akiva Goldman; Cast: Will Smith, Willow Smith, Alice Braga

Richard Matheson's 1954 post-Apocalyptic novel of the same name has also been adapted for the screen as *The Last Man On Earth* (1964), *The Omega Man* (1971) and *I Am Omega* (2007). On top of that its influence can clearly be evidenced in the likes of *Night Of The Living Dead* (1968), *Last Of The Living* (2009) and *I Am Virgin* (2010), among many, many others.

Tooled up with an estimated $150 million budget, this major studio outing from former music video director Lawrence apparently sought to - as its title suggests - bring the most faithful screen adaptation of the source material yet. It does a fair job of such ... until, in its theatrical cut at least, reaching a hideously compromised denouement.

But first, the plot. You know that feeling when you've been developing a potential cure for cancer, only for the knock-on effect of your biochemical creation to result in the majority of the populace being wiped out, the survivors transformed into ravenous ghouls? Yeah, scientist Smith is having one of *those* days. For whatever reason he's immune to the plague he's inadvertently inflicted upon humanity and so whiles away his hours experimenting on the infected in a bid to treat the situation.

Smith is atypically understated here. He's actually quite convincing in his plight, trademark frown notwithstanding, as he traverses the eerily barren Manhattan streets. By his side is his sole companion, a canine friend. Together they strive to steer clear of the ghouls - or "hemocytes" as they're known (trivia fans take note: the strange wailing sounds emitted by these sun-shy creatures were provided by rock vocalist Mike Patton).

There's a healthy amount of atmosphere evinced, tonally and visually, during the show's first hour. That's despite the glossy high-contrast sheen. The ambiguous morality at play is undeniably the screenplay's best hand: Smith is initially portrayed as the everyman hero but, as events progress, we realise that to the infected he's a serial killer feared in almost folklore proportions (giving fresh meaning to his titular "legend" status).

A clumsy action-heavy second half sees Lawrence forsake much of his conscientious scene-setting in favour of ticking boxes for the Multiplex brigade and giving Smith plenty of running around to do. It fails to answer questions which arise in earlier scenes and, considering the whopping great budget, these latter moments suffer from some shockingly bad CGI.

The "director's cut" reinstates a more faithful finale (no spoilers) and adds a little more weight in doing so.

I Never Left The White Room (2000)

Dir/Scr: Michael Todd Schneider; Cast: Michael Todd Schneider, Eric Boring, Tom Colbert

Several years in the making, Schneider's micro budget student project - originally entitled *My Crepitus*, prior to being re-edited for later (extremely limited) DVD releases in Sweden and the US - was shot on video and looks like shit as a result.

But, within a running time of little over an hour, it still manages to get beneath its viewer's skin.

Essentially nothing more than a chain of discrete, often surreal sequences of haunting stature, *White Room* trades technical finesse for jarring claustrophobic atmosphere while very loosely relaying the tale of a mental patient (Schneider himself) suffering violent visions - memories? - from the confines of his padded cell. Nightmares in a damaged brain, if you will.

Vignettes include the likes of a masturbating female bather being spied upon by a flaccid Schneider, and one victim's face receiving the brunt of ham-fisted axe savagery. If all that's needed to entice you to a film are full-frontal nudity and amateur gore, this will undoubtedly draw you in. Performances and special effects are lacking, though the crudely-shot action can at least boast of some deft editing.

Suffering from soft blurry visuals and a distorted audio throughout, *White Room* overcomes its grubby underground attributes by virtue of a strong experimental vibe running through its muddy veins. Various video techniques are toyed with - slow-motion, fast-motion, monochrome diversions etc - and the plot is not only non-linear but virtually non-existent.

Against all odds, it works as a disquieting, almost nauseating examination of madness, replete with explicitly representative demons and a convincing aura of squalor which helps render its strangeness as the *bad dream* equivalent of an impoverished arthouse picture.

Schneider would go on to embrace his indie alter-ego Maggot while landing a part in the notorious 2003 gore flick *August Underground's Mordum*. While having dipped his toes into directorial waters several times since (*... And Then I Helped* [2010], *Double Dose Of Terror!!* (2011]) via his own production company, MagGot Films, none of Schneider's output to date has proven to be quite so improbably beguiling as *White Room*.

I Spit On Your Grave 2 (2013)

Dir: Steven R Monroe; Scr: Neil Elman, Thomas Fenton; Cast: Jemma Dallender, Joe Absolom, Yavor Baharov

Monroe's pugnacious 2010 reworking of Meir Zarchi's reactionary exploitation classic *I Spit On Your Grave* (1978) proved surprisingly successful, on both commercial and critical fronts. Naturally, he returned with this sequel.

But where do you take a concept reliant on a formula so trusted that it's been used a template for virtually every rape-revenge flick made since? The answer is nowhere. The concept remains the same: men subject woman to prolonged sexual assault because, well, they're men; she survives her ordeal, recovers, and reappears to exact genital-bothering vengeance.

The only alternative, then, is to repeat the formula but paint it onto a larger canvas. This Monroe does, his victim in this instance being a pretty would-be fashion model (Dallender) who's abducted in New York and shipped off to Bulgaria where evil brothers Absolom and Baharov hold her captive, selling her wares to sadistic clients.

It's not just the location that's been expanded upon here, taking the action out of the sticks and into the ancient city of Sofia. The violence is considerably heightened too. Drugged with ketamine, handcuffed, raped, electrocuted between the legs with a Taser baton, spat on, kicked and punched in the face, buried alive … this girl is certainly ran through the mill by her captors. Her *European* captors, note, defiling their American victim without conscience or mercy … (just to fan the flames of so-called allegory).

Dallender is actually a British actress. She also featured in home-grown horror pictures *Community* (2012) and *The Mirror* (2014). She's superb: warm and open as the young hopeful of the early scenes; forcefully terrified during her tribulations; dead-eyed and resolute, tapping into her inner Christina Lindberg (*Thriller: A Cruel Picture*, 1973) you may say, once she's returned to turn the tables.

The rest of the cast turn in fine performances. Absolom, another Briton and known for recurring roles in long-running series' like "Doc Martin" and "EastEnders", brings 23 years of experience to the plate. Iffy accent aside, he impresses with his suggestion of barely contained menace which boils over horribly when provoked.

The first act of Elman and Fenton's screenplay invests in a kick against predictability: Dallender is credibly cautious as the single girl; in lesser hands the handyman neighbour could've been "in on it" but instead tries his utmost to help; the cops are for once sympathetic.

But, come the final thirty minutes, we're being invited to cheer on as a bad guy's knackers are crushed in a vice. Cathartic? Yes. Unforeseen? Not really.

Ich Seh, Ich Seh
See *Goodnight Mommy*

In 3 Tagen Bist Du Tot
See *Dead In Three Days*

In The House Of Flies (2012)

Dir: Gabriel Carrer; Scr: Angus McLellan; Cast: Lindsay Smith, Ryan Kotack, Henry Rollins

Smith and Kotack are young and in love. Following an afternoon of gallivanting round the local arcades and talking about marriage, the couple return to his car only to discover a strange chemical smell inside it that swiftly knocks them out. When they next awaken, it's in a purpose-built concrete room located in the basement of a secluded house.

Escape seems impossible. Their only hope of survival is the telephone stationed in the centre of their otherwise barren prison: their unseen captor (Rollins) rings at regular intervals, setting them tasks that – should they successfully complete them – will apparently set them free. But will Kotack go so far as to punch Smith in her belly, having just discovered she's pregnant?

Bookended by songs from vintage rock acts Saga and Brighton Rock, *In The House Of Flies* is set during the summer of 1988. It never overplays the evocation of era, doesn't force any fashion issues, and there's no suggestion that what we're watching may be based on actual events. The only logical reason for its setting, then, is to make the scenario more plausible – in a time before mobile telephones, UPS signals, CSI-style forensic wizardry and so on.

More interesting and timeless are the themes being examined as Rollins and his prisoners engage. He challenges Kotack frequently, questioning his machismo and probing his ability to defend what's most important now that he's potentially going to be a parent. Over time, he strips away at the veneer of his captive's principles to reveal some ugly truths. McLellan's script favours meditating on the gravities of loyalty, trust, duty and commitment over cheap torture-porn theatrics.

Casting Rollins as the captor's disembodied voice should've worked better, given his larger-than-life personality and deep-rooted understanding of emotional turmoil (check out his legacy as singer with hardcore punk band Black Flag or his father-baiting Rollins Band album "End Of Silence" for proof). Instead, he delivers a vocal performance of by-numbers facelessness, transforming his character into a weak clone of the *Saw* franchise's Jigsaw character (2004-2010).

Carrer directs his onscreen actors competently, eliciting sterling performances from the two young leads. Their relationship, both good and bad, feels real. Come the offbeat coda, you can't help but nod in agreement to a conclusion that's as out of left field as it is logical.

Alas, Carrer shows little in the way of visual imagination along the way and *In The House Of Flies* sags badly in the middle as a result.

Inbred (2011)

Dir: Alex Chandon; Scr: Alex Chandon, Paul Shrimpton; Cast: Jo Hartley, Seamus O'Neill, James Doherty

A group of young offenders are ferried by righteous care workers Hartley and Doherty to a Yorkshire village (the shooting location was Thirsk) where they're expected to carry out their community service. They soon discover the locals are not like normal people, and don't take kindly to strangers in their parts.

A reportedly arduous shoot was made easier by filming on the RED camera, ensuring the wonderfully widescreen outdoor settings were captured in fitting HD. Chandon works with his most proficient cast yet, while the screenplay is pleasingly tight. Measured against previous outings like *Drillbit* (1992) and *Cradle Of Fear* (2001), *Inbred* is his most technically adept endeavour to date.

But away from the photography and other such conventional merits (practised editing, Dave Andrews's fitting score, Melanie Light's perfect production design) this is a gore comedy of absurdist excesses.

A very British proposition - from the stuffy care workers to the yobbish youths they're in charge of, to the queasily racist counter-culture action and a show-stopping chorus of the Wurzels-esque ditty "Ee By Gum" - Chandon's film even boasts a bona fide home-grown soap star in the form of Dominic Brunt (TV's "Emmerdale" [1972 onwards]) and an oddly quaint slant to its gleeful irreverence not dissimilar to that found in the BBC's surreal comedy-horror show "The League Of Gentlemen" (1999-2002).

The right-wing undercurrents are there for budding reactionaries: references to everything from *Deliverance* (1972) to *Wrong Turn* (2003) abound. A final hour of continual sight gags, involving exploding sheep and a deliciously silly slice of home entertainment which manages to nod simultaneously to the Theatre du Grand Guignol *and* modern audiences' obsession with 3D, can't mask the underlying critique of the eternal divide between the North and South of England.

If none of that interests you, see this anyway for the barrage of torn limbs, decapitations, and punchlines reliant on shit and insidious uses for vegetables. *Inbred* sates the needs of gorehounds while at all times remembering to keep events funny, albeit in a refreshingly *politically incorrect* fashion. The only bit that doesn't really work is the cheap-looking prologue (replete with a cameo from cult favourite Emily Booth), which has precious little to do with the unfurling action.

The Inhabitants (2015)

Dir/Scr: Michael Rasmussen, Shawn Rasmussen; Cast: Michael Reed, Elise Couture, Rebecca Whitehurst

Young couple Reed and Couture buy Whitehurst's rundown Bed-and-Breakfast property in New England with the intention of restoring it for commerce. Reed keeps hold of his city job in order to make ends meet in the meantime; before long, he's called away on business and Couture is left alone in their new home. A home in which a child minder was hung for witchery some three hundred years earlier. A home where strange occurrences begin to scare the shit out of its newest landlady.

The Rasmussen siblings started their career in 2005 co-writing the twisting thriller *Long Distance*. Their real break came five years later when they were credited as screenwriters of John Carpenter's acclaimed horror *The Ward*. Their writer-directorial debut, 2013's *Dark Feed*, trod familiar ground – it, too, employed a psychiatric hospital setting – but showed promise which belied its meagre budget.

Their next project was this low-key spook show, which the co-filmmakers told me was largely influenced by movies like *Burnt Offerings* (1976), *The Haunting Of Julia* (1977) and *The Changeling* (1980).

In an age where haunted house flicks are almost as ten-a-penny as "found footage" spectacles and no-budget exercises in gonzo gore, the main assets here are the lead characters. The Rasmussens are switched-on enough to take time fleshing them out. As a result we get a warm, agreeable and convincing pair of protagonists. The early relationship enjoyed between Reed and Couture feels absolutely real.

Shot in – and, indeed, inspired by – co-producer Glenn Cooper's New England property (once owned by the Reverend Samuel Parris, whose daughter and niece made the initial accusations which led to the Salem witch trials), *The Inhabitants* has a strong look and benefits from a carefully measured build-up. The co-directors clearly favour drama over spectacle, though perhaps this is a budgetary necessity as this doesn't look like the kind of production that could afford to throw shedloads of dollars into special effects.

It's only when the overt scares come that proceedings succumb to cliché: bats fluttering ominously in attics, shadows darting furtively behind our oblivious leads, creaking doors. The spooky sound design is painfully obvious too, signposting the jumps at every turn.

Inland Empire (2006)

Dir/Scr: David Lynch; Cast: Laura Dern, Justin Theroux, Jeremy Irons

… or *INLAND EMPIRE*, the capital presentation an insistence enforced upon critics by Lynch when the film was first released.

Whether typed in upper or lower case letters, this film is a most curious prospect.

Ostensibly, it follows Dern - an over-the-hill actress who bags the coveted lead role in a new production, a Hollywood remake of a supposedly cursed Polish flick originally entitled "47". As she assumes her new role on set, her life begins to mirror events from the film-within-a-film's screenplay - as has been prophesised to her. Cue sordid affairs, tales of infertility and miscarriage, and nightmarish journeys through boxed rooms which may or may not represent compartments of Dern's increasingly disturbed mind.

And I haven't even mentioned the rabbits, who offer their own parallel narrative in-between each surreal sequence ...

Gleefully open to interpretation, *Inland Empire* sees Lynch at his most obscure: just type it into your search engine and prepare for page after page of people dissecting what each moment *may* mean. The abstract links between each set-piece, the apparent visual clues littered throughout ... not since 1997's *Lost Highway* has Lynch revelled so heartily in blurring truth and dream to such incomprehensible degrees.

Impromptu dance routines, cheap sets and extraordinary performances team to create an unnerving atmosphere as Dern's grasp on reality slides steadily out of view. Taken as a deranged, erratic soap opera of-sorts, *Inland Empire* works in the same way a bad dream digs its claws into your subconscious and refuses to let go.

Shot on digital video and running at three hours in length, *Inland Empire* feels conceived as a challenge on all fronts. It was filmed in fits and spurts over a number of years as and when the mood took Lynch. Later pieced together to follow a clandestinely woven thread, it could be that the end result only makes sense to the director's inner logic and those seeking to fully understand it have disappeared down their own rabbit holes in doing so.

The Innkeepers (2011)

Dir/Scr: Ti West; Cast: Sara Paxton, Pat Healy, Kelly McGillis

Based at, and shot in, the Yankee Pedlar Inn in Connecticut, West's follow-up to his fan favourite *The House Of The Devil* (2009) takes the slow-burn ethos of that minor hit and embroiders upon the sense of build-up to an extent that borders on tedium.

Paxton and Healy are employees of said hotel. It's on the verge of being closed down for good. They're aware of the rumours surrounding its haunted history and, as old guests return to enjoy one final stay during its death throes, they determine to capture paranormal activity on their handheld digital camera. What are those strange sounds? Are the increasingly strange occurrences all in Paxton's head? What's psychic guest McGillis's story? And so on.

There is, of course, plenty of scope for a successful ghost story within the context of post-millennial horror cinema. *The Others* (2001) is one excellent source of proof; *Lake Mungo* (2008) is another, albeit entirely different, example. The former is an austere, painterly masterclass in stylish understatement which builds to a satisfying rewind-and-watch-again twist. The latter haunts deep by virtue of its persuasive senses of loss and melancholy. *The Innkeepers* has precious few of these qualities.

What it does do is carefully drip-feed its measured pace and eschew the visceral thrills of the modern genre (in fact, its restraint makes the low-key *The House Of The Devil* look comparatively trashy). Which I have no problem with, other than the fact that West appears to favour this style as a niche to slot into rather than a legitimate means of complementing a story while maximising the spooks along the way. While a similar approach worked perfectly for the likes of Jack Clayton's *The Innocents* (1961) or seminal British made-for-TV horrors such as *A Warning To The Curious* and *The Stone Tape* (both 1972), they had an awful lot more going on for them. Their successes brings us back to what worked for *The Others* and *Lake Mungo*: an understanding of what it is that scares us, and of how to incrementally apply that tension with perspicacious cunning.

We get that West's stated intention was one of ambiguity. He's nailed it in that respect, right up until the final act. Look closely during the final scene for a subtle clue which points towards the truth. But it's all so vague leading up to that point, the characters so uninvolving and smug, and the screenplay so devoid of any genuine suspense or threat, that one can't help but imagine West ticking off boxes as he directs what he thinks a slow-burning mood piece *should* look like.

Invoked (2015)

Dir: Humberto Rosa, Thairon Mendes; Scr: Aaron Gibson, Humberto Rosa; Cast: Patrick Murphy, Kiera Rose Burke, Aaron Gibson

Having co-founded the company Red Line Filmes in 2009, Brazilian filmmakers Rosa and Mendes set about honing their craft on a series of short films. The most notable of these within the context of this book is undoubtedly 2011's sci-fi thriller *The Picture*. In a mere quarter-of-an-hour, it exuded considerable promise by way of ambition, style and originality.

Relocating in this instance from South America closer to Mendes' second home in Dublin, their commercial feature debut *Invoked* was filmed in the coastal Irish town of Sligo on a budget of just 2,000 Euros.

The story concerns a group of young revellers who sail out to an abandoned youth hostel on a quiet isle, where they plan a weekend of drinking, fucking and – for some reason – filming their initially mundane exploits on a HD camcorder. Following an uneventful sail out to the isle (captured for posterity in shaky style, of course, along with every other boring detail), the group settle in to tell each other tales of the hostel's grisly past. Inevitably this leads to a jokey, drunken séance intended to invoke the spirits of the malefactors executed by locals and buried on these very grounds many moons before.

We know from the start that these actions will have repercussions: the film opens with handheld footage of the guarda inspecting the derelict building while a text introduction claims we're about to witness "evidence pertaining to the case of 5 people that went missing in the west of Ireland whilst on vacation". Said introduction assures us that the footage, being leaked to the public after having baffled officials, has not been doctored in any fashion.

Oh dear. We're back in found-footage territory and the components are depressingly familiar. Five unlikeable characters in their mid-20s dick around, talk over one another, flirt and fight, while avoiding any attempts at creating personalities we can empathise with. Their shaky camera captures obscure details (the aforementioned boat journey; the non-event of searching the premises upon arrival). Without characterisation the slow build-up serves no purpose, a ploy made even more redundant by the film's final 30 minutes of clichéd night-cam pandemonium, unwatchable swirling camerawork, and – to cap it all – apparitions that appear to have strayed straight out of some J-Horror film from the late 1990s.

From a technical filmmaking stance, *Invoked* reveals that its co-directors are competent. But, from the overused introductory "disclaimer" onward, they seem pathological in their desire to exploit every one of this over-saturated sub-genre's tired platitudes.

Isis Rising: Curse Of The Lady Mummy (2013)

Dir: Lisa Palenica; Scr: Annie T Conlon, Lisa Palenica; Cast: Priya Rai, Randy Oppenheimer, Aria Song

Six of the most despicably arrogant, wisecracking students conceivable are led on a fieldtrip to a museum of Egyptian artefacts by professor Oppenheimer. While cavorting in its darkest crannies, they inadvertently awaken the spirit of goddess Isis (Rai) from her ancient slumber. Appearing as a smoke-hued apparition, it is now her bidding to possess each student in an attempt to have them murder others – her objective being to collect body parts required to resurrect her lover-cum-brother Osiris (Cameron Tevis).

An early outing for fledgling production house Tomcat Films, *Isis Rising* (unfortunate title, perhaps, given the current climate) is very much Palenica's film: along with directing and co-writing, she produces and co-stars. If I had to choose which one of these tasks comes most naturally to her, I'd have to say "none".

What's wrong with *Isis Rising*? Everything. Cheap unconvincing set design which, under superficial lighting, resembles a particularly cheap episode of TV series "Goosebumps" (1995-1998). The most awful, unrealistic digital effects work imaginable. Believe me, they're terrible. A script of indescribable stupidity, padded out with execrable scenes such as the museum's fat security guard (James Bartholet) wanking while watching the teens getting it on via a CCTV monitor. Performances seemingly designed to make you instantly detest everyone on screen.

Of the crap cast, only Rai has presence. She at least imbues her performance with a modicum of physicality. The Indian-born actress (known to her mum and dad as Anjeli Sipe) is best-known for her work in adult videos. Titles like *Big Wet Tits 8* (2009) and *American Cocksucking Sluts* (2011) should clue you in on where her talents lie. Aged 36 at the time of filming *Isis Rising*, it's easy to imagine her feeling the time was right to leave such shenanigans behind and go "legit". But, no, mainstream acting clearly isn't an option for her. Before long, she was back starring in the likes of *Pure MILF 2* and *My Friend's Hot Mom 38* (both 2013).

Very almost fun in terms of its sheer ineptness, *Isis Rising* is alas severely lacking in the levels of nudity or gore that the audience likely to tolerate exploitation films this cheap would expect.

It Follows (2014)

Dir/Scr: David Robert Mitchell; Cast: Maika Monroe, Kier Gilchrist, Jake Weary

Boyfriend Weary sleeps with Monroe, and then reveals that in doing so he has passed on a curse whereby she'll be stalked and potentially killed by a malevolent force that can take on any human guise – but only be seen by her. Her circle of friends agree to help her combat this jinx, the solution to which may include passing it to someone else via sex …

In keeping with the tradition of American genre flicks from the early 80s onwards, adults are strictly peripheral and events are fielded almost exclusively by teenaged protagonists. Mitchell acknowledges his love of 80s horror films in interviews, citing George A Romero and John Carpenter in particular as influences; the electronic score, provided by Disasterpeace (a.k.a. Richard Vreeland), could easily by off-cuts from any vintage Carpenter soundtrack.

Carefully paced and perceptively geared towards chills rather than gag-inducing gore, Mitchell's film follows the dream logic of the recurring childhood nightmares he based it upon. His nightly visions consisted of being hounded by a relentless pursuer – something not uncommon in genre cinema, as the likes of *Halloween* (1978) and *The Terminator* (1984) can attest.

The concepts of spectrophilia and the titular "It" serving as a metaphor for sexually transmitted infections were added to the director's screenplay during later drafts. They, however (and crucially), provide the film with its greatest dollops of food for thought. Stripped of such dwellings – and the intriguing notion that nookie is both the cause and the potential solution to the torment - *It Follows* would undeniably shrink in stature.

With or without such tantalising themes, however, there's no denying that this is an attractive retro-style distraction populated by unusually well-defined, agreeable characters and a sense of solidarity between them which modern films seldom indulge in.

It manages to be scary, too.

Boasting the advantage of an excellent cast and sublime cinematography, Mitchell's film – an international hit, unlike his preceding romcom flop *The Myth Of The American Sleepover* (2010) - was shot in Detroit on a reported budget of $2 million.

Jack And Diane (2012)

Dir/Scr: Bradley Rust Gray; Cast: Riley Keough, Juno Temple, Kylie Minogue

Temple suffers from nosebleeds and a recurring vision in which she perceives herself as being a monster. Keough (Elvis Presley's granddaughter!) is the modest slacker who meets her in a clothes store and quickly falls in love. Theirs is a short and tumultuous romance, further disrupted along the way by interfering relatives, tragic pasts and the unfortunate prospect of Temple's impending departure to study in France.

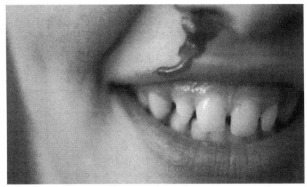

Often incorrectly billed as a "lesbian werewolf movie", *Jack And Diane* is far more accurately described as a melancholic tale of love between two individuals seeking to belong. While the hallucinatory creature effects - overseen by Gabriel Bartalos (*Dolls* [1987], *Basket Case 3* [1991] etc) - are notable, they're also in the main peripheral to the understated drama at play. Gray's concerned with meditating on his characters' complex emotional states, the allusions to Temple's beastly inner workings being little more than a metaphor for her sexual awakening.

The film spent over ten years in gestation Hell. Ellen Page was at one stage attached but abandoned ship as the production schedule stalled while her star in the meantime ascended. It must've slain Gray when the film was finally released to little fanfare and generally nonplussed reviews.

But despite its positive facets - credible performances from the agreeable leads, attractive cinematography, a cool score from Icelandic band mum - *Jack And Diane* is all-too-often bogged down by pretentious dialogue and a sense that it's trying too hard to appease the indie arthouse brigade.

Not even the odd moment of typically brilliant animation from The Quay Brothers (*Street Of Crocodiles* [1986], *Institute Benjamenta, Or This Dream People Call* Life [1995]) can save proceedings from being dour and unengaging.

Connoisseurs of fine music can at least console themselves in the fact that John Mellencamp's dreadful 1982 song (from which the film's title is surely lifted - Jack's a girl here, incidentally) doesn't feature.

Jennifer's Body (2009)

Dir: Karyn Kusama; Scr: Diablo Cody; Cast: Megan Fox, Amanda Seyfried, Adam Brody

Hot High School cheerleader Fox has become demonically possessed. She transforms into a succubus intent on killing her male classmates, leaving it up to dowdy pal Seyfried to curb the terror.

Cody arrived on the movie scene in 2007, penning the screenplay to the celebrated indie hit *Juno*. A rather twee coming-of-age comedy-drama, that film did at least boast a sterling performance from up-and-coming Ellen Page - and earned "cool" points for having its characters debate the qualities of Dario Argento's cinema over Herschell Gordon Lewis'.

Here, Cody flirts more overtly with the horror genre, by way of awkward comedy and even more iffy feminist motivations.

If Fox is cast for her beauty, then employing her is a valid move: riding high on the exposure she received from the Multiplex-pleasing *Transformers* (2007), she's painfully gorgeous here. Kusama's camera loves her too, ensuring we're never allowed to forget just how tempting she's meant to be. If, however, she's been cast for her personality ... well, unless Jennifer is meant to be cold and arrogant to the point of rendering her thoroughly unappealing, the results must be deemed a resounding failure.

Seyfried is better, earning our sympathies as the film's moral core. Even her plight is somewhat undermined, however, by heavy-handed allusions to the right to female empowerment. There's nothing clever or sly about Cody's by-numbers screenplay in this respect, nor in its rather obvious observations on High School politics. *Mean Girls* (2004) addressed the latter - and, to some extent, the former - in far more satisfying fashion.

The comedy is rarely funny. It's smug and sardonic; the characters are never warm enough to invite you in. As for the horror? While mildly gruesome at times, the film is curiously devoid of any tension whatsoever. It's probably fair to say, though, that the film was incorrectly marketed as a genre picture: it's a black comedy first and foremost, a pastiche.

Jennifer's Body is also an extremely mechanical film: it looks good, ticks boxes, crowbars the requisite subtext into its clichéd script and ... well, doesn't achieve much else.

But Fox looks great in it.

Jesus Christ Vampire Hunter (2001)

Dir/Scr: Lee Demarbre; Cast: Phil Caracas, Jeff Moffet, Erica Murton

Caracas is the messiah, brought back to Earth in modern times to cast judgement upon mankind. Before he can do that though, he has a slight problem on hand: a legion of lusty lesbian bloodsuckers in need of vanquishing. With the help of Mexican wrestler pal Moffet, can God's son use his kung-fu skills and save the day?

The action comes thick and fast in this goofy, likeable mish-mash of genres. Surprisingly well-choreographed combat sequences benefit further from adroit editing. Horror hounds won't find anything spooky on offer - I'm sure you'd sussed that on your own from the above synopsis - but there are enough genre motifs and iconography kicking about to make even the more cynical fans smile. Homages abound, Demarbre referencing everything from *Nosferatu: A Symphony Of Horror* (1922) and H P Lovecraft to Hammer films and apocalyptic '70s cinema.

As a comedy, the script is often amusing - daft, family-friendly gags in the main. The cast are agreeably energetic in their delivery of it. There's a great deal of physical humour being served up too, most of which is deftly executed.

Shot on weekends over a two-year period for a total estimated budget of 100,000 Canadian dollars (about £58,000.00), *Jesus Christ Vampire Hunter* makes great use of public places during set-pieces that were shot guerrilla-style: check out the unsuspecting picnickers observing agog as Jesus kicks the arses of bad guys around a car park one afternoon.

The film was lensed in Ottawa with Demarbre shooting on 16mm. This bold choice pays off: the look and feel is much akin to the low-budgeted '70s and '80s exploitation flicks Demarbre clearly has a lot of love for.

Oh, did I mention that this also finds time to challenge the principles of science being the new religion, along with subtle political swipes peeking through the jokes here, there and everywhere? More importantly, have I failed to bring it to your attention that, aside from everything else, this also happens to be ... a musical?! That's right! "I was born in a manger, doomed to live in danger" Caracas croons to the strains of Graham Collins's breezy score.

Bizarre. But undeniably entertaining.

Jiao Zi
See *Dumplings*

Junk (2000)

Dir/Scr: Atsushi Muroga; Cast: Miwa, Kaori Shimamura, Shu Ehara

A gang of jewel thieves find their way to an apparently abandoned factory, where they hope to sell their loot to the local Yakuza. Alas, the undead results of failed army experiments have been stored in the same building. Cue the bloodbath.

A heist, a mob of tough gangsters, a storehouse rendezvous ... *Junk*'s first act nods its head frantically in the direction of *Reservoir Dogs* (1992). Once the ghouls make their presence known, however, events take on a clear Lucio Fulci bent. Crusty, unconvincing monster make-up comes across as curiously endearing as the pace ups considerably and Muroga drags us through one spirited set-piece after another. A techno soundtrack underlines the unrelenting energy.

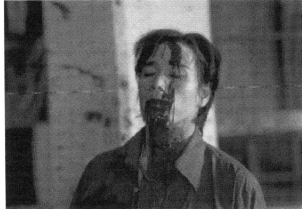

The special effects, by Anthony Grow and Masami Kobayashi, are fairly primitive. They do, however, manage to provide plenty of stabbing, gunshot wounds, flesh-tearing, entrail-spilling and cannibalism. All the things you'd hope for in a modern zombie flick.

If you're looking for assets like originality and well-drawn characters, you're in the wrong place. There are no surprises in terms of plot, this is a simple blood fest; none of the characters register as anything other than caricatures. That said, Miwa's performance as the magnetic 'zombie queen' stands out.

My understanding is that the American soldiers featured in the film where actual army men stationed in Japan at the time of the shoot. This makes sense, as their performances are woefully stilted and wooden. There are also some ill-advised moments of Japanese actors conversing in hard-to-decipher English - presumably squeezed into the film in a bid to attain greater appeal in the Western marketplace.

These are trifling matters, though, when the film as a whole is this much fun: fast-paced, darkly witty and frequently delivering the gruesome goods.

Junk: Shiryo-gari
See *Junk*

Ju-on: The Grudge (2002)

Dir/Scr: Takashi Shimizu; Cast: Megumi Okina, Misaki Ito, Takako Fuji

When social worker Okina makes a home visit to a new family, she becomes the subject of hauntings by vengeful ghost Fuji. Having been slain on the premises by her husband previously, Fuji now presides over the house. We learn more about these ghastly goings-on as Shimizu dispenses with linear storytelling and attempts to spin four separate yarns at once.

It has to be said, the narrative is all over the place as a result. Not only is it confused (and confusing), but it wreaks havoc with any sense of momentum: who do we identify with, for example, when the plot reduces to little more than vignettes wherein the lead character of each will almost inevitably fall victim to unfriendly apparitions?

Stylistically, *Ju-on: The Grudge* condenses all the rules of J-Horror into one: from the black-eyed child ghost, to the gaunt spectral female with black hair draped over her face, to the notion of an inanimate object (here, the house) acting as a portal for evil spirits, to the beastie under the bed, to the sudden split-second edits of ghastly visages flashing onto the screen, to the inventive sound design (Fuji's death rattle, a product of her having had her throat slit in life, is effective) ... They're all here.

In its favour, *Ju-on* delivers all of the above with both flair and fervour. It does succeed in being intermittently scary. Production design is fetching; the cast are uniformly reliable.

But, replete with set-ups so surreal that they become – in terms of logic – absurd, and bereft of a central character upon which we can emotionally attach ourselves, Shimizu's film is simply a button-pushing exercise. A proficient scare show that, upon a second viewing, reveals itself to be utterly ridiculous from beginning to end.

This film is the third in a series of linked features, but the first that was designed to be screened theatrically. Its two predecessors, also helmed by Shimizu - *Ju-on: The Curse* and *Ju-on: The Curse 2* (both 2000) – were made for Japanese television. Such was the popularity of this third instalment, a sequel soon followed (2003's *Ju-on: The Grudge 2*). We also got the inevitable Hollywood remake (*The Grudge*, 2004 – co-produced by Sam Raimi, but at the very least it kept Shimizu in the director's seat) and even a 2006 novelisation by Kei Ohishi.

K-Shop (2016)

Dir/Scr: Dan Pringle; Cast: Ziad Abaza, Ewen MacIntosh, Reece Noi

Bloodthirsty Butchers (1970), *Microwave Massacre* (1983), *The Texas Chain Saw Massacre Part 2* (1986), *Blood Diner* (1987), *The Untold Story* (1993), *Evil Feed* (2013) ...

You get the idea. Maniacs slaughtering their victims and processing them into food which is subsequently enjoyed by unwitting acquaintances or, specifically, customers. It's a fantastic concept – arguably, in terms of influence on cinema, traceable to the tale of demon barber Sweeney Todd, first told in the Victorian serial "The String of Pearls: A Romance" in 1846-47. Horror movies have gone on to exploit the notion umpteen times.

Pringle's feature debut seeks to cover such ground while exploring issues of Britain's drinking culture, its attitude towards immigrants, family honour and more. It's semi-successful.

Abaza is dependable as the young Turk who takes time out from University to tend to the family business – a late-night kebab shop in popular seaside haunt Bournemouth – following his father's death at the hands of violent drunks. An initially placid man, Abaza is drawn into an altercation with a punter when he catches them helping themselves to the food. Accidentally killing the would-be thief, he disposes of their bones and clothes in the nearby sea while cooking up their flesh and meat to sell on. Before long he's winning awards for his perfectly tenderised "lamb" kebabs ... but such attention brings with it a demand for fresh supplies.

This may all sound like ludicrous, campy comedy material. But, barring a few moments of plausible black humour, Pringle approaches his own screenplay with a commendably serious tone.

The plight of foreign workers providing services to inebriated Brits is detailed, allowing for plenty of commentary to be had on our nation's shameful penchant for scratch-the-surface racism. The footage of re-enacted nightlife is plentiful, exposing all of the binge-boozing, scrapping and vomiting for being as stupid as it truly is. In this regard, it's easy to see Abaza as a vigilante when pitted against the vile slobs he's dispensing of.

Overlong and yet paradoxically underdeveloped in terms of sub-plots (a romantic link in particular suffers), *K-Shop* is nevertheless an attractively shot, decently acted and absorbing film. It's never preachy, maintaining a cool distance in terms of moral judgement throughout – and is all the better for it.

Kill, Granny, Kill! (2014)

Dir: Jacob Ennis; Scr: Gregory W Brock, Jacob Ennis; Cast: Alicia M Clark, Donna Swensen, Dale Miller

The trashier elements of *The Texas Chain Saw Massacre*, *Deranged* (both 1974) and *Mother's Day* (1980) combine in this cheap and cheery backwoods hoot.

Clark answers an advertisement for an in-house home help, relocating to the sticks to tend to kind elderly Swensen's needs. Granny Swensen has but a few simple rules for her new aide to abide by: no swearing, no lewd TV and definitely no fornicating under her roof. All goes well until Clark's horny boyfriend, Jason Crowe, turns up looking to get his leg over. Unfortunately for these amorous youngsters, Swensen's puritanical obsessions don't extend to respecting the "thou shalt not kill" rule – and she's handy with an axe.

The screenplay is knowingly bunkum. Riddled with acerbic one-liners throughout, it allows for the spirited cast to have fun with their characters. Clark is most agreeable as the hapless carer; Swensen is brilliant as the old lady – at once doddery and gentle, callous and ravenous. TJ Park provides able support as the old dear's equally cannibalistic, psychotic grandson.

The dark humour of the script works well within this potentially clichéd setting. When the horror set-pieces come, they're satisfyingly serious in tone and benefit from the gory FX work of Jeremy Kinley and Dean Stephens.

Having seen and enjoyed Ennis' previous features *Stash* (2007) and *Red River* (2011), it's great to see how he's evolved here. Not only with regards to technical prowess – camerawork, editing, lighting etc are all highly efficient – but in terms of tighter control over his storytelling too. Of course, it's worth noting than co-writer Brock also acted as first assistant director on the film, as well as editing the action alongside Ennis ...

Relatively short at just over an hour in length, *Kill, Granny, Kill!* doesn't ask for your undivided attention. It's a simple throwback folly, and all the more fun for being so.

Killer Barbys Versus Dracula (2002)

Dir: Jesus Franco; Scr: Jesus Franco, Lina Romay, Jose Roberto Vila; Cast: Sylvia Superstar, Enrique Sarasola, Lina Romay

Franco's *Killer Barbys* (1996) followed the cartoonish exploits of its titular rock band, who fell afoul of a female vampire. Here, their concert at a Wild West park in Spain is interrupted by the arrival of a latent Dracula (Sarasola) – awoken from his slumber by one of their tunes, the appropriately titled "Wake Up". Amid the ensuing confusion, the Count sets about trying to convince locals that the actor portraying him at the festival is a fake, and becomes smitten with the band's leader (Superstar).

An interesting cast also gathers punk rocker Bela B, latter-day Franco regular Fata Morgana (*Vampire Junction* [2001]; *Snakewoman* [2005]), Carsten Frank (Ulli Lommel's *Zombie Nation* [2005]; Marian Dora's *Cannibal* [2006]) and Aldo Sambrell (*The Good, The Bad And The Ugly* [1966]; Lucio Fulci's *Silver Saddle* [1978]).

Shot on Betacam SP professional video, the aesthetic value is comparable to that of a cheap TV broadcast from the 1990s. Colour-filtered lighting and camp costumes bring a much-need aura of the theatrical to the aesthetic. The likes of Sarasola and Romay – Franco's muse, having previously featured in everything from *The Erotic Rites Of Frankenstein* (1973) and *Ilsa The Wicked Warden* (1977) to *Macumba Sexual* (1983) and *Mari-Cookie And The Killer Tarantula* (1998) for her future husband – ham up proceedings in a bid to accentuate flamboyance over skid row visuals.

In part, such ploys are successful. A certain comic-strip-type exuberance is achieved. Ultimately, however, it's impossible to watch this without lamenting how Franco was once a master of resource – how he could work with a miniscule budget and limited schedule, but still produce a lyrical and ethereal treat such as *Female Vampire* (1974) - but here is incapable of transcending his budgetary limitations. The end results are cheap-looking and often reek of amateurishness.

As a horror film, *KBVD* proffers little in the way of frights. Bloodletting is restrained, and any sense of Gothic ambience is accidentally realised. The sense of kitsch doesn't harm too greatly: indeed, it benefits the film's more comedic moments. Humour is of a decidedly European bent – silly and camp, a little old-fashioned.

The Barbys' songs have an agreeably melodic punk bounciness to them, reminiscent at times of a poppier Lunachicks. Soundtrack contributors include Superstar (her songwriting skills are credited to S Garcia – her birth-name being Sylvia Garcia Pinto), Bela B, Iggy Pop and even Franco himself.

Killing Words (2003)

Dir: Laura Mana; Scr: Laura Mana, Fernando de Felipe; Cast: Dario Grandinetti, Goya Toledo, Eric Bonicatto

The power of words and their meanings. It's a fascinating subject which also provided the foundations for Sion Sono's colourful *Guity Of Romance* (2011).

Here, Grandinetti is a self-professed serial killer whose latest intended victim is psychiatrist Toledo. She awakens bound to a chair in his carefully prepared apartment basement. He suggests, per her profession, that they engage in a game of wordplay – bouncing off each other with pertinent libretti which must follow the last one by sequence of thematic relevance and sharing a syllable of the preceding word. Should she falter, he threatens to pluck out her eye.

It's a conceit which allows for revelations to emerge about the couple's history, Grandinetti's validity as a psychopath and what actually qualifies as "the truth" for both aggressor and captive. More so, as the conversation between the two intensifies, clear allusions abound towards the themes of Fyodor Dostoyevsky's 1866 novel "Crime and Punishment": what makes a man capable of murder, and are such actions justified if one can argue the world would be a better place as a consequence?

Superb central performances, a steady pace and several revelatory twists help *Killing Words* grip. The script is based on Jordi Galceran's play and still feels at times a tad stifled by its stage intentions, but it's testament to Mana and her talented cast that events remain entertaining. Galceran went on to pen the screenplay for Jaume Balaguero's underrated *Fragile* (2005).

Given that this is a Spanish film, the English subtitles on export versions (I'm going by the US and UK DVD releases, as well as the cinema screening at Edinburgh's Dead By Dawn festival) excel in retaining the purpose of the narrative: they manage to adhere to Grandinetti's rules while making a connection which reveals a bigger picture in agreeably small doses.

A pivotal scene, involving a message Grandinetti leaves on an answer machine for the increasingly suspicious police, is clumsily handled (continuity surveyors will be shaking their fists at the screen). It's the one bum scene in an otherwise impressively tight film, which very almost irreparably undoes the plot's credibility. Thankfully there is enough ambiguity in the final act to help *Killing Words* survive this major faux pas. Just.

Mana graduated from acting (notable gigs include *Dobermann* [1997] and *Romasanta: The Werewolf Hunt* [2004]) and into direction. *Killing Words* remains her most exciting work, her subsequent efforts behind the camera amounting to insipid family dramas and TV movies.

Killjoy (2000)

Dir: Craig Ross Jr; Scr: Carl Washington; Cast: Angel Vargas, Vera Yell, William L Johnson

Kareem J Grimes is a put-upon geek, bullied daily by the cool kids in his rough Los Angeles 'hood. Unwisely, he has designs on Yell – girlfriend of Snoop Dogg lookalike Johnson, a particularly unpleasant wannabe gangster. When Johnson protects his reputation by giving him a beating simply for talking to Yell, Grimes retreats to his shithole apartment where he practices black magic.

Johnson murders Grimes shortly afterwards. One year later, the fruit of the latter's occult dabbling materialises in the form of a vengeful demon clown known as Killjoy (Vargas).

We've had black horror pictures before. *Blacula* (1972) remains justifiably iconic – along with the following year's equally valid sequel *Scream, Blacula, Scream* - while 1973's arty *Ganja And Hess* is actually quite brilliant. *Def By Temptation* (1990) is, er, an interesting addition to the cycle.

All of the above are masterpieces when viewed alongside this cheap, sorry mess.

Shot on a reported budget of $150,000.00, *Killjoy* bypasses any opportunity to comment on ghetto life or commission its horrors as a metaphor for the struggles of being young and black in modern America. Rather, it wallows in vexatious characters whose dumb dialogue forces them to behave like castoffs from *Menace II Society* (1993). Overly dark, ugly photography and direction which seems pathological in its bid to avoid tension at any cost, add to the failings.

If *Killjoy* has anything going for it, anything at all (I'm trying here, I really am), it's that the titular monster does actually have the potential to be creepy. Clowns are freaky at the best of times, and a decent horror film can get fair mileage out of them (the 1990 TV Movie "It"; Marcus Koch's *100 Tears* [2007] etc). But even this clown's admittedly sinister appearance soon loses its impact, such is Ross Jr's insistence on filling entire scenes with the creature when occasional glimpses would've been far more effective.

Remarkably, *Killjoy* has spawned three sequels to date. Mexican actor Vargas was tied into filming a domestic TV series when the first of these went into production in 2002, hence the title role was handed over to popular genre figure Trent Haaga. He's remained in the role ever since. The fourth instalment, 2012's *Killjoy Goes To Hell*, is by far the best of the entire series. But that's not saying much.

Kiss Of The Damned (2012)

Dir/Scr: Xan Cassavetes; Cast: Josephine de La Baume, Roxane Mesquida, Milo Ventimiglia

de La Baume falls for writer Ventimiglia while enjoying an extended stay at a friend's mansion. She soon reveals to him that she is in actual fact a vampire; during a bout of lovemaking she turns him into one too. Everyone's happy, until de La Baume's reckless sister Mesquida turns up with trouble in mind.

Xan – or Alexandra, per her birth certificate – is the daughter of late actor/filmmaker John Cassavetes and actress Gena Rowlands. That's a lot to live up to.

Fortunately there's considerable promise here. The plot may not on the surface seem significant but there's plenty of substance mined from the themes which brew within it: longing, decadence and loneliness. Shot on 35mm in a lovely wide 2.35:1 ratio, the results are often visually sumptuous. These themes and aesthetic values, married with the measured pace, affected performances and a keen sense of the erotic, suggest Jean Rollin's cinema as a primary influence. Cassavetes's film certainly has that same deeply personal vibe about it.

It's also easy to liken *Kiss Of The Damned* to Jim Jarmusch's *Only Lovers Left Alive* (2013). The synopses to both films are strikingly similar; both pander to the arthouse brigade over the average horror hound. That said, there is a dense atmosphere to be savoured here, as well as a fair amount of blood shed. Black humour and an understanding of the dark nature of desire also lift Cassavetes's film above its comparatively dour rival.

Slow in pace, elegiac in tone: some will recoil from its mannerisms and dismiss it as pretentious. For those willing to scratch the surface, *Kiss Of The Damned* will prove far more rewarding.

The film won the coveted Octopus d'Or prize at the 2013 Strasbourg European Fantastic Film Festival.

Konkurito
See *Concrete*

Laid To Rest (2009)

Dir/Scr: Robert Hall; Cast: Bobby Sue Luther, Nick Principe, Kevin Gage

Luther wakes up in a funeral home, trapped inside a coffin. Struggling encourages the casket to topple over, enabling her to flee. By the time she's rescued by passer-by Gage, she's well aware that a masked killer appropriately named Chromeskull (Principe) is stalking her.

Finding refuge in Gage's modest abode, Luther reveals she's suffering from amnesia due to a blow to the back of her head. Who is she, and why does this technology-savvy maniac (he wears a small video camera on his shoulder at all times in a bid to film his victims' tribulations before mailing the footage to the police) relentlessly pursue her?

Hall doesn't care to answer that second question. Instead, Chromeskull's origins and motivations remain obscured here – a la Michael Myer's unexplained penchant for carving up babysitters in *Halloween* (1978) or the titular character's nature in *The Hitcher* (1986). Some may bemoan the lack of backstory; others will argue it affords the villain greater menace. For the former, we learn a lot more about our monster in the 2011 sequel *Chromeskull: Laid To Rest 2*.

Polished in its finish and controlled in terms of editing, there's no denying that *Laid To Rest* boasts an accomplished sheen. It is perhaps a little too refined, however, to arrive at the levels of raw terror achieved in clear influences such as *Maniac* (1980). The tight 1.78:1 framing marries with cheap coloured lighting schemes to mimic the gloss of a modern US TV drama. Casting Lena Headey ("Game of Thrones", 2011 onwards),Thomas Dekker ("Terminator: The Sarah Connor Chronicles", 2008-09) and Richard Lynch ("The Fall Guy" [1983-84], "Airwolf" [1985] etc) in support roles keeps the spectre of the small screen in mind.

Model-turned-actress Luther was married to Hall at the time – a partnership that dissolved in 2010 – which helps explain why he cast someone so unconvincing as his lead. Her rendering of fear as Chromeskull terrorises her for the first time in the funeral home is little short of laughable. Gage is cast against type, his usually formidable presence somewhat neutered by the lack of the intensity he delivered in films like *Chaos* (2005).

Marc Varisco's Asylum FX ensemble provide the splashy (and mainly practical) effects: decapitations, faces hacked off, stabbings ... the more undemanding gorehound will revel in the well-executed violence, especially during the final hour, when the flimsy plot has all-but been discarded in favour of a continual succession of chases and set-pieces.

Lake Mungo (2008)

Dir/Scr: Joel Anderson; Cast: Rosie Traynor, David Pledger, Steve Jodrell

"Alice kept secrets …".

Pledger and Traynor are grieving parents, mourning the loss of their teenaged daughter (Talia Zucker) following a drowning incident at the local dam. Strange occurrences in their household – not least of all being the appearance of a ghost-like figure resembling the girl, which begins appearing on their son's photographs - prompt them to enlist the help of parapsychologist Jodrell. His investigations unearth revelations about Zucker's secret past.

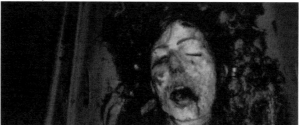

Shot chiefly in the style of a television documentary, *Lake Mungo* employs character interviews, faux news clips and fly-on-the-wall footage in collage fashion, judiciously drip-feeding the facts for patient viewers to ruminate over. Largely improvised performances lend events a naturalistic flow. The pace is slow, there are no jump scares, and the film is as much an emergent mystery as it is an understated ghost story.

Often labelled (dismissed?) as a "found footage" film, *Lake Mungo* does contain an element of handheld camcorder action – as filmed by Zucker's increasingly important-to-the-plot brother (Martin Sharpe). This is interwoven with moments shot on Super 8, 16mm, 35mm and even a mobile 'phone. Meticulously edited together, this array of visual sources keeps things stimulating even when not much appears to be happening on screen. They also help to put across another theme Anderson wants us to consider: how media can influence everyday decisions, and how it governs so much of what we nowadays accept as reality.

Stick with it. Anderson's directorial feature debut (following 2002's short "The Rotting Woman") is a confident, well-planned-out tale with more than a couple of successful twists waiting up its sleeve. Dealing effectively with themes of grief, loss and how to come to terms with it, communication and loneliness, its autumnal tone will hook you in … its chilling denouement will reward your forbearance.

The Landlord (2009)

Dir/Scr: Emil Hyde; Cast: Derek Dziak, Erin Myers, Rom Barkhordar

Dziak has been obliged to cater to the whims of two flesh-eating demons (Barkhordar and Lori Myers) since childhood. Now an adult, he rents his top floor apartment out to tenants who are unaware of the monsters lurking there waiting to feast on them. Complications arise in the form of a pair of inquisitive detectives (Ezekiel Brown and Kurt Ehrmann) and Dziak's growing feelings for latest lodger Myers.

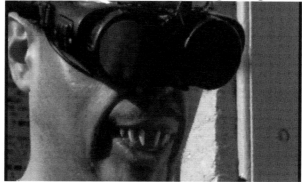

Hyde's enjoyably daft flick benefits from a sharp, witty script which finds Dziak on fine form as the landlord more irked at having to clean up the mess than the murders that cause it. His is one of many amiable performances which help the gags hit their mark with regularity. Barkhordar in particular is great fun, calling on his background as a voice artist to inject a cartoonish exuberance into his otherwise gormless character.

Criticisms seem harsh, but there are a couple. The storytelling is all over the place at times, with multiple lapses in logic and a sub-plot concerning Dziak's errant cop sister (Michelle Courvais) which never bonds with the rest of the film. A schizophrenic tone veers between the entertainingly silly (Barkhordar discovering the delights of the QVC shopping channel) and unexpectedly dark (moments of splashy, straight-faced violence).

Shot on HD video in a Chicago apartment with a budget of $22,000.00, *The Landlord* is dippy enough to become its feeble CGI and yet competent enough to suggest Hyde has potential to significantly develop his craft as a filmmaker.

Tempe Video's US DVD contained an excellent bonus feature: a built-in drinking game. Suggesting the viewer takes a drink each time someone dies onscreen, or a demon appears, or a recurring occultish symbol is glimpsed (similar to the Eibon pictogram in Lucio Fulci's *The Beyond* [1981]) during playback, following this to the letter would get you very drunk indeed.

The Last Horror Movie (2003)

Dir: Julian Richards; Scr: James Handel; Cast: Kevin Howarth, Mark Stevenson, Antonia Beamish

A wedding photographer by day, Howarth has been busy in his spare time crafting "an intelligent horror film". With the aid of sidekick Stevenson, this has involved murdering people for real and filming the deeds. A series of said killings have been recorded over a video rental cassette of a film called "The Last Horror Movie". The conceit here is that you, the viewer, have rented that title out and, minutes into viewing it, the programme is interrupted by Howarth's visage leering at you through the TV.

Yes, you are now the voyeur, challenged to remain seated and watch the several murders Howarth and Stevenson have collated for your delectation. These include stabbings, beatings, cannibalism, strangulation and a show-stopping scene in which one victim is set alight. After all, that's what you were looking for ... correct?

What is it that attracts a horror fan to the genre? Why are we compelled by violent drama? What if that violence was real? Questions posed by Howarth as the fourth wall is broken in various attempts to implicate us, a la *Man Bites Dog* (1992), in his actions.

The extent of what we learn about the effects of cinematic violence, the media's attitude towards it, or even about ourselves, is debatable. But Handel (working from a concept originally proffered by Richards) is careful to balance his philosophising against the drama: even when Howarth's monologues border on pretentious claptrap, there's enough going on visually to compensate.

Howarth is an animated lead, reasonably convincing as the arrogant, manic psychopath with delusions of his actions serving a greater purpose. He carries much of the film well, even pulling off a rather obvious twist finale. Richards was wise to work with him again on the criminally underseen *Summer Scars* (2007).

Of course, one clear setback is that the film came out just as video rental stores were rendered obsolete. The idea of hiring a tape only to find someone had recorded over it … well, unfortunately it missed out on being a timely concept by a good decade or so.

Late Phases (2014)

Dir: Adrian Garcia Bogliano; Scr: Eric Stolze; Cast: Nick Damici, Ethan Embry, Lance Guest

Blind war veteran Damici takes up residence in a small retirement community. Not long passes before he learns that his neighbours are being slaughtered one-by-one, the victims of apparent wild dog attacks. Following one such assault in his own home, Damici becomes convinced that the old folks' foe is something far more sinister.

Spanish director Bogliano first showed promise with 2008's unsparing rape-revenge shocker *I'll Never Die Alone*. In 2012, he made the disturbing metaphorical *Here Comes The Devil* – one of the unsung gems of post-millennial Spanish-language horrors (it's set in Mexico).

I was interested to see how the filmmaker would fare on his transition to filming in New York with an entirely English-speaking cast. The answer is, just fine.

Imbued with rich warm hues and warmer performances, *Late Phases* is a skilfully edited and amiably performed slice of horror with a slightly *retro* feel to it. Characterisation, exposition and tension are all given ample room to breathe, earlier scenes glued together by Damici's charismatic lead turn. Support comes from the always-dependable Tom Noonan (*Manhunter*, 1986), and Larry Fessenden – director of modern horror gems of his own such as *Habit* (1995) and *Wendigo* (2001), and a guy who doesn't traditionally involve himself in inadequate productions (he also acts as co-producer here).

Stolze (no, you're thinking of Eric *Stoltz*, the guy from *Mask* [1985] etc) lets dark humour and a sense of wistfulness – Damici's message to his estranged son, for example - add dimension to what is, in all other respects, an effective but straightforward werewolf picture. Meanwhile, Bogliano is savvy enough to prevent such distractions from taking the film into the realms of Steven Spielberg-style sentimentality.

A whiff of *Cocoon* (1985) here, a smidgeon of *Silver Bullet* (also 1985) there; however, *Late Phases* is its own beast. Robert Kurtzman and David Greathouse's creature effects designs may not be the most convincing, but that's a minor quibble regarding an otherwise highly enjoyable addition to the lycanthropic cinema cycle.

Laundry Man (2016)

Dir/Scr: Johan Vandewoestijne; Cast: Gunther Vanhuyse, Ignace Paepe, Sharon Slosse

Summoned to investigate strange smells emanating from a local neighbourhood, detectives discover an injured woman who claims to have been held captive by a serial killer. Taking his suspect, smarmy Vanhuyse, in for questioning, lead cop Paepe soon realises he's dealing with a remorseless madman. Vanhuyse confirms as such when he opens up to his interrogator, proudly recanting tales of previous transgressions. These anecdotes serve as the perfect excuse for a catalogue of increasingly sadistic flashbacks.

Vandewoestijne - not a name to attempt pronouncing while drunk - first burst onto the scene in 1986 with *Lucker The Necrophagus*, one of Belgium's most notorious horror films. He's hardly been a prolific director in the meantime: his only other credits between his controversial debut and this are the short *Bathroom Story* (2004) and comedy *Todeloo* (2014). In the three decades since his entrance film, however, his preoccupations appear to have remained largely the same: murder and necrophilia feature high in both *Lucker* and *Laundry Man*.

One victim's severed head is utilised by Vanhuyse for fellatio (it's been done before: *Bloodsucking Freaks* [1976], *Switchblade Romance* [2003], *The Hospital 2* [2015] ...). Others are raped, beaten with baseball bats, stabbed, have their throats slashed, and so on. Though Wesley Remory and Ceus Rob's FX work is pretty basic - more after-effects than actual lacerations - the blood is plentiful; Vanhuyse's sadistic delight in telling his victims how he's about to abuse them formidably ups the air of distaste.

Bodies are dismembered and discarded of in acid baths, a clear reference to one of the film's chief sources of inspiration: Hungarian-born pastor Andras Pandy, who in 1997 was convicted of slaughtering six members of his Belgian family. The other major influence on *Laundry Man* is Jeffrey Dahmer, the "Milwaukee Cannibal" who raped, murdered and dismembered seventeen men and boys between 1978 and 1991. Vandewoestijne takes these basics and updates the methods of luring victims to incorporate a mildly diverting cybersex sub-plot. It's certainly more credible than the references made throughout to Vanhuyse's parsimony (though this does reveal the meaning behind the film's title).

Picked up by America-based distributors SGL Entertainment on the strength of an early teaser trailer, certain stipulations were put in place: most significantly, they insisted that Vandewoestijne filmed in English. So, despite shooting in his home country with a largely Flemish cast, this is precisely what he did. This results in a lot of dubious performances but, overlook them, and this persists as a curiously affecting little beast.

The Lords Of Salem (2012)

Dir/Scr: Rob Zombie; Cast: Sheri Moon Zombie, Bruce Davison, Meg Foster

Hard rock radio DJ and recovering druggie Moon Zombie receives a strange package through the post, including a vinyl record by a group calling themselves The Lords. An attempt at playing it sees the disc spin backwards. Unwisely, Moon Zombie's radio colleague later decides to give it a whirl on air regardless. This time the record plays correctly – thus sending the women of Salem into a trance and, ultimately, resurrecting Foster's ancient coven of vengeful witches.

Shot in Salem, Massachusetts, Zombie has described his fifth feature film as "Ken Russell directing *The Shining* (1980)". He's certainly eager for us to know of his love for old-school horrors. In interviews, he also cited this work as an homage to the ethereal cinema of Jean Rollin (*Requiem For A Vampire* [1971], *Lips of Blood* [1975] etc). A somewhat vague approach to storyline, the occasional dreamlike image and a fair amount of female nudity are as close as he gets. The supporting cast is littered with notable names from the genre's past: Michael Berryman, Judy Geeson, Ken Foree, Dee Wallace, Lisa Marie …

Inter-titles break the action up into days, offering a semblance of structure to an otherwise rather obscure narrative. Predictably, Moon Zombie's troubled character becomes an integral part of what transpires. But, playing fast and loose with plot details, Zombie definitely sees this project as a more *fantastic* endeavour, an aural-visual experience unconcerned with trifling matters such as logic and cohesion.

Haunted Films - a Blumhouse Productions brand - had already given the world *Paranormal Activity* (2007) and *Insidious* (2010). They produced *The Lords Of Salem*, offering Zombie a $1.5 million budget and complete artistic freedom. However, the film suffered from a problematic production. Veteran TV actor Richard Lynch was cast as a 17th Century Reverend; due to ill-health and the onset of blindness, his scenes were unfilmable and had to be reshot using Andrew Prine (who had already been cast in another role). Lynch died of a heart attack in June 2012.

Other sequences were filmed but didn't come out well. However, lack of funding required Zombie to pare his script his down rather than reshoot them. Further cuts were made by the studio – one notable deleted scene involves a film-within-a-film containing cameos by Udo Kier, Camille Keaton and Clint Howard.

The end result is a highly flawed, at-times incomprehensible film with stylish visual hints of what might've been. Nice use of Mozart's music though.

The Lost (2006)

Dir/Scr: Chris Siverston; Cast: Marc Senter, Shay Ashtar, Alex Frost

Senter is a juvenile delinquent with trouble on his mind. One evening, for kicks, he shoots two women dead in cold blood. Pals Ashtar and Frost help him to cover the crime up. Four years pass and the murders are still officially unsolved – though local cops Michael Bowen and Ed Lauter remain determined to prove that their prime suspect, Senter, is guilty.

In the meantime, Senter has settled into a job as a local motel manager, where Lauter's young girlfriend (Megan Henning) has started working. The volatile Senter develops a crush on her, despite currently dating the equally deranged Robin Sydney …

The Lost is adapted for the screen from Jack Ketchum's novel of the same name. First-time director Siverston relocates the action from its original 1960s setting to the present day. Whether this is to obscure the more obvious references to Charles Schmid, a killer from the former era once dubbed "the Pied Piper of Tucson", or simply to save on production costs and avoid glaring anachronisms, who knows.

The shift in timeline doesn't harm the drama any. The plot is still filled with offbeat, often sleazy characters (even the cops are morally dubious). The violence comes in shocking fits and starts, Senter's enigmatic energy as the titular rebel without a clue propelling each stylishly shot set-piece forward in the meantime.

Ultimately though, like its source novel, *The Lost* is a character piece. Senter's reckless character, called Ray, is an aimless small-town loser who desperately looks to gain power in his otherwise pointless existence. Power over his weaker friends, power through deciding who lives and who dies. Power through fucking as many of the witless young fillies he happens upon while getting high and wandering around without apparent direction. He's not a Jason Vorhees, nor is he a Hannibal Lecter. He's fallible, an unprepared lout with a hot temper and psychopathic bent. In Senter's hands, he's also quite riveting.

There are no jump-scares or elongated chase scenes; the horror comes from the grim tone, matter-of-fact bleakness and dark violence.

A fine supporting cast also includes the likes of Dee Wallace, Erin Brown and Ruby Larocca.

The Love Witch (2016)

Dir/Scr: Anna Biller; Cast: Samantha Robinson, Gian Keys, Laura Waddell

Robinson is the modern-day enchantress of the title. She's been desperate to find herself a new man ever since her husband fucked off. To this end, she conjures up spells and love potions, and begins dating ostensibly eligible bachelors in the hope of ensnaring "the one". Should be a simple task for a sorceress … right? But no, things don't go quite to plan and Robinson's actions soon extend to murder.

The first things that'll strike you upon laying your eyes upon *The Love Witch* are its rich, retro-style aesthetics. Shot on 35mm, the film boasts wildly garish colour schemes, kitsch fashions and pop-art decor which scream "1960s/1970s EuroCine" from the off. Replete with a fittingly hip soundtrack penned by Biller - she also edits, produces, designs the interiors and costumes - this really does exceed in emulating the artistic vibe of classic genre trips from four or five decades earlier. Think: archetypal Technicolor splendour. And yet, modern tropes such as mobile telephones and contemporary vehicles place events squarely in a present setting. Any such anachronisms are gleefully intentional.

Labelled as a satire by critics but openly declared as something far more serious by Biller, *The Love Witch* carries a robust feminist message: women are willing to accept the men they love for what they are, while their male counterparts are weak, narcissistic, shallow creatures - they'll hold any imperfections against their partner and ultimately do the dirty. It's not that this sentiment is offensive, or even ridiculous, to me as a male viewer: my only problem with Biller's stance is how she feels the need to hammer it home time and time again. The message more or less becomes the film.

That aside, David Mullen's cinematography impresses throughout; for a feminist feature, there's a surprising amount of female nudity on offer. But, at 2 hours in length, Biller's trite premise would have benefited from an outside influence unafraid of editing without prejudice.

And if you're looking for something with menace, you'd best bring along a powerful magnifying glass.

The Loved Ones (2009)

Dir/Scr: Sean Byrne; Cast: Xavier Samuel, Robin McLeavy, Victoria Thaine

Samuel has been a messed-up pothead ever since being behind the wheel during a road accident which took his father's life. He finally finds happiness in the form of sweet-natured girlfriend Thaine. Unfortunately admirer McLeavy reacts badly to his rejection when she proposes they go to the local prom together. With the help of her equally unhinged dad, she kidnaps Samuel and traps him in her home – where a mock dance hall has been arranged, and drill-assisted lobotomy is on the cards. Can she have this boy all to herself, by hook or by crook?

Shot in Melbourne over a period of four weeks, *The Loved Ones* is a good-looking and inventive foray into torture territory. Tasmanian filmmaker Byrne had made several shorts prior to this feature debut, which indubitably have succoured him in demonstrating such an assured hand here.

The set designs are modest but impressive. McLeavy's home in particular benefits from a dungeon of *Grand Guignol* chic, hidden beneath the floorboards. It's populated by her former victims, their cannibalistic savagery recalling the climax of the preposterous *Bloodsucking Freaks* (1976).

You may recognise Samuel from the subsequent *Bait* (2012) and Bernard Rose's *Frankenstein* (2015). He makes for a strong lead here, cool enough to pull off attempts at offbeat humour and sincere enough to fret for. The real star of the show, though, is McLeavy. She's a revelation as his psychotic tormentor. In equal parts ferocious, insidiously collected and incongruously exposed: it's a role that perhaps didn't ask for depth on paper but profits greatly from what McLeavy brings to the plate. Her character's unconventionally hot too, which helps ...

The inclusion of an alt-rock soundtrack is the closest this one gets to cliché. The blackly comical tone acts as a perfect foil for the gruesomely realistic FX work of Justin Dix and his team. Trepanning, multiple stabbings, flesh-eating, salt being poured into open wounds ... prepare yourself for a wild time.

The film briefly flirted with notoriety when, in August 2012, the body of middle-aged Andrew Nall was found in his Chester flat. He'd been tortured to death – he was stabbed forty-nine times, cleaning fluid had been rubbed into his eyes etc. His best mate, horror-fixated alcoholic Gary George, had committed these transgressions in a crime recognised by his sentencing judge during the following March's trial as "aping the conduct in a film of which you were obsessed, namely *The Loved Ones*".

Lunacy (2005)

Dir/Scr: Jan Svankmajer; Cast: Pavel Liska, Jan Triska, Anna Geislerova

Czech filmmaker and artist Svankmajer made his name through a host of surreal short animated films which began in 1964 with *The Last Trick*. Among these triumphs of imagination were loose adaptations of Edgar Allen Poe's stories *The Fall Of The House Of Usher* (1980) and "The Pit and the Pendulum" (filmed as *The Pendulum, The Pit And Hope*, in 1983).

In 1988 he branched out into making feature-length films with the excellent *Alice*. With each successive feature, Svankmajer increasingly incorporated live-action into the subversive animated madness. By 2005, the drama being directed was predominantly live. Which brings us to *Lunacy*, and back to Poe: this film is informally based on two more of the master's stories - "The System of Doctor Tarr and Professor Fether", and "The Premature Burial". The works of the Marquis de Sade are also a clear influence.

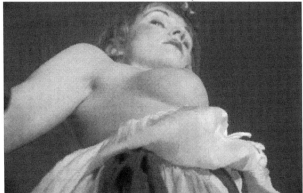

It finds virginal orphan Liska plagued by nightmares in which he's bound into a straitjacket (a metaphor for the confines of the puritanical). Claiming to be able to cure him, marquis Triska invites him to stay at

his chateau overnight. While there, Liska is mortified to witness a black mass orgy and a most peculiar funeral service. And yet he accepts Triska's subsequent invitation to a course of preventative therapy in the local asylum - primarily in the hope of rescuing Geislerova while he's there.

In past Svankmajer films, the actors have often let the side down. Happily, that's not the case here: Triska, in particular, is a compelling figure as he spits out monologues that are as pragmatic as they are blasphemous. The filmmaker is further aided by a barmy classical score and Juraj Galvanek's stunning cinematography. Marie Zemanova's flawless editing deserves special mention too, seamlessly marrying the live-action drama with episodes of nightmarish stop-motion animation involving slabs of raw meat (echoes of another Svankmajer short, 1988's *Meat Love*).

Ultimately it all acts as an address on which is the most effective way to exercise power: give your people freedom to a degree, or control them rigidly through restrictions and punishment for transgression. Whether such political deliberation interests you is a moot point: the film can easily be enjoyed either as a "philosophical horror film" (Svankmajer's description), on a purely visual level, or as a deranged ode to excess where nudity and gore are as frequent as the surreal puppet eyeballs and dancing hunks of pork.

Lunacy was the Czech Republic's official selection for Best Foreign Language Film at the 2007 Oscars (it lost out to the Austrian movie *The Counterfeiters*).

Madness Of Many (2013)

Dir/Scr: Kasper Juhl; Cast: Ellen Abrahamson, Alexandra Alegren, Dinna Ophelia Haeklund

Abrahamson is molested and starved by her parents as a child. Finally making her escape, she staggers into adulthood via prostitution and substance abuse. This leads her straight into the clutches of a group of strangers determined to test her limits of physical endurance. Some people are just plain unlucky.

Danish filmmaker Juhl was 22 when he completed *Madness Of Many*. Shot on a budget of 30,000 Danish Krone (a little over £3,000.00; just shy of $4,500.00), the film often looks a lot more accomplished than perhaps it has any right to. Kudos to the sparse yet striking set designs, along with Kuhl and Torben Greve's carefully considered cinematography. All-but drained of colour, the stark images employed throughout possess a knack for getting beneath the viewer's skin.

Another asset is Juhl's special effects work, which is often alarming in its gory conviction. Gouged eyes, an unflinching decapitation, a decimated face: Abrahamson and her fellow victims are certainly put through the wringer by their faceless assailants. Puking is genuine, lending the film a whiff of Lucifer Valentine's fetishist extremism (*Slaughtered Vomit Dolls* [2006] etc).

Narrative is an obvious weakness. Working within a virtually plotless framework, *Madness Of Many*'s abstract moments of violence are scarcely held together by four chapter headings ("Birth", "Between Two Kingdoms", "The Darkness Within", "Rebirth") and Abrahamson's inscrutable voiceover. Her portentous musings include the likes of "pain and suffering expands my consciousness to find peace", or mouthing "I am nothing" into the screen as she's being physically assaulted. What works for someone like punk poet Lydia Lunch (reference: *The Right Side Of My Brain* [1985]) becomes cringe-inducing here: it's horrible *film student* philosophising about the worth(lessness) of being, searching for a veracity to existence.

The barrage of torture, justified through the narration as a means to self-discovery, echoes *Martyrs* (2008). This comparison is reinforced by the similarities between the sparse torture chamber suffered by Abrahamson and the design of the final girl's prison in Pascal Laugier's vastly superior predecessor.

Does Abrahamson attain spiritual enlightenment? It's difficult to say, as her character isn't developed enough to warrant an arc.

Despite its shortcomings there's enough potential here to suggest that, should Juhl ever be given a decent budget to play with (and a decent script!), he could produce something special.

Malignant (2013)

Dir/Scr: Brian Avenet-Bradley; Cast: Brad Dourif, Gary Cairns, Nick Nicotera

Cairns sinks into alcoholism following the death of his cancer-stricken wife. Twisted scientist Dourif believes he can cure Cairns of his dependency, implanting him with an experimental creation that causes him to blackout and commit murders upon command whenever booze passes his lips.

Loss, mourning, addiction and basic human nature all come under Avenet-Bradley's microscope in what is a surprisingly literate, well-thought-out script. The most intriguing theme is that of culpability: if your hands commit the crime but your mind was manipulated by another's to do it, who is the guilty party?

A $2 million budget secures a reliable cast and an élan worthy of cable TV (not so much of a slur in this day and age). As far as the technical side goes, the film is up to snuff thanks to these production values and well-considered photography, though the visuals never become overly flashy. Even the violence is relatively subdued. Indeed, you have to wonder how much Dourif's fee may have been: the director refrains from undue displays of extravagance elsewhere.

Avenet-Bradley's preparation included researching themes of neurology and, specifically, lobotomy. It shows. But there's a thin line between demonstrating a knowledge of one's subject and overplaying the learned approach. The writer-director allows Dourif's rum dialogue to stray too far over that line on occasion.

Cairns is a believable lead, compensating somewhat for Dourif's tendency to overplay the "Dr Evil" role and Nicotera's ill-placed computer-savvy nerd of a friend. The latter's energetic swagger is at loggerheads with the otherwise bleak tone. While the mere concept may be preposterous – the relationship between doctor and subject being entirely implausible for starters – *Malignant* succeeds by virtue of its style and ability to intrigue.

The working title was *Black Butterflies*, in reference to the Gallic expression "les noir Papillions" - said to represent ill memories. Presumably this more intriguing moniker was cast aside due to a 2011 Ingrid Jonker biography of the same name (not to mention the 2008 thriller *Papillon Noir* – starring ex-footballer Eric Cantona – and the 2013 documentary *Les Papillons Noirs*).

Mama (2013)

Dir: Andres Muschietti; Scr: Andres Muschietti, Barbara Muschietti, Neil Cross; Cast: Jessica Chastain, Nikolaj Coster-Waldau, Daniel Kash

Stockbroker Coster-Waldau goes blood simple, murdering his co-workers and wife before abducting his own young daughters (Megan Charpentier and Isabelle Nelisse). Taking them into the woods, he unearths a remote cabin where he plans to kill the girls ... until supernatural forces intervene. Five years pass; the girls' uncle (also portrayed by Coster-Waldau) searches restlessly for them. He's eventually successful. It's believed the sisters have been surviving alone in the wilderness for the duration of their absence. They claim that a spectral figure they refer to as "mama" has been tending to their needs.

With the help of partner Chastain and doctor Kash, Coster-Waldau attempts to assimilate the girls into his home life and provide them with a fresh start. But dark forces appear to be at play here.

Co-produced by Guillermo Del Toro, the film was adapted from a 3-minute short of the same name - shot by Andres Muschietti in 2008. His sister Barbara jumped on board to help produce this feature version, along with co-writing the screenplay alongside Briton Cross (whose claim to fame is creating the popular TV series "Luther" [2010-2015]).

The notion of kids who've braved the elements to survive against all odds echoes incredible stories such as that of Australian teenager Matthew Allen, who endured nine weeks alone in the outback by drinking water from a creek and catching fish to eat. Reconditioning the feral girls once they're back in civilised surroundings allows room for astute human observations. Those which resonate the most are the reactions of Coster-Waldau's increasingly despairing partner Chastain as her instinct to protect what is hers begins to surface.

The affect the girls' incrementally odd behaviour has on the existing family unit, and Chastain's character arc as she deals with this by recoiling from the perceived threat, provides the heart of Muschietti's slick fear machine.

In fact, it's *Mama*'s supernatural components - more pronounced as events escalate - that don't work so well. In this regard, much of the action is clichéd (overly familiar scenarios; dumb reactions from characters who've clearly never seen a horror film) and overly reliant on jump-scares for cheap thrills.

Maniac On The Loose (2008)

Dir/Scr: Steve Hudgins; Cast: Nick Faust, Steve Hudgins, Jessica Dockrey

Faust oversees the daily running of an institute for the criminally insane. When one of the inmates escapes, he's desperate to shield the event from the media. This necessitates bringing said escapee back to the asylum as soon as possible. Help is at hand in the form of the hospital's lunatic janitor Hudgins.

Maniac On The Loose does, on the one hand, do what it says on the tin. But there is much, much more to this than there simply being a nutter amongst us.

The multi-stranded plot revels in introducing a multitude of shady characters, all with dark secrets of their own. From Dockrey's preparation for a blind date to Faust's desperate search for the person guilty of leaking news to the press, seemingly disparate storylines converge with skill as the action progresses. Told in a non-linear fashion, employing occasional flashbacks to good effect, it's impossible to expand on the plot to any great extent without giving away major spoilers.

Twists aplenty will keep you guessing which way this one's going to turn, right up until a triumphantly shocking climax. Along the way, Ron Elliott's attractive photography and some proficient editing lend style to what is otherwise obviously a cheap (reportedly $5,000.00) production.

Chris Cook's bloody special effects are crude but enjoyable in their own lo-fi manner.

Hudgins' strong screenplay is full of surprises, while seeking to serve up a balance of scares and offbeat humour. The film is successful in both departments. though impeded to a degree by some poor scripting and overly enthusiastic performances.

The founder member of the small Big Biting Pig Productions company (his business partner and fellow filmmaker, PJ Woodside, has a small role in this movie), it's been interesting to watch Hudgins evolve over several years: from the ungainliness of 2007's debut *The 3rd Floor* through films like *GoatSucker* (2009) and *Spirit Stalkers* (2012), right through to 2014's likeable, complex *The Caretakers*. He's honed his directorial skills somewhat over this period; as enjoyable as *Maniac On The Loose* is, if he'd have handed his excellent screenplay to a more competent filmmaker at the time, it could've made for essential viewing.

El Mascarado Massacre
See *Wrestlemaniac*

Masks (2011)

Dir/Scr: Andreas Marschall; Cast: Susen Ermich, Magdalena Ritter, Julita Witt

Struggling actress Ermich enrols at Berlin's renowned Matteusz Gdula academy, where isolation from the outside world is just one strange requirement the students must abide by. Despite a shadow hanging over the institute – it was founded by late occultist Gdula, whose extreme methods led to the deaths of several students in the 1970s – Ermich follows her ambition and succumbs to private classes, hallucinatory drugs and far worse as the school's devious plans gradually transpire.

Heavy debts to *Suspiria* (1977) are apparent from the off. Ermich's initial stroll towards the school, complete with frantic student fleeing as she arrives, is all-but a carbon copy of Jessica Harper's introduction to the Freiburg-based ballet academy of Dario Argento's classic. The similarities continue as events progress, *Masks* also nodding to general gialli throughout its operatic kill scenes and *Inferno* (1980) during a preposterous finale.

From the beautifully realised retro-style opening titles onwards, the word "homage" looms prominently in mind. But whereas something like *Amer* (2009) focused almost entirely on paying lip service to the audio and visuals of bygone genre cinema, and *Berberian Sound Studio* (2012) obsessed with deconstructing the appeal of 1970s Italian horror films for the arthouse brigade, Marschall takes his copious references and complements them with both an accessible plot and healthy doses of trashiness.

Hence, we have in Ermich a character we can relate to and fear for as she becomes consumed by the school's unholy atmosphere. Along the way, the trash factor is catered for via violent set-pieces and regular bouts of gratuitous nudity.

Beyond the surface, Marschall has fun dissecting the very nature of 'performance' while toying with the concept of masks as literal, mental and metaphorical tools of expression – both in reality and in play. The message isn't profound but does add some weight to what otherwise could've been dismissed as an attractive though ultimately vacuous fanboy exercise.

Meet Me There (2014)

Dir: Lex Lybrand; Scr: Brandon Stroud; Cast: Lisa Friedrich, Michael Foulk, Jill Thompson

Friedrich and Foulk have been lovers for three years. They're fundamentally happy together, though her inability to embrace intimacy is cause for concern. Their counsellor recommends they visit the small Texan town where Friedrich barely remembers growing up. The hope is this will help her to recall and come to terms with any potentially blocked-out trauma from her childhood, thus resolving her sexual dysfunction. And so, the road trip to Hell commences.

A grainy, self-consciously downplayed affair, *Meet Me There* revels in its stark indie aesthetics – from its carefully handpicked alt-rock score to the laconic pace and slacker droning of its two casually scruffy leads. This offbeat tone is an unconventional approach for the genre, Lyland adding to the transposition by applying greater emphasis on relationships than action. Stroud's screenplay, based on factual anecdotes imparted by friend Destiny D Talley, does a fair job of fleshing out characters while successfully obscuring the truth for the most part.

When Friedrich and Foulk finally reach their destination, a remote town populated by diffident religious types, the quirkiness continues with peripheral characters who wouldn't feel out of place in a David Lynch film. Only here do tell-tale signs of something darker peek through: shopkeepers threatening their visitors with guns, a twisted preacher (WWF wrestler Dustin "Gold-dust" Runnels, who acquits himself well), and a God-fearing aunt – Thompson – whose face is covered in unexplained cigarette burns ...

Regarding comic book artist Thompson (she designed the film's enticing poster campaign), she appears to be acting in a different genre of film to her co-stars. Whereas their mumble-core restraint fits with the gritty lo-fi mood, her theatrical hysteria brought to mind the crazed Marion Eaton in *Thundercrack!* (1975). It's a performance which feels at loggerheads with everyone else's.

Perhaps a tad too slow for some tastes, the final third of this short film – 77 minutes –picks the pace up somewhat with ritualistic cults and a reasonably well-executed woodlands chase. A dark, ambiguous finish reinforces the fact that these later scenes echo another recent bucolic horror, the British hit *Kill List* (2011).

Memories Of Murder (2003)

Dir: Joon Ho Bong; Scr: Joon Ho Bong, Sung-bo Shim; Cast: Sang-kyung Kim, Kang-ho Song, Roe-ha Kim

It's 1986, in the South Korean provincial town of Hwaeseong. Women have started being found slaughtered, having been raped and gagged with their own underwear. The community has never experienced a murderer this prolific and the cops are understandably eager to curb the ensuing public panic. Their investigations into the crimes are by equal turns brutal, ham-fisted and fruitless.

Though based on the true details of Korea's first recorded serial killer (racking up a total of ten known slayings between 1986 and 1991), Bong's film takes its primary cues from Kwang-rim Kim's 1996 play "Come to See Me" - also based on these shocking events. Bong has also stated in interviews that the movie's visual style owes a great deal to Alan Moore and Eddie Campbell's Jack the Ripper-based graphic novel "From Hell" (first serialised 1989-1996).

To this latter end, *Memories Of Murder* is extremely dark - both tonally and visually - while retaining an achingly gorgeous aesthetic (a shout-out is due to cinematographer Kim Hyung-koo, whose work here is exemplary), and populated by morally ambiguous characters. The cops, the ostensible heroes of the piece, are ineffectual thugs: prone to clumsily compromising crime scenes, beating the shit out of suspects and losing vital pieces of evidence. It's hard to know who to root for, while the fact that the killer has never been caught comes as no surprise.

A thread of malevolent humour runs through the intense, lengthy screenplay. It's necessary, otherwise we really wouldn't be able to identify with anyone. Beneath it all, Bong underscores everything with his trademark political observations: here, we see a Korea failing its people through lack of organisation and by refusing to embrace the knowhow of outside influences (the forensics methods employed by the local police are archaic even by late 80s standards).

The film went on to win numerous awards. These included Best Film at 2003's Korean Film Awards and First Prize at 2004's Festival du Film Policier de Cognac.

The Mexican Porn Massacre
See *Wrestlemaniac*

MindFlesh (2008)

Dir/Scr: Robert Pratten; Cast: Peter Bramhill, Carole Derrien, Steven Burrell

Based on New Yorker William Scheinman's 2008 novel "White Light", *MindFlesh* is an ambitious 72-minute effort which is not easy to adequately synopsise.

But I'll try. We follow taxi driver Bramhill who, thanks to a traumatic childhood event involving his mother, now has the gift of extrasensory perception. Or should that read "curse"?

These abilities have led to our protagonist repeatedly envisioning a strange female figure (Derrien) – an image he eventually becomes gript by. When waking from a nightmare results in very real bruising on his torso, Bramhill learns that his powers have unlocked a portal through which his obsessions and anxieties can manifest in reality. Sure enough, before long the lady of his visions becomes flesh … but so do the monsters representing his innermost fears.

Can he learn how to reverse this action before he and his closest acquaintances come to harm?

An odd riff on early David Cronenberg sci-fi/horror crossovers such as *The Brood* (1979) and Stuart Gordon's 1986 ode to similar otherworldliness *From Beyond*, Pratten's film is an enticing mix of straight-faced drama and low budget genre aspirations. Replete with its fair share of nudity and metaphysical ponderings, it's a dark but attractive proposition – and quite unlike any other British horror film of this Century (even Pratten's own *London Voodoo* [2004] was a completely different beast).

The plot incorporates inter-species sex and ominous stomach growths, keeping these Cronenbergian references coming, while suggesting an evolution through metamorphosis as the only viable way forward for Bramhill, and possibly for mankind.

A lot of this works, thanks to taut direction, agreeable aesthetics and solid performances. There are only the moments of ropy CGI which are capable of undermining what would've otherwise been a formidable effort.

Miss Violence (2013)

Dir: Alexandros Avranas; Scr: Alexandros Avranas, Kostas Peroulis; Cast: Themis Panou, Reni Pittaki, Eleni Roussinou

A Greek family's insular life comes under scrutiny when the eleven-year-old daughter (Chloe Bolota) throws herself from the home balcony. Her parents insist it was an accident. But could it have been suicide? If so, what prompted the girl to take her own life ... on her birthday?

In terms of concept, tone and its cool clean aesthetics, *Miss Violence* would play perfectly on a double bill with *Dogtooth* (2009). Both films have the studied feel of a Michael Haneke movie, replete with organic performances and measured, insidiously understated storytelling dynamics. The machinations of the Greek family, where the male rules the roost and what goes on behind closed doors remains that way, propel both films thematically.

Here we have a fundamentally cheerless tale where the man (Panou) provides for his family, on condition that they stay as virtual prisoners in the household. Ice cream is given as treats, the fridge is permanently stocked and occasional trips to a nearby beach serve as rewards when the kids do their homework well.

Avranas' observations go beyond the very Greek principle of "saving face" (even when we become aware of the horrors being endured within the family home, it's apparent that its inhabitants pool together in reporting a death on the premises as a mishap rather than withstand the public analysis news of a suicide would induce). More broadly, the director is offering commentary on modern life in general. Life which is bound by routine and restrictions, punctuated by the little rewards we allow ourselves periodically. The whole thing is taken to extremes here, naturally, peeking into a life devoid of the usual distractions and tied to an almost military-style regime.

The fact that the awful truth behind the daughter's death is no less appalling than the stifling control Panou keeps his family held under, affords *Miss Violence* the power to horrify without the aid of crazed slashers, gore or jump-scare tactics.

Mister Blades (2007)

Dir/Scr: Tom Lee Rutter; Cast: David James, Leandro D'Andrea, William Stafford

Under suspicion for the murder of his girlfriend, James watches helplessly as matters go from bad to worse when those around him - many of which are initially fellow suspects - also start getting killed. Stafford's sleazy journalist and D'Andrea's take-no-shit detective are just two of the oddball characters who enter the unfortunate's life at this juncture. Along with Mister Blades, a sinister figure dressed entirely in black and sporting an expressionless white mask at all times.

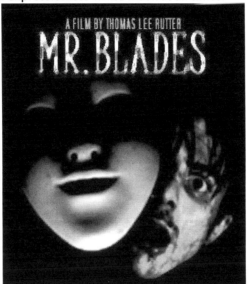

Told largely in flashback, *Mister Blades* also flirts stylistically with the conventions of the giallo genre. The *whodunit* plot elements work reasonably well, as does the non-linear approach. The titular black-clad character does its best to evoke the genre's more haunting imagery.

But there's only so much that can be achieved when shooting on standard definition video, in the West Midlands, on a reputed budget of just £200.00. With a lack of professional equipment such as boom mics and artificial lighting there is an aura of punkish primitivism to proceedings which I imagine Dario Argento would balk at. The irony is that *Mister Blades* is more entertaining than the bulk of the Maestro's latter-day output.

Performances are enjoyably lively, the slasher gore (overseen by Rutter) is surprisingly effective and, at seventy minutes in length, there's not a superfluous moment to be found. In terms of chronology, the film also evidences a marked development in competence when measured against Rutter's rudimentary 2006 feature debut *Full Moon Massacre*.

A welcome strain of pert humour runs throughout, which should hopefully assuage those bemoaning the understandably rough edges.

Look out for film journalist and indie cinema champion MJ Simpson too, who cameos as Stafford's volatile editor.

The Most Disturbed Person On Planet Earth (2013)

Dir: Thomas Extreme Cinemagore; Scr: not applicable; Cast: not applicable

One of my aims when writing these guides was to cover all aspects of 21st Century horror films. From the comedies and Hollywood remakes through extreme underground splatter, animation and world cinema works of art, to no-budget curiosities ... I'm hoping there's something for everyone within these pages.

One sub-genre that seems forever inexorably linked with horror is the shockumentary. And they don't come much more shocking than this.

Shockumentaries, incorporating an extreme strain of mondo movies, have been challenging viewers' sensibilities for decades. Paolo Cavara and Gualtiero Jacopetti popularised the genre in 1962 with the release of their racist expose on the bizarre and violent practices of "primitive" cultures, *Mondo Cane*. Since then we've had *Shocking Asia* (1976), *Faces Of Death* and *Brutes And Savages* (both 1978), *Faces Of Gore* (1999) ... the list is endless.

In these post-millennial times, however, the Internet has really upped the ante in terms of providing sick kicks for hungry violence seekers. Sites like Ogrish and bestgore quickly established themselves as go-to hosts of some of the most sickening authentic videos imaginable.

What Cinemagore has done is compile well over two hours of some of the Internet's most troublesome clips, and released them under the singular umbrella of what is commonly referred to as *MDPOPE*. There's no narrative (unless you include the titling of each sketch) and, unlike the aforementioned shockumentaries that it shares its ignoble appeal with, it doesn't even pretend to be designed to educate. It's a party tape, a wank fest for psychos.

So, why's it included here? As mentioned above, my intention is to cover all aspects of modern horror. This compilation is unabashedly horrific - and lest we forget that the very term "horror" is directly derived from the word horrific. Cinemagore's sole motivation, as the film's title suggests, is to disturb us. And this he does.

You want to see a Mexican chain saw massacre? Or a pregnant woman being hideously assaulted in a metallic bathtub? How about a cat forced into a blender and its bloodied remains then imbibed by its killers? People hacked to pieces; scat porn; animal and kiddie violence; a terrifying gang rape in an Asian prison; bloody tampon-eating; human-octopus sex Genki Genki-style; *2 Girls 1 Cup* (2007)? Nothing is simulated, nothing can be unseen. Be forewarned!

2014's follow-up, *The Most Disturbed Person On Planet Earth Part 2*, is - astoundingly - even more extreme.

Motivational Growth (2014)

Dir/Scr: Don Thacker; Cast: Adrian DiGiovanni, Jeffrey Combs, Danielle Doetsch

DiGiovanni has spent the last eighteen months growing a beard and living as a recluse in his fleapit home. His days are punctuated by hiding from his aggressive landlord (Pete Giovagnoli), enduring the occasional visit from food delivery monkeys and spying on pretty neighbour Doetsch through his peephole. Oh, and taking the odd shit. This latter pastime is a daily highlight.

When his sole companion - an old television set named Ken – explodes, it all gets too much for DiGiovanni and he attempts suicide. Alas, this fails and results in him lying on the bathroom floor staring at a mound of mould which has formed on the wall. Mould that begins talking to DiGiovanni, courtesy of Combs' distinctive vocal talents.

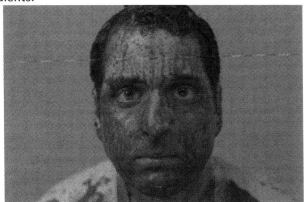

The mould begins whipping DiGiovanni's life back into shape: its stirring speeches inspire the guy to shave, clean his home and even start talking to Doetsch. But, for all the good that the fungus brings to DiGiovanni's life, it requires something sinister in return ...

An intriguing small-scale triumph, *Motivational Growth* marks both DiGiovanni and Thacker as talents to watch. The film employs a small but dedicated cast of quirky, interesting-looking characters – DiGiovanni's lead impressing through comic timing and emotional range, though not so much that the efforts of each beguiling support are overshadowed. A single-location setting benefits from its convincingly stinky set design.

The film's greatest strength, however, is the snappy, dialogue-heavy screenplay. It satirises modern society's over-reliance on television as both a companion and a learning tool. We could also easily read the mould as being a metaphor for the rot so many of us allow to set in to our day-to-day living. Thacker fills his script with smart one-liners, the likes of which hark back to acerbic classics of the 1980s such as *Repo Man* (1984) and *Heathers* (1988).

Alex Mauer's minimalist electronic score recalls vintage video games and TV shows. The practical FX work by Steve Tolin's team (a good old-fashioned foam latex creation for the mould) brings to mind lo-fi favourites of yesteryear like *Basket Case* (1981) and *TerrorVision* (1986). And yet *Motivational Growth* is set in current times, and deals with very contemporary issues such as loneliness, depression, modern living, media manipulation and more.

Perhaps a little too self-consciously "clever" in its occasionally smug delivery and tendency for unnecessary camerawork showmanship, the film is unlikely to achieve the cult status it so clearly desires. Nevertheless, *Motivational Growth* is an original, well-conceived and most of all entertaining little flick.

Mulholland Drive (2001)

Dir/Scr: David Lynch; Cast: Naomi Watts, Laura Harring, Justin Theroux

Originally envisaged as an offshoot of his hugely influential "Twin Peaks" TV series (1990-1991), Lynch winded up committing his initial vision of *Mulholland Drive* to celluloid in 1999. It was intended, at that point, as the pilot for a new television outing. Financiers ABC dropped it before the final edit was made; StudioCanal came to the rescue with extra funding which allowed the director to shoot additional scenes and build a conclusion-of-sorts onto his story, thus enabling the film to be sold as a standalone theatrical experience.

The fractured plot deliberately plays havoc with viewers' perceptions. Ostensibly it tells the tale of Watts, a struggling actress who pines for the love of best friend Harring. When she loses out on her attentions to budding movie director Theroux, Watts hires a hitman to kill her unrequited love. Or does she? The lines between reality and fantasy blur from this point onward as much of what has gone before is suggested as a dream, and a new story involving the same people – albeit with different names and truer characters – begins to evolve. Duality is a favourite theme of Lynch's; see also *Lost Highway* (1997).

Roger Ebert was typically astute in his review of *Mulholland Drive*, remarking of its dreamy logic "(it) lingers over what it finds fascinating, dismisses unpromising plotlines". It's a difficult film to synopsise; simply assessing its effectiveness is far simpler.

To this end, esteemed French magazine "Les Cahiers du Cinema" took a bold step in 2010 by naming Lynch's odyssey the best film of the noughties. This is easy to agree with, and not only due to the startling strengths on display in terms of Peter Deming's beautiful cinematography, Angelo Badalamenti's insidiously affecting score and Watt's achingly honest, career-consolidating performance. Its genius lies in its power to infuriate, confound and provoke its viewers. It's a film made to be dissected and debated over, long after the end titles have rolled.

If you struggle with the twisted narrative, fret not. The seamless, stylised merging of genres (noir, romance, thriller, horror – the final act, in Club Silencio, sees Lynch in full nightmare mode) works even for those unwilling or unable to decipher *Mulholland Drive*'s many maddening puzzles.

The Museum Of Wonders (2010)

Dir/Scr: Domiziano Cristopharo; Cast: Fabiano Lioi, Maria Rosaria Omaggio, Francesco Venditti

Little person Lioi runs the titular circus. He's oblivious to the tantrums and politics which occur backstage nightly, his energies being pooled into fawning over beautiful dancer Omaggio. She pays him no interest, preferring the attentions of strongman Venditti. However, upon learning of Lioi's inherited fortune, Omaggio and her lover conspire to dupe the petite ringmaster into marrying her.

The plot owes more than its pocket money to Todd Browning's astounding *Freaks* (1932). Cristopharo makes no attempt to disguise this unabashed act of theft.

But, visually at least, there are a great deal more influences in evidence here. The very first scene opens to the image of a pasty face staring at us from a night sky's moon. The camera then withdraws to reveal it as part of a stage act, as a heavily made-up woman croons in front of a blue velvet curtain and the moon backdrop. The song ends, dry mist engulfs the stage; when it clears, the woman has been replaced by a clown-faced ventriloquist performing to an auditorium of empty seats. Two minutes in and *The Museum Of Wonders* has already drawn comparisons to Georges Melies, David Lynch, Federico Fellini and Alexandro Jodorowsky.

The references continue. The surreal and oft-times minimalistic stage settings can't help but echo Rinse Dream-era Stephen Sayadian (*Café Flesh*, 1982, for example); meticulously arranged and coloured set designs evoke the fine painterly qualities of Peter Greenaway; the dreamlike oddity knowingly places itself somewhere between the cinema of Luis Bunuel and Jean Rollin.

Yes sir, Cristopharo has an impressive knowledge and understanding of the language of cinema – and he wants us to know it. However, such wanton showmanship – from the tearing of a clock from one character's chest calling to mind *The Holy Mountain* (1973), to the persistent utilisation of smoke and mirrors as obvious allusions to the façade of the theatre – undermines any sense of the dramatic. It's all very clever, yes. Up its own satisfied arse, definitely. But, without that emotional hook, the beautiful visuals (and they *are* gorgeous) soon become fallacious in their quests to stir emotion.

In terms of excess, *The Museum Of Wonders* reins itself in when compared to Cristopharo's *House Of Flesh Mannequins* (2009), a sadistic arthouse endeavour that would easily sate the torture-porn crowd in its uncut form. The emphasis here leans more towards warped humour (check out Ruggero Deodato in a cameo role as a bungling waiter). And yet, the tendency for style over substance strips away the warmth required for such comedic episodes to hit their mark.

Full marks for ambition Dom, if not for the rather apathy-inducing results.

Mutilation Mile (2009)

Dir/Scr: Ron Atkins; Cast: Lawrence Bucher, Daniel McCabe, Susan Bull

Apparently inspired by true events which stem back to 1993, *Mutilation Mile* sees brothers Bucher and McCabe embark upon an insane, forty-eight-hour killing spree while hunting for their beloved uncle's murderers. Fuelled by rage and cocaine, they scream a great deal while slaughtering prostitutes, drug dealers, bums ... anyone who gets in their way, in fact.

There is a lot of shouting in Atkins' film. And a load of profanity. A fuckload of fucking profanity. According to the film's Wikipedia page, there are 664 uses of the word "fuck" throughout. Which, for a movie just over eighty minutes in length, is ... impressive?

Mutilation Mile is similarly relentless when it comes to its violence. Once the scenario has been swiftly established, the film becomes little more than a fast-paced series of increasingly chaotic vignettes. Men and women are battered, tortured and worse: for unknown reasons, the latter definitely get the most severe mistreatment, with inflictions including knife terror and anal rape. The episodic approach could've resulted in something that got very boring very quickly. On the contrary, the constantly raised pulses (and voices) of both victims and aggressors, the persuasively gritty lo-fi aesthetics and a truly manic performance from McCabe - he looks like a tramp and behaves like he's off his tits on crystal meth - create an intoxicating, nervous energy that keeps growing and growing.

Essentially a one-man film machine, Atkins writes, directs, edits and shoots here. The only other crew member present on the Las Vegas shoot appears to have been Kimberly Bell (whose special effects are crude and basic, save for a startling moment of genital maiming). Kristian Day's electronic score complements the no-budget look well.

Atkins has several movies under his directorial belt, all firmly rooted within the genre. Arguably the best-known of these titles is 1997's *Schizophreniac: The Whore Mangler*. Despite its lack of plot and dubious penchant for sexual violence akin to *August Underground* (2001), however, *Mutilation Mile* is his most satisfying, accomplished feature to date.

Myortvye Docheri
See *Dead Daughters*

Nails (2003)

Dir/Scr: Andrey Iskanov; Cast: Alexander Shevchenko, Irina Nikitina, Svyatoslav Iliyasov

Hitman Shevchenko has grown jaded due to the excessive violence of his chosen vocation. He's miserable and he can't sleep. Drowning his sorrows in vodka and pills does little to assuage the pain. During one typically restless night he stumbles upon a magazine article extolling the virtues of trepanation - the act of puncturing the skull with small holes, thus exposing the brain's outer membrane (the dura mater) to relieve pressure and attain a higher state of contentment.

Shot on video for 10,000 Russian roubles, which is about £130.00, *Nails* follows its leading man's plight for sunnier climes and manages to be both gritty, and surreal, in doing so.

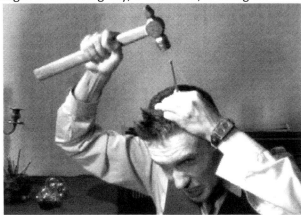

There's a slightly transgressive feel to proceedings. The grubby lo-fi aesthetics begin in black-and-white, accentuating the drudgery of our haunted protagonist's existence, and later burst into garish colours to signify enlightenment. It holds a queasy sense of squalor about it. The film's soundtrack follows suit in its signalling of the distinction between intolerable life and post-trepanning serenity: it's all incessant industrial churning until Shevchenko unlocks the door to happier times, at which point the music - a combined effort between Iskanov and his lead actor - becomes lighter, breezier.

Paradoxically, hammering happy holes into his cranium leads to Shevchenko seeing his life as it really is. Even the food he not only tolerated but enjoyed is realised as being shit through his freshly awakened eyes. Which, of course, means even more extreme measures are required if he is to ever achieve divine peace ...

The problem with *Nails* is that it opens with an intriguing premise but soon runs out of places to go. The film is only an hour long but would have been more effective had it been considerably shorter. And, considering it was sold as a gore flick, it's neither nasty nor proficient enough to satisfyingly nauseate the hardcore crowd it's aimed at. The special effects, again by Iskanov and Shevchenko, with a little help from co-star Nikitina, are especially revealing of the film's meagre budget.

Iskanov went on to nastier things, his most renowned work to date being the vicious semi-documentary *Philosophy Of A Knife* (2008) - an unflinching account of the atrocities perpetrated by the Japanese army's infamous Unit 31.

Trivia fans may be titillated to learn that the hitman's ringtone is Harry Bromley Davenport's synth-heavy main theme tune from cult 1982 movie *Xtro*.

Naina
See *Evil Eyes*

Nar Dyrene Drommer
See *When Animals Dream*

Necromance: A Love Story (2015)

Dir/Scr: Nekro Kaos; Cast: Nekro Kaos, Nekro Val Bundy, Nekro Scatogorophage

Spiritually and aesthetically akin to the German Underground's infamous *Snuff Tape Trilogy* of short films (2011-2014), the hour-long *Necromance* exists for the sole purpose of pushing the boundaries. And this it certainly does.

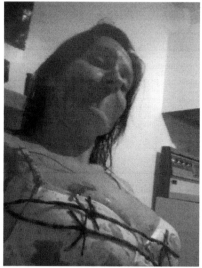

Virtually plotless, it opens with Bundy entering her home and nipping for a bath after preparing a cup of coffee. While soaking, masked assailant Kaos covertly slips a drug into the unsuspecting woman's cuppa. Before long she finds herself tied to a chair with barbed wire and abused in horrifying fashion, her tormentor ultimately killing her and leaving her corpse to rot in the bathtub. A couple of months later, a masked deviant returns (now portrayed by the demented Scatogorophage) to have sex with the rotten cadaver.

Kaos not only writes, directs and co-stars, but also handled the film's crude special effects work along with contributing — alongside Marc Butcher — to the lo-fi score. So it's apt that his film is independently released through his company, DIY Productions (hardcore collectors will have purchased the "gore cover" DVD, limited to just 20 copies).

Although the FX work is primitive, the film retains power thanks to Kaos' refusal to shy away from anything. This is not aspiring for art along the lines of *Nekromantik* (1987): this is categorically, unapologetically out to upset sensibilities. To this end, we get graphic masturbation (with the assistance of a corpse hand), explicit skull-fucking, and evil things done to the remains of a murdered child.

Savage and unsparing, the handheld HD video camerawork helps achieve a troubling sense of voyeurism, while the aggressor's pig mask and occasional echoes of a child's laughter on the soundtrack are undeniably disquieting.

It could be argued that there's social commentary to be found here: the notion that an individual can lie dead in their apartment unnoticed for several weeks could be a sobering denunciation against modern society. However, it's more likely that *Necromance* caters little for interpretation. Rather, it is what it is.

Convincingly foetid, the film was shot in the Canadian director's apartment over the November and December of 2014. The cold weather conditions were fought against with copious amounts of alcohol —

which may also account for Scatogorophage's performance being so brutal, his onscreen actions so excessive.

The Neon Demon (2016)

Dir/Scr: Nicolas Winding Refn; Cast: Elle Fanning, Christina Hendricks, Jena Malone

Fanning, in a role originally intended for Carey Mulligan, is the ambitious sixteen-year-old who moves to Los Angeles with dreams of becoming a model. Her rise in the fashion world there is meteoric, thanks to her coveted "deer in the headlights" look. But, as her competitors watch her ascent with increasing jealousy, she's about to realise that fame comes at a price.

Danish filmmaker Refn burst onto the scene at the age of twenty-four, with 1996's blistering crime flick *Pusher*. Its tight narrative, gritty realism and well-rounded characters paved the way for several similar films before the director took a turn towards the less linear with his surreal take on the prison life of career criminal Charles 'Bronson' Salvador, *Bronson* (2008). Narrative became even vaguer as the visuals continued to be paramount in *Valhalla Rising* (2009), *Drive* (2011) and *Only God Forgives* (2013). The latter even carried a dedication to Chilean surrealist Alexandro Jodorowsky.

The Neon Demon persists along these lines. Filmed on a $7 million budget, it's very much a film of two halves.

The opening hour works as an astute satire on the vacuous, catty and image-obsessed world of modelling, shot through in a manner which is both noirish (Refn's vision of LA echoes that of *Mulholland Drive* [2001]) and steeped in the gaudy primary colours of vintage *giallo*. The proceeding half descends into dreamlike fetishist horror replete with sexualised violence and kitschy cannibalism. It's like *Beyond The Valley Of The Dolls* (1970) meets *Blood And Black Lace* (1964), drenched in neon lights and shallow gore.

The movie was shot in chronological order. The final scenes were improvised on set. The results are often breathtaking to behold – special mention must go to Cliff Martinez's electronic score too, which exceeds his work on *Drive* in terms of multi-layered atmospheric style – but thematically as hollow as the minds of the characters inhabiting this world. Our obsession with beauty is unhealthy, destructive even. Hollywood is a vacuous, heartless place that will eat young wannabes alive (literally). We get it, Nicolas. Your metaphors hardly run deep.

Still, Fanning – younger sister of Dakota – is outstanding as the vulnerable, wide-eyed lead (even if her character doesn't really merit much sympathy). We're also treated to a convincingly sinister cameo turn from Keanu Reeves as a sleazy motel owner.

The concept had been gestating in the back of Refn's mind for a decade. It rose to the fore of his psyche when he shot a commercial for Gucci in 2012, with model Blake Lively sporting an old Hollywood glamour-style look while posing for fashion photographers. *The Neon Demon* was booed during its Cannes premiere and crashed at the box office (distributors Amazon Studios pulled its US theatrical release after two weeks, by which time takings were just $600,000.00). Ironically, it was trounced at cinemas by shark survival thriller *The Shallows* (also 2016) – starring none other than Blake Lively …

NF713 (2009)

Dir: China Hamilton; Scr: China Hamilton, Niki Flynn; Cast: China Hamilton, Niki Flynn

In an unspecified police state, Flynn has been arrested for handing out anti-establishment pamphlets on the street. In a bare room, she's tied to a chair and subjected to a barrage of verbal and physical abuse at the hands of Hamilton. Her initially softly-spoken tormentor ostensibly wants her to name her co-conspirators; as events unfold, we learn his true aim is to break her, reducing her to nothing more than the titular number.

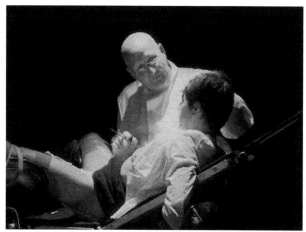

The single setting scenario and shot-on-video aesthetics afford proceedings a peculiar sense of unease. Flynn's torture is not simulated: she genuinely is being beaten, whipped, force-fed and electrocuted. She's also quizzed aggressively about her sex life in a bid to shame her through humiliation. Hamilton matches his verbal assaults with more physical sadism as Flynn is stripped, genitally tortured and forced to piss herself.

A Control & Reform Productions film, originally entitled *Enemy Of The State*, this 73-minute cheapie skirts around its political ideas, along with touching upon themes such as the principals of the Stockholm Syndrome phenomena and the very nature of torture itself. But if you're looking for true insight, or even a Sadean level of intellect, look elsewhere: this is a BDSM venture with little motivation other than to exploit the objectification and brutalisation of its female character.

Flynn was a prominent "spanking model", known in UK circles for her penchant for such punishment in fetish videos like *The Red Reformatory: Old Friends* (2007). Even she admitted, in her online blog, to being left broken and sobbing at the end of what sounds like a fairly gruelling shoot. However, it's important to note that all acts in the film were performed consensually – no matter how convincingly the performers may suggest to the contrary. Superficial likenesses could be drawn to Adam Rehmeier's *The Bunny Game* (2010) in this regard, wherein Rodleen Getsic welcomed all manner of abuse to be inflicted upon her – in the name of art, and of exorcising personal demons.

The British Board of Film Classification didn't like *NF713*. As with *The Bunny Game*, they rejected Hamilton's film outright. Their official statement argued that the film sought to "sexually arouse the viewer at the sight of a woman being sexually humiliated, tortured and abused".

Night Of The Wolf: Late Phases

See *Late Phases*

Nightmare Code (2014)

Dir: Mark Netter; Scr: Mark Netter, M J Rotondi; Cast: Andrew J West, Mei Melancon, Googy Gress

The horror genre has been no slouch when it comes to embracing the threat of a cyber-future and giving us fair warning that technology is, in fact, our enemy. From machinery turning against its creators (*The Terminator* [1984], *Hardware* [1990] etc) to the prospect of Big Brother watching our every move (too many to mention, but let's go with 2002's *My Little Eye*) and the potentially destructive powers of social media (*Unfriended*, 2014), the world of psychotronic cinema holds out little hope for post-millennial mankind. Even when technological advancements aren't being blamed for the apocalypse, they're increasingly used as a means through which to witness it (2015's *Jeruzalem*, for example, which is told entirely through the screen of a Google Glass headset).

Nightmare Code reinforces this dread of progression, this fear of change, while proffering a literal spin on the term "ghost in the machine".

Computer hacker West has mouths to feed and a costly court case looming over him. So he's quick to accept a job which involves repairing the code of a corrupted application designed to read people's emotions. For confidentiality purposes, this necessitates remaining isolated with a small team of techie types until the work is completed. Oh, did I mention that the code's original designer (Gress) went berserk and murdered several colleagues before turning his gun on himself?

It emerges the program being worked on is dangerously accurate in revealing people's insincerities. While wearing a specialised headset, the user is notified via onscreen text of how the person they're conversing with truly feels. Suddenly smiles are shown as disguising contempt, masked arousal is exposed, and so on. And once you realise how false those around you are, it's hard to hold on to your rationale - especially in such an enclosed environment. Matters are hardly helped by the fact that crazed Gress's spirit now resides within the code.

Ideas are expanded to incorporate moments of Cronenbergian surrealism, the most intriguing of which being the notion that the program evolves to a level where it can not only foresee future events but dictate how they will transpire. Prepare for plenty of mind-fucking sparring between reality and artificial intelligence.

Netter's flick looks great considering its modest budget of $80,000.00. Shot in HD, it utilises a voyeuristic surveillance-camera approach which often fragments into split-screen shenanigans. This could've become irritating very quickly, but the director employs such gimmickry wisely: the candid nature of each scene echoes "found footage" tactics; the slick editing and occasional cinematic score ensure the movie steers clear of that tired sub-genre's pratfalls.

There is the odd moment of ropy CGI which lets things down (the first appearance of Gress's ghost being an obvious low-point) but, on the whole, *Nightmare Code* expertly balances its human drama - a reliable cast, well-drawn characters - with an intriguingly paranoid concept.

Nikos The Impaler (2003)

Dir: Andreas Schnaas; Scr: Ted Geoghegan, Andreas Schnaas; Cast: Andreas Schnaas, Felissa Rose, Joe Zaso

Romanian barbarian Nikos (director Schnaas) was cornered by an angry mob and disembowelled half a dozen centuries ago. His legendary remains reside inside a crate, housed in a present-day New York museum hosting an exhibition on Romanian culture. This is also the scene of a gorily bungled robbery. When blood is spilt onto Nikos' mask, the murderous warrior is resurrected to embark on a fresh killing spree. After laying waste to most of the museum's residents he takes to the streets, targeting a local gay bar, a cinema – which is screening fellow Schnaas movie *Zombie Doom* (1999) at the time - and a gymnasium. Look out for cameos by Lloyd Kaufman and Debbie Rochon as Schnaas also terrorises a local video store.

Other noteworthy names among the cast include Tina Krause, punk rocker Bela B and Darian Caine. The latter is the subject of a show-stopping shower-based scene.

From the director of no-budget delights such as *Violent Shit* (1989) and *Anthropophagus 2000* (1999), it's probably safe to say *Nikos The Impaler* is precisely what you'd expect it to be. A breakneck pace, the thrash metal soundtrack, surprisingly well-choreographed battles filmed on a shoestring allowance. Oh, and lashings of extravagant gore ... The first twenty minutes alone boast more bloodshed and insane action than most films muster in their entire running times.

It's good fun, bolstered by upbeat performances and Marcus Koch's splatterific FX work. Limbs are hacked off left, right and centre; bodies are chopped in half; bloody beheadings and the pulping of skulls become the order of the day.

All of which is enough to qualify *Nikos* as a solid party feature. But as drama, it sadly tails off badly once we leave the museum. From that point onwards, the film feels formless and – as much as it's driven by its relentless action – soon drags as a result.

The look of the film is rough and unpolished, shot on entry-level digital video. Performances are atrocious, as are the puerile attempts at humour. This one really is all about the gore (good job there's oodles of it).

Nocturne Six (2014)

Dir: Charlton Jacob Jacques; Scr: Bill Freas; Cast: Nathaniel Jack, Jasmine Boyd, Nathan Witte

A TV news show runs an article on a secret government compound called Nocturne Six. The facility, we're told, was designed to train a motley crew of people with extra-sensory capabilities into elite "guardians". Guardians against what? Demons, trying to break into our world from parallel universes. Something terrible has occurred at the hideout: the bulk of the ensuing film employs 'found footage' aesthetics in a bid to explain what happened to the hapless superheroes.

This Canadian production scores points for its novel concept, ambitious streak and stylish visual élan. Working on a budget of just 25,000 Canadian dollars (£13,335; $19,500), Jacques and crew have toiled well on delivering a clearly focused, dark sci-fi look and feel to proceedings.

However, there are a list of shortcomings which threaten to undermine the production design's impressive work.

One major stumbling block is the badly recorded audio which soon becomes irksome. It doesn't help matters that the cast are largely flat in their deliveries, registering little interest in their dialogue or the supposed dangers their one-dimensional characters may be facing.

Once it's established that the guardians were at war with an inter-dimensional demon, Ceco Aliensa's creature effects are often obscured by flashing lights (someone pay the electricity bill!) and jump-edits. And what began as an intriguing idea is ultimately undone by Freas' screenplay leaving the viewer with far too many loose ends to ponder.

The occasional creepy moment keeps things watchable, along with the aforementioned agreeable visuals. But points for originality and style don't count for a great deal when measured against Nocturne Six's many weaknesses.

The Noonday Witch (2016)

Dir: Jiri Sadek; Scr: Michal Samir; Cast: Anna Geislerova, Karolina Lipowska, Zdenek Mucha

Inspired by Czech historian and writer Karel Jaromir Erben's poem "Polednice", taken from his 19th Century literary collection "Kytice z Povesti Narodnich", Sadek's film is an understated piece which seeks to remain faithful to its folklore origins while relocating the action to modern times.

Geislerova is the film's strongest asset, as the mother attempting to convince daughter Lipowska that her father is not dead but is working away, due to return some time soon. However, as the pair move into the village the late husband originated from, the girl starts to challenge her mother's version of events. All of which leads to Geislerova's grasp on sanity becoming strained, grief subconsciously overwhelming her as she endeavours to keep Lipowska in line by retelling the tale of the Noonday Witch: a she-devil said to materialise at the stroke of midday and snatch unruly kids from their parents.

I was excited to see a new horror film from what's now the Czech Republic. They're not exactly prolific within the genre, either nowadays or back when they were known as Czechoslovakia, but whenever they've gone balls-out they've done it with style: *The Cremator* (1969), *Valerie And Her Week Of Wonders* (1970), *Morgiana* (1972) ... they all spring immediately to mind.

Sadly *The Noonday Witch* doesn't rival any of the above titles. It looks beautiful, certainly, thanks to a combination of its sun-kissed straw field locales and Alexander Surkala's attentive photography. Performances are solid. Pacing isn't too much of an issue. The problem lies in the film's ability - or lack of - to tap into the primal fears it claims to exploit. There is no menace, no threat; concepts of parental psychosis, depression and coping with loss are underdeveloped. Characters are written too bluntly to merit our empathy.

Initial thematic similarities to *The Babadook* (2014) are far too fleeting to stick. Instead, this peters out rather quickly. It looks gorgeous but any subtle suspense built in its first half soon evaporates and we're left with a genteel drama incapable of surprises or scares.

A missed opportunity, albeit an attractively mounted one.

Nymphomaniac Volume 1 (2013)

Dir/Scr: Lars von Trier; Cast: Charlotte Gainsbourg, Stellan Skarsgard, Stacy Martin

Elderly scholar Skarsgard discovers Gainsbourg lying bloodied and unconscious in the alley behind his apartment. He takes her in. Over a cup of tea she regales him with tales of her troubled life. Using items in his room as prompts - a portrait of the Virgin Mary; a pistol-shaped stain on the wall - she races through her story in several chapters, Skarsgard all the while trying to comprehend her actions and assure her she's not the rotten egg she professes to be.

FORGET ABOUT LOVE

NYMPH()MANIAC

Gainsbourg's character is, in fact, a nymphomaniac. More to the point, she represents one facet of von Trier's personality. Her sense of lust, of mischief, of confrontation is easy to link with his approach to filmmaking (censor-baiting movies like *The Idiots* [1998] and *Antichrist* [2009]; the unwise pro-Nazi gestures during promotional appearances). Yet there is a sensitive, studious and observational side to the director that has enabled him to form some of the finest female roles of our generation (*Breaking The Waves* [1996]; *Dogville* [2003]; *Melancholia* [2011]). These aspects are reflected in Skarsgard's sympathetic, contemplative characteristics.

Period and location are deliberately indistinct. An impressive cast - Christian Slater as a paternal doctor; Uma Thurman as a frenzied wronged wife; Shia LaBeouf's baffling English accent - are out-acted by Martin as the nymph in flashbacks to her youth, her naive impishness perfectly conveying von Trier's playful attitude towards controversy here. Some vignettes are amusing (a wager between Martin and her pal to see who can bed the most strangers on a train, the victor's prize being a bag of sweets). Others are tasteless (deflowering by sodomy). All are explicit.

A fusion of actors' performances, computer graphics and porn-star stand-ins were seamlessly employed to create the graphic scenes of fellatio, masturbation and penetration. But don't bother bringing a box of tissues to your screening: the bulk of it is too dour, deliberately so, to titillate.

In serial style, *Volume 1* concludes with a preview of *Volume 2*. Both were released simultaneously.

Nymphomaniac Volume 2 (2013)

Dir/Scr: Lars von Trier; Cast: Charlotte Gainsbourg, Shia LaBeouf, Jamie Bell

Agony follows ecstasy. Gainsbourg's story takes increasingly dark turns as virginal Stellan Skarsgard listens on.

Angrier, more explicit and downbeat than the first volume, this closing instalment still zips along at a fair pace and maintains the director's teasing mood (Skarsgard's imagined versions of Gainsbourg's yarns become more outlandish; von Trier threatens to re-enact the opening trauma of his *Antichrist* [2009] before hitting his audience with an equally jolting though less violent fate for this film's child).

Some plot detours are far-fetched. Bell acts well as an otherwise unlikely service to downtrodden housewives looking to be beaten for pleasure. Gainsbourg's late entry into the debt collection profession seemingly only exists to afford von Trier the opportunity to repulse viewers with an ill thought-out argument in favour of would-be paedophiles. Even Skarsgard, by this juncture our voice as well as one side of the director's ego, has trouble swallowing this last morsel. Pun intended ...

Disappointingly predictable music cues aside (Talking Heads' "Burning Down The House" during an episode of arson), *Volume 2* ups the ante in terms of both sex and trauma as it descends uncompromisingly towards the return to Gainsbourg's original, broken discovery in that alley. Memorable characters, dashed attempts at marriage and redemption, and pretentious psychological ramblings that are thankfully tempered by self-effacing humour help push things along.

The savage consequences of Gainsbourg's inability to leave her genitalia alone echoes the body horror cinema of early David Cronenberg (*Shivers* [1975]; *The Brood* [1979] etc) or Marina de Van's more recent *In My Skin* (2002).

Though the finale feels at first rushed and unsatisfactory, upon reflection it poses an intriguing ambiguity as to whether Gainsbourg has conquered her demon ... or indeed, learned anything over the course of the preceding evening.

But what do *we* learn? Not a great deal. Sex can be great, but can also be destructive if our lives become governed by it. Psychological profiles are in place from childhood. Von Trier makes a better sensationalist than he does philosopher. If you're looking for an insightful look into the machinations of sex addiction, you may find yourself better served by 2011's *Shame*.

The film's theatrical version (both volumes combined) was four hours long. A director's cut surfaced mere months later, adding ninety minutes - more Slater, more sex, and a gory DIY abortion which gives anything on the UK "video nasties" list a good run for its money. The latter is preferable, especially if you want to appreciate how this could be construed as a horror film through these eyes, though the original workprint apparently ran at a whopping seven hours in length.

Oculus (2013)

Dir: Mike Flanagan; Scr: Mike Flanagan, Jeff Howard; Cast: Brenton Thwaites, Karen Gillan, Miguel Sandoval

Traumatised after killing his psychotic father as a child, young adult Thwaites is finally released from the institution that's been tending to his mental wounds and taken into the care of sister Gillan. Almost immediately, she alerts him to a mirror that daddy brought into the family home many moons ago - and which she suggests is the cause of all the bad luck they've thus far endured (including the murder of their mother at their patriarch's hands). The mirror is evil, Gillan insists. And lo, she's recently located its whereabouts at an auction, where she's procured it in the hope that Thwaites will help her destroy it once and for all.

Flanagan followed up his minor indie hit *Absentia* (2011) with this relatively low-budgeted studio picture (the stated budget is $5 million). What results is a measured, tight and resolutely old-school foray into *spooky shenanigans* territory. If you're in need of cheap gore or signposted jump-scares, you'd best scuttle off elsewhere.

Well-thought-out camera angles, a keenly judged atmosphere of brooding menace and a fine balance of subtle chills help *Oculus* build almost surreptitiously in terms of overall impact. Gillan - who made her name between 2008 and 2013 as Doctor Who's redheaded sidekick in the long-running TV show of the same name - is key to the successfully mounted drama, delivering a performance which in equal portions evokes vulnerability and barely restrained mania. She straddles ambiguity with guarded assurance. Unsurprisingly, this promising actress has since gone on to bigger things: *The Big Short* (2015), *Guardians Of The Galaxy Volume 2* (2017) ...

Oculus triumphs not only due to its solid cast and low-key approach, but in large part also because of its skilfully played vagueness. The mirror is employed as metaphors for the varying interpretations of events in life, for the emulation of reality and as a window into the complex arenas of identity and duality. Indeed, does the mirror actually exist in this case at all?

Haunted looking-glasses have served the horror genre well over time: from the chilling segments of celebrated portmanteaus *Dead Of Night* (1945) and *From Beyond The Grave* (1974), to the likes of *The Boogey Man* (1980) and *Into The Mirror* (2003, along with its 2008 remake *Mirrors*). *Oculus* is worthy in joining an impressive list of effective mirror-based fright shows.

One Missed Call (2003)

Dir: Takashi Miike; Scr: Minako Daira, Alexander Von David; Cast: Kou Shibasaki, Kazue Fukiishi, Shin'ichi Tsutsumi

The rumour perpetuates about a woman who had died "full of hate", and who now kills others by reaching them supernaturally through their mobile 'phones. Legend has it she spreads from one 'phone memory to the next, each recipient receiving a call from themselves dated two days into the future – anticipating the exact time that person will die.

When Fukiishi becomes the latest to receive the dreaded call, best pal Shibasaki teams up with detective Tsutsumi in a bid to source the root of the evil and save her life.

Based on Yasushi Akimoto's novel "Chakushin Ari", Miike's film explores the modern obsession with mobile telephones and digital media in general. On a broader scale, *One Missed Call* can be viewed as a critique against modern Japanese society at large: an overpopulated country whose people value electronic communications over physical interaction. Within the realms of contemporary Asian horror cinema, this film's premise also follows a trend where paranormal malevolence assaults the material world by means of electrical appliances: *Ring* (1998), *Pulse* (2001) etc (not such a novel concept, perhaps, as Wes Craven explored similar territory back in 1989's *Shocker*).

It would be fair to anticipate, then, that *One Missed Call* would be another formulaic J-Horror offering. Certainly it plays close to convention with its Yurei-style ghost and flash-frame edits of grisly imagery designed to shock. But this is Miike at the helm, and he knows how to separate his horror from the herd – as evidenced in earlier masterpieces such as *Audition* (1999) and *Gozu* (2003).

Under his tutelage, we get strong likeable performances from the typically young leads (though Fukiishi is the stronger at expressing heightened emotions, and so perhaps would've been a better lead than Shibasaki) and a keenly observed pace which builds the scares gradually. Despite the presence of the aforementioned expected motifs, the action is largely cliché-free thanks to the director's creative use of camera and editing. The finale is a tad baffling, of course, as they often are in Miike's cinema.

There's a 2005 sequel, and an American remake from 2008. Trust me, leave both be.

Only Lovers Left Alive (2013)

Dir/Scr: Jim Jarmusch; Cast: Tilda Swinton, Tom Hiddleston, Mia Wasikowska

Listless vampire musician Hiddleston – a poor man's Michael Fassbender, who he replaced early into the production - is reunited with similarly blood-dependent lover Swinton and all seems well for a time. That is, until her wild younger sister Wasikowska arrives to upset the proverbial applecart.

The story bears no relation to that of Dale Wallis' 1964 counter-culture novel of the same name, though Jarmusch has acknowledged that his title serves as a loose homage. If you look closely at the photos on Hiddleston's wall you'll even glimpse a portrait of filmmaker Nicholas Ray, who was once set to adapt Wallis' tale for the big screen. Tribute is big on the auteur's agenda: other references include Samuel Beckett, Luis Bunuel, Nikola Tesla and Jean Michel Basquiat – to name but a few of the many. The lead characters are named after Mark Twain's 1905 satirical piece "The Diaries of Adam and Eve", and not the biblical figures.

The director describes *Only Lovers Left Alive* as "a crypto-vampire love story". It's easy to concede to it being poetic, while its motivation appears to be the examination of what it is that drives us onward … even when life has reached a monotonous low. If you're familiar with Jarmusch's cinema – *Mystery Train* (1989), *Dead Man* (1995) etc – you'll not only know that he's acclaimed by many as one of the last truly great indie US filmmakers, but also have a fair idea of what to expect. If not, let me clue you in: drawling performances, pretty visuals, an air of pretention, a cool soundtrack.

Music plays a big part in the director's art. It's integral to the plot here, of course (as are the arts in general – it's suggested that centuries-old vampires are responsible for creating works attributed to the mortal likes of William Shakespeare and Franz Schubert). Note how every instance of music being played by the characters utilises vinyl (a medium that has since become very trendy again). Jarmusch's band SQURL provide the main score, while an eclectic array of sounds are also provided by the likes of Wanda Jackson, Yasmine Hamdan and Black Rebel Motorcycle Club.

Famously against compromising – reportedly, Jarmusch removed all scenes of "action" when his producers asked for more – he did however relent upon realising he couldn't secure the budget needed to shoot on his preferred medium of film. Through low lighting and filtered lenses, he was able to achieve his desired look with an Arri Alexa HD digital camera.

Orozco El Embalsamador
See Orozco The Embalmer

Orozco The Embalmer (2001)

Dir/Scr: Kiyotaka Tsurisaki; Cast: Froilan Orozco

A film where the tagline to the notorious *Snuff* (1975) seems quite appropriate: "Filmed in South America … where life is cheap!".

Feeding a lifelong fascination for photographing images of death, Tsurisaki travelled to Colombia in the mid-1990s. He settled in the notorious El Catucho area of the country's capital city, Bogota, where poverty and crime are commonplace. It's here that he met middle-aged Orozco, a former police inspector who had by that time moved on to an apparently even more cheerless vocation: preserving and beautifying cadavers in preparation of their funerals.

During his career, Orozco reportedly handled over fifty thousand corpses. In a metropolis like Bogota, he was never short of work: the grim opening scenes of this documentary reveal a city where bodies lying bloodied in the streets are walked over nonchalantly by locals who see this type of atrocity all too often.

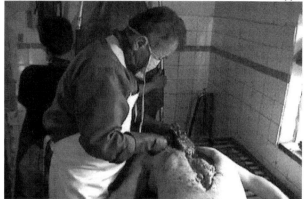

On the one hand, *Orozco The Embalmer* serves as an oddly affecting character study. In it, the mortician talks us not only through his daily processes but also his views on life and death. A warmth in his eyes contradicts the dismissive approach his work appears to possess. His attitude is casual on the surface, and yet as events progress he emerges as a decent man who did invest true care into his work. The reality of his grim surroundings is witnessed through the melancholy evident behind his smile.

Keeping on that same hand, Tsurisaki's camera captures – over the course of five years - both the monotony of Orozco's daily routine and a distinct acceptance of the poverty and violence with which the Bogota locals live. No matter whether you're man, woman or infant (the corpses being tended to here start from a *very* early age), regardless your background or profession, we all end up in the same place. When life ends, what we each amount to is a pile of flesh and bones – and we're all at the mercy of someone like Orozco. There's a lot of food for thought on offer.

Now. Let's take a look at that other hand. Tsurisaki has supplemented his income previously by helming the occasional *pink eiga* entry (Japanese erotica, often with a sadomasochistic bent). His direction here retains that corruptive streak: nothing is spared from his handheld video camera, as it zooms in on lifeless genitalia and films Ozorco's every scalpel slice with unwavering conviction.

All of which would perhaps bypass accusations of exploitation, were it not for the use of library music which flits between atmospheric industrial dirges and strings of the ominous, horror movie variety. Combined with the barrage of matter-of-fact unsimulated grisliness, all presented as a virtually plotless string of vignettes, *Orozco The Embalmer* slots easily into that most ignoble of modern horror offshoots, the shockumentary (*Shocking Asia* [1976], *Faces Of Death* [1978] etc).

It's a captivating, thought-provoking and ultimately depressing film – and it's definitely not for those with weak constitutions.

Orozco died of natural causes shortly after Tsurisaki's film was completed.

Orphan (2009)

Dir: Jaume Collet-Serra; Scr: Alex Mace, David Leslie Johnson; Cast: Vera Farmiga, Peter Sarsgaard, Isabelle Fuhrman

Married couple Sarsgaard and Farmiga have their share of problems. She's a recovering alcoholic, their third child was recently stillborn and their relationship has suffered ever since. Bafflingly, they decide that their lives will be enhanced by adopting nine-year-old Russian orphan Fuhrman. Their younger daughter takes to her; their son, a little older, does not.

Before long, Farmiga grows suspicious of Fuhrman too: the girl possesses an unusual amount of sexual knowledge for someone her age, and is increasingly violent at school. When her concerns are raised, Sarsgaard refuses to take them on board. Some people insist on learning things the hard way ...

Killer kids have been a staple ingredient of the genre for decades: *The Bad Seed* (1956), *Village Of The Damned* (1960) and *The Omen* (1976) are but three priceless examples deserving of immediate attention. *Orphan* feels especially faithful to the spirit of the latter, while embracing its own trashy excesses with such aplomb during its final hour that it borders on becoming pastiche.

Collet-Serra had rankled fan feathers with his glossy, OTT remake of *House Of Wax* (2005) – co-starring Paris Hilton! He claws back a degree of credibility here by virtue of some delicious moments of dark humour and those later set-pieces which, while by that point it could be argued the film has degenerated into formulaic action, are so overblown that they can't fail to be hugely entertaining.

A $20 million budget certainly assists in lending the film a sheen suited to the big screen and blu-ray showmanship. Farmiga brings necessary gravitas as the frantic mother whose own troubles have those around her doubting her every word. Sarsgaard, in comparison, is there to look good and occasionally frown.

The UK tagline read "You'll never guess her secret". Which is a bit unfortunate, because all that makes you do is second-guess the twist from the start. Even if you do suss what's going on (I think I got it about midway through), it makes for such an audacious turn of events that you can't help but smile regardless.

The Others (2001)

Dir/Scr: Alejandro Amenabar; Cast: Nicole Kidman, Alakina Mann, James Bentley

Kidman tends to her photosensitive children Mann and Bentley in a seemingly deserted Jersey mansion towards the end of the Second World War. It's here that she awaits the safe return of her military husband (Christopher Eccleston). The arrival of three servants – including veteran British comic Eric Sykes in a straight role – coincides with strange occurrences around the house. Mann speaks of having seen ghosts, everyday items are conspicuously misplaced, the curtains are stolen much to the sunlight-intolerant kids' horror. Should Kidman believe her daughter's claims of unseen "intruders" in their midst?

Expanded by Amenabar from a short story of the same name which formed an episode of the excellent anthology series "Armchair Theatre" in 1970 (and which was also developed into the 1973 film *Voices*),

The Others is a polished $17 million production complete with an A-list lead and agreeably austere approach to its spooky storytelling. It's easy to liken it to superior ghost story *The Innocents* (1961).

Amenabar had already proven his skill in engineering frights with *Thesis* (1996). Here he hones his craft further, delivering one of the classiest, most restrained and yet convincingly eerie period pieces in recent memory. There is no gore. No sex. No profanity. We don't need those in this case. Even when you've sussed out the obvious twist, proceedings remain classy enough to keep you glued - and the reveal carries a weighty emotional kick regardless.

Kidman is unexpectedly great as the fiercely protective, increasingly vulnerable lead. The Australian actress, and former Mrs Tom Cruise, is a world away from insipid swill like *Moulin Rouge!* (2001) here.

The film went on to win eight Goya Awards – Spain's answer to the Oscars – including Best Director and Best Film. Notably, it was the first English-language film to ever receive the latter accolade.

You know your film's a hit when Bollywood remake it too: the better-than-it-sounds *Hum Kaun Hai?* (2004) refers.

Ouija (2014)

Dir: Stiles White; Scr: Stiles White, Juliet Snowden; Cast: Olivia Cooke, Ana Cato, Daren Kagasoff

White is one of a long line of special effects artists who've graduated to directing later in their careers (Tom Savini and Stan Winston also spring to mind). Having worked on the FX for a number of films including *Interview With The Vampire: The Vampire Chronicles* (1994), *The Relic* (1997) and *The Sixth Sense* (1999), White progressed to screenwriting with titles like *Boogeyman* (2005) and *The Possession* (2012) to his credit. This latter effort was co-written by Snowden. Her creative partnership with White was evidently strong enough for the pair to reconvene on the latter's directorial debut.

Based upon a popular board game, itself spawned of the titular spiritual communicatory device which harks back to 1890, the film is, well ... flawed. It tells of a group of teenaged friends, led by Cooke, who gather round said board to perform a séance in the hope of contacting their recently deceased pal (Shelley Hennig). Hennig, it transpires, committed suicide shortly after she herself had been fooling around in matters of a Ouija nature ...

Oh, what secrets will this bunch of suspiciously mature-looking "teens" unearth, and who will come a cropper as a consequence? Stick around, if you must, to find out.

Dabbling in the game of Ouija is a rites-of-passage that almost every kid has indulged in at one time. Turn the lights down low, hold hands and speak to the dead in a grave tone - while trying your best not to giggle. We all know the drill. If you think it sounds like the kind of thing that would struggle to elicit screams from today's (supposedly) sophisticated audiences, you'd be right. At least, it's startlingly free from scares in the hands of novice White and his slick $5 million budget, controlled from the wings, no doubt, by co-funders like Platinum Dunes (Michael Bay's company) and Hasbro Studios. That's right! The toy and board-game folk who brought you the likes of My Little Pony and Transformers ...

An attractive cast are as dull as dirty dishwater, not one of them being capable of breathing life into the predictably one-dimensional script. We don't fear for their safety at any point, nor are we aghast at any of the so-called revelations in store.

Filmed in an uninspired manner more suited to late-night TV, *Ouija* drags along aimlessly with only signposted jump-scares to occasionally wake its flagging viewers up. Not even a cameo from the excellent Lin Shaye (shot in post-production following disappointing test-screening reactions) can save this donkey.

But what do I know? The film performed well at the box office and a follow-up, 2016's *Ouija: Origin Of Evil*, was soon announced.

The Pact (2012)

Dir/Scr: Nicholas McCarthy; Cast: Caity Lotz, Casper Van Dien, Haley Hudson

With her mother's funeral looming, estranged Lotz is cajoled into returning to the family home for the first time in years. Bad childhood memories soon resurface as a sinister presence is felt in the old house. When Lotz's sister and cousin go missing, detective Van Dien suspects her of foul play. He gradually acknowledges the sensation of a malevolent force on the premises. Cue medium Hudson, drafted in to contact the mother's ghost - the true culprit, according to strung-out Lotz - and locate the missing persons' whereabouts.

McCarthy began making short films in 2004 with the well-received *Maid*. His fourth effort, 2011's *The Pact*, was a tense 11-minute ghost story starring Jewel Staite. It became a hit on the festival circuit, winning particular praise at that year's Sundance shindig. This led to securing the financial backing required to develop the concept to feature length.

Citing the likes of Dario Argento and Val Lewton among his influences, McCarthy makes a seamless transition to feature direction here. Not only is his film visually eloquent and beautifully coloured, the perfectly paced story is told with a confident fluidity a lot of more experienced filmmakers fail to master.

Lotz takes over the helm from Staite and is a suitable replacement. Her balance of vulnerability and edgy instability plays out as convincingly ambiguous throughout. Hudson is just as good as the initially cool psychic. She gets to flex her acting muscles impressively during the film's latter half. Even Van Dien, cheesily handsome star of Paul Verhoeven's *Starship Troopers* (1997), puts in a strong, understated turn. The acclaim he won wasn't, however, sufficient to keep his career from stooping to the level of appearing in shitfests like *Sharktopus Versus Whalewolf* by 2015.

The Pact delights in its attractive set design and photography, assured build-up and persuasive twist. Co-directors Dallas Richard Hallam and Patrick Horvath's 2014 sequel, *The Pact II*, tried to stay true to this winning formula - but it's an undeniably lesser film.

Palabras Encadenadas
See *Killing Words*

Paradise Lost (2006)

Dir: John Stockwell; Scr: Michael Arlen Ross; Cast: Josh Duhamel, Melissa George, Olivia Wilde

A trio of backpacking Americans meet up with three foreign travellers and soon enough, following an unlikely run of bad luck, the group becomes stranded in Brazil. While searching for a way to get home, they stumble across an idyllic beach. The locals there sure are friendly, inviting the sextet to party until the early hours. Alas, there is an ulterior motive behind this affability - and our protagonists awake the next morning to find themselves in a world of shit.

George, a veteran of Australian television, went on to find moderate fame in 2007's *30 Days Of Night*. Duhamel, meanwhile, scored big with a prominent role in the same year's *Transformers*. Both have maintained fairly successful careers since but that hasn't been enough to encourage more of a cult following for this film. Which should give you a good indication of just how mediocre it is.

It all looks very pretty though. Indeed, the first hour plays more or less like a tourism reel for Brazilian 18-30 holidays (if they exist?). The sun-kissed locales, perfectly toned bodies and abundance of young actors in either snug shorts or even tighter-fitting bikinis are undeniably easy on the eye.

However, an attractive sheen can only distract from the one-dimensional characters and absence of action for so long. When proceedings do finally pick up and our leads discover they've been lured into an organ-harvesting ruse, Stockwell sadly fails to capitalise on the potential for claustrophobic tension and instead plays events out in tired, by-the-numbers fashion.

There's scant trace of conscience in the xenophobic subtext: *Paradise Lost* makes use of America's post-9/11 fear of foreigners (a la *Hostel* [2005]), only to avoid any social commentary in favour of pantomime villainy and unlikely chase scenes.

Considering Stockwell is a prolific actor on the small screen, he does nothing to elicit charisma from his dull cast. Too stingy with its gore to even qualify as torture-porn, *Paradise* Lost is left with very little to offer.

Paranormal Entity (2009)

Dir/Scr: Shane Van Dyke; Cast: Shane Van Dyke, Erin Marie Hogan, Fia Perera

"Prepare to see the actual footage of the supernatural events leading to the 2008 'murder' of Samantha Finley". Okay. Prepared.

Well, that's what the UK press release advised for this extremely cheap (and exceedingly quick) cash-in on Oren Peli's surprise hit *Paranormal Activity* (2007). Taking no chances on their demographic missing the connection, British DVD distributors Anchor Bay even graced this film with cover art almost identical to its box office-bothering inspiration.

The situation is this: Van Dyke has been arrested for the above murder, and subsequently has committed suicide while in custody. All the while, he protested his innocence. After the fact, the cops have retrieved homemade video footage of his which suggests his stories of supernatural terrorisation may have been true. The recordings are divided into individual segments which signify nights in Van Dyke's family home (he films everything, every monotonous detail, on his handheld digicam – so don't go into this curious to see what Dick Van Dyke's grandson [or even Barry Van Dyke's son] looks like, because you'll be none the wiser). Living with sister Hogan and mother Perera, there's not much for Van Dyke's camera to initially report. But then the strangeness begins: weird scribing found in furniture, unexplained bumps in the night.

Giving the "found footage" sub-genre a bad name (if that's possible?), *Paranormal Entity* stacks cliché upon cliché over eighty tiresome minutes. It's devoid of suspense, hackneyed in delivery and clumsy in execution (I'm not going to list the numerous continuity flaws here). If there is a saving grace, it's that its two female leads aren't utterly terrible in their thankless roles. But, really, that's a small compliment.

It should come as no surprise that this is derivative, bargain basement fare of the worst kind: it comes from The Global Asylum, a production company who've had a hand in well over a hundred films since the year 2000 – the titles of which include *Snakes On A Train*, *The Da Vinci Treasure* (both 2006) and *Mega Shark Versus Crocosaurus* (2010).

Perseveration (2013)

Dir/Scr: Adam Sotelo; Cast: Josh Potter, Peter Beck, Chelsea Levine

A young boy is held captive by demented priest Beck, a cult leader who thinks nothing of skull-fucking decapitated nun's heads in-between raping and beating the child. Eventually, the lad gets his hands on a claw hammer, doles out some violent retribution and escapes. But the damage has been done. As an adult, he (Potter) is now a killer every bit as sadistic as his former captor. We watch as he butchers victims to the tune of his own twisted religious beliefs, utilising pliers, pickaxes and even a baseball bat with barbed-wire wrapping to full effect.

Reportedly filmed on a budget of just $5,000, this crowd-funded effort shows promise from debut director Sotelo. There's an arty slant to it, lots of considered and slightly surreal imagery, without events ever becoming bogged down in arthouse stuffiness. The sound design at times is striking in its impact - scary and disturbing - while Justin Taylor's impressive FX work goes against the meagre budget he was playing with.

Opting to add dialogue in post-production is an odd choice. But it pays off in a weird way which often lends events a curious, dream-like quality. Coupled with the disembodied voices filling Potter's head with occasionally portentous spiritual diatribe, the echoed post-dubbed spoken moments come across like something that shouldn't work but, strangely, do.

Split into three chapters, the film chronicles Potter's trajectory from victim to aggressor. Sotelo fills the screen with religious motifs and blasphemous imagery, ramming home the evils of organised religion, along with the notion that violence breeds violence. Hardly revelatory musings, but in a film with as little character development as this, that's hardly surprising.

If you're not interested in such matters, or the astute artistic compositions, relax: the film delivers gore and depravity in spades. It opens with an obdurate pre-credits scene depicting a backstreet abortion, for Heaven's sake. The first act goes on to shock due to the child actor being so young - seven, at a guess? Later on, we get necrophilia, rape, decapitation, beatings, disembowelment ... the list goes on.

Sotelo, who has proven popular in the industry providing masks and props via his company Crypt Creations, had announced intentions to make more films following positive reviews for *Perseveration* (not a commonly used word, so I don't feel too patronising while explaining that it refers to someone who continues to repeat certain actions from their former life despite having suffered brain injury - in this case, Potter's dedication to continuing the cycle of abuse he'd suffered in the name of Christianity). Alas, Taylor's untimely death in May 2015 has seen the fledgling filmmaker withdraw from embarking on fresh productions to date.

Pieces Of Talent (2014)

Dir: Joe Stauffer; Scr: Joe Stauffer, David Long; Cast: David Long, Kristi Ray, Barbara Weetman

Struggling actress Ray takes a job as a cocktail waitress in a strip bar, helping to support herself and her ailing mother. Witnessing an altercation between a club bouncer and seemingly innocent passer-by Long, she intervenes. A friendship develops between Ray and Long - who, coincidentally, proclaims himself to be a filmmaker. Naturally she accepts his invite to take part in his next production. Oh dear, oh dear ...

We've seen scenarios like this one before: two ostensibly similar films of recent lineage are *Penance* (2009) and *Starry Eyes* (2014). The former takes the struggling waitress premise and hurls it down a tunnel of Nazi experimentation and torture. The latter shares a heroine whose own craving for fame leads her into dark territory. Despite treading a well-worn path, Stauffer's effort has strengths which help it rise above the norm.

For a start there are its considered pace and highly articulate visuals, allowing an arthouse quality to permeate proceedings. A generous dose of foreshadowing clues lends events a lyrical edge, while the solid lead performances build character identification and plausibility of situation with skill. Ray is extremely likeable and convincing as the wannabe prepared to put any misgivings to one side in the hope of realising her dream. Long - appearing, effectively, as himself - makes for a disconcerting psycho with curious motivations.

The film was marketed as a gore flick. It does get very bloody at times - Tony Rosen's practical FX work is excellent - but it's worth noting that, for the most part, this is a slow-moving, absorbing study of an industry which mercilessly manipulates those desperate enough to want to be a part of it. The body count is low.

Based on the 2006 short film "The David Long Story", *Pieces Of Talent* was shot over the course of four years. A great deal of deliberation has gone into its look and thematic arc, all of which pays off well. Hats off especially to Stauffer who, along with directing and co-writing, also edited the film, handled the striking cinematography and even composed its ambient score.

A Plague So Pleasant (2013)

Dir: Benjamin Roberds, Jordan Reyes; Scr: Benjamin Roberds; Cast: David Chandler, Maxwell Moody, Eva Boehnke

Based one year on from a zombie apocalypse, *A Plague So Pleasant* suggests that – unlike other films charmed by this premise – the panic lasted a mere twelve hours, by which time survivors had realised the undead were docile creatures if left alone.

Within this situation live slacker pals Moody and Chandler, and the latter's sister Boehnke. She stills pays daily visits to the quarantine field containing her zombified ex-boyfriend. Desperate for her to move on, Chandler encourages Moody to set about wooing her. When this fails, drastic measures are required to permanently erase the ex-boyfriend. Alas, this breaks one very vital rule of coping in this post-apocalypse environment: never harm a zombie. If you do, the rest of them will group together and retaliate against mankind. This is particularly bad news as, given that even those dying from natural causes are inclined to return as ghouls, the undead far outnumber the living.

The monochrome photography of *A Plague*'s opening third does its best to recall *Night Of The Living Dead* (1968) by way of pin-sharp digital visuals; a humorous bent, taking in episodes such as Chandler having to attend an "undead awareness" course at his workplace, can't help but bring to mind *Shaun Of The Dead* (2004); the kinetic bursts of colourful zombie action during the final forty minutes owe much to TV's "The Walking Dead" (2010 onwards). And yet, there is an individuality to proceedings achieved by virtue of painstaking cinematography, amiable performances and a contemplative script.

What begins as a dark comedy swiftly moves into more menacing territory as the zombies attack and the co-directors' haunting, ambient score becomes more pronounced. The camerawork is brisk but focused, its most extraordinary moment being an over-Chandler's-shoulder view of the devastation he's unwittingly instigated. The action is gory, relying mostly on Tylar Carver's enjoyably rudimentary practical effects. The best of these is a convincingly gross blind ghoul, nicknamed "Bacon Face" for reasons that will become clear upon viewing.

Reportedly made for just $1,400.00, *A Plague So Pleasant* shows potential from its young filmmakers.

Planet Terror (2007)

Dir/Scr: Robert Rodriguez; Cast: Rose McGowan, Freddy Rodriguez, Josh Brolin

Inhabitants and passers-by of a typical Smallsville, USA, band together when a chemical leak at the nearby military base starts turning locals into demented zombies.

Elaborated upon from a thirty-page script Rodriguez had begun developing back in 1998, *Planet Terror* represents the Texan-born filmmaker's contribution to Miramax's "Grindhouse" double-bill - the other film, of course, being Quentin Tarantino's *Death Proof* from the same year (covered in Volume One). It's tough deciding which one fails the most.

Both can't help but come across as smug vanity projects, their grinning mainstream directors frantically trying to earn "cool" points by assuring us of their fanboy knowledge credentials. Both are guilty of reinventing the grindhouse ethos in a manner which doesn't truly reflect their inspirations (were there ever such mash-ups of sub-genres that were so cluttered with half-baked ideas and self-consciously hammy performances?). Both operate under the misconception that surf rock, bad-ass females and faux distress on the film are what the grindhouse spirit was all about.

Perhaps Rodriguez's film edges it. Partly because it takes the zombie concept and, rather than opting for the obvious route of cloying George A Romero's seminal works, it more closely echoes Umberto Lenzi's entertainingly batty *Nightmare City* (1980). Partly because it has the more interesting cast of the two: supporting roles from Bruce Willis, Michael Biehn, Jeff Fahey, Cheech Marin and Tom Savini provide more entertainment value than their director's self-congratulatory script merits.

So, no, it's not *utter* toss. Brolin is great fun as an abusive husband while Marley Shelton is a hilarious, sexy standout as his beleaguered wife. KNB EFX Group's make-up effects are satisfyingly exaggerated and gross. The pace never flags, and those looking for quotable lines will be in heaven.

But, from that nudge-nudge-wink-wink casting to Nouvelle Vague's jazzy cover version of Dead Kennedys' "Too Drunk To Fuck", from the chick with a machine gun moulded onto her leg stump to the guy who collects the freshly hacked-out testes of his victims, this is desperate to win your affections. Off-puttingly so.

Polednice
See *The Noonday Witch*

Poltergay (2006)

Dir: Eric Lavaine; Scr: Hector Cabello Reyes, Eric Lavaine; Cast: Clovis Cornillac, Julie Depardieu, Lionel Abelanski

In the 1970s, France's premier gay nightclub closed its doors forever when a faulty foam machine exploded, taking the lives of its five campest dancers. Thirty years on, oblivious lovers Cornillac and Depardieu - yes, Gerard's daughter - buy a new home, which just happens to have been built on the nightclub's former spot.

In no time Depardieu has been summoned away and Cornillac is left home alone. A red-blooded Italian hunk, when not working on a construction site, he likes a beer and game of pool with his buddy: *that's* how much of a man's man he is. However, there's a quintet of gay ghouls who're about to begin employing the power of suggestion upon him. Their antics include taking Polaroid snaps of Cornillac's bare arse in the shower and wolf-whistling whenever he bends over at his pool table. Even upon her return, Depardieu cannot see the penis the ghosts have chalked on her wall, or hear them as they taunt her lover with invites to the joys of homosexuality.

On the one hand, this French flick is extremely silly. It takes a premise daft enough to have stemmed from the mind of someone like Lloyd Kaufman and gleefully explores every preposterous avenue - poltergeists that enjoy dancing nightly to a scratched vinyl copy of Boney M's "Rasputin" is just the beginning ...

But then, it would be unjust to dismiss *Poltergay* as throwaway fluff. It's very well-made on a technical level - it looks fabulous (the Gothic exterior of the old house at dusk provides a highlight), is attentively edited and boasts some fantastic sound design. The film also benefits greatly from a host of affable, heartfelt performances. Cornillac finds the equilibrium between animated reaction and strong stoic reasoning; Depardieu plays it straight and consequently brings some vital heart to proceedings. Of the ghouls, Jean-Michel Lahmi stands out as their bickering, boogieing ringleader.

The gay gags do become tiresome after an hour or so. But beneath the mirth there's the hint that *Poltergay* is challenging stereotypes and asking whether there's a little bit of sexual curiosity in all of us.

The Possession Of Michael King (2014)

Dir/Scr: David Jung; Cast: Shane Johnson, Ella Anderson, Cara Pifko

Documentarian Johnson is a devout atheist. Upon losing his wife in a tragic accident, he becomes obsessed with challenging concepts of good and evil, of life after death and the like, in his latest filmmaking project.

Hiring a pal as his cameraman, Johnson sets out interviewing various acolytes of the dark arts (a lapsed priest, devil-worshipping weirdoes, a necromancer and so on) while inviting them to direct any of their so-called hexes upon him. His intention is to debunk each one, thus proving that there is no spiritual world and his wife is gone forever. Which must be comforting for his young daughter Anderson, I'd imagine.

As the film's title cannily reveals, Johnson's reckless flirtation with such nefarious practices lands him in deep shit. More reassurance for his grieving daughter, having to watch her dad transform from the inside-out into a seething, red-eyed, sweaty monstrosity capable of pulling a knife on her ...

Filmed in a faux-documentary style, replete with handheld footage, regular breaking of the fourth wall and surveillance camera inserts to cover more unlikely angles, *The Possession Of Michael King* takes a saturated sub-genre and attempts to bring something new to it via the art of "found footage" tropes. Only, that market's rammed too. So much so that all Jung really achieves is to showcase the clichés running rampant throughout both fields. Throw in blaring jolts on the soundtrack designed to make you leap out of your skin, and it's almost as if this one's *striving* to be predictable at every turn.

In its favour, Johnson proffers a credible character arc in the titular role. From arrogant sceptic to frightened victim, his is a journey which allows for a wide array of emotions to be explored. What's not probed so well are the film's potentially intriguing themes, which Jung fails to cover to any satisfying degree. Science versus religion, good versus evil, the concept of the afterlife ... there's plenty of scope for rumination here; instead we get a gory, incrementally silly and slightly disheartening (why would the father of a young girl, still mourning the death of her mother, volunteer himself for what amounts to slow suicide?) take on tired possession conventions. Still, at least there's no pea soup vomit or spider-walking.

The Poughkeepsie Tapes (2007)

Dir: John Erick Dowdle; Scr: John Erick Dowdle, Drew Dowdle; Cast: Ben Messmer, Stacy Chbosky, Samantha Robson

An attractive city in the state of New York, Poughkeepsie is rocked when local police unearth a host of videotapes detailing a serial killer's decade-long reign of terror. The recordings detail carefully planned abductions, rapes and murders – in one segment, an unconscious woman's belly is sliced open, her husband's severed head is inserted into the C-section opening, and the woman is roused awake once she's been sewn back up.

The Poughkeepsie Tapes presents itself in the form of a cable television news programme, merging interviews with occasional clips from the fictional killer's 2,800 hours' worth of video footage. Even Ted Bundy (Todd Cahoon) pops up at one point, offering his thoughts on the murderer's motivations.

As the hunt for the perpetrator intensifies (his face remains hidden at all times; he tampers with each crime scene to an extent that even psychological profiles are hard to build), the film focuses more on Chbosky – a victim he'd kidnapped and held captive for a number of years prior to her being rescued by cops.

From graphic throat-slashings, misery and debasement, to the chilling snatching of an eight-year-old girl, Dowdle's film aims to shock. It's all expertly edited together, boasts credible performances and whatnot, but … its primary concern is to jolt its audience with a catalogue of suffering. Bombarding the viewer with scene after scene of distress has a nullifying effect, however, and the film comes perilously close to losing momentum by its midway point. It manages to hold the attention, just.

For reasons that remain unclear, the film was advertised as "coming soon" in 2007 but sat on a shelf until 2014 when it finally enjoyed a brief on-demand release. A blu-ray release finally transpired in 2017.

Something of a family affair, *The Poughkeepsie Tapes* was co-written and produced by Dowdle's brother Drew, while Chbosky is the director's wife. The Dowdle brothers went on to develop their documentary-style of genre filmmaking in *Quarantine* (2008) and *As Above, So Below* (2014).

Psycho Beach Party (2000)

Dir: Robert Lee King; Scr: Charles Busch; Cast: Lauren Ambrose, Thomas Gibson, Beth Broderick

We're in Malibu and it's the 1960s. Beach parties are the 'in' thing, which is where surfing hottie Ambrose really comes into her own. However, there's a dark side to her persona – a foul-mouthed, cantankerous alter-ego that rears its ugly head every now and again, threatening to undermine her everyday popularity. Worse still, the bodies of those in Ambrose's social circle start to pile up, a fresh kill occurring each time her alter-ego takes a hold. Could she unwittingly be responsible for the murders? Or is someone close to her using her condition as a cover for their own dastardly deeds?

Based on Busch's stage play of the same name, in which he played Ambrose's role himself, *Psycho Beach Party* is a gleefully camp exercise in colourful, silly homage. Homage to the beach party movies popularised by AIP in the 1960s (*Beach Party* [1963], *Bikini Beach* [1964] etc), and homage to the often convoluted whodunits of the early-80s slasher genre (1982's *Slumber Party Massacre* and so on). The two are blended together surprisingly well.

Despite a $1.5 million budget, access to the soundstage employed during production was clearly limited, as most scenes were shot in either single or double takes to save time. Considering this, the cast do a fair job of maintaining their high-spirited deliveries. Characters are broad, certainly, but conveyed with equal degrees of consistency and verve.

The emphasis is on loud facial expressions and catty one-liners, all akin to vintage John Waters fare. Busch gets to play a female role again, albeit lower down the cast this time. As a thriller the film does at least remember to populate itself with several likely suspects, a couple of gory kills involving castration and dismemberment, and a twist reveal.

Perhaps the biggest point of interest, outside of its agreeable surf soundtrack, is the inclusion of a pre-fame Amy Adams in a supporting role. Watch out for her getting her bikini bottoms ripped off – a scene she was reportedly unhappy about having to perform.

Purgatory Road (2017)

Dir: Mark Savage; Scr: Mark Savage, Tom Parnell; Cast: Gary Cairns, Luke Albright, Trista Robinson

Mischievously claiming to have been based on a fictitious "banned novel" by "Kevin Everett", Australia-born filmmaker Savage's Mississippi-based road trip tells of two disturbed brothers - Cairns and Albright - who steer a travelling confessional through the state's most rural passages.

Troubled by a house robbery which occurred in their youth, subsequently leading to their parents' apparent double suicide, the boys accept donations in return for ex-communicated priest Cairns listening to local folk confess their sins. Their mission is to replace the life savings that were stolen from their father on that fateful night. However, so strong are Cairns' views on theft that any such transgressions are met with swift justice - usually involving his six-inch blade. Those who've merely involved themselves in voyeurism, affairs or even sex with goats - "I named her Gertrude after my wife" reasons the horny widower, "to be honest, in the dark, it ain't all that different" - are given their Hail Mary instructions and sent on their merry way.

An inquisitive local sheriff, a love interest for Albright and the arrival of a mysterious brunette (Robinson) with a dark past which links her to the boys, help form the plot of what could've otherwise festered in an episodic and shapeless succession of enjoyable vignettes.

Purgatory Road is beautifully shot. It makes great use of its pastoral exteriors (including a standout chase through deserted farm grounds), while vivid colour correction proffers a wealth of cool blue, red and green hues for interior sequences, lending events a frequent visual recall of prime Mario Bava and even top-tier Lucio Fulci. There's a striking opening composition too, depicting a child emerging from shadows in the midst of hyper-stylised blue lighting, which can't help but bring to mind a pivotal moment from Agusti Villaronga's troubling (but excellent) *In A Glass Cage* (1986) - an acknowledged favourite of Savage's.

Glen Gabriel's understated score acts as a perfect companion piece to the script's dry dark humour and the highly proficient cast's focus on creating memorable characters, affording *Purgatory Road* a distinct whiff of 90s indie cinema - replete with unexpected moments of short, sharp and cruel violence.

Speaking of which, FX artists Marcus Koch and Cat Bernier-Sowell deliver the gory goods, ensuring this is Savage's most visceral film since *Defenceless: A Blood Symphony* (2004). Their talents allow for gun shootings, stabbings, dismemberment and hints at necrophilia amid a polished morality tale that finds depth and food for thought beneath its punctuating set-pieces.

The Purge (2013)

Dir/Scr: James DeMonaco; Cast: Ethan Hawke, Lena Headey, Max Burkholder

The tagline read "One night a year, all crime is legal". It's a concept so high that Don Simpson (infamous late producer of single-line-synopsis blockbusters like *Top Gun* [1986] and *The Rock* [1996]) would've been proud.

The general idea is that, by the year 2022, crime and overpopulation have become so problematic that the American government initiates an annual event whereby anything goes for twelve long hours. Of course, there are flaws in this philosophy: just ask Hawke, Headey and their children, innocently caught in the midst of the ensuing mayhem. Fortunately the former happens to be a specialist in home security systems ...

Effectively a home invasion film with an added talking-point gimmick, *The Purge* captured the public's imagination upon its theatrical release. Disregarding its premise (which, be honest, doesn't hold up to logical scrutiny), it's a taut and visually involving horror-thriller set at a stirring, unflagging pace. Characters are one-dimensional with silly dialogue to match – choice moment is Headey bawling "We're gonna play the rest of this night in motherfucking peace ... anyone have a problem with that?". The action is bone-crunching but considerately crowd-pleasing at the same time: we're positively encouraged to cheer along to Hawke's progressively more violent acts of vigilante bloodshed. As a slice of tense action where the brain is best disengaged in order to enjoy, DeMonaco's film works well.

It's less successful when it comes to matters of social and political commentary. What does this preposterous concept achieve, even if we're willing to believe that a future government would legalise murder and rape once a year? Well, we're invited to swallow the notion that every other day of the calendar is blissfully crime-free as a result. Because that's what would happen, *naturally* ... all the criminals would store their aggression in anticipation of looting and killing at will once in a blue moon. Yeah, right!

The improbable gives way to the implausible as the action gets more and more convoluted. But if you like your thrills with a fair degree of spit and polish applied, and don't care for the virtues of a credible screenplay, *The Purge* may well titillate you.

Its sequel – 2014's *The Purge: Anarchy* – crossed over more overtly into John Carpenter action style a la *Assault On Precinct 13* (1976).

Queen Of Earth (2015)

Dir/Scr: Alex Ross Perry; Cast: Elizabeth Moss, Katherine Waterston, Patrick Fugit

Co-producer Moss excels as a young woman still overcoming the loss of her father when beau Kentucky Audley gives her the boot. Her annual jaunt to old pal Waterston's country retreat suggests an opportunity for recovery. But the girls have drifted apart in recent times and their strained relations, along with constant reminders of her ex-lover (he'd joined her at Waterston's lake house the year before), begin to take their toll on Moss. Factor in handsome neighbour Fugit's singular attention towards her friend, and Moss's mental deterioration rapidly accelerates. Adding to this implosive scenario is Waterston, who has a troubled past of her own to contend with.

Perry's earlier film *Listen Up Philip* (2014) ably displayed his knack for tapping into human behaviour along with exploring its potential to form and deform relationships. Perhaps the best thing about that movie though was Moss's assured, convincing supporting role as the lead character's long-suffering partner.

Both director and actor show signs of growth here, making for a more mature - albeit darker - proposition.

Shot on 16mm and devoid for the most part of telltale era-specific detail, *Queen Of Earth* is an incredibly welcoming retro-style psychological drama addressing the issues of mental illness and failed friendships in gratifyingly understated fashion. There is little spectacle: the pleasure lies in its languid pacing, those drawn-out moments where faces tell their own stories during elongated passages of tense silence. Some will become absorbed in this approach; others may swiftly feel alienated by the absence of conventional action.

Perry is not averse to tossing in moments of pitch-black humour. The scathing dialogue as the tension between the two leads heats up makes for a fine example of this. But this remains a serious drama at heart, almost entirely reliant on its fiercely brave, open performances.

It's easy to liken *Queen Of Earth* to Ingmar Bergman's *Persona* (1966), given the shared considered approach of subtle manipulation on its way to achieving rich tragi-drama. John D Hancock's *Let's Scare Jessica To Death* (1971) deserves a nod too: not only for the lakeside setting and 70s-esque vibe, but also Keegan DeWitt's insidious score - the closest thing to melodrama here - and the incremental aura of paranoia enveloping Moss as she edges evermore persuasively towards total breakdown. The naturalistic performances and candid handheld camerawork share the sense of intimacy explored in the best works of John Cassavetes - in particular the similarly themed *A Woman Under The Influence* (1974). The film would also play well on a triple bill alongside two early Robert Altman examinations of damaged women: *That Cold Day In The Park* (1969) and *Images* (1972).

A beautiful, beguiling, thought-provoking film.

The Quiet Ones (2014)

Dir: John Pogue; Scr: John Pogue, Craig Rosenberg, Oren Moverman; Cast: Jared Harris, Sam Claflin, Olivia Cooke

England, 1974. College professor Harris enlists two of his hornier students, along with working-class trainee cameraman Claflin, to help him prove that ghosts are negative energy which have been manifested by disturbed individuals. Having recently rescued young orphan Cooke from an asylum, the plan is for this small team to retreat with her to a remote country house and conduct experiments aimed at bringing out her inner demons. "Cure the individual" Harris coos, "and you can cure all mankind".

Inevitably, the plan goes tits up.

Hammer's continued search for a good old-fashioned spook show worthy of capitalising on the success they enjoyed with *The Woman In Black* (2012) led to this curious hybrid of 70s-tinged ghost story and modern found-footage tropes.

The era is evoked lazily by way of dated drab fashions, copious smoking of cigarettes and an inordinate amount of Slade on the soundtrack. None of the characters, save for Claflin's, merit our sympathies. Harris comes across as a sleazeball with unclear motivations behind his actions; his two pupils (Rory Fleck-Byrne and Erin Richards) just want to fuck and fight. Pogue has clearly instructed Cooke to behave in sinister fashion, something she does with an ill-fittingly theatrical verve.

And why oh why does Claflin's 16mm footage look so scratchy when ran through a projector mere moments after having been shot? More clumsiness.

With three people working on the screenplay (itself based on an original treatment by Tom de Ville) you'd be forgiven for expecting better than tosh like "EMF level two increased" and "we can't have non-believers in this house ... it's a destructive energy in a constructive space", recited in laughably earnest manner.

The Quiet Ones actually purports to be loosely based on fact. *Very* loosely would be more accurate: in 1972, Dr Alan Robert George Owen led a team of Canadian parapsychologists through The Philip Experiment - an attempt to manifest a ghost which ended inconclusively. And here, the similarities end.

Pogue's film is at least a very handsome-looking production, slickly put together while making good use of its estimated £150,000.00 budget. But it's terribly twee fare, unconvincing at every turn as a fright flick (a key moment midway through is ruined by a really shitty CGI effect; the final act plays it safe with unscary retreads of earlier, superior films, and Cooke's clichéd portrayal of demonic possession).

Rabid Love (2013)

Dir/Scr: Paul J Porter; Cast: Hayley Derryberry, Brandon Stacy, Josh Hammond

Five college graduates head out to the sticks for one final weekend together before going their separate ways in life. They've hired a cabin in the middle of nowhere (the film was shot largely on location in Kansas) where they intend to indulge in a spot of hunting in-between fucking, playing truth-or-dare ... the usual stuff. They pick up a friendly stranger (Stacy) en route, who decides to stick around for the weekend. All seems to be going well ... Until the local sheriff pops in to warn of a bear loose in the nearby woods, and Derryberry's beau (played by director Porter) begins acting oddly.

When members of the group start disappearing, only for their mangled bodies to be found a short while later, the survivors understandably panic. But who, or what, is killing them off one-by-one? Is it the aforementioned bear? Has one of the many hunters who've been attracted to the area in the hope of slaying said beast gone crazy? Or is all of this simply happening in one character's head?

While *Rabid Love* kicks off rather inauspiciously (it's set in the 1980s, which ties in with it initially playing as homage to the likes of *Friday The 13th* [1980] and *The Evil Dead* [1981]), it develops via a few nifty twists midway through which raise it above predictable slasher conventions.

Porter's screenplay elaborates on an original story by Derryberry (who unsurprisingly gets cast as the final girl). It's a perceptive piece, with equal amounts of humour and sincerity during the first act which help us identify with the protagonists. The cast are all proficient; these guys are a likeable bunch.

The $100,000.00 budget is used modestly but effectively, the film appearing slick and attractive while avoiding unnecessary flashiness. It also benefits from an interesting soundtrack - including the likes of Gene the Werewolf, Racecat and The Harmless Doves - which serves up a mix of era-appropriate synth pop, raucous rock and mellow trip-hop.

Relatively low on nudity and gore, and slow to get going, *Rabid Love* nevertheless emerges as a satisfying homage to both 80s cult cinema and survivalist horror.

Ratline (2011)

Dir: Eric Stanze; Scr: Eric Stanze, Jason Christ; Cast: Emily Haack, Jason Christ, Sarah Swofford

Though less prolific than it was in the late 1990s and early 2000s (with titles such as *Ice From The Sun* [1999], *Scrapbook* [2000] and *Deadwood Park* [2007] under their belt), it's heartening to see Stanze's Wicked Pixel Cinema production company can still knock out the odd gem.

Haack and her half-sister (Alex Del Monacco) are on the run following a bungled heist. With villains pursuing them, they hole up in the sleepy Missouri town of Hermann, taking shelter in local landlady Swofford's abode. But she's not without problems of her own: her grandfather's ties to a mythical Nazi artefact attract the attentions of out-of-towner Christ, a psychopath with an agenda.

Ratline is filled with subplots and twists, so much so that it's virtually impossible to adequately synopsise. Part of the fun is just letting it take you along for the ride, as it breathlessly soars through sleazy set-pieces and gleefully baffles – its multiple strands not truly coming together until the final third.

Along the way the action gets wildly gory. There is some great practical effects work to be enjoyed from Jim Wayer and Chris Belt. A healthy dose of nudity keeps that sleaze factor up too.

Stanze has three decades of experience behind a camera and it shows. He makes great visual use of his Missouri and Illinois locations – a scenic cemetery, a dishevelled school, annual festivities held in one Missouri town being shot in, and so forth. Avoiding that cheap digital look which blights so many low-budget flicks, the director imbues a sense of style into every frame. The black-and-white newsreel footage, featuring an amusing cameo from the director, is a welcome touch too.

Raw (2016)

Dir/Scr: Julia Ducournau; Cast: Garance Marillier, Ella Rumpf, Rabah Nait Oufella

Diffident teenager Marillier enrols at the same veterinary school attended by older sister Rumpf. Her seemingly peaceful existence is soon shattered by a series of cruel initiation demands imposed upon her: required to dress like a slut for class; forced to wear nappies; drenched in animal blood a la *Carrie* (1976); compelled to eat a raw rabbit kidney.

All of which awakens something in the introverted vegetarian. She develops a rash which leads to her skin peeling. An insatiable taste for meat becomes too irresistible to fend off. Hitherto unrealised carnal desires are violently sated.

Transformation comes both literally - the shedding of skin being symbolic of the caterpillar erupting from its chrysalis as a butterfly - and figuratively. The correlations between cannibalistic violence and urgent sexual needs are obvious but they're handled by Ducournau with a deftness of hand which lends *Raw* a healthy amount of artistic worth.

219

The French director's feature debut premiered to critical acclaim at Cannes in May 2016. By the September, there were reports of it provoking walkouts and, more bizarrely, faintings among its audience during a screening at the Toronto International Film Festival. While it certainly is gruesome on occasion (even the sound effects can be harrowing), this over-reaction threatens to obfuscate the fact that *Raw* is a work of considerable restraint and intelligence.

At its heart are a couple of commendable performances. In many ways brave, it is however more pertinent to note how appropriately understated Marillier is. She elicits our sympathies even as her bloodlust grows drunkenly out of control: her confusion and curiosity have us spellbound throughout. Rumpf, meanwhile, is impressively adept at straddling that fine line between being the helpful older sibling (well, she loans her sis a skimpy dress for "slut" day) and a cold, calculating nemesis, with persuasive magnetism.

The school itself is a sparsely decorated, clinically austere offering of cool blue hues. Adults are rarely seen, creating a universe in which it's feasible that Marillier can both suffer such cruelty at the hands of fellow students, and develop the most disturbing Gallic body-horror fascination since *In My Skin* (2002).

Beautifully shot and carefully paced, *Raw* - much like werewolf flick *Ginger Snaps* (2000) - uses the genre to comment upon female sexuality, sexual awakening and what it means to be bonded as siblings.

It's a great film. Albeit a sad one. There's only the unwise coda - featuring a cameo from Laurent Lucas - that spoils the mood.

Red Room 2 (2000)

Dir/Scr: Daisuke Yamanouchi; Cast: Miyuki Kato, Yukio Kokago, Salmon Sakeyama

Yamanouchi's original *Red Room* (1999) holds the distinction of being one of the first horror films to explore the phenomena of cruel TV game shows within a contemporary, voyeuristic setting. A Japanese production, it could easily be read as a satire on home-grown tests of fortitude such as the 1980s series "Za Gaman" ("Endurance"). In that, contestants were pushed to the limits of physical and mental torture, all in the name of entertainment.

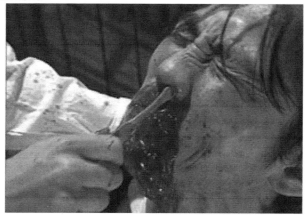

Yamanouchi's concept took things several steps further. *Red Room* pitted four contestants against one another in a single room, where we were invited to watch a la reality show "Big Brother" as they drew cards. In each round, the one with the lowest card was placed into a cage and subjected to a form of torture they must survive to stay in with a chance of making it to the end and claiming the $1 million prize.

Red Room 2, as its generic title suggests, offers more of the same. The lo-fi digital video aesthetics are retained; the formula for how the action unfurls is largely unchanged. A combination of stripped-down production design, measured lighting and unfussy camerawork help maintain its predecessor's reality TV show vibe. Fumio Kaneko's electronic score pulsates effectively throughout.

In many ways, it's preferable that Yamanouchi didn't feel the need to expand on his concept and explain its origins, or graduate to shooting on film and alter the tenor felt in his shocking first instalment. But the results are definitely diluted by the sense of déjà vu such familiarity provokes.

Yamanouchi attempts to stifle such apathy with increased character development and, naturally, torture sequences which raise the bar above its predecessor's brutality. One character is compelled to fist a pregnant competitor's vagina, culminating in him reaching deep inside and tearing out the foetus; another is forced to eat a bowl of vomit; what sounds ludicrous on paper – a contestant's nasal passages are scrubbed clean with a toothbrush – actually escalates into being one of the film's nastiest moments.

A clear stylistic descendent of the original *Guinea Pig* series of low budget gore films (1985-1989), the *Red Room* films are perhaps too cheap and crude to truly nauseate. They remain, in their own ways, harrowing examinations of a modern world populated by people driven by a lust for the quick fortune reality shows promise them.

As for former pornographer Yamanouchi, his finest work remains the troubling *Muzan-E* (1999).

Red, White And Blue (2010)

Dir/Scr: Simon Rumley; Cast: Amanda Fuller, Marc Senter, Noah Taylor

Raped at age four, Fuller has grown into a disaffected young woman given to trawling bars at night in search of one-night-stands. A glimmer of hope comes in the form of Taylor, who – despite an air of barely contained anger – shows potential to be something more to her than a fleeting fuck.

Matters are complicated by the return of rocker Senter, whose unprotected tryst with Fuller has led to him being diagnosed as having AIDS. He's not happy. Not least of all because he's just donated blood to his cancer-stricken mother.

Certainly, it seems that Fuller's past has caught up with her. It's perhaps small consolation that Taylor is psychotic, having been discharged from military service under a cloud of mystery while serving in Iraq.

Red, White And Blue opens on a downer and never cheers up. Its first act is largely dialogue-free as we follow the troubled Fuller through her joyless routine of casual sex and self-loathing. Taylor's arrival into her life is met with the caveat that he used to torture animals as a kid; Senter is a victim whose intentions are violent from the start.

Drab colour schemes, languid moments of contemplative silence, soulless rutting … Rumley's film, set in Texas, is one of hopelessness and subversion. As a revenge thriller, which it ultimately becomes, it turns conventions on its head: Fuller's victim is an antagonist who's been intentionally spreading her disease among unwitting lovers; Senter, her aggressor, is a fundamentally good guy driven to passionate hatred via extreme circumstances; Taylor, who is the crusader setting out to avenge whatever wrongdoing has befallen his beloved Fuller, is a crazed fantasist just looking for an excuse to maim and torture.

Inspecting the protagonists, one can only conclude that Rumley's title is highly ironic. The colours of the American flag are said to represent valour (red), purity (white) and justice (blue); it would take a skewered view to find such attributes in their actions.

Considerately shot and keenly performed, *Red, White And Blue* nevertheless doesn't offer its viewer an easy ride. Its grim demeanour is unrelentingly oppressive, while as a character study it becomes undone by odd editorial choices (the shift of focus from Fuller to Senter midway through proceedings is schematically flawed). Come the savage denouement, the graphic violence may estrange those who'd been perceiving this as a dour arthouse feature.

The Redsin Tower (2006)

Dir: Fred Vogel; Sr: Fred Vogel, Shelby Lyn Vogel; Cast: Bethany Newell, Perry Tiberio, Jessica Kennedy

When their party is folded by the police, a group of young revellers search for a more low-key venue to resume drinking in. This leads them to the Redsin tower, a local landmark infamously rumoured to be haunted.

While our witless protagonists settle in to the titular building's basement, unstable Tiberio gets busy trying to locate them. He has a bone to pick with ex-girlfriend Newell. The longer it takes him to find them, the more murderous his rage becomes. Meanwhile, the party is about to find out just how haunted the tower is ...

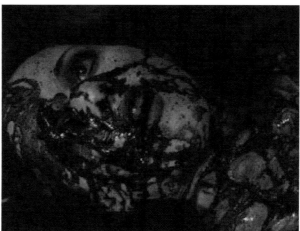

Vogel sprung onto the horror scene with his troublesome faux-snuff atrocity *August Underground* (2001). It marked the arrival of a ferociously hardcore director and his impressive FX crew, collectively working under the banner of Toetag Pictures.

Following on from the similarly rough-around-the-edges *August Underground's Mordum* (2003), Vogel promised that his next feature would be made along more conventional lines. No handheld camerawork, no home movie-style primitiveness.

Shooting on a Panasonic DVX-100A MiniDV camera, the results are semi-successful. While the camerawork is fluid and well-framed, also benefiting from efficient editing, it's an unfortunate truth that a great deal of the action is badly lit. Inevitably there is still a "cheapness" to the look too.

Toetag's effects work, overseen by Vogel collaborator Jerami Cruise, are excellent for the most part. The two problems facing gorehounds though are that (a) you have to wait an insanely long time for the bloodshed to arrive, and (b) when it does come, a hefty amount of it is virtually obscured by the insufficient lighting.

The premise lifts from *Night Of The Demons* (1988) and, to a degree, *Intruder* (1989). Meshing both synopses together probably sounded like a sure-fire winner on paper. In reality, Vogel's dialogue and characters don't intrigue enough to carry both plots. Poor quality acting lets the side down further – though Newell gets a reprieve in this department, emerging as the only person worth giving a hoot about.

La Region Salvaje
See *The Untamed*

Reise Nach Agatis
See *Voyage To Agatis*

Resident Evil (2002)

Dir/Scr: Paul W S Anderson; Cast: Milla Jovovich, Michelle Rodriguez, Colin Salmon

In an alternate future, the ubiquitous Umbrella Corporation has the monopoly on supplying computer technology, healthcare and medical products to the people. Behind the scenes, they bolster their funds by conducting top-secret research into genetics and viral weaponry on behalf of the American army. When one such experiment goes awry, an elite military unit is sent to quietly quell the situation. However, upon reaching their secluded facility destination, they discover its occupants have become infected by a newly formed virus. Side-effects largely consist of mutating into ravenous zombie-like creatures. One seemingly unharmed survivor is amnesiac Jovovich ...

Shot across German and Canadian locations on a reported budget of $33 million, *Resident Evil* saw Anderson - who'd previously helmed the underrated *Event Horizon* (1997) - return to the sci-fi-horror genre with a script based on 1996's best-selling Japanese video game of the same name. A stunt crew of twenty-nine, several established FX teams and the pulling power of model-turned-actress Jovovich (still in favour following her breakthrough success in Luc Besson's *The Fifth Element* [1997]) all assisted the British director in his plight.

Allusions to Lewis Carroll's perennial favourite "Alice in Wonderland" abound. Jovovich's character is named Alice; the computer system that must be destroyed if there is to be any hope of curbing the virus is dubbed the Red Queen; references to white rabbits and looking glasses jump out during key sequences. Not that any of this adds any great substance to proceedings. Just observing ...

Of course, *Resident Evil* exists as a zombie actioner. There are just enough canine critters and lonely walks down darkened corridors to keep the game's purists content. Set and sound design are the outright winners on the technical front, while feisty Rodriguez - a self-proclaimed fan of the source material - steals every scene she's in. None of it is scary, but it's always easy on the eye and never fails to deliver on its promise of highly efficient brain-in-neutral entertainment.

The film was sufficiently successful, raking in $40 million at the US box office alone. A number of sequels and animated spin-offs predictably followed.

Resurrecting The Street Walker (2009)

Dir/Scr: Ozgur Uyanik; Cast: James Powell, Tom Shaw, Lorna Beckett

Powell longs to be more than the mere runner for a small-time film production company. Upon searching their vaults he discovers an unfinished horror film entitled "The Street Walker". Seeing potential in the project and learning that its original director committed suicide, Powell embarks on completing the film himself. In the meantime, pal Shaw decides to make a video diary of Powell's plight.

Turkish-born Uyanik's British film is an interesting and ambitious one. It's essentially a character study, an examination of how one man's obsession leads to mental breakdown. We follow a couple of stories which run concurrently - Shaw is documenting Powell, who in turn is researching a dead filmmaker while becoming consumed by the freshly unearthed movie. So we have multiple timelines here: the original film-within-a-film stems from the 1980s; Shaw's footage of Powell's increasingly fraught psyche over the course of several months; present-day retrospective interviews with associates.

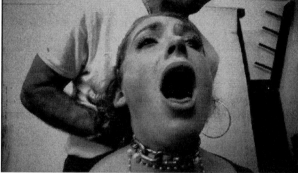

Such elaborate storytelling is bold. However, it could easily spell disaster for all but the most focused of directors. For the most part, Uyanik pulls it off with aplomb. Assisted by a fine cast - Powell excels - and some convincingly grainy footage from the violent faux film of yore, his script is well-paced and tight enough to bring everything together without mess or undue contrivance.

The faux-documentary approach and enveloping present-tense interviews echo the style of Pat Higgins' *The Devil's Music* (2008). It's also interesting to note that both films offer commentary on artists whose creative obsessions develop into something more disturbing, more destructive. In Higgins' film, it's the music industry that comes under the microscope. Uyanik muses over the filmmaking process - having been a runner himself, much of what we see has a reek of authenticity about it.

Definitely worth a look.

The Returned
See *They Came Back*

Les Revenants

See *They Came Back*

Revenge Is Her Middle Name (2011)

Dir/Scr: Anthony Matthews; Cast: Lissa Brennan, Michael Todd Schneider, Douglass Bell

Drug addicted prostitute Brennan learns she's pregnant and decides to seek a way out of her Hellish existence. She ropes her partner, fellow junkie Schneider, into aiding her in a heist which they hope will fund a better life. Inevitably, this goes wrong. Vulgar pimp Bell punishes Brennan's betrayal by having several of his henchmen brutally gang-rape her. Having taken time to lick her wounds and re-evaluate her life, she goes after the gang seeking vengeance …

The rape-revenge sub-genre was a formidable force within the realms of 1970s exploitation cinema. Titles like *Thriller: A Cruel Picture* (1973), *Rape Squad* (1974) and *I Spit On Your Grave* (1978) pushed the censors' relaxed views on onscreen sexual violence to the max. In doing so, they found an audience prepared to wallow in the objectification and abuse of female characters, safe in the knowledge that the moral equilibrium would be restored via a denouement offering the victim – and viewers – some cathartic form of retribution.

An age of anti-violence censorship groups and political correctness all-but halted the production of such films during the 1980s and 1990s (one dramatic exception being Abel Ferrara's startling *Ms 45* [1981]). Come the 21st Century, those who grew up discovering such decadent grindhouse movies on VHS were ready to pay homage via their own films. And so, the rape-revenge flick was reborn through the likes of *Hora* (2009), Steven R Monroe's *I Spit* remake (2010) etc.

In terms of plotting, New Zealand-born Matthews' feature debut – a continuation of a theme explored in his earlier short "The Night Stinger" – doesn't promise much innovation. Even its characters' names (Turbo, Tony the Grave Digger, Mutton Chop and so on) sound like rejects from what was arguably the biggest mainstream hit of this ignoble cinematic wave, *Death Wish* (1974). What *Revenge* lacks in originality it compensates for in style.

Welcome use of colour-filtered lighting lends measures a cinematic quality. Editing is adroit, serving the flab-free narrative well at each turn. Excellent performances are a boon. Brennan's especially good: she goes from junkie, through reformed mother-to-be, to dead-eyed vengeful vessel with persuasive conviction. Bell lets the side down a tad, his broad portrayal of villainy coming straight out of a bad Blaxploitation movie.

Matthews has fun with his expletive-riddled script, upping the crazed pitch to the point that the cruel rape scene is – thankfully – almost comedic in its excess. Once the mainly expositional first act is over, the blood flows freely during a hate-fuelled final act involving throat-slashing, castration, dismemberment and more.

The practical gore effects are splashy and impressive, as you'd expect from FX supervisor Jerami Cruise. The Toetag Pictures regular also co-produces. Matthews had previously worked as a part of the Toetag production team on *The Redsin Tower* (2006) and *Murder Collection Volume 1* (2009), along with taking on the odd acting gig with them.

Hopefully he'll get to direct more of his own features, as *Revenge* shows considerable promise.

Ricky 6 (2000)

Dir/Scr: Peter Filardi; Cast: Vincent Kartheiser, Chad Christ, Sabine Singh

The account of troubled teenager Ricky Kasso's descent into bloody murder was the most chilling middle-American true crime story of 1984. Upon discovering his friend Gary Lauwers had stolen several bags of PCP from him, Kasso lured him into local woods with two more pals on the promise of getting high. Instead, there followed an evening of prolonged torture in which Lauwers was beaten, stabbed multiple times and even had his eyeballs sliced open. During the ordeal Kasso commanded Lauwers to pledge his love for Satan – something the seventeen-year-old refused to do even as death loomed large.

The fact that Long Island youth Kasso was a Satan-worshipping metal-head (he was wearing an AC/DC T-shirt at the time of his arrest) made it inevitable that filmmakers would be attracted to translating this tale of drugs, alienation and mindless brutality to the screen.

Tommy Turner and David Wojnarowicz got there first with 1985's short transgressive masterpiece *Where Evil Dwells*. Cult filmmaker Jim Van Bebber added lashings of nasty gore for his own interpretation, the bludgeoning *My Sweet Satan* (1994: again, a short). 1997'S *Black Circle Boys*, directed by Matthew Carnahan, was a tepid "inspired by" drama most notable for providing former boy-band star Donnie Wahlberg with an early role. 2000's Discovery Channel premiere *Satan In The Suburbs* offered a hybrid of earnest documentary and cheesy re-enactments.

Filardi's film stands as the mostly highly-thought-of filmic account of the crime, as well perhaps the least seen. Perhaps the two go hand-in-hand: a lot of this movie's standing is owed to its relative scarcity (an alleged dispute between producers has prevented it from thus far attaining wide release). Were it more commonly known, it's debatable whether its reputation would be so bold.

That's not to say this is a bad film. On the contrary, Kartheiser is excellent as the disaffected delinquent – renamed Ricky Cowen here – and on many occasions Filardi stays faithful to the facts, or at least accurate as per David St Clair's sometimes mistrusted 1987 book on the subject "Say You Love Satan". I was also pleasantly surprised to hear mainstream metal bands like Iron Maiden, Dio and Van Halen on the soundtrack.

The melancholic mood conspires with articulate performances and a steady, slow-burn screenplay to build a profile which finds us experiencing sympathy towards Kartheiser – even as his penchant for evil grows more apparent.

However, grislier aspects of the crime are overlooked here (Filardi shies away from the eyeball violence, or the fact that the victim had rocks rammed down his throat). The story is delivered more as a drama than a horror: at times, it feels like we're watching one of those mid-afternoon made-for-TV biographies. Overcome these minor misgivings though, and *Ricky 6* provides ample food for thought.

Rossa Venezia (2003)

Dir/Scr: Andreas Bethmann; Cast: Natalie Balini, Marianna Berucci, Sabine Ironheart

Balini returns home one afternoon to find her husband in bed with another woman. Having made mincemeat of the pair of them, she's farmed off to a tough prison – where ten years of gruelling rape and torture await. Upon her release, Balini has developed a hatred of women and sets about luring prostitutes to her old marital home for seduction and slaughter.

Bethmann has carved a name for himself over the last two decades, not only as the head honcho of the excellent X-Rated Kultvideo DVD label but as prime purveyor of German Underground Splatter Porn. Films such as *Der Todesengel* (1998) and *Prison Of Hell: K3* (2009) are typical examples of his output: cheap, shot-on-video productions bolstered by explicit sex, women-in-prison motifs and crude gore.

Rossa Venezia is his epic. He's responsible for writing, directing, editing, producing and photographing it. The "Hardcore Export" version is a sprawling 155-minute marathon, almost an hour longer than its softer "Director's Cut" variant. In its complete form, we get an abundance of graphic lesbian sex (most of the actresses look like junkies) and a disconcerting amount of vaginal violence: cunts are punished by truncheons, electrified dildos, knives and even drills.

Too much time is spent on the prison storyline, making the viewer wait for what seems like an age for the gory revenge set-pieces to transpire. In fairness, they come with agreeable regularity from that point onwards. The fucking is frequently ugly but well-shot; the gore is basic but applied with considerable gusto. Alas, Olaf Ittenbach – who's provided effects on several of Bethmann's productions – was unavailable: the inferior FX work is supplied by Tim Jonas.

It's clear that Bethmann is heavily influenced by the sleazy exploitation cinema of Jesus Franco. The first hour of the film often recalls the likes of *Women Behind Bars* (1975) in its bare interior designs, unsightly nudity and clunking pace. Once Balini is freed to kill again, a procession of sex-death vignettes bring to mind the mechanics of *She Killed In Ecstasy* (1971), albeit with precious little of that film's finesse. Not one to labour a point, Bethmann also casts Franco and wife Lina Romay as one of Balini's victim's parents. Despite their roles being little more than cameos, Romay finds time to get naked ...

This German production was lensed in and around Venice, though the locations are inconsequential to both plot and the film's cheap aesthetic.

S & M: Les Sadiques (2016)

Dir: Alex Bakshaev; Scr: Alex Bakshaev, Sarnt Utamachote; Cast: Nadine Pape, Sandra Bourdonnec, Kevin Kopacka

Runaway student Pape arrives in a snow-covered Berlin, is declined a bed for the evening by her loved-up gay friend and is almost raped by a horny barman. Fate seems kinder when photographer Bourdonnec discovers Pape dossing in a stairwell and offers her a place to stay. Fuelled by a mutual hatred of men, the girls soon embark on a relationship dictated by Bourdonnec's love of kinky sex and domination. A date night in which they lure a rentboy (Bang Viet Pham) to their apartment so the *maitresse* can guide her new protégé through asphyxiating lovers without harming them ends disastrously, only serving to intensify the bond these girls share.

All good things sour, however, and the turning point here comes when Bourdonnec orders Pape to go out and find a new male to act as their "sex toy". Though reluctant, Pape remains obedient - ultimately happening upon, and falling for, nightclub crooner Kopacka. A passionate affair ensues. But Bourdonnec is unaccustomed to not having control, and takes drastic measures to restore the equilibrium.

The greatest perk of reviewing indie cinema is getting to watch a filmmaker who's shown potential from the start, as they mature. Bakshaev is a prime example of this. From *Naked Trip* (2008), through *Bittersweet* (2009) and *The Devil Of Kreuzberg* (2015), his growth has been remarkable - a pleasure to have witnessed. *S & M* is his most accomplished film to date.

Shot without permits over several nights utilising a snowy Berlin to great effect, the major surprise is that the film's budget is estimated as being just 250 Euros. Surprising, because Bakshaev's photography is great: he captures many images beautifully (everything from wintry landscapes to decrepit buildings and streetlamps lighting up otherwise lifeless streets) while successfully exposing the city as one of anonymity. Surprising, because the cast give their all, delivering fearless and persuasive performances across the board. Look out for prolific German character actor Harry Baer in a small role as Pape's uncle too.

Though a little coy in its depiction of sadomasochistic practices, the film does explore the politics of such - the power games between participants; Kopacka's introduction to rough sex which he soon develops a taste for, just as Pape begins craving affection from him; Pape's own sexual awakening which liberates her, destroys her and prepares her for rebirth in equal measures.

With his strongest narrative to date, and a great ambient score which alternates successfully between 80s-style electronica and jazzy piano interludes, Bakshaev really impresses on every level. The film is dedicated to Jess Franco (and his frequent chronicler Robert Monell). The Franco influence is evident: lesbian leads, a vampirish quality to their nocturnal activities, minimal dialogue, stylised symbolism, a dreamlike quality to proceedings.

But Bakshaev's film literacy extends further. Expect references to Rainer Werner Fassbinder, Barbet Schroeder and Lord knows who else. Alongside generous doses of nudity and violence, of course.

Sadi-Scream
See *Sadi-Screem*

Sadi-Screem (2007)

Dir/Scr: Kanzo Matsuura; Cast: Minori Magokoro, Yoshino Terumasa, Yusaku Tayama

Matsuura has made a name for himself in recent years as the insanely prolific director of a cheap "Super Heroine" series (*Demonic Heroine In Peril* [2005]; *A Fistful Of Fuku* [2008] etc) which cheekily preys upon any fetish for curiously naïve cosplay kinkiness.

But the filmmaker has a darker side. This is clearly exhibited in the 70-minute trawl through sadistic sexual abuse and low-rent gore which is *Sadi-Screem*.

Employing the aptitudes of adult performer Magokoro – you can catch her in such delights as Sex *Tape Of My Wife* (2008) – Matsuura's thinly-plotted flick initially borrows from Daisuke Yamanouchi's *Muzan-E* (1999), before descending into a cavalcade of physical abuse and near-hardcore porn.

The demure Magokoro portrays a journalist who's alerted to a refuse collector rumoured to enjoy a side-line disposing of corpses for the local yakuza. With the help of two male assistants, Magokoro sets about obtaining an interview with her subject. He's sufficiently suspicious of her motives to request that she conducts the interview in nothing more than her underwear. Even then, her interviewee is doubtful enough to probe her more closely, searching for the microphone she's hidden inside her vagina.

Of course, this all ends quite horrifically for our trio of reporters. The men get off relatively lightly, being simply bludgeoned to death with machetes. For Magokoro, there are more transgressive terrors in store. A fingering in the anus soon becomes the least of her concerns.

Low on production values and shot with little in the way of visual flair, *Sadi-Screem* is however unexpectedly well-acted and considerately edited to boot. Should these be attributes you're looking for while consulting a film in which the lead actress gets her nipples crushed in a clamp, or is disembowelled then fucked while trying to keep her exposed intestines from spilling out of her open stomach.

Disconcertingly, the film concludes with Magokoro writhing around in what appears to be post-rape ecstasy: this may be Matsuura's way of reassuring his audience that no harm has come to his actress (unnecessary, given that the practical FX work isn't terribly convincing), but also implies her gradual acceptance and arousal at the hands of her aggressors.

Sadi-Screem was the first of five increasingly violent instalments, all obsessed with the annihilation of helpless female characters, which were spawned in 2007. The series tends to be collectively known to Western audiences as *Sadi-Scream*.

Salinui Cheuok
See *Memories Of Murder*

Satan (2006)

Dir: Kim Chapiron; Scr: Christian Chapiron, Kim Chapiron; Cast: Roxane Mesquida, Olivier Bartelemy, Vincent Cassel

Three insufferable city lads (Bartelemy, Ladj Ly and Nico Le Phat Tan) take to the town one Christmas Eve for a night of predictably obnoxious revelry. Following a ruckus outside a Parisian nightclub, they hook up with sexy Mesquida who suggests they can continue to party at her secluded farmhouse. Of course, they take the bait.

Upon arrival, they're greeted by Cassel's weird caretaker - a gurning simpleton with clear sexual designs on Bartelemy - and tales of a pact with the devil which resulted in an evil offspring being borne unto the family. Lost and far from home, the friends cast any notion of ill-foreboding to one side and continue to make merry. But for how long?

Satan starts boisterously - in a disco - and continues to assault the earlobes throughout. Shouting, screaming, raucous laughter, blaring beats, screeching car tyres, barking dogs: Chapiron's feature debut will most definitely keep viewers alert during its relatively brief running time.

Therein lies one of *Satan*'s fundamental problems. Without quiet passages, the intended later "shock" scenes never stand out as they should. Horror needs to build to have its required impact, whereas here a cartoonish excess from the first scene onwards dictates that Chapiron's maiden venture cruises on one level (fever pitch) throughout. The effect soon becomes nullifying.

On the plus side, we get impressive art design once the action is relocated to the farmhouse. The detailed decor recalls that of *The Texas Chain Saw Massacre* (1974), with the added chill of creepy dolls littered amongst its clutter. The three male protagonists exonerate themselves sufficiently considering their lack of experience in front of the camera, having previously only made a couple of shorts and music videos with Chapiron for their communal production company Kourtrajme.

Cassel, on the other hand, hams things up bizarrely as the feral stooge. Yes, dark humour is prevalent (a canny juxtaposition against Chapiron's commentary on France's classist and racial issues of the time), but ... the revered thespian proffers an outlandishly exaggerated performance. Coupled with the ghastly personalities of his visitors. it makes it difficult to fret over how events will pan out.

A great deal of *Satan*'s crude conversations revolve around sex. And yet the film is curiously coy when it comes to the depiction of the act itself. Restraint is also applied to the acts of onscreen violence. More than anything, Chapiron appears to be aspiring for "cool" status: much of the early aesthetics most closely resemble a music promo clip. The director is only semi-successful in his overall plight.

Look out for Cassel's off-screen wife Monica Bellucci in a brief but integral final-act cameo.

Satan Hates You (2010)

Dir/Scr: James Felix McKenney; Cast: Don Wood, Christine Spencer, Larry Fessenden

Alcoholic deviant Wood and promiscuous, pill-popping pregnant teen Spencer are observed by demons – led by producer Fessenden – who ultimately seek to claim their souls. On the opposing side of the moral spectrum, a pair of cheery Christians hope to sway our protagonists' inclinations towards redemption.

Illicit trysts in toilets, murder and even abortion factor into McKenney's attractively shot, fundamentally silly diversion.

The eternal conflict between good and evil as they battle to win our mortal thoughts is an ancient concept. Here, it's given a workout that exhibits all the subtlety and finesse of a cartoon. Complete with smoking jacket and sub-Jack Nicholson leer, Fessenden makes for a caricature devil. His nemesis, Godly Angus Scrimm (the iconic Tall Man from the *Phantasm* films [1979 - 2016]) is no less skittish in delivery.

Billed as an homage to "end of days" horror films of the 1970s, a trend of the era popularised by *The Exorcist* (1973) and *The Omen* (1976), *Satan Hates You* actually works best as a satire of Christian propaganda: the concept that God loves all sinners (but condemns the sin, as is true of strict Catholic schooling) is merrily bandied about between each increasingly daft set-piece scene. Though the use of evangelist speeches emanating from background TV screens throughout is a mite heavy-handed, even for a film this broadly played out.

Whether curious moviegoers are going to embrace such a message while being bombarded by scenes of rape, vomit, bloodied afterbirths and some of the most fervent overacting this side of a soap opera, is anybody's guess.

Caught somewhere between dark comedy and grindhouse tribute, *Satan Hates You* comes across as a conflicted, uneven film which never fully delivers on its initial promise. Still, cameos from horror stalwarts such as Michael Berryman, Debbie Rochon and Reggie Bannister should keep fans engaged.

Satan's Playground (2006)

Dir/Scr: Dante Tomaselli; Cast: Felissa Rose, Ellen Sandweiss, Irma St Paule

As travelling troupes go, this is an intriguing gathering: Rose (star of *Sleepaway Camp*, 1983), her partner, their autistic son, Sandweiss (*The Evil Dead*, 1981) and her baby.

What could possibly go wrong? Well, they could break down in the proximity of St Paule's remote, ramshackle home. She could wind up being the head of one of the most demented family of killers this side of *The Texas Chain Saw Massacre* (1974). And everyone could be living in fear of the fabled Jersey Devil, believed to be roaming the surrounding land with a hunger for human flesh.

Spoiler alert: things *do* go wrong.

Tomaselli is a talented director unafraid of embracing abstract narrative ploys in his pursuit of achieving "absolute" cinema: horror films that are propelled by their atmosphere and visuals, rather than a strong plot or any consistent thread of logic.

It's a brave step to take in an era where a great deal of fans seem happy to be fed formulaic swill. *Satan's Playground* has a few tricks up its sleeve to appease the more cynical viewer: a cast containing genre favourites such as Sandweiss, Rose and *Chain Saw*'s Edwin Neal; lots of considerately composed, highly atmospheric compositions; a screenplay that strives more than usual to maintain a linear path for the benefit of the lazy.

And yet, despite its many assets and the fact that Tomaselli is here working with a bigger budget than before (reportedly $1 million), there are many who hate this for its clumsily acted old-school homages and "nightmare logic" (the director's own term). Oh, and the fact that the Jersey Devil is never explicitly shown. It's a shame how expressionism, even of the modestly budgeted variety, gets dismissed so readily in these times.

For the more adventurous, *Satan's Playground* serves a keen blend of retro vibes and moderate gore. It also shows one of the current century's more interesting breakthrough genre directors gaining in both confidence and proficiency.

A cousin of filmmaker Alfred Sole, Tomaselli is – at the time of writing – attached to helming a remake of the former's 1976 stunner *Alice Sweet Alice*. Hopes are high.

Say You Love Satan
See *Ricky 6*

Schoolgirl In Cement
See *Concrete*

Screaming Dead (2003)

Dir/Scr: Brett Piper; Cast: Erin Brown, Joseph Farrell, Rachael Robbins

Sleazy fashion photographer Farrell has a penchant for the kinky. What better way to indulge this than to hire three shapely models (fronted by Brown), and entice them to a shoot at an abandoned asylum – where Farrell's preferred bondage scenarios are passed off as being part of his latest "study in terror" project? What he didn't count on was the malevolent ghost (Kevin G Shinnick) still haunting the grounds.

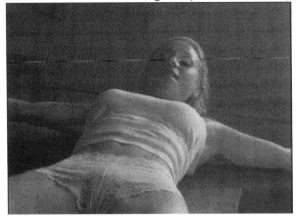

Piper's screenplay is dialogue-heavy. While this affords Farrell a degree of amusingly sexist abuse screamed in his models' directions (this baseness is accentuated further by his proclivity for spying on the girls via hidden cameras at bedtime), the abundance of otherwise non-consequential discourse results in a sluggish pace. Attempts by the director to address issues of exploitation are half-hearted, while the decision to shy away from humour prevents the viewer from siding with the cast's amateurish deliveries.

Despite being shot on location at an actual disused sanatorium in Marlboro, New Jersey, *Screaming Dead* is also curiously devoid of atmosphere. It limps along through one cheaply executed scene of tame nudity to the next. All the while we patiently await the promise of demonic possession. Admittedly, Farrell's eventual transformation into a sadistic killer becomes the unintentionally comical highpoint of the film.

The odd trice of Argentoesque lighting; the sight of Brown – best-known as her Seduction Cinema alias Misty Mundae, by which name she appears here – chained naked and covered in blood: such moments keep the film vaguely interesting on a purely visual level. Alas, the CGI of the final third is lamentable. It's a shame that Piper was coerced by producers E.I. Independent Cinema into employing digital technology, as the more simplistic Claymation effects of his earlier efforts such as *Psyclops* (2002) were far more endearing.

A more camp delivery would've perhaps demonstrated that *Screaming Dead* knew its limitations. As it stands, the film takes itself too seriously for something that ultimately offers little other than minor nudity and gore over the course of ninety long minutes.

See No Evil (2006)

Dir: Gregory Dark; Scr: Dan Madigan; Cast: Glenn Jacobs, Samantha Noble, Christina Vidal

A derelict hotel is marked out as a future shelter for the homeless and several young offenders are charged with laying down the groundwork for its conversion. Unluckily for them, the place is also the latest stomping ground for unstoppable killer Jacob Goodnight (Jacobs).

A wafer-thin premise fits neatly with the no-frills direction: this is a throwback to stalk 'n' slash teenkill movies of the 1980s, pure and simple. Sub-plots are hackneyed but serve to bolster the running time somewhat: Vidal is abducted by Jacobs, prompting an unlikely rush of loyalty among her fellow delinquents as they fight to get her back; Steven Vidler – a former lawman-turned-community service supervisor - also happens to be the cop who put a bullet in Jacobs' skull many moons earlier.

Monochrome flashbacks providing expositional details on the killer's penchant for tearing out his victims' eyes are a given (a domineering mother torturing her son into the belief that promiscuity equals evil – *again*?!). In truth, they add little to Jacobs' character ... but they do, along with some effective handheld point-of-view shots later into proceedings, allow Dark scope to flex his stylistic muscles a little.

Speaking of muscle, 7-foot behemoth Jacobs - better-known as American Wrestling star Kane – makes for a persuasively imposing villain. The script, which was written with him in mind, wisely demands little more than grunts from the man. Restricted to grimaces and scowls, he pulls of his role with presence and aplomb.

In comparison, the protagonists are little more than one-dimensional fodder. Insufficiently fleshed-out, laboured with clichéd lines of dialogue and hammered neatly into stereotypical templates, there's not one character worthy of rooting for. So, the only tension we're likely to feel is in anticipation of Jacobs' increasingly gory kills.

Shot on location in Australia over the course of 32 days, an $8 million budget (the film was co-produced by WWE) ensures two things: production design is excellent, and the violence is kept on the right side of an R-rating. The money men want their mainstream palatability.

Dark has had an interesting career. From directing his third film, the seminal adult flick *New Wave Hookers* in 1985 (infamously featuring an underage Traci Lords), followed by a slew of unusually creative porn movies – 1996's *Sex Freaks* is a highpoint – he's always displayed a keen eye for style. His progression into music videos felt natural, gaining respectability as he worked with the likes of Britney Spears and Xzibit. At the age of 49, he made this transition into "legit" filmmaking but has hardly been prolific since – his only other feature to date being 2009's poorly received *Frenemy*.

A sequel, *See No Evil 2*, followed in 2014. This was co-directed by sisters Jen and Sylvia Soska, who went some way to disproving the claims of those who'd over-rated their so-so *American Mary* (2012) that they're the saviours of modern horror.

Sei Mong Se Jun
See *Ab-Normal Beauty*

Sella Turcica (2011)

Dir: Fred Vogel; Scr: Fred Vogel, Shelby Vogel, Don Moore; Cast: Camille Keaton, Damien A Maruscak, Harvey Daniels

Military man Maruscak returns home from serving his country in Afghanistan. He's wheelchair-bound and deathly grey, but has no recollection of how he came to be in this state. As the day progresses, his family

– headed by mother Keaton – look on as he deteriorates further: black fluids ooze from random orifices; his pasty white complexion worsens; cognitive skills rapidly diminish.

What is the truth behind Maruscak's condition, and what implications will it have on his gathered family? Stay awake, if you can, and all will be revealed.

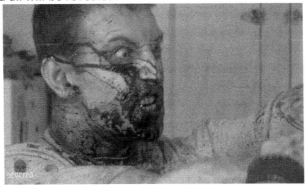

From Fred Vogel's Toetag Pictures team, who previously brought us the raw faux-snuff *August Underground* trilogy (2001-2007) and the more polished *The Redsin Tower* (2006), *Sella Turcica* is motivated by a clear anti-war message while drawing obvious influence from Bob Clark's excellent *Deathdream* (1974).

But it's dreadfully slow.

The quiet, considered build-up perhaps wouldn't be such an issue if (a) performances weren't so iffy and (b) the sound hadn't been so crappily recorded. But it's difficult to care about characters when the actors portraying them don't seem remotely invested in their script. And, even when we do get someone on the screen with a little life in them – Maruscak is decent, I'll give him that – it's a bind to have to strain your ears in a bid to decipher what's being said beneath the muffled audio.

Still, we're talking about a film shot on a Sony HDW-F900 camera for a reported $20,000.00. Keeping that in mind, *Sella Turcica* frequently looks impressive. It eventually leads to a predictably gory climax which, as you'd expect from the Toetag chaps, is very competently staged. And it's great to see Keaton (*What Have You Done To Solange?*, 1972; *I Spit On Your Grave*, 1978; etc) back working in the genre after 18 years of shunning it (since working with Vogel, she's embraced her cult status and appeared in several more micro-budget horror flicks).

But the film is too long to sustain intrigue, the actors too inexperienced to elaborate on the modestly beguiling premise. The audio problems really do detract from any tension being aimed at, especially when Marucsak's condition degenerates further and his monologues become grating illegible drawls.

And, in a film whose tone suggests it wants us to buy into the reality of the situation, the lapses in logic are fatal. For example, no-one thinks to ring the emergency services as Marucsak all-but dies in front of them. The closest we get is towards the end, a little late in the day methinks, when the family half-heartedly call their doctor … but get through to his answer machine. Do they then try another number – like, call for an ambulance, perhaps? No. *Why would they?*

Senseless (2008)

Dir/Scr: Simon Hynd; Cast: Jason Behr, Emma Catherwood, Joe Ferrara

Based on Stona Fitch's 2001 novel of the same name, *Senseless* opens with arrogant American tradesman Behr's abduction upon exiting a business meeting in Glasgow.

He wakes in a plain white room. A bed sits in one corner; a CCTV camera hangs from another. The only other furnishing is a sole chair. Shades of *Oldboy* (2003) as Behr, unaware of why he's being held captive or who by, whiles his time away exercising. Eventually masked antagonist Ferrara enters, explaining that Behr is now the star of a reality show in which viewers can watch his torture online. His assailants plot to remove each of his senses one by one over the course of several weeks. Behr's only hope is that his audience halt the brutality by pledging sufficiently towards his captors' fundraising appeal.

The simplistic production design and minimal exposition do little to assuage initial fears that *Senseless* is dragging us back into torture porn territory. But there's more to this Glasgow-based production than meets the eye.

There's an enjoyable irony to be had in the fact that Behr made his name as a star on US television, in programmes like "Dawson's Creek" (1998-1999) and "Roswell High" (1999-2002), before winding up here as the main attraction of an altogether different – though no more tortuous – small-screen show. It's perhaps a shame that his character is too flawed, too brutally corporate, to root for.

Predictably his priorities do change somewhat as his suffering intensifies. Meanwhile Ferrara comes to revel in his position as host of the show: Hynd is afforded ample scope to comment on the anonymity allowed by the Internet, and our complicity as voyeurs in seeking out vicarious thrills via online clips.

Though quite bloodthirsty as it progresses, *Senseless* is more interesting when viewed as a commentary on the above and more. Reality TV is an easy target, and one which has also provided the inspiration for other modern horrors such as *My Little Eye* (2002), *Saw 2* (2005) etc.

Behr represents American Globalisation and the consumer culture it's heralded in with it. His aggressors are fitted with symbolic foreign accents (broken English, indistinct in terms of origin): allusions to conflicts of recent years – the threat of Eastern terrorism which looms large over capitalist Western countries post-911 - are clear from the start. The proceeding torture footage seems all the more prescient nowadays given the regularity of prisoners' executions broadcast as propaganda by outfits such as ISIS.

Ironically the film was distributed on UK DVD by a company called ISIS Ltd ...

Session 9 (2001)

Dir: Brad Anderson; Scr: Brad Anderson, Stephen Gevedon; Cast: David Caruso, Peter Mullan, Josh Lucas

An asbestos abatement team enter into a disused asylum where they intend to work their magic, casting aside any personal differences they may have while doing so. Extramarital affairs, the pressures of newly appointed parenthood and the discovery of riches hidden behind a wall of the hospital: all matters which factor into our all-male protagonists' reactions once one of their group, a would-be lawyer (Gevedon), unearths the tape-recordings of a former patient's interview sessions. An apparent victim of dissociative identity disorder, the voice on the tape has multiple personalities – including, significantly, that of a child called Simon. As the killings begin, Anderson's ambiguous direction asks: are they the work of demonic possession, or a hidden mental illness within the crew?

There are many things to recommend when considering *Session 9*. It's unhurried pace and insidious atmosphere, ably sustaining an aura of suspense that never lets up. A reliance on strong performances and astute characterisation, both of which strike a deeper chord as the tourniquet of fear tightens around our necks. A plot with enough subtleties to ensure it's open to interpretation, eliciting joyous post-viewing debates.

For all that Caruso, Mullan, Larry Fessenden et al effectively get beneath our skin by acting their socks off, the character of greatest impact is most certainly the location itself. Anderson based the entire concept around Danvers State Hospital in Massachusetts, which he would drive past daily while travelling to an earlier day job. It's a formidable presence – also used as a partial setting for the 1958 Jean Simmons vehicle *Home Before Dark* – filled with dark, foreboding corridors, ominous shadows looming large across its eerily barren rooms, and dank decaying décor. Despite having limited access to its splendour due to structural damage rendering most of its interiors as unsafe, Anderson gains ample mileage from the building.

Perhaps a little too vague at times for its own good (Anderson isn't overly concerned by filling out plot holes or explaining passing overheard conversations), *Session 9* still succeeds in overcoming its proto-HD aesthetics and providing some solid cerebral spooks.

Anderson went on to direct the likes of *The Machinist* (2004) and *Transsiberian* (2008), before returning to sinister madhouse territory with 2014's star-studded *Stonehearst Asylum*. He's yet to produce anything that convinces as menacingly as *Session 9*.

Shadow Of The Vampire (2000)

Dir: E Elias Merhige; Scr: Steven Katz; Cast: Willem Dafoe, John Malkovich, Udo Kier

What if Max Schreck, the actor who portrayed the monster in F W Murnau's seminal *Nosferatu: A Symphony Of Horror* (1922), really was a vampire?

That's the bold conceit of Merhige's arty film, his first feature in a decade following on from the disturbing, surreal masterpiece *Begotten* (1990). Here, he adopts a far more accessible filmic style – on the surface, at least – while attempting to explain certain tragedies that befell the shoot of Murnau's take on Bram Stoker's "Dracula" novel, and create a new myth.

In a role apparently written with him in mind, Dafoe excels as Schreck: the thespian of mysterious background who becomes increasingly immersed in his performance as Count Orlock (Murnau and co were prohibited from using the "Dracula" name by members of Stoker's estate). It's not just that his rakish appearance, awkward posturing and gaunt features suit the character so well, nor that the similarities are alarming once Dafoe's head has been shaven. The actor carries his performance with equal degrees of wide-eyed menace and sly humour. His body language is deliberate and coiled, like an animal furtively preparing to strike upon its prey.

Malkovich convinces as Murnau. He's a monster of a different kind; determined to get his film made, against all odds and irrespective of who gets hurt along the way. His one stipulation is that Dafoe mustn't kill his leading lady, Catherine McCormack, until filming has been completed.

Whereas *Begotten* was experimental, extreme and often incomprehensible, *Shadow Of The Vampire* finds sometime music video director Merhige having fun within the confines of a "studio picture". Kier and co-star Cary Elwes return to the arena of bloodsucking cinema, having previously appeared in *Blood For Dracula* (1974) and *Bram Stoker's Dracula* (1992) respectively. Music from John Williams' score for John Badham's acclaimed *Dracula* (1979) can be heard at various points throughout.

Sheitan
See *Satan*

Shin Akai Misshitsu (Heya): Kowareta Ningyo-Tachi
See *Red Room 2*

Sileni
See *Lunacy*

The Sins Of Dracula (2014)

Dir/Scr: Richard Griffin; Cast: Michael Thurber, Jamie Dufault, Sarah Nicklin

Devout churchgoer and choirboy Dufault is encouraged by girlfriend Nicklin to join in with her at the local amateur dramatics society. The troupe comprises of an array of social misfits, all of whom seem to have been put on God's Earth for the sole purpose of antagonising Dufault: the flirtatious gay, the promiscuous slut etc. Collectively, they're oblivious to the fact that the guy running their show (Steven O'Broin) is in allegiance with the Prince of Darkness himself (Thurber). It's all simply a ploy, apparently, to get some sinful blood into the Count in a bid to resurrect him – anticipating his bid for World domination.

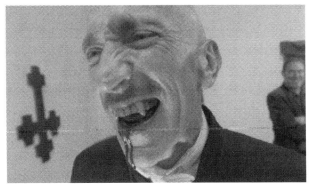

Griffin is a modern filmmaker of some note. Not only is he hugely prolific (over twenty feature efforts under his belt since 2000) but he's proven time and again how he can make an attractive, well-oiled film on a budget. Plus, his balancing act between the knowingly camp and respectfully retro never fails to appeal – check out the likes of *Nun Of That* (2008), *The Disco Exorcist* (2011) and *Frankenstein's Hungry Dead* (2013) for proof.

The Sins Of Dracula isn't one of his best films (perhaps the aforementioned *Exorcist* takes that honour, or the same year's more sober *Exhumed*). But it's still a lot of fun.

Griffin has his regulars, among which are Dufault and the ever-reliable Thurber. A sense of the theatre is enjoyably evident in their energetic performances, the one-liners of Griffin's script successfully treading a fine line between smart and stupid in such capable hands.

Tone, pacing and visuals are other things Griffin doesn't have to worry about - he makes their slick execution seem effortless. But it's this adeptness that also frustrates: Griffin makes quick, micro-budgeted films very well but just think of what he could achieve if he took more time on a project. Perhaps his set-piece scenes would resonate further, as the mild violence and coy sex of *Dracula* left this viewer wanting.

Skinned Deep (2004)

Dir/Scr: Gabriel Bartalos; Cast: Jason Dugre, Warwick Davis, Kurt Carley

A family suffers a puncture while driving through a rural part of America. Calling at the nearest house hoping to use the owner's telephone, they happen upon the strangest brood of psychopaths imaginable. Among the antagonists are plate-throwing speedball Davis and the appropriately named Brain (Dugre), who sports an enormous exposed thinkbox.

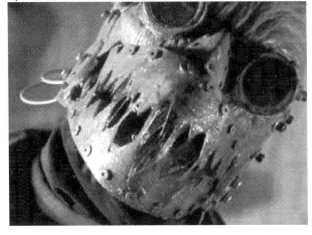

The premise may initially resemble that of *The Texas Chain Saw Massacre* (1974). But throw in a gang of violent bikers, an elderly nutcase with a bad case of the shakes (Allen Richard) and oodles of gore, and you have one uniquely deranged flick on your hands.

Bartalos has been servicing the genre since the mid 1980s as a special make-up effects artist. In particular, he's worked on several of Frank Henenlotter's deranged masterpieces including *Brain Damage* (1988), *Frankenhooker* (1990) and *Bad Biology* (2008) – he also acted as executive producer on the latter. *Skinned Deep* marks his directorial debut and, naturally, his own Atlantic West Effects studio handle the FX.

Resultantly a great deal of the effects have that familiar punkish, rubbery quality to them – not to mention, they're often cartoonish in their grisliness too.

Having previously directed a music video for veteran punk band The Damned, it's little surprise that their bassist and sometime solo artist Captain Sensible contributes to the wacky soundtrack. Another name of note is "Famous Monsters of Filmland" founder Forrest J Ackerman, who appears in a minor role.

The film is bookended by two striking sequences: it opens to the image of unsimulated scarification, and climaxes with one actress screaming repeatedly over the end credits.

None of it makes much sense. Who cares? If you like your horror laced with comedy, bad acting and an absurd amount of energy, then *Skinned Deep* should pique your interest. If you also have a taste for the surreal, then this is definitely for you.

If anything, Bartalos' second directorial feature, 2013's *Saint Bernard*, was even stranger.

Slagt Mig Nogen
See *Slaughter Me Naked*

Slaughter Me Naked (2015)

Dir/Scr: Sune Rolf Jensen; Cast: Dominik Metzger, Sune Rolf Jensen, Kasper Juhl

A masked killer (Metzger) stalks the streets, bedsits and bedrooms of Denmark, butchering his slacker quarries without remorse. His seemingly random motives are given a semblance of reason later into proceedings, as we gain some insight into his tortured background.

Jensen filmed his provocatively-titled feature debut for just 5,000 Danish Kroner (around £627). Though shot in HD, its aesthetic values are often extremely low-rent. The generally dark photography and grainy finish make things appear as though this was made on video in the late 1980s or early 1990s for the most part. This aura of cut-price filmmaking extends to the primitive practical effects work and some decidedly amateur-hour performances during the first third.

None of which prevents *Slaughter Me Naked* from being a highly enjoyable way of wasting 65 minutes.

Divided into several chapters, each one is effectively little more than a set-piece serving up a short passage of build-up before culminating in scenes of gialloesque nudity and gore. Metzger wears black gloves and a white faceless mask while conducting his attacks, echoing Mario Bava's seminal *Blood And Black Lace* (1964).

The violence is mainly of the blade-in-the-dark variety during the first couple of chapters. Appearing to have been shot in chronological order, the film becomes both more efficient and ambitious as it progresses. Jensen surprises on occasion with unexpected moments of nastiness such a bathroom-based rape scene, and a prolonged home invasion segment which wallows in its victims' grieving a little too convincingly. This intense 16-minute sequence - which could also be known as "the worst birthday party ever" - suggests that, given better resources, Jensen could be capable of producing something very potent indeed.

Look out for the director-writer-editor-producer-cinematographer himself enjoying a cameo as a struggling artist, and also fellow indie filmmaker Kasper Juhl as one victim lucky enough to enjoy sex with a hot blonde just moments before receiving his comeuppance.

Slither (2006)

Dir/Scr: James Gunn; Cast: Nathan Fillion, Elizabeth Banks, Michael Rooker

A meteorite crash-lands on the outskirts of a small American town. Rooker is first to stumble across the fallout, instantly finding himself infected by a worm-like alien parasite as a result.

He initially shrugs off the beginnings of a visible mutation as being "a bee sting", but wife Banks swiftly suspects something far more sinister is afoot. She enlists the help of local sheriff Fillion: soon, they have widespread chaos on their hands as Rooker embarks on a mission to contaminate, impregnate or devour everyone in sight.

Slither marries the camp action of colourful B-movie classics like *The Blob* (1958) with the gleeful gore FX of 80s flicks comparable to, well, *The Blob* remake (1988). That it does so with true wit is what makes it so infectiously entertaining.

Gunn wears his influences on his sleeve throughout. On paper the plot bears resemblance to *Night Of The Creeps* (1986). The plentiful visual references include nods to monster movies such as *The Thing* (1982) and *Tremors* (1990). Homage is paid to Jacques Tourneur, Stephen King and Frank Henenlotter (whose *Brain Damage* [1988] can be viewed as another source of stimulus). These tributes come in the form of local character names. In a nod to the director's days spent working for Troma Studios in the 1990s, *The Toxic Avenger* (1984) can be seen playing on a television at one point.

The unrelenting pace stops only to allow for regular bouts of satisfyingly gooey creature effects – a successful blend of foam latex, animatronics and CGI – and rapid-fire one-liners like "If I weren't about to shit my pants right now, I'd be fascinated". Gunn's cast nail the pulpy tone; Fillion in particular delivers each of his lines with caustic glee.

From writing and producing the irreverent *Tromeo And Juliet* (1996) through penning the screenplays for mainstream hits *Scooby-Doo* (2002) and the *Dawn Of The Dead* remake (2004), to writing and directing the tongue-in-cheek Hollywood blockbuster *Guardians Of The Galaxy* (2014), Gunn's career has been a curious and interesting one. And he's remained a nice chap during the journey, so it's great to see him achieve such deserved success.

Snowtown (2011)

Dir: Justin Kurzel; Scr: Shaun Grant, Justin Kurzel; Cast: Lucas Pittaway, Daniel Henshall, Louise Harris

On May 20th 1999, the Australian authorities made public a most gruesome discovery: the remains of several bodies, found in barrels of acid located in Snowtown, almost a hundred miles north of Adelaide - where most had been killed some time beforehand. A lengthy trial ensued, eventually ruling that John Bunting was responsible for eleven murders (a twelfth remains unproven due to a lack of forensic evidence) along with the young accomplices he'd roped in to helping him.

Kurzel's startling feature debut examines Bunting's arrival and influence in an impoverished northern suburb of Adelaide. Portrayed with equal parts charm and venom by the extraordinary Henshall, he ingratiates himself into the life and home of single mother Harris and becomes an unconventional father figure to her downtrodden teenaged son Pittaway. In no time, his bigotry is rubbing off on the lad and he's encouraging him to assist with the casual brutalisation of local gays and paedophiles.

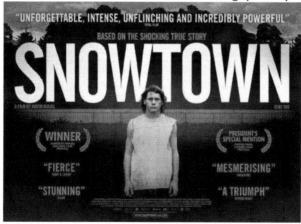

Henshall spent six weeks living in the same community in a bid to get a feel for his character. Kurzel interviewed dozens of neighbours from the era, along with extensively researching definitive books like Debi Marshall's "Killing for Pleasure" and Andrew McGarry's "The Snowtown Murders". Such punctilious preparation has paid off: *Snowtown* feels terribly authentic.

From its on-location setting to the use of mainly non-professional actors who give astoundingly naturalistic performances across the board, the level of low-key realism achieved is nothing short of remarkable. And, given the nature of the story being told, harrowing.

In fact, if anything goes against the excellent *Snowtown* - more so than the mumbled script or loose manner in which characters are introduced to proceedings - it's its unrelentingly bleak tone. The film wallows in misery (poverty, child abuse, rape) from the very start, right up until its ominous final scene. From the dead-eyed boredom of its chain-smoking characters to the oppressively dull colour palettes, there is no respite: Kurzel's commitment to demonstrating the hopelessness of living in evil's shadow is formidable, but will undoubtedly alienate some.

Though never needlessly graphic, there is one standout sequence of bathroom-based torture which will stay with you for days afterwards. Such is its cruel, flawlessly acted intensity.

Much darker and more affecting than 2010's ostensibly similar *Animal Kingdom* (another Oz crime flick), *Snowtown* went on to win several prizes at the Australian Academy of Cinema and Television Arts Awards ceremony, held at Sydney Opera House and designed to honour "outstanding achievements" in the Australian arts. The Academy has good taste.

The Snowtown Murders
See *Snowtown*

Snuff 102 (2007)

Dir/Scr: Mariano Peralta; Cast: Yamila Greco, Silvia Paz, Eduardo Poli

Echoes of *Hardcore* (1979), *Thesis* (1996) and *8mm* (1999) abound as journalist Greco – inspired by a serial killer case she's just covered –delves deeper into the nature of violent fetishism by negotiating the world of extreme online pornography.

This leads to her requesting an interview with film critic Poli. Unluckily, he's a sadistic butcher himself … Greco now finds herself intended as his next victim (victim number 102, in fact). The remainder of the film largely alternates between segments of their interview, philosophising over what draws people to view such violent imagery, and footage of the journalist held at Poli's whim with two other hapless abductees – visibly pregnant 100 (Andrea Alfonso) and 101 (Paz).

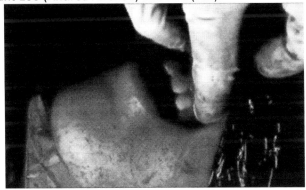

Snuff 102 is a slow film populated by an unpredicted amount of dialogue, much of which aspires to examine the nature of visceral thrill-seeking. One of the film's taglines is "why be moral … if we can remain anonymous?": it's a fitting summation of the themes Peralta is addressing. Morality, the irresponsible sensationalism of modern media, pornography, our inert hunger for violence. *Snuff 102* takes a stab at commenting on all of these issues.

Such conscientious allusions are somewhat belittled by the penchant for graphic violence. Along with early genuine footage of a Mosul beheading conducted by the Iraqi insurgent group known as Jamaat Ansar al-Sunnah, monkey experimentation horror and a pig being slaughtered, the convincingly simulated terror also includes an unforgettable moment of horrendous dental torture. Ouch.

This Argentinean thriller premiered at its home country's Mar Del Plata Film Festival, where it's reported that Peralta was assaulted by an irate audience member. The offending scene concerned the brutalisation of victim 100: she's punched repeatedly, choked with a plastic bag over her head, has her swollen belly stomped on numerous times, several fingers chopped off and is pissed on. This all occurs long before her aggressor gets round to killing her.

Contrary to popular misconception, however, this isn't another "faux snuff" film. It's a cleverly edited, multi-camera affair with a challenging narrative and a plot that does reach a credible conclusion (though some have bemoaned the non-downbeat outcome).

The physical abuse witnessed is horrific, obviously, but Peralta is clever enough to employ grain, dimly-lit sets and slick cutaways which result in a degree of the atrocities being suggested rather than overtly shown. Still, the average viewer will consider this a rough ride.

At the time of writing, Peralta has a sequel in development: *Snuff 102.2*.

Snuff Killer – La Morte In Diretta
See *Snuff Trap*

Snuff-Movie (2005)

Dir/Scr: Bernard Rose; Cast: Jeroen Krabbe, Lisa Enos, Terri Harrison

Horror director Krabbe's heavily pregnant wife was one of several people slaughtered during a home invasion by crazed cultists in the 1960s. Since then, he's developed an ever-more reclusive approach towards both life and filmmaking. Stepping out from his own shadow, he determines to make new art – but on his terms. Auditions are undertaken in clandestine fashion, the successful applicants being at the mercy of Krabbe's remote home and a surreal filming style which blurs art with reality.

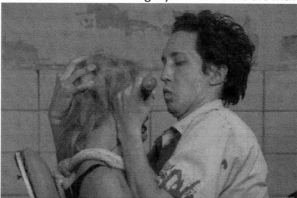

Rose made two of the most satisfying, cerebral horror films in recent memory – *Paperhouse* (1988) and *Candyman* (1992). Both beg the viewer to look further than their spooky surfaces and discover a multi-layered festival of troubled characters, deep-rooted personal anxieties and a cultured delimitation of the nature of modern myth-telling.

How does the British auteur go one further? Well, with *Snuff-Movie* the answer is to extend a treatise on the manner in which the camera manipulates the facts. As such, we're thrown into a film-within-a-film-within-a-film situation where reality and fiction are often impossible to distinguish from one another, and cast members perform multiple roles as the viewer is thrown deeper into Rose's self-conscious rabbit hole.

Those expecting a faux snuff flick, or even some cheap shot-on-video excuse for violence a la *August Underground* (2001) can forget it. The film does serve up its share of gore and nudity (thanks, Ms Enos), but Rose is more preoccupied with addressing the manipulative superficiality of horror cinema – and the media in general - by exploring various styles (Hammer-esque monster pictures; post-modern internet safety phobias etc) and smugly parading their absurdities before his camera. Cue patently fake cadavers, overblown death performances, ketchup used for blood and so on.

There are a host of self-referential genre films out there: *Fright Night* (1985), *Scream* (1996), *Funny Games* (1997) etc. *Snuff-Movie* is laughable in its repeated attempts at saying something "worthy". The effect is also nullifying, constantly distancing us from any sense of emotional involvement.

Krabbe stands head and shoulders above a largely mediocre cast, serving up a chilling performance of persuasive intensity. Everyone else is wooden and failing in impact. Ironically though, come the final act's anticipated revelation, this may well be the case of Rose hammering his point home.

Snuff Trap (2003)

Dir: Bruno Mattei; Scr: Bruno Mattei, Giovanni Paolucci; Cast: Carla Solaro, Anita Auer, Federica Garuti

Mattei began his film career in the 1950s working as an editor for the likes of Jesus Franco. Graduating to directing his own features in the early 1970s, he remained insanely prolific throughout the next four decades. Despite a reputation for technical ineptitude, poor production values and bulking films out with ill-fitting stock footage, his oeuvre has retained a cult appeal in terms of sheer entertainment. If nothing else, Mattei was willing to try his hand at all manner of exploitation cinema: shockumentary (*Mondo Erotico* [1973]), Nazisploitation (*SS Girls* [1977]), living dead horrors (*Zombie Creeping Flesh* [1980]), Nunsploitation (*The Other Hell* [1981]), women-in-prison films (*Women's Prison Massacre* [1983]), erotic thrillers (*Dangerous Attraction* [1993]) … he covered the lot, usually working under any of several regular pseudonyms.

Here, he tackles the thorny subject matter of the snuff movie while directing as Pierre Le Blanc.

In what amounts to little more than a thinly-veiled take on Joel Schumacher's *8mm* (1999), the plot follows politician's wife Solaro as she traverses the seedy underbelly of Europe in search of kidnapped stepdaughter Garuti. With reason to believe an underground porn ring have the girl in their clutches, Solaro shows considerable resolve as she throws herself into prostitution in a bid to get closer to the truth: fellating one contact, taking a good hiding to prove her readiness for sadomasochism … *this* is commitment to the cause.

All of which leads her to the preposterously entertaining Auer, hamming things up marvellously as the cartoon villain Dr Hades.

En route, we get a great deal of the anticipated travelogue footage – Mattei making full use of his Hamburg, Paris and Amsterdam locations for padding purposes. If you're looking for sleaze (you're reading this review: the likelihood is you are) you may be disappointed. While there is sex and minor gore – the baddies are creating snuff films for wealthy clients, after all – it's all relatively tepid in terms of this traditionally troublesome sub-genre.

Still, the upbeat conclusion is satisfyingly daft and the shot-on-video aesthetics lend events a fortuitous air of menace.

Mattei was diagnosed as having a brain tumour in 2007. He underwent surgery to remove it but, following complications, fell into a coma and never recovered. He died aged 75.

Spaceship Terror (2011)

Dir/Scr: Harry Tchinski; Cast: Kristen Springer, Jay Wesley Cochran, Lacey Blair

A group of decidedly unglamorous female astronauts and their male commander crash-land on a remote planet, the latter suffering severe injuries in the collision. Their distress signal is soon answered by a freighter ship. Once boarding, however, they discover that they are at the mercy of its pilot - sadistic killer Cochran. His idea of fun is a game in which he smears the ship's walls with a number written in the blood of each victim. The last remaining "contestant" is given the chance to key these numbers into a computer. If they guess the sequence correctly, they gain access to an escape pod and leave with their life intact. If not, they too are to be tortured and slain.

The fact that Cochran's character is called Captain Terror and, in his bloody apron, looks like a reject from *Hostel* (2005) may suggest low expectations are wise. On the contrary, *Spaceship Terror* - abysmal title aside - has more to recommend it than you may think.

Interior set design is impressive in its detail, the grimy corridors and dingy medical bay that acts as a "safe zone" for the women being authentically claustrophobic. Dialogue allows for each character to be fleshed out more than is usual for this type of fare, while the space setting adds a fresh slant to the traditional slasher/torture porn approach.

Practical effects are generally good. One character has her nipple bitten off; another is electrocuted while naked. Legs are amputated without anaesthetic. The impact of such scenes is heightened by Eric Brindenbaker's moody score and a strong HD aesthetic.

However. Performances are inconsistent, with only Springer really convincing as one of Cochran's prey. The reported $200,000.00 budget can't overcome the shoddy CGI employed towards laughable exterior shots. And there's no denying that the plot - which goes so far as to have Cochran riddle his ship with booby traps - seems overly keen on reminding its viewer of the *Saw* franchise (2004-2010).

Splinter (2008)

Dir: Toby Wilkins; Scr: Ian Shorr, Kai Barry; Cast: Jill Wagner, Paulo Costanzo, Shea Whigham

A romantic break in the Oklahoma hills turns into a nightmare for Wagner and Costanzo. It's bad enough that they're accosted by on-the-run criminal Whigham and his junkie girlfriend (Rachel Kerbs). What's worse is when their car runs over a splinter parasite, a mould-based organism hungry for blood and capable of absorbing the corpses of its victims – thus transforming them into lethal hosts. Holing up in the nearest petrol station, the four mismatched protagonists prepare themselves for one very long night …

The siege scenario immediately brings to mind *Night Of The Living Dead* (1968). An alien creature that takes hold of its human hosts and mutates them into deadly monsters? You must be thinking of *The Thing* (1982) too, surely. In fact – from the scene where one character's arm is amputated in an attempt at stopping the splinter infection from spreading (hello, *Day Of The* Dead [1985]) to a predictably flame-engulfed finale (how countless horror movies used to end, before the arse felt out of decently-budgeted filmmaking) – *Splinter* doesn't score highly on points of originality.

Instead, Wilkins' feature debut (following several comedic shorts) focuses on a no-frills drive that lends events the enjoyable pulp vibe of a B-movie. Characters are mechanical – though, conveniently for the plot, Costanzo is cast as a biology graduate – and it hardly matters: this is all about the monster.

The decision to pare back on CGI and use practical effects where possible instead is something I applaud Wilkins for. We know we're in good hands, given his prolific experience as a visual effects artist, and his supervisory role in that department here. Quite why, though, *Splinter* had to adopt such quick-fire editing and shaky camerawork during its set-piece gore scenes, I don't know. Actually, I can guess: to disguise any shortcomings in this modestly budgeted sleeper's FX work. The results are highly irritating.

Still, that gripe aside, *Splinter* offers an undemanding flab-free evening's entertainment. The final-frame twist is perhaps one cliché too far, but by then the film has you on side.

Starry Eyes (2014)

Dir/Scr: Kevin Kolsch, Dennis Widmyer; Cast: Alexandra Essoe, Amanda Fuller, Fabianne Therese

A waitress by day, Essoe dreams of making it in Hollywood. A bizarre audition for a role in a new horror film – "The Silver Scream" – leads to that all-important call-back. Ditching her day job in preparation for her second meeting with the casting directors, Essoe plunges headlong into a nightmare of increasingly challenging screen tests, mental instability and surreal violence.

Kolsch and Widmyer attack the Hollywood system while asking their audience "how far would *you* go to realise your dreams?" before crossing over into soul-selling territory akin to *Faust* (1926) during the film's final moments. Along the way, Essoe's troubled starlet begs success in a physically gruelling, psychologically demanding manner recalling Natalie Portman's turn in *Black Swan* (2010).

Much like in that film, *Starry Eyes* also asserts the consummate performer's ability to metamorphose into an alternative identity: in a word, the film is about transformation.

Essoe is to this film what Angela Bettis was to *May* (2002) and Jocelin Donahue was to *The House Of The Devil* (2009): a relative unknown announcing her talent to the genre, proffering a performance so assured, so multi-faceted (vulnerable; sexy; resilient; true) that it's impossible to imagine anyone else delivering the role so well.

The shame here is that the supporting players don't make much impression. Louis Dezseran is underused as a persuasively lecherous movie producer. Essoe's pals, meanwhile – including sincere Fuller and catty Therese – do little more than pose by a pool behaving like faceless hipsters.

Come the inevitably blood-soaked climax (a disappointingly unimaginative final act, given the intriguing first hour), you realise you don't care if these people fall victim to Essoe's stab-happy delirium.

Yet another successful Kickstarter story, *Starry Eyes* was fortunate enough to have DVD distributors Dark Sky Films on board as co-producers and 'Fight Club' author Chuck Palahniuk as a link when it came to online sponsors (Widmyer runs the writer's official website).

Stitches (2012)

Dir: Conor McMahon; Scr: Conor McMahon, David O'Brien; Cast: Ross Noble, Tommy Knight, Gemma-Leah Devereux

Noble is the titular children's entertainer, who finds himself up against a tough crowd when performing at young Tommy's tenth birthday party. The kids are suitably unimpressed with his old-hat routine and decide to play a prank on Stitches. Tying the clown's shoelaces together, Tommy is left traumatised when his trick takes a tragic turn.

Several years later, and Tommy has grown into the likeable Knight. His mother is out of town for his latest birthday and so his pals coerce him into hosting a house party. A load of teens gather to drink, get high and get screwed. What better time for Stitches to return from the grave and claim his revenge against Knight and co?

So, the story is not only wafer-thin but also incapable of holding up against even fleeting scrutiny. It's hardly original and there are few surprises to be had along the way. The teen characters are largely stereotypical types: the jittery lead, the decent-hearted love interest (Devereux), the impish fat kid, the slut etc.

However. *Stitches* has quite a few things working in its favour. For one, the kids actually look their ages (not the usual thirty-year-olds-playing-teenagers that we used to get in 80s slashers). They're also a likeable bunch. Then there's the gore. Aoife Noonan and Ben O'Connor rely mainly on practical effects for their set-piece grisliness, and deliver the goods in the form of splashy decapitations, dismemberments, stabbings and more. There are only a couple of instances of unconvincing CGI that let the side down.

The icing on the cake is Noble. The Geordie stand-up comedian is renowned for his surreal, largely improvised shows. Here, he sticks to a script while managing to expand on its lame humour by virtue of body language and facial expressions. He's even able to make the dumb Freddy-esque one-liners, which accompany each murder, work.

Funny, gory and unabashedly catering for the post-pub crowd, *Stitches* provides solid, unchallenging entertainment.

Stockholm Syndrome (2008)

Dir: Ryan Cavalline; Scr: Ryan Cavalline, Jason Senior; Cast: Jason Senior, Lisa Marano, Eddie Benevich

The trade of human trafficking comes under the spotlight in this no-budget cousin of Eli Roth's *Hostel* (2005).

It focuses on an underground organization concerned with kidnapping nubile young fillies. They imprison their captives and subject them to forms of torture so brutal that they've been transformed into subservient slaves by the time they are sold on.

Now, let's refer to Wikipedia (!) for a nicely bite-sized reminder as to what "Stockholm Syndrome" actually is: "a psychological phenomenon ... in which hostages express empathy and sympathy, and have positive feelings towards their captors, sometimes to the point of defending and identifying with (them)". You know you're in trouble when the filmmakers don't even understand the title of their own movie.

That incongruity aside, it has to be said that none of *Stockholm Syndrome* appears to have been very well thought-through. Why, for example, would a crime syndicate batter their prisoners so severely – to death in some cases – when they are, in fact, theirs to sell on?

Devoid of characterisation, scrimping on production values and ridiculously light on plot (I'm being generous, before you ask "what plot?"), *Stockholm Syndrome* also suffers from video-quality visuals and terminally inconsistent audio.

The most forgiving gorehounds may find some thrills to be had in the unconvincing staging of delights such as blowtorch torture and a forced abortion. We have "Frank Effects" to thank for realising such delights. For some unknown reason, one of the syndicate's clients is a deranged priest (Todd Proesl) who likes to cleanse his female victims by ramming a homemade sex toy of deadly persuasion where the sun never shines. Inevitably, *Stockholm Syndrome* throws in a healthy amount of gratuitous nudity, ensuring all exploitative boxes are ticked.

Other films from Cavalline include *Dead Body Man* (2004), *House Of Carnage* (2006) and *Day Of The Ax* (2007). As you can probably deduce from their titles alone, they're all extremely cheap exercises in gore.

Not to be confused with CJ Schmidt's film of the same name, which was also made in 2008.

The Strangers (2008)

Dir/Scr: Bryan Bertino; Cast: Liv Tyler, Scott Speedman, Gemma Ward

Speedman takes Tyler to his father's isolated summer home overnight. They're retiring there following on from a party they've attended, where his marriage proposal didn't go as planned. The night begins with Tyler accounting for her lack of readiness and develops to a stage where the couple are starting to make inroads towards emotional reconnection.

But then comes a knock at the door. Speedman turns Ward away, insisting that the person she's asking for doesn't live there. However, Ward and her two pals - Kip Weeks and Laura Margolis - are not about to call things a night.

And so begins a long night ahead for our confused protagonists. Bertino's directorial debut enters 'home invasion' territory a la *In Cold Blood* (1967) and *Funny Games* (1997). Inevitably, due to the timing of its release and some remarkable plot similarities, the film was also likened to French-Romanian hoodie horror *Them* (2006). It carries that familiar whiff of right-wing scare tactics about it (beware the random violence of today's vile youth!).

Away from such comparisons, *The Strangers* profits from a strong opening act in which its lead characters are unexpectedly well-drawn and an intriguing scenario is proffered. Though many of the final hour's frights are effectively staged, it remains true that the film becomes less interesting the moment Ward hammers on the front door.

Why? Because from this point onwards little of what unfurls is credible. If you were reconciling with your loved one and a stranger started pounding ominously on your door at 4am, would you answer their call? Further decisions of a dubious nature plague our protagonists (choosing to canvas the house separately is never wise, for example). These incidences undermine Bertino's otherwise competently-staged frissons.

In some respects the film harks back to early Wes Craven classics *The Last House On The Left* (1972) and *The Hills Have Eyes* (1977): the setting clearly strives to evoke the 1970s; the late Craven was a champion of "Hell-comes-to-your-house" terrors; as is the case here, he also had his everyman leads forced to tap into their primal instincts in a bid to outfight their comparatively feral aggressors.

Tyler and Speedman are strong and likeable in their roles. The kids behind the masks, devoid of background or personality (we never even fully see their faces), are reliably unapologetic. The most haunting moment of the film comes when Tyler asks them why they are tormenting her so, to which Ward replies "because you were home".

Similarities to finer details of the notorious Keddie Resort murders which took place in California, in April 1981, abound during the film's final act. Despite this, Bertino maintains that the concept stems from an experience he encountered as a youth, where a would-be burglar scouted his neighbourhood knocking on doors - including the director's family home - asking for someone who didn't reside there.

Survival Of The Dead (2009)

Dir/Scr: George A Romero; Cast: Alan Van Sprang, Richard Fitzpatrick, Kenneth Welsh

A sixth 'Dead' film from Mr Romero, *Survival* is based several weeks after the events of 2007's *Diary Of The Dead* and holds the distinction of being the first in the series to carry a character (Van Sprang's) over from its predecessor.

It tells of a small platoon of surviving National Guardsmen – led by Van Sprang - who answer a broadcast invitation to start a new life on the promised safe-haven of Plum Island. However it transpires that the Island, unofficially governed by misguided zombie conservationist Fitzpatrick, is infested with the hungry undead. Of course.

The ensuing violence serves as a backdrop to a central plot involving an ongoing dispute between Fitzpatrick and rival neighbour Welsh, both of whom have conflicting ideas on how best to deal with the undead on their island. Yet again, Romero's commentary boils down to man's inability to work alongside his fellow man in times of crisis: humanity is doomed en masse.

Shot in Canada on a reported $4 million budget, Romero employs the high-definition sheen of the Red One camera to fair effect, shooting in 'scope similar to 2005's inferior *Land Of The Dead.* Here at least he has a firmer grasp over the visuals, making for – if nothing else – a relatively attractive picture.

The flaws are conspicuous. Gorehounds aren't going to be happy with SPIN VFX's clumsily rendered moments of CGI; the KNB EFX team do a better job with their passages of messy flesh-munching (including the greedy devouring of a horse). In terms of casting, a largely faceless bunch have been employed which results in very little emotional attachment on the viewers' behalf. And, as mentioned above, the fact that Romero seemingly has nothing insightful left to offer on the zombie topic renders this whole exercise somewhat pointless.

Obviously when measured against the classic triptych that is *Night Of The Living Dead* (1968), *Dawn Of The Dead* (1978) and *Day Of The Dead* (1985), *Survival* shows a downslide in terms of both style and content. It may take some time to find an audience. However, when that time arrives, and in spite of the aforementioned shortcomings, it is actually worthy of reassessment. Keen cinematography, a handful of well-edited action sequences and Fitzpatrick's standout performances ensure *Survival* isn't quite the unmitigated debacle many reviewers claimed it to be.

Sweeney Todd: The Demon Barber Of Fleet Street (2007)

Dir: Tim Burton; Scr: John Logan, Christopher Bond; Cast: Johnny Depp, Helena Bonham Carter, Sacha Baron Cohen

Based on Stephen Sondheim and Hugh Wheeler's original 1979 musical of the same name, Burton's adaptation seeks to marry his absurdist style with the Grand Guignol flavour of classic Hammer films.

Depp takes the lead role (of course – this is a Tim Burton film after all). He's a barber, setting up stock in 19th Century London, where he gets busy murdering his more unsavoury clients with a cutthroat razor blade. Neighbouring cook Bonham Carter is happy to help dispose of the bodies, grinding their flesh into mince and selling it on in her pies.

This lavish Dreamworks production was originally steered by Sam Mendes (*American Beauty* [1999]; *Skyfall* [2012]). When he jumped ship, Burton replaced him and thus finally got to realise a dream he'd been harbouring for over thirty years: bringing one of his favourite musicals to the cinema.

He does a fair job in some respects. The production design not only recreates the era but impresses at every turn: both the custom-built sets and computer-generated landscapes consistently impress. Depp can't carry a tune but knows how to wing it by virtue of pure charisma. Bonham Carter (another stable element of modern Burton films, even since the dissolution of their marriage in 2014) is predictably kooky as the wide-eyed surrogate mother-of-sorts. Baron Cohen – famous for his brand of comedy which finds its punchlines in the reactions of unwitting foils (see *Ali G Indahouse* [2002], *Borat* [2006] etc) – steals the show as Depp's flamboyant rival.

Alas, the songs aren't memorable. They don't carry that cheesy hook you look for in musicals (which this very much is: there's not a line of spoken dialogue). Hence the air of pantomime does grate after a while, and the horror is pushed to the back of concerns – save for a few moments of enjoyably gory ridiculousness, there is little to titillate the buds of fear fans.

Taeter City: Take A Tour In The City Of Cannibal Dictatorship (2012)

Dir/Scr: Giulio De Santi; Cast: Riccardo Valentini, Santiago Ortaez, Wilmar Zimosa

Every wondered what would happen if someone attempted to marry the operatic violence of vintage Italian horror movies with the breathless, kinetic cyberpunk madness of Japanese Manga comic books? On a budget? Wonder no more.

From De Santi, one half of the creative force behind the splatterific *Adam Chaplin* (2011), comes *Taeter City*: a furiously paced, nonsensical but highly spirited romp through paranoid dystopian scenarios.

It tells of a near-future where a new law enforcement regime is working extremely well in the titular metropolis. Here, the government have developed a revolutionary system which uses radio waves capable not only of predicting who society's criminals are, but also adept at controlling their brain reflexes and compelling them to commit splashy suicides on demand. Specialised cops known as "bikers" clean up the subsequent mess, selling the corpses to fast food chains who regurgitate them out to consumers as processed burgers.

The streets are crime-free and big business is booming as a consequence. Everyone's a winner. Until ... a problem with the program controlling the radio waves causes them to turn criminals more demented, and stronger, than ever before. Three bikers - Valentini, Ortaez and Zimosa - are assigned the unenviable task of restoring order to Taeter City.

There's very little characterisation to speak of; the screenplay is all over the place. But I suspect De Santi isn't unduly concerned with such trifling matters: his film is all about style and action. And it offers an abundance of both.

Dismemberments, head-crushings, exploding torsos ... De Santi never lets up with the unrelenting violence, set to a cheap 80s-esque backdrop of blue-hued sci-fi darkness (the likes of *Blade Runner* [1982] and *The Terminator* [1984] are clear stylistic influences, right down to Razzaw's winning synth-led score). David Borg Lopez oversees the impressively prolific practical FX work; it tries hard to counteract some ropy CGI along the way.

Shot on HD, *Taeter City* looks amazing but is utter claptrap in terms of logic and comprehensible storytelling. Its pace is so breakneck, its gory zeal so boundless, that you may not even notice the lack of plot until the closing titles have played out. Which must mark this film out, in some bizarre sense, as a success.

The Taking
See *The Taking Of Deborah Logan*

The Taking Of Deborah Logan (2014)

Dir: Adam Robitel; Scr: Adam Robitel, Gavin Heffernan; Cast: Jill Larson, Anne Ramsay, Michelle Ang

PHD student Ang's documentary crew follow the titular character (Larson) as she succumbs to the effects of Alzheimer's disease. The crew's initial focus is not only on her suffering, but the impact her illness is having on her prime carer, daughter Ramsay. Events unfurl as you'd expect, until Larson begins speaking in a foreign tongue and obsessing over sacrificial snakes. Could it be that she's been possessed by a cannibalistic physician of old?

The film's early theme of living with dementia is handled with a reassuring degree of sensitivity. Alzheimer's disease is a troubling subject matter, it being something that's affected many of us indirectly: the effects are portrayed with authenticity here (Larson's violent outbursts, brought on by the frustration of her failing memory; her physical decline as she begins to resemble a walking corpse) without ever crossing the line into overblown theatrics. Kudos to Larson for a brave, nuanced performance in this regard.

In fact, all principal cast members are aided in their quest to provide necessarily naturalistic performances be their combined previous experience on the small screen. The three central actresses in particular are great. It's encouraging to see such strongly written female characters within the genre. Ramsay is believably strong yet crucially capable of convincing as the carer whose own sanity slowly deteriorates from the pressure placed upon her, a la *The Babadook* (2014). Ang makes it known early-on that one of her own relatives suffered from dementia, and that her motivations for making the film are nothing but respectful: her character is pleasingly free from mercenary concerns. There is a truth about their convictions, all of which Robitel and Heffernan allocate time towards highlighting during the first act, which makes these people feel real.

The Taking Of Deborah Logan is an extremely assured feature debut from Robitel. While adopting the arguably tired convention of a faux documentary-style, the director handles his first-person POV shots with subtle intelligence: employing use of security camera recordings as well as handheld footage is one way of restricting the nausea-inducing shaky-cam effect of other "found footage" flicks.

The preliminary premise is harrowing; the build-up is slow and creepy. Robitel feeds on our innate fears of aging, of mental and physical deterioration, of death. Wily use of camera, editing and lighting help to evoke subtle scares along the way. While the film is low on visceral thrills (happily, given its restrained nature), one of the most jarring moments many will discuss after the fact is a gruesome instance of self-harming.

Following such a considered set-up and deliberately paced first hour, the film's final act descends into more conventional frights – jump-scares, split-second flash-frames and so forth.

A-list director Bryan Singer (*X-Men* [2000]; *Superman Returns* [2006]) was instrumental in getting the film made, acting as co-producer.

Taxidermia (2006)

Dir: Gyorgy Palfi; Scr: Gyorgy Palfi, Zsofia Ruttkay; Cast: Csaba Czene, Gergely Trocsanyi, Marc Bischoff

Palfi's film, based on short stories by Lajos Parti, leads us through specific moments in the lives of three men, each representing a different generation of the same family. Czene tends to a lieutenant's chores on a remote farmhouse during the Second World War. In his free time he dreams of his cock shooting fiery loads and has sex with pigs. The son he sires is born with a piglet's tail, and grows to become professional speed-eater Trocsanyi. Further down the lineage we meet taxidermist Bischoff, obsessed with his own anatomy while tending to his cartoonishly obese father (Trocsanyi in a fat suit).

Fake vomiting, explicit sex, hideous exposed flesh, jarring violence ... Palfi's film is stunning enough aesthetically to overcome such ugly content and emerge as, paradoxically, a rather beautiful viewing experience. Its meticulous production design often recalls the dreamlike surrealism of Terry Gilliam and extends to an original, quirky sound design (unsurprisingly, given Palfi also helmed the hiccup-heavy oddity *Hukkle* [2002]).

The film tackles the machinations of the human body in a manner which is at once fascinated and repulsed by its subject. Themes include self-obsession with appearance; greed; gluttony and desire. Palfi has a rather unsympathetic view of humanity it would seem, his ultimate observation being that we are what we inherit —humans being an avaricious race, our fates are mapped out for us.

Imagine an unholy, CGI-enhanced hybrid of Dusan Makavejev's *Sweet Movie* (1974) and Andrei Tarkovsky's *Mirror* (1975), and you'll not be far off. The only thing that robs the film of any emotional punch is its ill-considered stabs at humour.

A primarily Hungarian production, with assistance from French and Austrian sources, *Taxidermia* was Hungary's official entry into the Best Foreign Language Film category at the 2008 Academy Awards. It was trumped by Austria's entry, *The Counterfeiters*.

Tell Me How I Die (2016)

Dir: D J Viola; Scr: James Hibberd, D J Viola, Rob Warren Thomas; Cast: Virginia Gardner, William Mapother, Nathan Kress

A group of students volunteer to take part in a clinical drug trial which, naturally, necessitates that they move out to a secluded facility where they must remain for several weeks. As one of them puts it, it's "summer camp with drugs". Except it's winter and snow covers the surrounding hills.

The drug administered to each kid is designed to enhance memory. However, Gardner soon discovers she's become afflicted with a most disconcerting side-effect: she can predict her fellow volunteers' deaths. Which wouldn't be so bad if she could foresee them dying of old age; rather, she's convinced that a killer is lurking on the complex grounds.

Sure enough, the murders begin and soon everyone is a suspect.

A graduate of directing music documentaries and the 2010-2011 TV series "Elvira's Movie Macabre", Viola brings a keen eye for visual panache to his cinematic debut. The snow-swept exteriors are impressive, benefiting from lush aerial shots which give the audience a fair indication of the facility's isolated position while feeding our eyes with widescreen splendour. It's odd then that a number of the interior shots are badly framed and too dimly-lit.

The attractive cast look more like models than students, though the screenplay does afford them the usual stereotypical traits: the slut, the bookworm, the slacker, the jock etc. They're not given much to do for the first forty minutes - indeed, it's a relief when someone starts bumping them off.

Alas, it's at this juncture that the co-writers fail to fully explore their initially intriguing concept - it transpires that the killer can also see into the future. Instead they lead us through a final hour of tired slasher movie tropes. The anaemic approach to gore, coupled with the pretty cast and slick production values, place this one squarely in the tradition of mainstream horror fluff like *I Know What You Did Last Summer* (1997) and *Valentine* (2001).

For more successful post-millennial films with a similar premise, try out *The Facility* and *Bloodwork* (both 2012).

Terror Nation (2010)

Dir: Shane Mather; Scr: John Shand; Cast: Andy Callaghan, Ivan Brady, Claire-Louise Catterall

A gang of hoodlums wreak havoc across rural England before reaching their remote rendezvous destination, a ghost town where they are doomed to become victims of a deadly government experiment.

The tribulations that Mather suffered with his previous film, 2007's *Fantacide* (unreliable distribution promises; one cast member chasing the director for their share of imaginary profits), account for *Nation*'s darker tone. Humour still features through the caustic gangland dialogue, but the overall ambience is more sinister than what has been proffered before.

Another reason for the film's fraught atmosphere is the mid-shoot walkout of the FX artist (Mather's brother Dean), leaving the production with a shortage of intended splatter set-pieces. The director's cut, which emerged several months after an initial online DVD release, fixed this with some seamless re-shoots which bolstered the film's splashy content. It seems the filmmaker learned a fair amount about the art of squibs and bloodletting from his sibling.

But there's more than gore to *Terror Nation*. The plot is an enjoyably paranoid cold war-type yarn that reads not unlike a feature-length, potty-mouthed episode of TV's "The Twilight Zone". Mather's preferred themes of moral and artistic freedom are explored once again. The cast – which, for the first time, includes experienced actors – command screen presence and ensure Mather's script runs tightly at all times. The director even gets to homage *The Wild Bunch* (1969), a personal favourite of his, in the explosive finale.

Shot on DV and reined in by a tiny budget, *Terror Nation* lacks the veneer of much lesser studio pictures. But it demonstrates a continued development in Mather's skills as director, editor, actor, writer and composer. Give the man a decent budget and a crossover into the mainstream seems inevitable.

The Texas Vibrator Massacre (2008)

Dir/Scr: Rob Rotten; Cast: Roxy DeVille, Ruby Knox, Eric Swiss

Five young adults (it really is pointless trying to dupe you into accepting them as being teenagers) embark on a road trip across Texas, only to break down and eventually fall foul of the world's worst farming family. Two of their group are killed off early; the remaining three are forced to endure the perverse torments of Leatherface (Swiss) and siblings on their grandpa's secluded ranch.

It goes without saying that this is a riff on Tobe Hooper's seminal *The Texas Chain Saw Massacre* (1974). Albeit, it's not the first fuck film to take on the classic: 1998's *The Texas Dildo Masquerade* got there first.

This being a creation of Rotten's Punx Productions stable (2006's *Porn Of The Dead* etc), you should know to expect a lot of hardcore rutting and a whole slew of tattooed flesh along the way - including director Rotten, who appears as a family member long enough to show off his inked dick. Daisy Tanks as one of the victims provides the obligatory punk chick quota, complete with body piercings and luminous hair.

Wisely, Rotten has discarded the off-putting death metal soundtrack of old here. Music on this occasion comes from rockabilly group The Straight 8's. Also, there are greater senses of both storyline (ie, there is one) and pacing. Of course, this is a porno, and as a result the bonking is still paramount - but Rotten at least shows an interest in delivering the gory goods too.

Hence we get severed limbs, stabbings and - inevitably - a vibrator attached to a lethal whirring contraption, employed to penetrate one actress and effectively fuck her to death while geysers of blood shoot from her crotch.

In terms of nookie, it's all well-shot and energetic. Curiously for a modern production, the performers steer clear of anal sex.

A distressed "grindhouse" look delivers on the requisite faux scratches and grain. There's even a twist ending to look forward to, which allows for the added pleasure of veteran adult star Herschel Savage (*Debbie Does Dallas* [1978] etc) turning up in a fully-clothed cameo.

Despite its surprisingly good-natured vibe, this was rejected outright by the British Board of Film Classification in 2008. They felt that the film eroticised sexual and sexualised violence "to a highly significant degree" and were also perturbed by the fact that some of its (non-related) performers acted out a fictional incest scenario.

The Theatre Bizarre (2011)

Dir: Various; Scr: Various; Cast: Udo Kier, Virginia Newcomb, Catriona MacColl

The collective brainchild of production companies Severin Films, Nightscape Entertainment and Quota Productions, this portmanteau piece seeks to showcase several of the 21st Century's most promising genre directors. The results are predictably uneven.

It all begins with a rather unconvincing framing device in which Newcomb happens upon a local cinema, seemingly derelict, only to garner privileged entry via insidious owner Kier who introduces her to six tales of the macabre.

A couple travelling through France fall foul of a vivacious witch; a promiscuous lover's dreams filter into his waking world with sinister repercussions; a character who feeds on other's memories discovers the best way to do so is by extracting the vitreous fluid from their eyes, and so on. Naturally, the wraparound story builds to a nasty twist of its own.

Despite credible production values and a fair amount of well-executed gore, it doesn't seem harsh to suggest you could've expected a lot more from the talent involved. Contributing directors are David Gregory (*Plague Town*, 2008), Buddy Giovinazzo (*Combat Shock*, 1984), Karim Hussain (*Subconscious Cruelty*, 2000), Douglas Buck (*Cutting Moments,* 1997), Richard Stanley (*Hardware*, 1990), Tom Savini (*Night Of The Living Dead*, 1990) and Jeremy Kasten (*The Wizard Of Gore* remake, 2007).

Along with Kier and MacColl, the cast includes other genre favourites such as Debbie Rochon, Lynn Lowry and Elissa Dowling.

So, why does it all fall short of expectations? Specifically, it's in the writing. There are no less than nine screenwriters involved (including five of the directors; Stanley worked with Scarlett Amaris and Emiliano Ranzani to adapt Clark Ashton Smith's 1938 story "The Mother of Toads").

Inconsistencies abound in any horror anthology. Here, though, they are more prominent than usual. From the arthouse of Buck's disquieting, poignant "The Accident" through the cerebral gore of Hussain's "Vision Stains" to the hardboiled paranoia of Giovinazzo's "I Love You", the tone never follows from one short tale to the next. Savini's "Wet Dreams" goes for a blend of comedy-horror; Gregory's "Sweets" aims to gross us out.

In isolation, each tale has points of interest: solid performances, intriguing premises, moments of dark surrealism. Grouped together, they rob each other of cumulative suspense or identity. The results are, taken as a whole, erratic and underwhelming.

They Came Back (2004)

Dir: Robin Campillo; Scr: Robin Campillo, Brigitte Tijou; Cast: Geraldine Pailhas, Jonathan Zaccai, Frederic Pierrot

Residents of a small French town are shocked to discover the deceased are returning to life. The locals deal with the return of their loved ones by trying to reintegrate them back into society. As the film progresses, we focus on three families and the emotional dilemmas at hand.

The arrival of the returnees is unexplained, and Campillo shows no interest in filling in such gaps. Rather, he seeks to hypothesise over the practicalities to be dealt with. Do the dead have entitlement to reclaiming their old jobs, for example? How will they fit into the adapted regimes of their respective families? And do their reanimated dispositions require special medical provisions?

A sombre, low-key tenor is imbued. The subject matter is handled in a thoughtful and thought-provoking fashion; the somnambulistic performances work in harmony with the slow and eerie mood.

Boasting a premise notably similar to that of Akihiko Shiota's 2002 film *Yomigaeri*, *They Came Back* retains an identity of its own due to a leaning more towards political and dour social musings. It will of course disappoint those seeking out their next zombie gorefest: those looking for a gut-muncher along the lines of *Zombie Flesh Eaters* (1979) are forewarned.

Quite what we learn about the afterlife is debatable, come *They Came Back*'s enigmatic conclusion. Again, Campillo's interests appear to lie elsewhere: examinations of loss, coping, immigration (the allegory of a government struggling to accommodate an influx of new arrivals), love and faith rule the day.

The film was rereleased onto DVD in 2013 where it was retitled as *The Returned*. This was in keeping with the French TV series of the same name (a literal translation of the film's original French title, *Les Revenants*) which became an unexpected international hit in 2012.

Tin Can Man (2007)

Dir/Scr: Ivan Kavanagh; Cast: Patrick O'Donnell, Michael Parle, Emma Eliza Regan

O'Donnell is down on his luck. His girlfriend has just left him for another man, and he's in danger of losing his job. A job he hates, granted, but one which he nevertheless needs. Enter neighbour Parle, a charismatic presence who proclaims to have been in an accident and is in urgent need of using O'Donnell's 'phone. Having gained entry to O'Donnell's home, however, Parle refuses to leave – and begins to manipulate his neighbour's life, first through sadistic conversation and later via a string of increasingly nightmarish journeys into the dark heart of reality.

Shot in ascetic black-and-white, *Tin Can Man* was filmed in Ireland on a meagre budget of just 10,000 Euros. The dimly lit monochrome approach is a winner, while the tendency to frame everything tightly results in an effectively claustrophobic ambience: the impression is given that each character is constantly enshrouded in darkness. Whether by default or design, Kavanagh's film is effectively eerie as a consequence.

City life is not only lonely, it's dangerous ...

A surrealist streak increases in intensity as the canny plot develops, its leaning towards psychological horror incorporating elements of slasher violence and even moments of unexpected absurdist comedy. The largely gore-free visuals recall early David Lynch (*Eraserhead* [1977] is an obvious reference point), while echoes of *The Texas Chain Saw Massacre* (1974) can also be felt during key moments best not mentioned here.

The sound design is even more fabulous than the consciously antediluvian look. Calliopes on a film's score are always going to be jolting, and here their presence resounds against an escalating sense of unease which culminates with the arrival of a figure sure to give sufferers of coulrophobia a reason to scream.

O'Donnell and Parle are the glue that holds events together. The former is highly credible as the underdog whose life has rallied against him, partially because he doesn't have the backbone to fight against the kicks life's giving him; the latter is a formidably insidious character, compellingly capable of pulling an individual out of their comfort zone and embarking them upon a trip to Hell they'll never forget.

Tin Can Man enjoyed its premiere at the Sydney Underground Film Festival in 2007, and later screened to acclaim at the Dublin Film Festival in 2012. It finally won a DVD release stateside in 2014 courtesy of BrinkVision. It deserves a wider audience.

Train To Busan (2016)

Dir/Scr: Sang-ho Yeon; Cast: Yoo Gong, Soo-an Kim, Sung Gyeong

Gong insists on accompanying his visiting daughter Kim on her return journey from Seoul to her mother, his ex-wife, in Busan. He hopes the ride will give him time to build bridges and rekindle their relationship. That's all very well but try telling that to the woman who boards their train at the last minute. She's contaminated with an unknown virus. When she bites another passenger, they too become infected. Before long, the speeding train has become a battleground between frantic survivors and rabid zombies.

Busan is the live-action debut of accomplished animation director Yeon (*The King Of Pigs* [2011], *The Fake* [2013]). It's a solid first batting, a 2-hour action-horror hybrid that rarely pauses for breath.

Yeon shows little interest in elaborating on why his film is overrun with zombies. There are fleeting references made, both verbally and visually, to a leakage having occurred at a nearby biochemical plant. But he makes no effort to revisit this plot point at any later juncture: his focus is squarely on capturing the ensuing chaos.

In this respect, each set-piece is skilfully choreographed. Lee Hyung-deok's cinematography is fluid and controlled, stepping back from the violent shaky-cam style popularised by modern action directors like Paul Greengrass (*The Bourne Identity* [2002]). This allows for a clear grasp of what's going on to be enjoyed at all times.

The zombies move fast, lunging at their human prey in spastic bursts of ravenous energy. The FX work is modern and efficient. It straddles the line between practical and computer-generated imagery without causing too much distraction. In an unusual move (but an entirely plausible one, given the scenario) there are no guns evident.

Gong handles his character's dramatic arc from apathetic businessman to reluctant hero well; Kim, just ten years old at the time of shooting, is persuasive as the diffident daughter pining for his love. The whole 'estranged parent-child' set-up is nothing new and, indeed, Yeon is unafraid of flirting with cliché: the train's colourful passengers are caricatures of disaster movie staples, what with the pregnant lady, her belligerent husband, the young lovers, the doddery old ladies and so on. The melodrama provided by their individual relationships is typical of Korean cinema.

For all its unremitting pace, *Busan* is overly long. It's not once scary and it runs out of ideas as it approaches its slightly underwhelming finale. The commentary on its country's class divides and uncaring government is so ephemeral that it barely registers. But if you're willing to overlook all that and take it for the persistent zombie actioner it is, it can't help but entertain.

Yeon's *Seoul Station* (also 2016) is an animated feature with an almost identical storyline, the events of which take place a day before the happenings of *Busan*. It serves as more of a curious companion piece than a prequel: it too avoids offering any developed explanation for what's going on.

The Transfiguration (2016)

Dir/Scr: Michael O'Shea; Cast: Eric Ruffin, Chloe Levine, Aaron Clifton Moten

O'Shea's feature debut is a confident endeavour, examining the internal machinations of a lonely youth who may or may not be a vampire. Ruffin, the bullied teen in question, certainly believes himself to be one, and is prone to feeding on victims once-monthly to sate his self-perceived hunger.

Into his unhappy existence enters Levine. She's a modest girl and fellow orphan, who's newly moved into Ruffin's apartment block. She shares his sense of feeling like one of life's outsiders. Over time she penetrates Ruffin's cool exterior and an admittedly unlikely romance develops. But at what cost?

References to bloodsucker films of yore are rife, whether via being viewed on Ruffin's television or while he's dissecting their merits with his new girlfriend. Look forward to nods towards *Nosferatu: A Symphony Of Horror* (1922), *The Lost Boys* (1987), *Near Dark* (1987) and even *Twilight* (2008).

The film's gritty realism and ambiguous meshing of folklore tropes with a major suggestion of its protagonist being nothing more than a deluded fledgling serial killer strongly evoke memories of George A Romero's must-see *Martin* (1978). The autumnal love story, married with a notion of parents who are either absent, ill or abusive, and a cool indie vibe, beg comparisons to the superior *Let The Right One In* (2008).

Shot on a Canon C500 camera in full HD, the film captures its deserted world in stylish and haunting fashion. Devotedly lensed and taking great care to accurately convey the urban isolation felt while living on the grimy outskirts of New York, *The Transfiguration* is a gauged character study which nevertheless suffers from occasional pacing issues before reaching its rather underwhelming conclusion.

Performances are solid but characterisation is lacking. We get that Ruffin is melancholic and wayward but, while there asides to his poorly mother, late father and sickly brother, there is also precious little insight into why he's developed vampiric tendencies.

Perhaps it matters that Ruffin is black. Maybe it's relevant that his victims are white, or that his Brooklyn upbringing is blighted by those who yell "freak" at him and are given at times to urinate on him. Racial commentary is brushed against, but never with any authority or convincing sense of insight.

We're left with a reasonably interesting and good-looking, albeit low-key, indie drama which is easier to admire than be thoroughly entertained by.

Turistas
See *Paradise Lost*

Tusk (2014)

Dir/Scr: Kevin Smith; Cast: Justin Long, Haley Joel Osment, Genesis Rodriguez

Podcast presenter Long travels out into the Canadian sticks to conduct an interview with elusive seafarer Michael Parks. It transpires that Parks has lured his guest there in order to help him solve "a riddle older than the sphinx": are all men walruses at heart?

This rather flimsy conundrum serves as the purpose for Parks' subsequent imprisonment and surgical torture of Long, in a bid to transform him – physically and mentally – into the aforementioned creature.

In the meantime, girlfriend Rodriguez and best pal Osment embark on a quest to find the missing Long.

Smith made his name in the 1990s with comedies like *Clerks* (1994) and *Chasing Amy* (1997). His mix of irreverent humour, slacker characters (usually with some kind of comic book interest) and shoegazing alt-rock soundtracks soon became tiresome. In 2011, even Smith appeared to want to grow up, as he wrote and directed the more serious-minded thriller *Red State*.

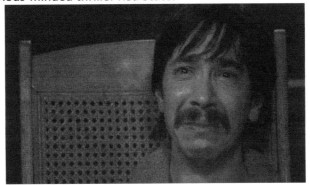

Despite its ludicrous premise, there was hope that *Tusk* would find the filmmaker venturing further into dark territory. For the first half at least, this optimism is rewarded with some tense exchanges between terrified abductee and sinister captor. The sparse sets are dimly lit; Long conveys fear in palpable fashion; editing and dialogue ensure any humour is more than balanced out by the quietly brooding tension. Even the silly scenario becomes temporarily plausible – largely thanks to Parks' persuasive, show-stealing turn.

But then, the film shifts gear. Johnny Depp arrives in an absurd cameo as a bungling detective with a French-Canadian accent of stupefying calamity. To shoehorn your mate into your film is one thing, but to do so in such a clumsy manner that the tone of the remaining action is entirely transformed, reeks of Freshman-style ineptitude.

The film simply falls apart, crumbling beneath the weight of its own synopsis – a concept apparently borne of Smith's own podcast ramblings – and ultimately failing as either comedy or horror.

Tusk is the first in an intended "True North" trilogy. The second, *Yoga Hosers*, and third, *Moose Jaws*, were announced as going into production in late 2015.

Ubaldo Terzani Horror Show (2010)

Dir/Scr: Gabriele Albanesi; Cast: Giuseppe Soleri, Paolo Sassanelli, Laura Gigante

Budding filmmaker and horror movie obsessive Soleri is desperate to have one of his scripts developed. No-one's listening, until a seasoned producer suggests he collaborates with the acclaimed titular genre author (Sassanelli). Accepting the invitation, this involves Soleri moving in to Sassanelli's spooky mansion for a week. His host is odd enough, but events are about to get a great deal more sinister as the author invites Soleri's girlfriend Gigante along for the ride – and turns his attentions towards seducing her.

It's no lie that Italy has produced some of the finest horror filmmakers of recent decades. Riccardo Freda (*The Terror Of Dr Hichcock*, 1962), Mario Bava (*Black Sabbath*, 1963), Sergio Martino (*Torso*, 1973), Dario Argento (*Suspiria*, 1977), Lucio Fulci (*The Beyond*, 1981), Michele Soavi (*Cemetery Man*, 1994) etc. But that latter film is widely regarded as the country's last great genre outing. Hopes were high, then, when early signs suggested *Ubaldo Terzani Horror Show* was a return to spaghetti nightmares of old.

It's halfway successful in its plight.

Albanesi endearingly wears his heart on his sleeve, ensuring Soleri's apartment walls are covered in posters for films such as *Strip Nude For Your Killer* (1975) and Argento's *Opera* (1987). Our protagonist also wears a T-shirt proudly declaring "Fulci lives". One thing's for sure, Albanesi aims to get fans on side from the start.

The two leads are excellent in their roles, trading off one another with palpable intensity suggesting a power game of persuasive, perverse twists is to follow. But the film falters here, such is the problematic pacing during its first act. Things rarely get going along the psychological lines Albanesi is clearly striving for, mainly due to a clunky script and the unfortunate cheapening effect of the HD photography (robbing the film of its anticipated stylised look).

On the plus side, events build to a gruesomely tense finale once one-too-many narcotics-infused set-pieces have been endured. Legendary gore maestro Sergio Stivaletti makes good of his reputation (*Demons* [1985], *The Church* [1989] etc) with some sterling, grisly practical FX work.

The Uh-Oh! Show (2009)

Dir/Scr: Herschell Gordon Lewis; Cast: Nevada Caldwell, Joel D Wynkoop, Broward 'Eclipse' Holsey

Searching for something new with which to lure young audiences to the theatres, the late Lewis made a transition in the early 1960s from soft erotica and bawdy capers like *The Adventures Of Lucky Pierre* (1961) to eye-popping gore. His first attempt at revolting shocked juveniles was a hit: 1963's video nasty-to-be *Blood Feast*.

Though none of Lewis' subsequent splatter films achieved the same level of success, and despite several forays into more explicit adult territory in the meantime (*Black Love*, 1971, etc), the likeable former teacher has come to be known as The Godfather of Gore.

Following 1972's *The Gore Gore Girls*, Lewis ended a thirty-year break from filmmaking with the long-rumoured *Blood Feast 2: All U Can Eat* (2002). Despite its mixed reception, it wasn't long before the director announced another project. *The Uh-Oh! Show* (the working title was *Herschell Gordon Lewis' Grim Fairy Tales*) finally surfaced, in rough form - it first premiered at Abertoir Film Festival in South Wales, minus music cues and still awaiting the completion of some effects - in 2009, the year Lewis turned eighty.

The plot revolves around the titular cable TV show. In it, bubbly contestants are in with the chance of winning large sums of money for correctly answering host Wynkoop's trivial questions. Should they respond incorrectly, a wheel is spun to determine which limb they must lose, there and then. A la Lewis' earlier *The Wizard Of Gore* (1970), the audience assumes the onstage action is fake ... until reporter Caldwell's boyfriend goes missing after his appearance on the show. As she investigates the matter further, I'm sure readers won't be surprised to learn what she unearths.

Retaining the vibe of *Blood Feast 2*, *The Uh-Oh! Show* settles on a tone so comedic, so camp, that you can't help but feel Lewis is apologising in advance to those who dismiss his efforts as inept. You know what you're in for when Troma president Lloyd Kaufman cameos as a pimp.

Any commentary on modern media's use of violence as an audience-grabber is consequently trite (as well as being hypocritical, given that Lewis owes his status to a legacy of crude gore).

Garish in design, though not as funny as it thinks it is nor as gory as it needs to be, *The Uh-Oh! Show* is populated by disposable cartoon characters and a script that desperately requires rewrites by someone tuned in to current tastes. At least the special effects, from Marcus Koch and co, are pretty decent: knowingly exaggerated appendage-hacking, decapitation, intestinal-tearing and the like are to be anticipated.

Lewis passed away in his sleep on 26 September 2016, aged 90. RIP Herschell.

Under The Shadow (2016)

Dir/Scr: Babak Anvari; Cast: Narges Rashidi, Avin Manshadi, Bobby Naderi

Iran, 1988. The country is living under Ayatollah Khomeini's reign. Prevented from returning to medical school due to her affiliations with the liberal opposition, and forced to wear a chador in public, Rashidi's only solace is within her family home. Even there, there are restrictions. She has to hide her Jane Fonda workout videotapes whenever visitors call; husband Naderi and daughter Manshadi hint at psychological problems having been suffered by Rashidi in the past.

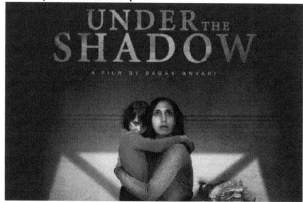

When Naderi is called to serve in the war against Iraq, mother and daughter shrink further into their apartment. Complete with masking tape across its windows to prevent the glass from shattering during air raids, the place becomes less of a sanctuary and more of a prison for them.

A crack in the ceiling emits insidious black shadows; Naderi appears in physical and aural visions, berating Rashidi for her failings as a mother. Is she cracking up, or are supernatural forces truly at play?

It's a question which UK-based debut filmmaker Anvari successfully avoids addressing for the most part, enjoying instead an agreeably ambiguous stance not dissimilar to that proffered in the tonally reminiscent *The Babadook* (2014).

Anvari draws from his own memories of growing up in war-torn Tehran, bringing authentic frissons to the everyday lives of people living under the constant threat of attack. Home no longer equals safety. Here, this is not only because of the frighteningly close bomb-drops serving as reminders that bricks and mortar will not protect against the enemy, but also due to Manshadi's palpable dread of being alone with her increasingly erratic mother.

Midway through, the hunt for a child's missing toy has never been so tense. Rashidi turns their place upside-down, the resultant disarray acting as an obvious but effective metaphor for her chaotic mental state. With or without the spectre of a possible djinn presence, we relate to the fear she's living in.

Avoiding jump-scares, *Under The Shadow* gets good mileage wringing tension from issues such as maternal anxieties and feminist repression. Kit Fraser's polished cinematography and Chris Barwell's tight editing help things along nicely, as do excellent performances across the board.

The Undertow (2003)

Dir/Scr: Jeremy Wallace; Cast: Emily Haack, Jason Christ, Trudy Bequette

Several city-savvy twenty-somethings embark on a break into the sticks, their destination being the backwoods town of Old Mines. All they care for is a weekend of river rafting. Along the way, a local sheriff pulls them over and forces them to sit on the road while he empties their beer cans onto the asphalt. Making a pit-stop for fuel a short while after finds country girl Bequette ominously cawing at them "maybe me and my brother will see you guys later". Then there's the altercation with the town loony upon arrival. Sometimes it pays to take heed of such omens, turn around and fuck off home.

But, no. This bunch ignore all the signs and continue headfirst into a disaster zone: fronted by the local mayor, this puritanical community doesn't take kindly to heathen outsiders infiltrating its sheltered tranquillity. So much so that a hooded brute known only as "The Boy" (Doc Brown) is set upon our protagonists without mercy.

Originally conceived as a comedy which was to be titled *The Float Trip Massacre*, its co-producers – Christ, Chris Belt, Ron Bonk and Eric Stanze – decided on an eleventh-hour tonal change along with a more appropriately foreboding title. Good decisions.

Stanze (director of *Scrapbook*, 2000) also edited and shot the film: his experience shines, lending events an air of rigid, attractive professionalism. Though shot on the now-primitive Sony DCR-VX1000, the look achieved is a satisfyingly gritty one akin to authentic Super 8mm. A handful of murky night scenes aside, it all looks extremely good (the audio hasn't been recorded so well, admittedly).

Cranium-crushing, throat-tearing, eye-gouging ... a meagre budget doesn't stop *The Undertow* from delivering the nasty goods. The final act, bolstered by some manic screaming, oodles of blood and Wallace's eerie score, works alarmingly well.

The Undertow is an unexpectedly effective addition to the cycle of films which have been intent on revisiting counter-culture terrors such as *Deliverance* (1972) and *The Hills Have Eyes* (1977) in recent years. It works because it keeps things simple: its derivative – and, on paper, rather dull – plot is wisely pared down to little more than a springboard from which tension and violent set-pieces arise. It comes to hardly matter that the killer so closely resembles Jason Voorhees circa *Friday The 13th Part 2* (1981) ...

Underworld (2003)

Dir: Len Wiseman; Scr: Danny McBride; Cast: Kate Beckinsale, Michael Sheen, Scott Speedman

The war between vampires and werewolves rages on in Underworld, though thankfully this isn't as sappy as the awful *Twilight* (2008). Not quite.

In it, vampire warrior Beckinsale – a go-to slayer of lycanthropes – falls for Speedman, an apparent mortal who for some unknown reason is relentlessly pursued by the hairy beasts. Could it be that he holds the key to ending this ongoing conflict for good? Or is this simply "Romeo And Juliet" reinvented for the Playstation generation?

Beckinsale – daughter of late British comedy actor Richard ("Rising Damp" [1974-78], "Porridge" [1974-79]) - has flirted with the horror genre before and since, having appeared in the likes of *Haunted* (1995), *Vacancy* (2007) and *Stonehearst Asylum* (2014) ... along with each *Underworld* sequel. She certainly possesses the physique and hardened glamour for such a role, and yet is curiously devoid of impact on this occasion. We don't get to know her character; we never really care beyond admiring her shape, and prowess during the combat scenes.

Still, she copes admirably opposite her onscreen nemesis Sheen – who's typically good – despite this married couple being separated off-screen at the time (to add to the mix, Beckinsale fell for Wiseman during the shoot and later married *him*).

Beyond her performance, this is hokum. Through and through. It has a degree of daft charm to it and the action set-pieces are competently staged (especially for a first-time feature director). But it's also a bloated, slick, videogame-esque action-horror hybrid that has more in common with *Blade* (1998) or *The Matrix* (1999) than anything intended to puts the shits up you.

Authoress Nancy A Collins was successful in being granted an out-of-court settlement when she claimed *Underworld*'s plot was painfully similar to that of her frankly terrible short story "The Love Of Monsters".

Unfriended (2014)

Dir: Levan Gabriadze; Scr: Nelson Greaves; Cast: Shelley Hennig, Heather Sossaman, Jacob Wysocki

A teenaged girl commits suicide after embarrassing footage of her drunk is posted online. One year later, a group of her friends begin receiving intimidating messages from the dead girl's Facebook account. Forced to stay at their computers and play sadistic games which threaten to expose each members' darkest secrets, the pals desperately try to fathom who's behind the sinister stalking ... as one by one, they're unceremoniously picked off.

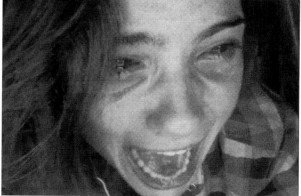

Shot on a $1 million budget, *Unfriended* owes a great deal of its commercial success (it played widely in cinemas) to two things: its timely theme of cyber-bullying, and the novel approach of having all of the action viewed on Hennig's laptop screen in real time.

Kudos to Gabriadze for managing to make the finished article much less tedious than that last sentence must sound. Through the utilisation of various social media outlets - Facebook, Skype, Chatroulette etc - the conversational drive of the protagonists is kept fluid throughout.

We get decent performances too, even if the characters being portrayed are hardly the sympathetic kind. The wronged girl is dismissed by almost all of her friends as someone deserving of her ill fate, while they themselves seem preoccupied with either substance abuse, vacuous acts of vanity or aping rapists for fun. Is it really wrong of me to have felt nothing once each of them started kicking the bucket?

The initial premise is the thing that works best. However, while its anti-bullying message for the textspeak generation is commendable, there's little denying that Greaves and Gabriadze force the issue on more than one occasion.

Still, the first two thirds of *Unfriended* build well. It comes undone later into proceedings, when events take on a more supernatural turn and clumsy horror tropes - including a couple of predictable jump-scares - become the order of the day.

Ultimately, Russian-born Gabriadze's film surfaces as a rather conventional slasher movie (the "one-year-ago-to-this-day" trigger event; the line-up of annoying teen victims) updated to cater towards today's online generation, complete with a self-conscious message warning against the perils of living one's life through social media.

Unholy Ground (2016)

Dir/Scr: Gunther Brandl; Cast: Jurgen Lill, Katharina Buchberger, Nadja Holz

Fleeting visual echoes of *Witchfinder General* (1968) as a group of soldiers happen upon a small village in the heart of rural Sweden during the country's conflicts with Russia in the 18th Century. One of their party is injured and in need of medical assistance. At first, the villagers - predominantly female - seem a little peculiar. As their stay extends, the military men realise they've stumbled upon Hell on Earth, a hotbed of perverse sexual mores and Satanic reverence.

Brandl writes, directs, produces and co-stars in this micro-budget (6,000 Euros) DIY effort, shooting on digital HD with a tiny crew which includes family members Helmut and Monika. It looks cheap for the most part but undeniably achieves an unlikely degree of style at the same time. The midnight orgies and black mass scenes are well-lit and colourful, enjoying an almost psychedelic sense of hysteria about them. Day scenes are less convincing, especially whenever a cast member is required to speak.

Fortunately, that's not all the clunky actors do. There's a fair amount of disrobing and fucking to be witnessed too. Brandl's film comes in two versions: a gory 'uncut' version and the 'X-rated director's cut', which throws in a generous serving of hardcore pornography (including the dubious sight of Brandl, as a monk, getting fellated by a demonically possessed nun). Also, I never knew shaven crotches were such a big thing among 18th Century women ...

One female character is pinned down and raped by a tentacled beast during a scene which simultaneously pays homage to *The Evil Dead* (1981) and Manga comics. Elsewhere the beginners' level gore resembles the early works of Olaf Ittenbach (*Black Past* [1989], *The Burning Moon* [1992} etc).

Oddly enjoyable.

The Untamed (2016)

Dir: Amat Escalante; Scr: Amat Escalante, Gibran Portela; Cast: Ruth Ramos, Jesus Meza, Eden Villavicencio

Escalante's previous feature, 2013's *Heli*, thrust upon its viewers a harrowing snapshot of life in an impoverished Mexican town, centring on one family who fall foul of local drug dealers. A tale of poverty, lawlessness, military rule and bodies that go missing without explanation or an investigation into their whereabouts, the movie made international news as a hard-hitting expose on its country's contemporary issues. In the longer term, it remains a talking point among fans of gruelling moments in modern cinema, infamous for its scene in which one victim's bollocks are graphically set alight.

The Untamed exhibits more polish and focus, but is similarly politically driven.

A troubled married couple, the wife's brother - who's having an affair with her husband - and a woman he treats at the local hospital are entwined by the discovery of an extra-terrestrial being which hides in a cabin in the nearby woods. This entity becomes a source of great physical pleasure and sexual enlightenment for each of them, which in turn threatens to ultimately destroy them.

Escalante's film is a delicately measured one. Its lingering opening shot of a meteorite approaching Earth (serving to explain how the alien arrived in the Mexican state of Guanajuato) soon gives way to a deliberately paced drama which concentrates more on the protagonists' strained relationships and quiet despair than any otherworldly aspects lurking for some time on the periphery.

Certainly, Igor Figueroa and Fernando Heftye's score is sombre and subtly menacing; the woodlands are filled with atmospheric dry ice fog. Cinematographer Manuel Alberto Claro imbues each scene with the same muted colours and sense of isolation that he brought to Lars Von Trier's *Melancholia* (2011). Shades of *The Man Who Fell To Earth* (1976) and *Stalker* (1979) are also evident.

But, until the final third, Escalante is more concerned with examining sexual mores in modern Mexico, and in particular the dominance of a woman's need to procure contentment. It's easy to compare the film's content - a warring couple, infidelity, an erotic alien encounter - with that of Andrej Zulawski's masterful *Possession* (1981). Yet this triumphs as being unique enough, both visually and in terms of tone, to stand singular; its ties to its own country's curious politics resonate on a different level.

270

As events unfurl into ever darker territory and genre conventions grow more prominent, *The Untamed* becomes arguably less engrossing. But stick with it for an abrupt finale which will spark enthusiastic discussion afterwards.

The film won a clutch of awards, including a Silver Lion prize for Escalante as Best Director at the 2016 Venice Film Festival and the Best Film accolade at 2017's Sydney Film Festival.

Upsidedown Cross (2014)

Dir: William Hellfire; Scr: William Hellfire, Mike Hunchback; Cast: Erin Russ, Colleen Cohan, David Yow

Following an extended period of homelessness, prostitution and drug addiction, wayward Russ moves in with her puritanical mother (Cohan) hoping to rehabilitate herself. There's a flaw in this plan: Cohan is a religious nutjob who attributes her daughter's withdrawal symptoms to demonic possession. Her solution is to hire shady preacher Yow to enter her house and perform a most unorthodox exorcism.

Hellfire began his career in the late 1990s. Shooting on video, titles like *Infamous Bondage Murders* and *The Duct Tape Killer* (both 1998) were at times funded by fetishists who dictated online what content these films should include. Arguably his most well-known movie from this era is 1999's *Duck! The Carbine High Massacre* - a $5,000.00 satire made in the wake of the Columbine High School shootings in April of that year. As the new century arrived, Hellfire started alternating his time between making more cheapie opportunistic flicks (*Orgasm Torture In Satan's Rape Clinic* [2004] isn't as amazing as it may sound) and producing bonus features for cult DVD releases.

Then, following the release of his softcore comedy *Cloak & Shag Her* in 2008, all went quiet. *Upsidedown Cross* broke the silence and - although familiar themes of sexual deviance and the evils of religion remain - it's like nothing else in the director's canon.

Shot in under a week, this is Hellfire's magnum opus. For a start, the consciously tight photography is startlingly effective in its claustrophobia-inducing impact. A measured pace allows for the unremittingly bleak tone to really hammer each miserable set-piece home. Aided by a fearless performance from Russ - at once vulnerable and resolute - the seriousness with which Hellfire unerringly approaches his subject is most impressive.

Free from jump-scares or ill-fitting scenes of gross-out gore, *Upsidedown Cross* is instead all about characterisation and atmosphere. Both of which it brings in spades. Alongside Russ's stunning turn, Yow - singer with defunct noise-rock legends The Jesus Lizard - excels as the creepy holy man, delivering intense monologues with troubling conviction. Cohan channels her inner Piper Laurie (*Carrie*, 1976) as the psychotic zealot you'd really like to punch.

Well-shot, superbly restrained and flawlessly performed (apparently Hellfire contacted Yow on Facebook asking him to appear in the film), *Upsidedown Cross* signifies a remarkable progression in the director's prowess. Sure, the final act is a tad predictable, but it's powerful nevertheless. More please, William!

Vacancy (2007)

Dir: Nimrod Antal; Scr: Mark L Smith; Cast: Kate Beckinsale, Luke Wilson, Frank Whaley

Born in America but of Hungarian descent, Antal returned to the country of his forefathers to kick-start his feature-length directorial career with 2003's excellent *Kontroll*. Since then he's reconvened to the US but has walked a tricky path of eclectic choices, including *Predators* (2010) and the much-maligned *Metallica Through The Never* (2013). To date, *Vacancy* is his biggest commercial hit.

Beckinsale and Wilson are reasonably convincing as a married couple on the verge of divorce. Having suffered the loss of their son in the recent past, they've grown apart and allowed their relationship to reach the level of incessant bickering. Despite this, we first meet them as they're travelling home together from her parents' anniversary party. After almost hitting what he believes to be a raccoon in the road, Wilson's car breaks down. It's night-time and they're in the middle of nowhere. Fortunately for them, or so they think, there is a motel nearby.

Upon discovery of a series of videotapes in their room, alas, the couple realises they are scheduled to follow in the footsteps of previous tenants by becoming the unwilling stars of the motel owners' next snuff movie. Fucking hell, I don't know about you but all I want is a decent night's kip when I'm staying overnight somewhere.

So, the estranged co-stars must work together if they're to outwit the building's numerous surveillance cameras and nasty antagonists lurking outside.

Earlier scenes where the couple struggle to get along within a small space and gripe to motel manager Whaley over issues such as noisy neighbours, cockroaches and whatnot work best. By the midway point, *Vacancy* has morphed into a by-the-numbers horror-action hybrid fuelled by a complete absence of originality and disconcertingly one-dimensional characters. Both actors do their best but are saddled with a ludicrous script in which the wife goes from scaredy-cat to shit-kicker in record time and the husband's notion of heroism consists of complaints and wide-eyed fretting. The choices they make are unlikely at every turn. This lack of credibility soon destabilises any tension Antal had until then been building.

The straight-to-video prequel, 2008's *Vacancy 2: The Final Cut*, is similarly mediocre.

Vampire Junction (2001)

Dir/Scr: Jess Franco; Cast: Lina Romay, Samantha Olsen, Fata Morgana

An entry in the Spanish director's latter-day, generally ill-regarded One Shot Productions phase.

Roving reporter Romay travels to the Old West town of Shit City, where she's been summoned to interview doctor Spencer (Steve Barrymore) about the strange goings-on there. She locates her subject in the saloon; his beguiling wife Olsen insists that Romay stays overnight. By doing so, she subjects herself to nightmares detailing lesbian vampire trysts. Waking up to the discovery of Spencer's murder, Romay determines to stay and investigate further – determined to solve the crime and explain the reasons for her continuing, increasingly penetrative hallucinations.

Or something like that. Franco's films have long-since carried an air of surrealism about them. But whereas seminal earlier works of his like *Vampyros Lesbos* (1971) maintained just enough command of their narrative qualities to appease those without such arthouse tolerances, *Junction* soon abandons all efforts of coherence and wallows instead in its chintzy dreamlike flow.

The languid pace is complemented by fatigued performances and scene after scene of odd, seemingly unconnected images or insufficiently explored plot strands. Why does Romay never pursue her interview with Spencer, for example? Why are characters introduced in a narrative haze, and never woven into later events?

The Western element is never explained either, though it's likely that Franco simply adapted his screenplay around the fact that he had access to a disused film set in Malaga. By doing so, Franco's film enters a small but interesting sub-genre – the vampire Western - which also includes the likes of *Billy The Kid Versus Dracula* (1966) and *Near Dark* (1987). In fairness to it, *Junction* utilises its resources to moderately stylish effect.

Sandwiched between *Vampire Blues* (1999) and *Incubus* (2002) in the Franco canon, long-times fans will know what to expect: psychedelic colours and crude optical effects achieved on a penny-pinching budget; copious amounts of ugly female nudity; a confused plot desperately trying to make sense of itself through the murky shot-on-video aesthetics.

Plus points include a strong sense of allure in the form of Olsen, and a show-stopping nightmare sequence in which two females gyrate against each other naked - graduating to shaving each other's groins in graphic, bloody fashion.

Vanished
See *YellowBrickRoad*

V/H/S (2012)

Dir: Adam Wingard, David Bruckner, Ti West, Glenn McQuaid, Joe Swanberg, Radio Silence; Scr: Simon Barrett, David Bruckner, Radio Silence, Glenn McQuaid, Ti West, Nicholas Tecosky; Cast: Hannah Fierman, Norma C Quinones, Helen Rogers

Set in 1998, for no obvious reason other than to justify the utilisation of lo-fi technology, *V/H/S* takes the tried-and-tested anthology format and applies it to a love of shot-on-video terrors.

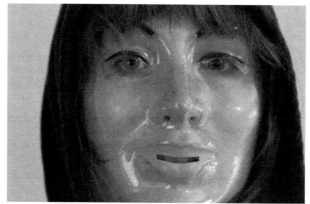

The framing narrative, directed by Wingard, concerns a gang of young hoodlums who are hired to break into a house and retrieve a specific videocassette. Upon entry, they discover the occupant dead in the living room, along with hundreds of unmarked VHS tapes. Setting about gathering them together, a member of the party is intrigued by what their contents may be and sneaks off to watch one alone.

The bulk of the remaining film focuses on five low-resolution shorts, as screened on the deceased guy's television.

Bruckner's "Amateur Night" pits a group of horny aspiring pornographers against a particularly ferocious succubus (Fierman). The results are chaotic and gory, though their impact is lessened somewhat by the wildly shaky camera work. West falls short of the mystique applied to his feature-length works with the lacklustre "Second Honeymoon". A hammy script and signposted "twist" effectively neuter this rushed effort. "Tuesday The 17th", from McQuaid, starts life as a typical teens-in-woods exercise, but boasts a couple of surprise plot detours and interesting use of tracking errors to obscure its monster's visage.

Swanberg's "The Sickening Thing That Happened To Emily When She Was Younger" is better than its overlong, misleading title suggests. It's the first flourish of real creativity on offer, Rogers starring as an increasingly fraught young woman who shares reservations about both her health and her seemingly haunted apartment via computer video chats with her sympathetic boyfriend. A claustrophobic atmosphere, some successful scares and a novel screenplay which manages to marry disparate subjects like alien incubation and schizo-affective disorder within a tight running time, all help this one to impress.

"10/31/98" concludes the shorts. It's a dark, bloody and incomplete-feeling endeavour from Radio Silence (a collective consisting of Matt Bettinelli-Olpin, Tyler Gillett, Justin Martinez and Chad Villella). Pranksters enter a haunted house on Halloween night, bad things happen. More shaky point-of-view camerawork abounds.

Wingard's concluding wraparound is nonsense.

The brainchild of Brad Miska, founder of popular reviews site Bloody Disgusting, *V/H/S* premiered at the 2012 Sundance Film Festival. Two people reportedly fainted during the screening. Which seems … unlikely.

Still, for all that the film is overlong, inconsistent and only occasionally inspired, it was successful enough to spawn two sequels to date: 2013's *V/H/S 2* and 2014's *V/H/S: Viral*. Directors involved across these films include the likes of Eduardo Sanchez, Gareth Evans and Nacho Vigalondo. Wingard was the only returnee from the original film (he directs a segment of *V/H/S 2*).

Victima 102
See *Snuff 102*

Vile (2011)

Dir: Taylor Sheridan; Scr: Eric Jay Beck, Rob Kowsaluk; Cast: Eric Jay Beck, April Matson, Akeem Smith

A group of strangers awaken to find themselves trapped together in a life-threatening situation …

Saw (2004) has a lot to answer for, as evidenced by a whole plethora of cheap derivatives in recent years. *Aquarium* (2004), *Breathing Room* (2008), *Hunger* (2009), *Nine Dead* (2010), *Would You Rather* (2012): take your pick of the cheap knock-offs, quick to capitalise on the notion of capturing characters in a conveniently confined environment and pitting them against gruelling tasks in the name of delivering requisite scenes of torture for our delectation. *Vile* can be added to that cycle.

… while adding nothing to the fray.

Its premise at least possesses a gimmick: this disparate bunch have been gathered so their captors can acquire naturally produced chemicals from their brains, in order to create a powerful drug which is storming the underground market. The chemicals involved are those generated when the body experiences great pain: a vial has been attached to each unwitting captive's neck in a bid to house whatever fluids their cranium releases under stress.

Naturally, we get a chief abductor addressing our bewildered protagonists via video message, explaining that they have twenty-four hours to inflict pheromone-inducing agony upon each other, otherwise they die (it may have been easier to simply torture these unfortunates directly and get it within ten minutes?). As the clock ticks away, the group's reticence gradually dissipates as they resolve to punch, stab and even castrate each other in the hope of living to see another day.

The resolve of the human spirit. A base instinct to pursue life. Are these the things *Vile* is addressing? Possibly. Or it may be that former actor Sheridan et al are simply latching on to a trend for self-contained torture-porn which shows no sign of flagging any time soon.

To assess, then. Performances are adequate if unremarkable. Characterisation is absent – we learn the bare minimum about each representative (one girl is distinguished as being pregnant … but that's all we ever learn about her). Violence is frequent, though the harshest gore often occurs off-screen. A twist ending is both obvious and clumsily executed. And no-one satisfactorily explores the fact that the same desired hormonal chemicals could've been obtained through making each other orgasm …

All told, there's little to recommend.

Villa Captive (2011)

Dir/Scr: Emmanuel Silvestre; Cast: Emilie Delaunay, Dario Lado, Derek Evans

French adult actress Delaunay temporarily drops her popular porn pseudonym of Liza Del Sierra – former triumphs include *Manuel's French Fucking Vacation* and *Fantasstic* (both 2010) - to frontline this softcore rape-revenge flick under her birth name.

Perhaps ironically, then, she portrays a burned-out porn star in need of a vacation. Supposedly incognito while chilling in a luxury Florida villa, her topless sunbathing garners the unwelcome attention of her landlord's adolescent son and his lowlife pals. They recognise her from previous wank fests and decide that, as she's bound to be wealthy, they should rob her secluded retreat. Her unexpected presence at the scene of the intended crime escalates matters into the realms of home invasion and sexual assault. Of course, she duly opts to retaliate.

Shot on the Canon 5D camera, *Villa Captive* looks impressively sharp and detailed. Intelligent colour correction has taken place in post-production, safeguarding the film against that cheap digital look. United with accomplished editing and an effective score, this helps Silvestre's film comes across as highly proficient on a technical level.

Despite this, fans will undoubtedly measure its success purely upon how shocking it can be. It's being sold to the people who elevated *I Spit On Your Grave* (1978) to cult status, after all.

As such, the film falls short of titillating its target audience's taste-buds. The sexual violence is toned down in comparison to Meir Zarchi's clear source of inspiration, and decidedly tame when presented alongside modern efforts such as *Gutterballs* (2008) or even *The Hospital* (2013). Considering her onscreen legacy, it's interesting to note that Delaunay remains clothed for most of the running time and Silvestre shies away from depicting the rapes in any manner which is alarming or even censor-baiting. Even the climactic scenes of retribution, relegated largely to the film's final ten minutes, are bashful in their preference for implied bloodshed.

Delaunay is unpredictably strong in the lead role though: hers is a performance of both candour and resilience, capable of getting the audience onside from an early point. It's a shame she fell straight back into after-hours efforts like *Cum Fart Cocktails 9* (2012) and *Naughty Double Penetration* (2015). I suppose, as a performer, you go where the money is …

The Visit (2015)

Dir/Scr: M Night Shyamalan; Cast: Olivia DeJonge, Ed Oxenbould, Deanna Dunagan

Single mother Kathryn Hann hasn't spoken to her parents in fifteen years, following an incident that she'd rather not share with her children DeJonge and Oxenbould. Seeking a week's respite with her new beau, she sees this as the perfect time to respond to an email from her folks and drop the kids off with them for a short stay. DeJonge decides to film events on her digital camera.

But as the kids settle in to their grandparents' secluded home, they realise all is not as it seems.

Indian-born Shyamalan first grabbed our attention with his third directorial effort, 1999's *The Sixth Sense* - a taut mystery with a much-discussed twist which not only helped bring slick supernatural content back to the fore of mainstream marketability, but also revealed Bruce Willis as a credible actor. The film was a critical and commercial smash. Since then, however, the writer-director's career has been startlingly erratic. 2000's *Unbreakable* was a respectable follow-up; later efforts such as *Lady In The Water* (2006), *The Happening* (2008) and *The Last Airbender* (2009) were lambasted by the press and suffered at the box office.

Shyamalan bounced back with *The Visit*, a much more low-key affair than recent flops, working with a self-funded budget of $5 million. He stated in interviews at the time that this approach allowed him complete artistic control over the end product – insinuating that studio interference was to blame for preceding failures.

He may be right. *The Visit* is his most rewarding picture since 1999. We still get the anticipated twist, which works, but it's the climb towards it that's so much fun. The kids are knowingly annoying (especially Oxenbould, whose character has a penchant for creating terrible improvised raps); Dunagan and Peter McRobbie are excellent as the increasingly sinister old folks. The balance of tone between comedy – funny - and incremental unease – convincing - is deftly straddled by Shyamalan. He keeps his premise simple and tense, employing the potentially hackneyed documentary-style approach to good, raw effect.

It just goes to show, you should never write a filmmaker off ...

Vittra
See *Wither*

Vomit Gore 4
See *Black Mass Of The Nazi Sex Wizard*

The Void (2016)

Dir/Scr: Jeremy Gillespie, Steven Kostanski; Cast: Aaron Poole, Kenneth Welsh, Daniel Fathers

Astron-6 components Gillespie and Kostanski - see also *The Editor* (2014) - concocted this simulacrum of 1980s horror flicks as a departure from the more comical tenor provided by the aforementioned group's efforts. Here, the tone is darker, more staid.

Poole is the cop who enters into a world of continual headaches when he rescues an incapacitated man (Evan Stern) from the scene of a farmhouse bloodbath. Taking him to the understaffed hospital where his estranged wife works, Poole is swiftly thrust into the role of reluctant hero when hooded figures surround the building. Their arrival prompts patients to start morphing into tentacled creatures, while an alternate domain is discovered in the infirmary's basement.

Direct involvement in earlier cult favourites such as *Manborg* and *Father's Day* (both 2011) clearly helped the co-directors raise over $80,000.00 via crowd-funding site Indiegogo. This worked towards making this a lavish homage, rammed to the gills with striking production design, noteworthy lighting and cartoonishly gory practical FX work overseen by Gillespie.

It's a fun affair, frequently engaging, but there are imperfections.

The script doesn't care too much for its characters. They're all fairly one-dimensional and never truly expanded upon. Hence we feel no obligation to empathise with their increasingly outlandish predicament. Cult actor Art Hindle (*The Brood*, 1979) turns up in an extended cameo and is the most interesting screen presence felt.

Then there's the plotting. Although imparted in linear fashion, we're often left in the dark as to the motivations of key figures - the occult group lurking outside, for example - and subplots such as one concerning the plight of missing children are never satisfactorily explored. It's easy to become confused by what's going on, should you make the mistake of looking for conventional explanations.

Finally, the film struggles to carry off its ambition of surfacing as a finely balanced merging of homage and fresh cinema, by insisting on being almost overbearingly referential. John Carpenter is clearly an influence - the skeleton staff protecting their hospital overnight from outside invaders brings to mind *Assault On Precinct 13* (1976) while the cultish figures echo similar imagery from 1987's *Prince Of Darkness*. Elsewhere, there are nods to *Alien* (1979), *The Beyond* (1981) and *The Thing* (1982). Perhaps most dominant though are the frequent references to the works of HP Lovecraft: specifically, short stories "The Call Of Cthulhu" (1926) and "The Dunwich Horror" (1928), and the novella "The Shadow Over Innsmouth" (1931).

If you're simply looking for stylishly rendered atmosphere and some competent old-school gore, however, *The Void* should meet your requirements.

Voodoo Curse - Legba's Rache (2009)

Dir/Scr: Stefan Svahn; Cast: Gordon Racker, Daniel Flugger, Suzanne Svahn

A marked technical improvement when measured against his 2005 debut *The Lost Way Of The Zombies*, *Voodoo Curse* sees all-rounder Svahn (he directs, writes, produces, edits, photographs and co-stars in this film, along with handling the splashy effects work) find his stylistic rhythm while delivering a fast-paced, enjoyably old-school living dead chompathon.

Racker is the young Goth suffering from recurring nightmares which may or may not be premonitions. Despite reservations, he's coerced by pal Flugger into following a bunch of their metalhead friends to a local cemetery, where they hope to take a shitload of drugs and communicate with the dead using a recently discovered book of spells.

Three guesses as to what happens next? One word: zombies!

Once the dead have risen, the action is relentlessly piled on. Characters are one-dimensional for the most part, but that's okay: they only exist to be torn apart anyway. Cue lots of decapitations, flesh-eating and ripping of unconvincing intestines. The pace and quick-fire succession of hokey gore recall Andrea Bianchi's *Burial Ground* (1981) while the crusty, ambling ghouls are definitely a throwback to the heydays of Giannetto De Rossi and Lucio Fulci (*Zombie Flesh Eaters* [1979]; *The House By The Cemetery* [1981] etc. One character is even named Dr Freudstein in a nod to the latter film). It's little surprise that Svahn appears to have focused more on becoming an FX artist in recent years - I really need to check out his work on *Turbo Zombi - Tampons Of The Dead* (2011)!

Perhaps a little too insubstantial to merit its feature-length running time, and not always capable of disguising the limitations of its 2,300 Euros budget, *Voodoo Curse* is nevertheless an entertaining and likeable addition to the ever-growing German splatter cycle. Svahn's DIY aesthetics pay off, his lead actors are agreeable and the gore is righteous enough to distract from the instances of bad metal on the soundtrack.

Voyage To Agatis (2010)

Dir/Scr: Marian Dora; Cast: Thomas Goersch, Tatjana Paige Muller, Janna Lisa Dombrowsky

Middle-aged couple Goersch and Muller decide to put the zing back into their marriage by inviting hot young Slovenian Dombrowsky for a ride on their yacht. Inexplicably keen to get it on with the jaded twosome, the striking filly gets a lot more than she bargained for as rape, degradation and murder become the afternoon's highlights.

The mysterious Dora has crafted a solid reputation as Germany's prime purveyor of transgressive art-horror hybrids in recent years. *Cannibal* (2006), a loose retelling of a gobsmacking actual event from 2001 where 39-year-old Armin Meiwes successfully advertised online for a "victim" willing to be murdered and eaten, was as repulsive in its cock-butchery as it was pretentious in its lingering close-ups of mating snails; 2009's *The Angel's Melancholy* proffered a sprawling, symbolism-heavy delayering of his country's psyche, replete with unconscionable sexual sadism and non-simulated violence against animals.

With *Agatis* – an extension of a concept explored in his 2002 short *Caribbean Sunrise* - the elusive filmmaker's approach is slightly more accessible: a running time of little over an hour necessitates that the pace is punchier than in previous efforts, and the only instance of animal cruelty comes in the form of the gutting of a sea cucumber.

The largely improvised plot – developed from an original idea by the film's producer Adrian d'Angelo – owes much to Ruggero Deodato's *Waves Of Lust* (1975), which itself is indebted to Roman Polanski's brilliant *Knife In The Water* (1962). As with those films, a sense of claustrophobia is expertly fostered by setting the action on the solitude of a small boat out at sea.

In Dora's hands, however, Deodato and Polanski's themes of dominance, deception and role-play are spurned in favour of unsparing brutality. Any points being made are recondite: the need to inflict suffering to curb one's own pain (Goersh is quickly established as a violent, unfulfilled drunk) is one possible reading; man's pathological corruption of that which is pure - as represented by Dombrowsky's virginal white dress and shaven genitalia - is another.

Sexual assault, multiple stab wounds ,vaginal mutilation and nipple-maiming will keep the misanthropists happy. Full credit to Dora, his special effects are highly convincing.

Filmed around Croatia over the course of three days in late 2008, *Agatis* gains from sun-kissed exteriors, whispered passages of poetry and oneiric images of battered dolls floating esoterically in the sea. Despite being shot on low-grade video and containing bookending scenes of barbaric violence caught through sharply edited bursts of handheld camerawork, the film on balance succeeds as an attractive visual proposition as a consequence.

Apparently a surgeon by day (which perhaps explains the relentless morbidity of his cinematic works), Dora also provides a paradoxically soothing score under the pseudonym of Transmitted Dreams. This lends a deeper illusion of elegance to his persuasively nihilistic tale.

The VVitch: A New England Folktale
See *The Witch*

The Wailing (2016)

Dir/Scr: Hong-jin Na; Cast: Kwak Do-won, Chun Woo-hee, Hwang Jung-min

Residents of a small village in the Korean mountains are falling ill. Symptoms include violent outbursts, delirium and eventual death. Local policeman Do-won initially puts the outbreak down to people eating wild mushrooms. But then villager Woo-hee suggests that the illnesses coincide with the arrival of a Japanese stranger (Jun Kunimura) in their midst.

With the help of shaman Jung-min, Do-won begins to investigate Kunimura's remote home. Their pursuit of the elusive stranger intensifies when Do-won's daughter becomes the latest victim of the mystery sickness.

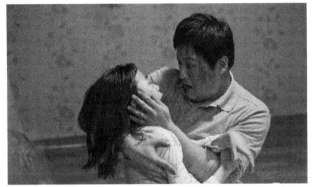

Following a couple of shorts at the start of his career, South Korean filmmaker Hong-jin Na's rise in prominence has been unabated since his feature debut, *The Chaser*, in 2008. 2010's *The Yellow Sea* consolidated his reputation as "one to watch", and the promise continues with *The Wailing* - his biggest commercial success to date.

But the film is not without its issues. For a genre flick it's long at 156 minutes in length. Which, in itself, isn't a problem - only, there's not enough going on to justify this running time (it could easily have been trimmed by a half-hour). And for all its meticulous visual style and expert moments of emotional manipulation, it can't be denied that the screenplay loses its train of thought on more than one occasion during the final hour, resulting in plot-holes galore.

On a happier note, the film is compelling enough during playback to ensure this latter shortcoming doesn't register until reflecting back on your viewing. Performances are uniformly strong; not-so-subtle moments of humour bring a necessary element of human warmth to proceedings; a mood of impending dread is expertly composed and sustained.

At its heart lie themes of faith, folklore and community. Forgive its lapses of focus and *The Wailing* still succeeds as stirring, thought-provoking cinema - while delivering one of cinema's most exhilerating exorcisms. Hong-jin Na's star continues to rise.

Wake The Witch (2010)

Dir/Scr: Dorothy Booream; Cast: Stefanie Tapio, Rachel Lien, Martin Kenna

Blamed for a spate of child killings, a woman is branded as a witch by angry townsfolk. Their vengeance is severe: her body is wrapped in chains and dragged to local woods, where she's hanged and buried. A hundred years pass, the legend of said witch gathering momentum among fresh generations in the meantime.

This brings us to the present day, where we meet photography student Tapio and her pals. They're out scouring their local woods for suitable shooting locations when they happen upon an old chain, thus prompting a discussion about the legend. Unwittingly, the girls "awaken" the wronged spirit: before long, they notice their families and friends behaving oddly, coming down with inexplicable ailments and so on. Oh, and who are those vampiric figures, emerging in the woods occasionally wearing bad make-up and hooded sweaters?

You may well ask. Telling a clear story is not one of Booream's strong points. It all starts off simply enough, then trundles off into largely irrelevant sub-plots as Tapio struggles to tolerate her boyfriend and her friends get ratty around their relatives. I'm all for fleshing-out characters, but it needs to serve a purpose. Alas, *Wake The Witch* spends an age on redundant side-stories which, thanks to a poor script, uninvolving characters and inexperienced acting, add nothing of dramatic relevance or emotional weight.

Shot in Lincoln, Nebraska on a JVC HD camera (the GY-HD250U, for the nerds) and a budget of $10,000.00, the film does at least look decent; Chad Haufschild's cinematography makes fair use of the exterior locations. But, at almost two hours in length, this is far too long. It barely holds the attention, such is the lack of empathy we feel for the fundamentally boring protagonists. There's a complete absence of threat as a consequence.

It's also safe to assume that the film is set in the present. So, does Booream really believe that people were being castigated as witches as recently as in 1910?

Booream says she was influenced by Japanese horror cinema, and that she wanted to emulate its skill for creating suspense "with a minimal palette". *Wake The Witch* seems designed to test the fortitude of even the most forgiving viewer. James Oliva's subtle score and some respectable photography aren't enough to make it worth your time.

Watch Out (2008)

Dir: Steve Balderson; Scr: Steve Balderson, Joseph Suglia; Cast: Matt Riddlehoover, Amy Kelly, Peter Stickles

Riddlehoover excels as a narcissistic yuppie on his way to a job interview at an out-of-town college. Along the way, he's propositioned by suitors of both sexes – all of whom he rebuffs. He is, in fact, autosexual: completely, utterly in love with himself.

So much so that the film's most memorable scenes find Riddlehoover taking self-appreciation to its absurdist extremes. Masturbating to video footage of himself wanking; strapping a photo of his own face onto a blow-up doll in preparation of then fucking it; pulling his pud while drooling over polaroid pictures of his own dick … welcome to the height of vanity.

That really is all there is to the plot, at least for the first fifty minutes or so. Riddlehoover's narration is frequently amusing as he clues us in on the extent of his disgust for the inferiority he sees everywhere around him, his obliviously clueless rants at times echoing those of Christian Bale's in *American Psycho* (2000). Played out in vignette-style, the whole thing hinges massively on its central performance: fortunately it's in good hands. Riddlehoover – who went on to become a notable director of intelligent gay cinema (*Scenes From A Gay Marriage* [2012], *Paternity Leave* [2015] etc) – plays it all with just enough charm and comic timing to make a fundamentally despicable character curiously endearing.

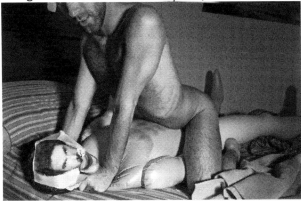

Split into two acts, the second one is relatively short – twenty minutes – and successfully jolts the viewer by dramatically changing the tone. This is where the film becomes a horror picture, incorporating scenes of toe amputation and enforced penis-eating.

There's a distinct air of John Waters' cinema here. Flashback sequences detailing how Riddlehoover's parents tried unsuccessfully to arrange his deflowering at the hands of a prostitute are reminiscent of the Baltimore auteur's earlier works such as *Female Trouble* (1974); the present-tense action, well-shot and sardonic, owes more to the slightly more refined style of *Serial Mom* (1994) or *Pecker* (1998).

Set in Michigan but filmed without permits around Wamego, Kansas, *Watch Out* is based on Suglia's 2006 novel of the same name. The movie premiered at London's Raindance Film Festival in October 2008 where it was nominated for Best International Feature. It lost out to Marcos Jorge's *Estomago: A Gastronomic Story* (2007).

Wendigo (2001)

Dir/Scr: Larry Fessenden; Cast: Jake Weber, Patricia Clarkson, John Speredakos

Weber needs a break from his stressful city job. To this end he takes wife Clarkson and their son (the excellent Erik Per Sullivan) into the Catskills on vacation. En route he runs a deer down; local hunter Speredakos is enraged that the beast *he* was tracking has been slain. Upon arriving at their cabin retreat, the family is perturbed to discover the hunter is their neighbour.

But that's not all. Why is their cabin littered with bullet holes? Who was the man who gave Sullivan a wooden figurine of an Indian spirit called The Wendigo, only to vanish moments later?

Fessenden takes the North American native legend of an evil spirit said to possess humans and imbue them with cannibalistic traits, and imprints it into the mind of impressionable Sullivan. While the audience witnesses a less ambiguous solution to the odd occurrences which follow – rationalising that Speredakos and cohorts are most likely responsible for the bad tidings befalling Weber's brood – the young boy sees everything as a direct action of the titular monster.

Does the creature exist? Are the boy's qualms due to be vindicated? These are moot points. What works so effectively here is how Fessenden presents the action from the kid's perspective, making either plot outcome seem feasible while successfully encouraging us to share in Sullivan's fear.

Shot on 16mm, *Wendigo*'s grainy look works in its favour. It adds a dark, gritty quality which perfectly complements the film's bleak, genuinely spooky mood. Fessenden takes his time letting the plot unfurl, focusing on believable characters and strong performances, allowing for that ambiguity over the nature of events to really sink in.

With a convincing villain in Speredakos and fine haunting photography from Terry Stacey, *Wendigo* holds up well for the bulk of its running time. There's only the final act's reliance on providing hallucinogenic thrills that threatens to undermine the earlier folklore-led abstruseness.

What We Do In The Shadows (2014)

Dir/Scr: Jemaine Clement, Taika Waititi; Cast: Jonny Brugh, Jemaine Clement, Taika Waititi

A mockumentary from the team behind New Zealand TV comedy show "Flight of the Conchords" (2007-2009). I'll admit it – I was sceptical.

A film crew are given privileged access to the home of four flatmates. They're there to document their day-to-day life. The usual tribulations blight this group: disputes over the household chore rota (can they finally get Brugh to wash their mounting pile of dirty dishes?); communal trips out to the local nightclub and the drama that inevitably ensues; the headache of taking in a new roomie and discovering whether they're capable of getting along with an already-established ensemble. It's "rites of passage" stuff with one major difference … these flatmates are vampires.

Whittled down from purportedly over 120 hours of largely improvised footage, Clement and Waititi deliver a fast-paced succession of situational sketches. Some have consequently argued that *Shadows* is plotless. However, a narrative does emerge as events progress – specifically relating to an impending ball (The Unholy Masquerade) which the bloodsuckers are gearing towards attending, and the promise of all loose ends being tied up there. These include Clement's historical troubles with a nemesis referred to as The Beast (Elena Stejko).

Along the way, there are successful gags concerning ongoing spats with a rival gang of werewolves (vampires versus lycanthropes: realised with much more success here than in 2008's *Twilight*), gross things done to a sandwich, Brugh's erotic dance ... Too many to mention, in fact.

Indeed, the jokes far outweigh the customary tropes expected of the genre: go into this expecting a comedy, rather than a full-blown horror flick, and you're a lot less likely to come away feeling short-changed. Though that's not to say clichés aren't explored and demystified along the way, geysers of blood aren't sprayed across the screen, or flatmate Petyr (Ben Fransham) doesn't make for a superb homage to Barlow, the lead vampire from Tobe Hooper's *Salem's Lot* (1979).

It's all throwaway, of course – and a tad smug at times too (Mr Brugh, stop looking like you want to laugh at yourself) – but ultimately it's difficult not to warm to this 21st Century overhaul of genre conventions.

Even if the under-seen Belgian film *Vampires* (2010) did do it first.

When Animals Dream (2014)

Dir: Jonas Alexander Arnby; Scr: Rasmus Birch; Cast: Sonia Suhl, Lars Mikkelsen, Sonja Richter

This Danish-French co-production is the most absorbing werewolf-as-metaphor-for-sexual-awakening picture since 2000's *Ginger Snaps*.

Set in an icily cool Denmark (shot in the small town of Agger), it tells of subdued teenager Suhl, whose life is dedicated to caring for wheelchair-bound mother Richter and depressive father Mikkelsen. Why do the locals of their sleepy fishing village look upon them with such suspicion? How come the family doctor continually injects Richter with drugs to keep her frail? What are those strange rashes and hairy growths suddenly appearing on Suhl's body? Questions, questions ...

The pace is relaxed, the photography austere and arctic. Performances are subtly nuanced. Much like another recent Scandinavian horror hit, 2008's *Let The Right One In*, *When Animals Dream* is as much an art film as it is a genre flick.

Also, as with that movie, Arnby's film weaves an offbeat romance successfully into its tale. Here, Suhl is awakened by the attentions of sincere suitor Jakob Oftebro. Theirs is a tender courtship which builds into a love-against-odds affair not entirely removed to that at the centre of William Shakespeare's 1597 tragedy "Romeo And Juliet".

The sexual hunger ignited in the otherwise reserved Suhl, along with the physical transformations brought about by going through puberty, are palpable allusions to the lycanthropic legacy suggested as her fate. Interestingly, the film also bears (very) loose comparison to Walerian Borowczyk's *The Beast* (1975): both examine a family coping with a hereditary illness which manifests itself in grotesque corporeal form.

Less visceral and more psychological, a blind buy from *wolfman* devotees may result in initial disappointment. But stick with this languid, painstaking event and your patience will be rewarded. *When Animals Dream* may be light on shocks and gore but it builds a sense of unease in cogent style.

Only the make-up effects during the final act can undermine what is an otherwise thoroughly involving, appropriately restrained meditation on internal growth, anxiety, repressed emotions and - in the case of Suhl's colleagues when she starts work at the local fish processing plant - a community reluctant to co-exist with different cultures. Timely.

White God (2014)

Dir: Kornel Mundruczo; Scr: Kornel Mundruczo, Viktoria Petranyi, Kata Weber; Cast: Zsofia Psotta, Sandor Zsoter, Lili Horvath

Hungary's official entry into the Best Foreign Language Film category at the 2015 Academy Awards delivers a curious blend of authentic World Cinema polemic and polished action.

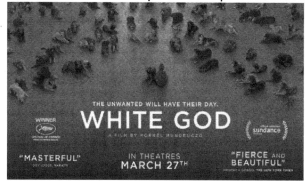

It tells of Psotta, a thirteen-year-old girl whose beloved dog is kicked out onto the mean streets by her estranged father Zsoter. The catalyst is a new (fictitious) tax introduced by the government imposing upon people housing mixed-breed canines. The remainder of the film divides its running time between Psotta's plight to reunite with her wandering pet and the tribulations of the peripatetic beast. To this end, we're privy to hideous organised dog fights, the threat of the local pound, and the systematic abuse endured by dogs at the hands of ignorant human adults …

Such is the suffering of lead pet Hagen (portrayed by twin shelter veterans Body and Luke, skilfully trained into delivering staggering performances) that he eventually rallies round a huge pack of similarly maltreated canines and spearheads a violent revolt.

White God is ostensibly a cautionary tale of how the oppressed and outcast may someday rise up against their oppressors. Marcell Rev's assured, attractive cinematography affords events a glossy finish which, alongside the inclusion of Franz Liszt's stirring "Hungarian Rhapsody Number 2" and a tautly edited latter half, makes a compelling argument for Mundruczo's intentions of this also crossing over as a mainstream-appeasing action film.

Indubitably, the Budapest setting creates a convincing environment in which social divides and state oppression can easily be envisaged. At the same time, Mundruczo desires to exhilarate (often through disturbingly cruel set-pieces), proffering a slick and tense thriller design which merges social commentary and visceral reaction in a style somewhat similar to *Rise Of The Planet Of The Apes* (2011).

Like that film, the violent action flirts perilously close to full-on horror as events progress. Furthermore, Mundruczo's film can be likened to templates such as 1971's *Willard* (one child's emotional connection to their pet, pitted against a vengeful nature's rampage), Samuel Fuller's *White Dog* from 1982 (can love conquer conditioning?) and Alfred Hitchcock's celebrated 1963 eco-horror *The Birds* (a cunning collective mentality; the mass assaults as the animal kingdom has its revenge upon man).

274 dogs were used in total, all of which were recruited from various animal shelters. This set a new world record for the most dogs employed in any single film. The scenes in which they attack en masse are undeniably as consummate as they are seemingly feral.

The final scene – which, after two hours of a story told in flashback, returns us to the opening image – is beautifully photographed and peculiarly poignant.

Despite losing out on the Oscar to Poland's excellent *Ida* (2013), *White God* got lucky at the 2014 Cannes Film Festival, picking up the Un Certain Regard prize awarded annually to promising new filmmakers.

Wired
See *Hanger*

The Witch (2015)

Dir/Scr: Robert Eggers; Cast: Ralph Ineson, Anya Taylor-Joy, Kate Dickie

New England, in the 17th Century. Ineson's family are ran out of their village by a court order, such are their oppressive, overly puritanical principles. Upon settling into the neighbouring woods, the clan are thrown into further turmoil when the youngest of the brood – a baby boy – goes missing. Suspicion is initially cast upon the infant's teenaged sibling, a show-stealing Taylor-Joy. But, as the family's luck goes from bad to worse, they begin to believe that the legend of a local witch is true … and that they are suffering under her curse.

Filmed in Canada, *The Witch* is an absorbingly slow and atmospheric delight which relies heavily on ambiguity for much of its running time. The Enochian dialect may require time for some viewers to adjust to, but its use is an admirable attempt at evoking the setting. Thankfully, there are no obvious anachronisms to spoil this effect.

Themes of grief, trust, the comfort of religion and the sanctity of family are examined in satisfying detail. Those hoping for regular bursts of gore or shock-tactics will find precious little to high-five. There are few easy answers proffered herein, and *The Witch* plays out more agreeably as a result.

Understated for the large part in terms of theatrics, there is however a creeping sense of dread successfully induced through ethereal visuals, stunning sound design and an intelligent focus on the rising to the fore of familial anxieties which keep in-group paranoia prominent throughout. Indeed, it's only the revealing conclusion that robs the film somewhat of the power it builds en route.

That's not to take anything away from first-time feature director Eggers, or his committed cast – including an impressive Ineson, who's a million miles removed here from his immortalisation of the womanising prat Finchy in Ricky Gervais' UK sitcom "The Office" (2001-2003).

While not quite the outright classic many have claimed it to be, *The Witch* compels from an early juncture and continues to hold the attention well.

The Witches Hammer (2006)

Dir/Scr: Jim Eaves; Cast: Claudia Coulter, Stephanie Beacham, Tina Barnes

Coulter wakes from a physical assault only to discover she's become the subject of a top secret agency's latest experiment. Equipped with a newfound thirst for blood and a healthy disposition of immortality (unless she happens to get decapitated or pierced through the heart), she's trained over the course of the ensuing year into becoming a highly skilled vampire assassin.

Eventually falling into the hands of Beacham's rival agency, she's tasked with her most dangerous mission yet: rescue the titular ancient book, capable of raising the dead, from the clutches of evil bloodsucker Hugo (Tom Dover).

Lazy comparisons alert: it's *Nikita* (1990) meets *Blade* (1998), via *Underworld* (2003), in this cheap actioner from the director of *Bane* (2008).

The scene is set for beginners' level CGI, ropy home video aesthetics and hand-to-hand fight scenes which I'd guess were prepared for by watching hours of "Mortal Kombat" videogame footage. Throw in a British screen icon (Beacham – *The Nightcomers* [1971], *House Of Mortal Sin* [1976] etc), regular bouts of gore and model-turned-actress Coulter in a tight-fitting leather outfit, and you get a film which is as entertaining as it is rough around the edges.

Mark Conrad Chambers' throbbing, energetic score complements the daft action set-pieces – which also carry a hint of *The Matrix* (1999) about them – while the high-spirited performances compensate for any clumsiness in Eaves' frequently silly script. Tonally, the cast embrace the cartoonish vibe and run with it.

A couple of unnecessary flashback sequences highlight the film's lack of budget; peripheral performers often can't act for toffee.

But, overall, *The Witches Hammer* overcomes any obvious limitations to emerge as a professional-looking, fluently paced and thoroughly engaging slice of madcap fun.

Wither (2012)

Dir: Sonny Laguna, Tommy Wiklund; Scr: Sonny Laguna, David Liljeblad, Tommy Wiklund; Cast: Patrik Almkvist, Lisa Henni, Patrick Saxe

Loved-up couple Almkvist and Henni invite their friends to a secluded cabin in the woods for a weekend of merry-making. One by one the revellers become possessed by something evil lurking within the cabin's cellar. Much bloodshed ensues.

Yes, yes. There are distinct similarities between the synopsis above and that of *The Evil Dead* (1981). But, for all that *Wither* lacks originality in its storytelling, it emerges as a more sincere prospect than the far bigger budgeted official remake of Sam Raimi's indie hit, 2013's imaginatively titled *Evil Dead* (well, they dropped the *The* ...).

Shot on location in Knivsta for 300,000 Swedish Krona - about £27,000 pounds - there is a raw energy to Laguna and Wiklund's approach which can't help but encourage viewers to get on side. Oh, and a Hell of a lot of gore.

On that front, *Wither* excels. The special effects, courtesy of the filmmakers along with Goran Lundstrom, Leo Thorn and their respective teams, are excellent. Gooey, convincing, practical: their efforts achieve everything you'd hope for from a modern-day demonic possession film. Naturally, instances of bodily dismemberment are a given.

If anything, *Wither* is darker, grittier than the film it's so brazenly paying homage to. Any humour is much less evident. But we still get creative camerawork, spirited performances and - once the slow start has ran its course - a breakneck pace during the final hour. Shot in HD on a Canon 7D camera, it looks great too.

The film's domestic title is *Vittra*. This refers to a creature which is a mainstay in terms of Norse folklore: an underground-dwelling beast akin to a troll or evil spirit, preying on animals and humans whenever its peace has been disturbed. So, now you know.

Forgive this one for its righteous pilfering; embrace it for a final act of insane gore and screaming galore.

The Wolfman (2010)

Dir: Joe Johnston; Scr: Andrew Kevin Walker, David Self; Cast: Benicio Del Toro, Emily Blunt, Anthony Hopkins

Following his release from an asylum, Del Toro has travelled the globe in a bid to escape his tormented past. He's lured home to his father Hopkins' estate by the pleas of Blunt, his missing brother's fiancée. The search for the absent sibling ends bloodily. Inspector Aberline (Hugo Weaving) snoops around as Del Toro familiarises himself with his family's curse - and unearths a fate from which he can't escape.

Shot on 35mm around several locations in the South of England, on a reported budget of $150 million, *The Wolfman* is nothing if not lavish. From Danny Elfman's sweeping score (not one of his more memorable efforts, it has to be said) to the A-list casting and immaculate production design, the refined aesthetics scream out "Hollywood" sheen at every juncture.

Special effects are supervised by the legendary Rick Baker. He oversees a team of over fifty artists, bringing him back to the realms of lycanthropic cinema: in 1981 he won the first ever Academy Award for Best Make-Up, for his work on that year's superior *An American Werewolf In London*.

Johnston is comfortable working with special effects on a large scale. His directorial resume also includes *Jumanji* (1995) and *Jurassic Park 3* (2001). What he's not so well-versed in is the theatre of horror. Perhaps due to a box office necessity, his werewolf shenanigans are largely toothless and pretty, positing themselves somewhere between the mainstream fantasy of 2004's *Van Helsing* and the dour navel-gazing tedium of the *Twilight* series (2008-2012).

Del Toro acts as if such fare is beneath him; Hopkins hams it up as only he can. Blunt makes for an attractive if somewhat uninspiring love interest. As the intense detective, Weaving by default becomes the best of a fairly mediocre bunch.

There's precious little threat to be found here. No sense of menace. The film spends an inordinate amount of time on exposition and conveying the scope of its production. When the drama finally kicks in it's a tad too late and lifeless to engage. Viewers are advised to stick to 1941's original Universal monster movie classic instead.

Wound (2010)

Dir/Scr: David Blyth, Cast: Kate O'Rourke, Te Kaea Beri, Campbell Cooley

Unhinged O'Rourke's life becomes even more complicated when the daughter she thought had been stillborn turns up on her doorstep. Is Beri real, or a product of O'Rourke's crumbling imagination?

Abuse at the hands of an incestuous parent which leads to psychosis later in life: we've had it before, one noteworthy entry being Matt Cimber's brilliant *The Witch Who Came From The Sea* (1976). Blyth explores the same theme but in a completely contrasting manner. Whereas *Witch* flirted lightly with surrealism during its mainly conventional, dialogue-heavy plot, *Wound* adopts a far more abstract approach, favouring nightmarish visuals and broken logic over the spoken word – to the point where narrative is all-but non-existent come the midway point.

Decidedly obscure in terms of storytelling, Blyth proffers a descent into a Hell where the difference between reality and hallucination is as muddled as the lead character's mind. Tonally, this is a startlingly bleak proposition from beginning to end – a world away from the dark humour of Blyth's best-known genre picture, 1984's mad scientist romp *Death Warmed Up*. Concepts of guilt, loss, revenge and sadness are poured over in po-faced fashion. A very early graphic castration lets us know what we're in for. *Wound* rarely lets up from there: rape, mother-daughter nipple sucking, a gory throat-slashing, the ritualistic humiliation of O'Rourke by her boss ... Prepare for an unhealthy amount of angst. Along with a wild, bloody birth scene involving a giant vagina ...

O'Rourke is excellent, holding the madness together with her steely stare while displaying a fine range of believable emotions. Without her, I feel this would've fallen apart entirely.

Considering he's been making movies, on-and-off, since the mid 1970s, Blyth's hand often comes across like that of a novice film student here. References to Shakespeare's "The Tempest" and Greek mythology are horribly heavy-handed; the cheap arty feel to each composition reeks of someone desperately striving to attain a level of the experimental which remains out of their budgetary reach.

For a 77-minute film, it's also a slow-moving affair. The unrelenting misery being conveyed doesn't help the cause. Perhaps it's this tenor that the New Zealand press objected to, to the point of calling (unsuccessfully) to get the film banned there. As much as they beg for controversy, the cavalcade of extreme images are too clumsily realised to provoke outrage on their own.

According to Breaking Glass Pictures' press kit which accompanied their US DVD release, the late Ken Russell – *The Devils* (1971), *Gothic* (1986) etc – heralded *Wound* as being "a masterpiece". It isn't.

Wrestlemaniac (2006)

Dir/Scr: Jesse Baget; Cast: Adam Huss, Jeremy Radin, Rey Misterio Sr

A group of young Scooby Doo-esque adults drive through Mexico looking for a suitable location to shoot their calling-card porno. The typical stereotypes fill their van: the slutty airhead actresses (including WWE diva Leyla Milani); the witless fat cameraman; the pot-smoking slacker couple who are along for the ride purely because the wheels happen to belong to them; the opportunistic director who cares more for getting his film made than for the wellbeing of his cast ...

Stopping at a petrol station, the sextet are warned away from nearby ghost-town La Sangre de Dios (trivia fans take note: this translates as The Blood of God). Legend has it that this was the last known whereabouts of Mexico's greatest wrestler - El Mascarado (Misterio Sr) - who went blood simple and began killing his opponents many moons ago. Ignoring this caution, ringleader Huss steers his group through the town's gates and determines to shoot his film in the local bar. You know what happens next ...?

Okay, the plot is pure hokum and doesn't stand up to close scrutiny. Lapses in logic abound throughout. Nor is any of this original: teens fall off the map and end up as bait for a psycho in weirdsville? What *Wrestlemaniac* does, then, is take a basic stalk 'n' slash formula and marries it successfully with a taut, flab-free screenplay and some rich sun-kissed photography which makes great use of the orange-hued Mexican locations.

Toss in plenty of bronzed female flesh, pert breasts and gushing gore, and this zippy 73-minute slice of nonsense should please most. To boot, Misterio Sr - alias Miguel Angel Lopez Diaz, a popular professional *luchador* - makes for a striking, authentically menacing adversary for our ditzy, sex-obsessed protagonists.

Not to be confused with the painful 2008 comedy of the same name, Baget's film emerges as good undemanding fun.

X Game (2010)

Dir: Yohei Fukuda; Scr: Mari Asato, Yoichi Minamikawa; Cast: Hirofumi Araki, Tetsuya Yoshiike, Kazuyuki Aijima

Based on Yusuke Yamada's novel.

Four former school bullies awake trapped in a mock-up of their old classroom. A hooded figure looms over them as the holographic image of their late teacher forces them to play the titular endurance game. There are thirteen levels: in each one a victim and a perpetrator are chosen, and various forms of maltreatment are doled out. Each round has its own suggestive name: "Milk Chugging", "Thumb Tacks", "Clothes Pin" and so on. If the victims tolerate their suffering, the game moves forward; if not, they are branded with a poker (its head signifying the "X" in the game's title) ... and *then* the game moves forward.

As the film progresses we learn more of each protagonist and, via flashbacks, how they relentlessly tormented a female pupil years earlier with the same game. The more recent suicide of their former tutor provides clues as to who's responsible for their current predicament.

A stylised revenge thriller with echoes of Daisuke Yamanouchi's much less-polished *Red Room* films (1999 and 2000), *X Game* takes time to introduce us to four individuals so questionable that, by the time they're aware of what's going on, it's hard not to view their antagonist's motives as vigilantism.

The drama gains from refined visuals and a solid cast, as well as more focus on character than you'd usually find in films of this ilk. There's a decent twist too. For the hardcore horror crowd, things do get grisly on occasion – pins digging into skin, people jumping arse-first onto nasty-looking nails, a meal consisting of maggot-corrupted rice etc.

Most imposing of all is how Fukuda (director of *Tokyo Gore School* [2009], *Death Tube: Broadcast Murder Show* [2010] etc) hits us with a harsh fact of life: bullies often shrug off their actions once they've become bored with their subjects, forgetting not only the pain they've caused but – in many cases – their prey's existence; for the victim, the scars remain.

A sequel followed in 2012, the imaginatively titled *X Game 2*.

X Gemu
See *X Game*

XX (2017)

Dir/Scr: Jovanka Vuckovic, Roxanne Benjamin, Annie Clark, Karyn Kusama; Cast: Natalie Brown, Melanie Lynskey, Breeda Wool, Christina Kirk

As the chromosomal referencing title suggests, *XX* is a statement of intent rallying in favour of there being more opportunities for female directors in the horror industry. Production commenced in October 2014, with names such as Mary Harron, Jennifer Lynch and the late Antonia Bird originally attached to this anthology.

The end results present four stories, all centred on strong female characters, all sharing a similar warm aesthetic thanks to the employment of the Red Epic Dragon camera across the board, and a familiar autumnal piano-led score which features throughout.

Vuckovic's "The Box", based on a story by Jack Ketchum, opens events. Brown is the mother who watches almost impassively as her son refuses to eat, following an encounter with a stranger on a train where the boy was allowed a glimpse into the gift box resting on the mysterious passenger's lap. The matriarchal role of family provider is made explicit here, in one hallucinatory sequence where mother literally feeds her brood - they gather round to feast on the flesh stripped from her thigh. Brown smiles with satisfaction as her loved ones tuck in. At the heart of this solemn piece is a woman so desperate to understand her children, to connect with them, that she loses sight of how to save them. Getting on their level becomes all, even after death.

"The Birthday Party" follows, courtesy of Benjamin and Clark (the latter is better-known as singer-songwriter St Vincent). This is lighter in tone, a dark comedy of errors as an increasingly frantic Lynskey tries to hide her husband's corpse while the guests start to arrive for her daughter's birthday jubilations. This is smart, smooth and engaging - but seems ill-fitting when considered alongside its three bedfellows. Still, Lynskey shines as the exasperated, well-meaning and typically practical mother.

Benjamin returns with "Don't Fall". Despite some stunning desert locations and a truly terrifying monster, this one falls oddly flat. There's no real sentiment to be found; it's more of a straight example of bloody, jump-scare-heavy showmanship.

Heavy nods to *Rosemary's Baby* (1968) abound throughout Kusama's "Her Only Living Son". Kirk convinces as the overly-protective mother of a quite eighteen-year-old lad, determined to protect him from his errant father. It's a slow-builder, but a worthy, creepy end to proceedings.

Each segment is bookended by Jan Svankmajer-esque stop-motion episodes offering a nightmarish slant on traditional doll's house tropes, brought to us by Mexican animator Sofia Carrillo.

YellowBrickRoad (2010)

Dir/Scr: Jesse Holland, Andy Mitton; Cast: Cassidy Freeman, Anessa Ramsey, Clark Freeman

1940: the small population of Friar, New Hampshire, took whatever they could carry, leaving their homes and lives behind, and wandered deep up a mountain trail in search of … who knows what. The point is they effectively disappeared, an army search managing to recover only the bodies of those who'd been butchered by an unknown entity en route.

Fast-forward to 2008. A group of historic researchers determine to embark upon the trail in pursuit of the truth. Curiosity kills.

What's most impressive about this backwoods-based effort is not its intriguing premise (fans of folk horror can liken it to the tale of The Pied Piper, or the strange true story of English colonists who disappeared from Roanoke Island, off the North Carolina coast, in the late 16th century), but its focus on psychological uneasiness over more obvious scares. Set at a deliberately slow pace which stirs echoes of Roman Polanski's drip-fed early dramas (the filmmakers have acknowledged the controversial director as an influence), the film adopts a minimalistic approach which works in its favour. *YellowBrickRoad* takes time in introducing its characters and then thrusting bouts of paranoia and understated insecurities upon them. The fear here is an age-old one – the unknown – and the longer the screenplay adheres to that concept, the better the film is.

There are a few inexperienced, camera-conscious performances along the way, while a share of the dialogue struggles to convince. But if you can overlook these common obstacles of low-budget movie-making, *YellowBrickRoad* emerges as a largely proficient, occasionally scary treat.

Minor gore punctuates later scenes as Holland and Mitton eventually subscribe to audience expectancies: the final act is undeniably underwhelming.

Renny Harlin's 2013 effort *The Dyatlov Pass Incident* proffered a similar premise, albeit with none of the subtleties contained herein.

Yeti: Curse Of The Snow Demon (2008)

Dir: Paul Ziller; Scr: Rafael Jordan; Cast: Marc Menard, Carly Pope, Adam O'Byrne

A plane carries a team of American high school students, en route to playing an important football game in Japan. Alas, a severe thunderstorm leads to said plane crashing in the Himalayas. Shade of *Alive* (1993) surface as the survivors initially pull together and, inevitably, agonise over whether it's permissible to eat the remains of their fallen teammates.

But then, a potentially bigger problem rears its ugly head. Yep, the abominable snowman (Ukrainian muscleman Taras Kostyuk in an unconvincing costume)! Can the surviving few outwit this woolly beast, keep themselves fed and fight off the sub-zero elements while a rescue party makes its way to them?

Yeti is riddled with stupidity. From shivering sportsmen frantically searching for something to start a fire with while plane debris blatantly burns around them, to people leaving corpses fully clothed while the living are freezing their nuts off. Prepare for lots of dire CGI, including truly horrid footage of the titular monster leaping Super Mario-style over trees. Hang your heads, Yard Dog FX. Viewers are also in store for workmanlike photography which makes little effort to pass the Vancouver shooting locations off as Asia, and moments of sheer daft action. The guy who uses a dead pal's severed arm as a splint to support his own broken leg is particularly resourceful. All of this results in a film of audaciously low quality.

It's fun. And, for all its silliness, it's unexpectedly mean-spirited too: Jordan's screenplay is merciless in its disposal of injured parties. The wounded don't last long and their comrades do little to help the situation.

The original story was the brainchild of co-executive producer Mark L Lester, a man who knows how to make masterful exploitation cinema - *Class Of 1984* (1982) and *Commando* (1985) refer. Ziller, meanwhile, is best-known for his directorial debut, 1990's tongue-in-cheek slasher *Pledge Night* (1990). Hardly a classic. Indeed, it's probably most notable for featuring Anthrax frontman Joey Belladonna among its cast. But don't expect anything of even that calibre here.

Ostensibly made for television (this film has Sci-Fi Channel written all over it, which is precisely where it premiered in America), *Yeti* actually enjoyed its maiden screening at the Cannes Film Festival in May 2008. I wonder how that went down …

You Belong To Me (2007)

Dir/Scr: Sam Zalutsky; Cast: Daniel Sauli, Patti D'Arbanville, Julien Lucas

Sauli's obsession with on-off lover Lucas leads to him discovering his beau lives a separate life in a Brooklyn apartment, where he resides happily with his full-time boyfriend. A chance meeting with landlady D'Arbanville leads to Sauli moving into the same tenement block. Unconcerned by the fact that the previous tenant of his new shithole room left without their belongings or medication, his mind is singularly on remaining close to the object of his affection.

But then, strange things happen. Deaf mute neighbour Stuart (Howard Sherman, zombie Bub in *Day Of The Dead* [1985] – credited here as Sherman Howard) is a frighteningly aggressive proposition. And what are those strange groaning sounds coming from the apartment below Sauli's –D'Arbanville's own personal haunt?

A combination of the simple set-up, string-based score and eccentric characters have led many to liken this film's low-key thriller dynamics to those of Alfred Hitchcock. In truth, it lacks his wit and is more reminiscent of the paranoia evoked in early Roman Polanski jewels such as *Repulsion* (1965) and *The Tenant* (1976). But, however dubious Sauli's intentions may be during the first act of *You Belong To Me*, his fragile disposition is not the only threat: he soon realises he's renting the flat from Hell.

All of which lends the title a deliciously double-edged purpose (who belongs to who?) while Zalutsky metes out an assured, measured pace with a satisfying lack of need for melodrama. The mood is subtly downbeat, the tension builds surreptitiously; all temptation towards resorting to bursts of crowd-pleasing violence is avoided.

Sauli is good, suitably understated, in facially relaying his reserved anxieties. D'Arbanville has this sussed: she's a powerhouse of horribly plausible malevolence, most frightening when she's acting her sweetest. They bounce off each other well.

The final act is something of an anti-climax but that shouldn't dissuade the curious from checking this stylish, restrained thriller out.

The Zombie Diaries (2006)

Dir/Scr: Michael Bartlett, Kevin Gates; Cast: Russell Jones, Imogen Church, Craig Stovin

An unidentified pandemic has overcome much of the population. Again. This time, it's off to rural England where we're privy to video diaries shot by three groups of survivors: their stories intertwine come the unlikely conclusion.

Shot on mini-DV with a reported budget of £8,000.00, *The Zombie Diaries* opens with an interesting montage of news reports revealing how the airborne virus has travelled from Asia to the UK (echoes of the then-topical bird flu crisis). Hospitals are closing their doors and the Army have taken to the streets in a bid to contain the growing sense of confusion. Footage of panicked city dwellers wearing protective masks as they go about their daily business intrigues, as does the suggestion that this film is going to reflect the undead threat from a credible, post-9/11 perspective.

Then comes the individual diaries. Actually, there's very little here to constitute what you'd call a "video diary": the random scenes of folk wandering around darkened places, shooting the occasional ghoul and so on, are more akin to any of the countless found-footage flicks we've witnessed in the wake of *The Blair Witch Project* (1999). Wooden acting robs several moments of their intended faux-realism; it also puts paid to many attempts at eliciting tension.

An episodic pace, and lack of clearly distinguished lead characters to identify with, are two more problems. On the plus side, we get decent special effects from Mike Peel, Scott Orr and Cesar Alonso. Bartlett and Gates know how to create atmosphere. The restrained use of violence helps the occasional bursts of gore attain greater impact.

Pacing is always agreeable; the diaries proffer short snapshots of the survivors' plights over the course of a couple of months.

The final scene predictably infers that the living are perhaps the real monsters, as opposed to the undead, and that surviving the viral outbreak gives way to a fate worse than death.

Zombie Infection (2011)

Dir: Alexander Sharoglazov; Scr: Alexander Sharoglazov, Rod Sweitzer; Cast: Ted Vernon, Richard Vidan, Rod Sweitzer

The US army tests its latest biochemical agent out on a small Russian village, leaking it into their water supply. Lo and behold, whoever drinks from the nearby stream soon mutates into a hideously deformed, flesh-eating zombie. Caught in the ensuing mayhem is Vernon, an American soldier on vacation to visit his long-lost brother.

Directing under the more English-friendly moniker of Alex Wesley, Russian filmmaker Sharoglazov's feature debut follows reputation-consolidating shorts like *Guts And Gore* (2004) and *Tumors* (2011). It expands his style in terms of both scope and execution.

Zombie Infection has been shot across Russian, American, German and Italian locations. The digital photography works best during the atmospheric Siberian-based passages, conveying a persuasively cold, foreboding atmosphere. The remainder of the footage struggles to achieve such impact, though that's not due to lack of effort on the director's part: his aesthetic eye is consistently on the money, utilising imaginative camerawork and adroit editing.

Alas, the badly-framed subtitles and poorly synchronised audio undo a fair portion of that hard work.

Still, the film delivers in terms of righteous - practical - FX work. The director handles this alongside Vasily Agapov and together their results are unremittingly splashy. At seventy minutes in length, there's no flab in *Zombie Infection* either: it gets down to business without delay and rarely lets up from there.

Sharoglazov's self-professed obsession with 1988 pot-boiler *Scarecrows* has led to him casting its co-stars Vernon and Vidan in his own movie. We also get cameos from Claudio Fargasso, director of *Troll 2* (1990), and German gore purveyor Andreas Schnaas (*Anthropophagus 2000* [1999], *Nikos The Impaler* [2003] etc). This has prompted some to declare the film as "the 'expendables' of horror" (a reference to Sylvester Stallone's 2010 hit *The Expendables*, the cast of which read like a 'who's who' of action movies). But, really, no. *Zombie Infection* is no such thing.

Another notable name among the film's credits is that of Harry Bromley-Davenport. The director of cult favourite *Xtro* (1982) not only has a small role in the film as a doctor but also co-wrote its electronic score.

Zomebieland (2009)

Dir: Ruben Fleischer; Scr: Rhett Reese, Paul Wernick; Cast: Jesse Eisenberg, Emma Stone, Woody Harrelson

Timid student Eisenberg negotiates the post-Apocalyptic wasteland formerly known as America, living by a code of thirty-odd strict rules ("don't be a hero", "avoid public restrooms" etc) to help him outsmart the living corpses he sees everywhere. Teaming up with Twinkie-loving tough guy Harrelson, he embarks on a road trip in search of his family. Along the way they pick up fellow survivors Stone and her younger sister, who've heard of an L.A.-based amusement park rumoured to be zombie-free.

Zombieland took inspiration from the videogame 'Left 4 Dead 2' and was originally conceived as the pilot for an intended TV show. Seeing the potential in the screenplay, its makers developed their efforts into a feature film. A reported $23 million budget helped their plight.

It's essentially a road movie, a journey both literal and metaphorical for our protagonists as they progress from bickering and trivial irks (Harrelson *really* wants a Twinkie) to forming a curious bond with one another. The sardonic one-liners come thick and fast; the zombie attacks, occasional set-pieces which at times feel like little more than afterthoughts on Reese and Wernick's part, are tempered by humour and a keen eye on securing that all-important R-rating stateside.

Lacking in many of the social observations made by George A Romero in something like *Dawn Of The Dead* (1978), *Zombieland* manages to in equal parts come across as tepid, trite and oddly agreeable once the lack of hardcore horror thrills has been accepted. The cast are good: Harrelson hasn't had this much fun chewing scenery since *Natural Born Killers* (1994).

Able support comes from Amber Heard and, most notably, Bill Murray as an undead version of himself. His extended cameo appearance is the highlight of the film. Fair play to Murray: he accepted the offer of featuring as a zombie, where actors such as Joe Pesci, Matthew McConaughey and Jean-Claude Van Damme declined.

Zone Of The Dead (2009)

Dir: Milan Konjevic, Milan Todorovic; Scr: Milan Konjevic; Cast: Ken Foree, Kristina Klebe, Emilio Roso

Kudos for making an undead movie while avoiding use of the word "zombie" in its title and *still* making it into the 'Z' category of an A-Z. Unfortunately, falling into that trap of using the most common alternative – having your film called *(Anything) Of The Dead* – wipes out favourable first impressions.

But, as I've by now hopefully established, I'll approach anything with an open mind. Sometimes there's disappointment, other times pleasant surprise … but everything is viewed with an equal degree of cautious optimism.

Which brings us to this Serbian-Spanish-Italian co-production. It's shot in Pancevo and Belgrade, effectively validating its claim of being Serbia's first ever zombie flick. Starring Foree, lead protagonist of the iconic *Dawn Of The Dead* (1978), no less.

He portrays an Interpol agent – working his last shift before taking retirement (!) – who's tasked, along with rookie partner Klebe, with transferring dangerous criminal Roso across Serbia. This coincides with a chemical leak which transforms passers-by into flesh-eating mutants. Holing themselves inside an abandoned police station, our protagonists resolve to work with their violent prisoner in a bid to survive the night and reach a nearby river … where they anticipate making their escape.

You may have noticed a plot similarity to *Assault On Precinct 13* (1976) in there. Indeed, alongside George A Romero, the filmmakers cite John Carpenter as a major influence …

Foree likes to eat. I know this: I met him at Edinburgh's Dead By Dawn festival several years ago, where he spent the entire time gleefully tucking into the cakes being sold at the food bar. I also know this because that's the only way to explain him appearing in this film.

He practically sleepwalks his way to his paycheck, only stirring slightly when required to participate in a wry homage to *Dawn* when one character unwisely suggests shacking up in a shopping mall for safety.

It's a rare moment of humour in an otherwise straight-faced and non-ironic take on the living dead which manages to waste not only its biggest-name actor but also its potentially ambient Balkan locations.

The HD photography is drab, often overly dark. For some reason, the co-directors have chosen to shake their cameras about violently during the frequent zombie attacks, rendering them virtually unwatchable. It's a shame because Miroslav Lakobrija's crusty make-up effects look satisfyingly old-school … whenever you can make them out.

Konjevic's script, from a story by Todorovic and co-star Vukota Brajovic, is laughable in both its predictability and shamelessly ridiculous dialogue. The latter is made more apparent by a Serbian supporting cast who collectively speak in broken English accents (complete with amusingly inappropriate facial expressions).

Are the zombies slow, menacing ghouls or rabid, fast-paced psychopaths? Both, thanks to a lack of directorial focus.

With sound editing issues galore and a woeful lack of pacing, this really is a chore to sit through. And yet, it's delivered with such earnest conviction; there's no trace of its makers having gone down the cynical "so bad it's good" route.

Appendix

2LDK
9 Lives Of Mara
100 Feet
2001 Maniacs
Ab-Normal Beauty
The ABCs Of Death 2
Abducted By The Daleks
Adam Chaplin
Aftershock
Alleluia
Amber Alert
American Guinea Pig: Bouquet Of Guts And Gore
Amerikan Holokaust
Among The Living
Apartment 1303
Applecart
Ascension
Atroz
Attack Of The Cockface Killer
The Autopsy Of Jane Doe
Bacterium
Bad Meat
Baskin
Beyond Re-Animator
Beyond The Black Rainbow
Beyond The Rave
Birdemic: Shock And Terror
Black Mass Of The Nazi Sex Wizard
The Black Waters Of Echo's Pond
Blood Oath
Blood Of The Werewolf
Bloodrape
Bug
Buried
Buzz Saw
Cabin Fever
The Cabin In The Woods
Camp Massacre
Capture Kill Release
The Card Player
Cat Sick Blues
Chained
The Children
A Christmas Horror Story
Citizen Toxie: The Toxic Avenger IV
Claustrofobia
The Cloth
Cloverfield
Clown
Cold Grip
Colin
Concrete

The Conjuring
The Cottage
The Crazies
Creepshow 3
Daddy's Little Girl
Dard Divorce
The Day Of The Dead
Dead Birds
Dead Clowns
Dead Daughters
Dead In Three Days
Dead Man's Shoes
Deadly Revisions
Death Factory
Deathgasm
Deliver Us From Evil
The Devil Of Kreuzberg
Diary Of The Dead
Donkey Punch
Don't You Recognise Me?
Dumplings
Ed Gein
The Editor
Evil Aliens
Evil Dead
Evil Eyes
The Evil Within
The Eyes Of My Mother
The Fall Of The Louse Of Usher
Family Portraits: A Trilogy Of America
Fear Clinic
Feed
Fetus
Films From A Broken Mind
Final Destination
Flowers
Fluid Boy
The Forbidden Four
Forced Entry
Found
Francesca
Freezer
Friend Request
Frontier(s)
Frustre
Game Over
The Gateway Meat
German Angst
Get Out
A Girl Walks Home Alone At Night
Goodnight Mommy
Graveyard Of The Living Dead
The Greasy Strangler
The Green Inferno

Green Room
Grotesk
Grub Girl
Gun Woman
Gut
Hack Job
The Hagstone Demon
Hanger
Hangman
Hate Crime
Head Case
Headless
Her Name Was Torment
The Hexecutioners
Hidden In The Woods
The Hills Have Eyes
Holocaust Cannibal
The Host
The Hours Of The Day
House At The End Of The Street
House Of The Dead
House On The Hill
Housebound
The Human Centipede 3: The Final Sequence
I Am A Ghost
I Am Legend
I Never Left The White Room
I Spit On Your Grave 2
In The House Of Flies
Inbred
The Inhabitants
Inland Empire
The Innkeepers
Invoked
Isis Rising: Curse Of The Lady Mummy
It Follows
Jack And Diane
Jennifer's Body
Jesus Christ Vampire Hunter
Junk
Ju-on: The Grudge
K-Shop
Kill, Granny, Kill!
Killer Barbys Versus Dracula
Killing Words
Killjoy
Kiss Of The Damned
Laid To Rest
Lake Mungo
The Landlord
The Last Horror Movie
Late Phases
Laundry Man
The Lords Of Salem

The Lost
The Love Witch
The Loved Ones
Lunacy
Madness Of Many
Malignant
Mama
Maniac On The Loose
Masks
Meet Me There
Memories Of Murder
MindFlesh
Miss Violence
Mister Blades
The Most Disturbed Person On Planet Earth
Motivational Growth
Mulholland Drive
The Museum Of Wonders
Mutilation Mile
Nails
Necromance: A Love Story
The Neon Demon
NF713
Nightmare Code
Nikos The Impaler
Nocturne Six
The Noonday Witch
Nymphomaniac Volume 1
Nymphomaniac Volume 2
Oculus
One Missed Call
Only Lovers Left Alive
Orozco The Embalmer
Orphan
The Others
Ouija
The Pact
Paradise Lost
Paranormal Entity
Perseveration
Pieces Of Talent
A Plague So Pleasant
Planet Terror
Poltergay
The Possession Of Michael King
The Poughkeepsie Tapes
Psycho Beach Party
Purgatory Road
The Purge
Queen Of Earth
The Quiet Ones
Rabid Love
Ratline
Raw

Red Room 2
Red, White And Blue
The Redsin Tower
Resident Evil
Resurrecting The Street Walker
Revenge Is Her Middle Name
Ricky 6
Rossa Venezia
S & M: Les Sadiques
Sadi-Screem
Satan
Satan Hates You
Satan's Playground
Screaming Dead
See No Evil
Sella Turcica
Session 9
Shadow Of The Vampire
The Sins Of Dracula
Skinned Deep
Slaughter Me Naked
Slither
Snowtown
Snuff 102
Snuff-Movie
Snuff Trap
Spaceship Terror
Splinter
Starry Eyes
Stitches
Stockholm Syndrome
The Strangers
Survival Of The Dead
Sweeney Todd: The Demon Barber Of Fleet Street
Taeter City: Take A Tour In The City Of Cannibal Dictatorship
The Taking Of Deborah Logan
Taxidermia
Tell Me How I Die
Terror Nation
The Texas Vibrator Massacre
The Theatre Bizarre
They Came Back
Tin Can Man
Train To Busan
The Transfiguration
Tusk
Ubaldo Terzani Horror Show
The Uh-Oh! Show
Under The Shadow
The Undertow
Underworld
Unfriended
Unholy Ground
The Untamed

Upsidedown Cross
Vacancy
Vampire Junction
V/H/S
Vile
Villa Captive
The Visit
The Void
Voodoo Curse - Legba's Rache
Voyage To Agatis
The Wailing
Wake The Witch
Watch Out
Wendigo
What We Do In The Shadows
When Animals Dream
White God
The Witch
The Witches Hammer
Wither
The Wolfman
Wound
Wrestlemaniac
X Game
XX
YellowBrickRoad
Yeti: Curse Of The Snow Demon
You Belong To Me
The Zombie Diaries
Zombie Infection
Zombieland
Zone Of The Dead

Printed in Great Britain
by Amazon